Running
Through the Ages

This book is dedicated to
everyone I have ever run with,

but especially to Tom Polk,
a good runner and a true friend.

# Running Through the Ages

*by* EDWARD S. SEARS

McFarland & Company, Inc., Publishers
*Jefferson, North Carolina, and London*

**Library of Congress Cataloguing-in-Publication Data**

Sears, Edward S. (Edward Seldon), 1943–
    Running through the ages / by Edward S. Sears.
      p.  cm.
    Includes bibliographical references and index.
    ISBN 0-7864-0971-1 (illustrated case binding : 50# alkaline paper)
    1. Running—History.   I. Title.
  GV1061.S38   2001
  796.42'09—dc21                           2001037055

British Library cataloguing data are available

Manufactured in the United States of America

*On the cover:* Greek Stadion runners of the fourth century B.C. *(from
Edward Norman Gardiner,* Greek Athletic Sports and Festivals, *1910)*

*McFarland & Company, Inc., Publishers*
  *Box 611, Jefferson, North Carolina 28640*
   *www.mcfarlandpub.com*

# Table of Contents

# Acknowledgments

In researching and writing this book, I was fortunate to have the help of several experts. I could not have written the book, especially the 19th century sections, without the generous help of British mystery writer and running historian Peter Lovesey. He answered my countless questions and provided me with much material from his files. He also read and commented on most of the manuscript. Best of all, he encouraged me to see the project through to the end.

I would also like to thank Dr. David Carrier, a biologist at the University of Utah, for reviewing and commenting on running by prehumans described in Section I. Much of that section is based on his work.

Dr. Stephen Miller sent me a video that was very useful in understanding the operation of the Hysplex starting mechanism used by the ancient Greeks. Dr. Dahn Shaulis read and commented on the six-day racing section and graciously provided information on female pedestrians, including all of his Amy Howard material. John Cumming sent me a list of 19th century illustrated American sporting journals that was very helpful.

Several others were also generous with their time and assistance. I would like to thank Bill Mallon for reviewing the sprints and Chris Kuykandal for his comments on the history of the mile. Andy Milroy, Bredo Bernsen and Trond Olav Svendsen were very helpful in sorting out the career of the mysterious ultra runner Mensen Ernst. Joe Henderson of *Runner's World* gave valuable advice on publishing the manuscript, and Jon Hendershott of *Track & Field News* provided suggestions on finding photos.

The bibliography lists sources that I thought were especially helpful and would be good starting points for those wanting to pursue running history further. Other important works are mentioned in the text.

# Introduction

This book covers the most important runners and races from prehuman times to the year 2000. It was written for runners but should also be of interest to students, coaches, historians—anyone who wants to know more about the history, lore and legend of running.

I began this project in the early 1990s when I was unable to find a source that covered the complete history of running. Several books dealt with various time periods, mostly modern, but none covered running from its beginning. I decided to start with the running of prehumans because they define us as runners. From them we evolved the distinctly human traits of being relatively slow but excellent distance runners. The need for prehumans to run long distances to obtain food provided the basis for the human feats of running marathon and longer distances that are common through the ages.

While some ancient writers, such as Homer, considered swiftness of foot to be the most highly prized trait a man could have, the ancients seldom recorded the details of foot races. This began to change

with improvements in timekeeping in the 17th and 18th centuries which allowed runners to compare their performances with previous ones of the same distance. By about 1800, newspapers, magazines and books began to include detailed accounts of running feats and matches. From the mid 1800s on, there are multiple sources for most of the important running events in Britain and the USA.

In order to keep this book to a manageable size, it was necessary to limit it to the greatest runners of each era. Many excellent runners, who were not quite the best of their day, had to be omitted, but that is the nature of running. The victor may become a legend while the second place finisher, even if he or she loses by inches, is usually soon forgotten. It is also possible that I omitted some great runners because their feats were never recorded in the literature available to me.

This book concentrates on the human aspect of running—what made each great runner stand out from others of his or her era. Some of the runners I describe will be familiar to almost everyone, but others, especially the 19th and early 20th century professionals, will be new to most of today's running enthusiasts. Professional runners, called "pedestrians" in the 19th century, have been overlooked by many writers. This is partly from lack of information. In order to get future races at reasonable betting odds, the best professionals tried to keep their true abilities secret. Only rarely — when they had to go all-out to win an important race — did the public or the press see them at their best.

Because professional running involved gambling, race fixing and unruly crowds it was scorned by most of the upper classes both in England and America. Amateurism ruled in both countries from the 1880s to 1980s. Although amateurism had some admirable qualities, it was far from perfect. Initially it was restricted to the upper classes and under-the-table payments to the best runners were common from the beginning. Today no stigma is attached to being a professional runner and I believe the feats of the professionals of old should share equal billing with those of the amateurs of their time.

The stories of many of the great runners of the past are both moving and motivating. Many of the champions fully justified the public acclaim they received and can still serve as heros and role models for today's runners. My choices of runners to include and the coverage allotted to each was most influenced by: (1) A runner's performances compared with others of his or her era; (2) What their contemporaries— primarily sports writers and fellow athletes— thought of them.

To really appreciate the runners in this book, do not be overly influenced by the fast times of today's elite runners. Times run in the 19th century may seem ponderously slow today, but in all likelihood so will today's performances a hundred years from now. Try to judge these men and women by the standards, techniques and limitations of their eras and keep in mind that they had

no incentive to run any faster than was necessary to be the best of their day.

Training methods have had a major influence on the running performances achieved during various eras. Where possible I give examples of the training methods of the time. Unfortunately, training methods were often poorly reported or sometimes closely-guarded secrets.

Technical improvements, such as starting blocks and better tracks, also help to explain why today's runners are faster than the runners of old. Summaries of innovations that improved running performances are presented in each section.

Running records can also be roughly correlated with population size. The more elite runners there are, the greater the probability that someone will come along who can break the old record. World population, which was 900 million in 1800, grew to 1.7 billion in 1900, then mushroomed to six billion by 2000. The number of countries participating in running at its highest levels also grew rapidly in the 20th century.

Knowing that a running feat is possible also influences running performances. Up until 1954 when Roger Bannister broke the four-minute mile, no one knew for sure that it was possible. Australian John Landy, a rival of Bannister's, was quoted as saying "I wasn't prepared for anyone to break 4:00. I had begun to believe it was a very difficult target and it might take ten years or so to get there. Then I thought if he did it, perhaps it wasn't such a barrier and I could do it." A month and a half after Bannister, Landy became the second sub-four-minute miler by running 3:57.9. Others quickly followed.

All times for running events in this book are given as originally taken with fractions of seconds expressed as ½, ¼, ⅕, etc. Tenths of a second are given with a decimal, e.g., (10.1 seconds). Hundredths of seconds, e.g., (10.01 seconds) represent "automatic timing." Distances are given first in English units followed by a conversion to metric units.

# I

# Running by
# Pre- and Early Humans
# (5,000,000–200,000 B.C.)

*"Eat, or be eaten." In those days, mankind had to rely on legs to be in a position to carry out the first part or evade the latter. So everyone ran and ate; when they failed to run fast or far enough they met the eater and subsequent proceedings no longer interested them.*

— Arthur Newton (1928)

Running can be defined as fast loco-motion, where, for an instant, all of the runner's feet leave the ground. Although some of us take pride in our running, even the fastest of us can be out-sprinted by a horse, a dog, or even a cat. Where we really excel, as a species, is running long distances. Of all the animals on Earth, humans can run the farthest. Why this is so cannot be explained with certainty, but the trait is of such importance in defining us as runners that it deserves an effort to explain it.

## Life in the Trees

About 65 million years ago when dinosaurs roamed the earth, mammals were no more than small rat-like creatures. Some catastrophic event — probably a large meteor impact — destroyed the dinosaurs but allowed mammals to survive. Mammals grew larger, diversified and flourished. One branch excelled at fast running — the horse and antelope are good examples. These animals became adapted for fast running mainly to escape predators.

3

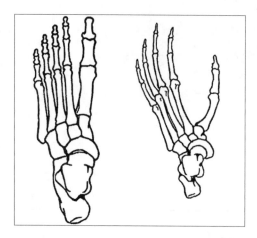

*Illustration 1:* **The human foot on the left evolved for walking and running, the chimpanzee foot on the right for climbing (drawing by author).**

At the same time another group of mammals—the primates—began adapting to life in the trees. About 40 million years ago these creatures' forelimbs became hands with opposable thumbs for grasping. During the next 30 million years they became more acrobatic, able to swing from branches and walk through the trees. This method of moving about led to a semierect posture such as apes have today. Life in the trees laid the foundation for upright walking and running on the ground. Prehumans and apes are believed to have split from a common tree-dwelling ancestor about 7.5 million years ago, although no trace of this human-ape ancestor has yet been found.

## Becoming Bipedal

Prehumans evolved a novel method of moving about. They became bipedal. Scientists are unsure why this ability to walk and run on two legs evolved in our ancestors, but the reason may be related to the climate changes that occurred in Africa. The once-dense forests thinned, and by seven million years ago large patches of grassy areas, or savanna, dominated the East African landscape, our ancestral home.

Bipedalism may have been useful for traveling and hunting on these grassy areas. At any rate, becoming bipedal placed a tremendous burden on the prehuman's spine and feet. The spine had to support the cantilevered body and two feet had to do the work previously done by four.

According to Dr. Dudley Morton in *Evolution of the Human Foot* (1964), man's ancestral foot was adapted to life in the trees. It was probably similar to the chimpanzee's foot shown in Illustration 1 and was hand-like. One of its main purposes was to grasp branches. When this flexible, grasping foot was forced to adapt to walking and running on the ground, it became more rigid and arched for efficient propulsion and shock absorption. The big toe lost its grasping function, became aligned with the other toes, and along with the second toe, became longer and stronger. The other toes were not needed to walk or run and became smaller.

David Carrier, an evolutionary biologist at the University of Utah, has pointed out that human toes evolved to act like a set of gears allowing us to walk and run more efficiently. During a step, the foot acts like a lever. One lever arm runs from the calf muscle to the ankle. This lever arm transfers force to a second lever arm, which runs from the ankle to the point where force is applied to the ground. Running on your heels, the ratio of the two lever arms is low because the distance from the ankle to where the force is applied to the ground is relatively short. When you switch to running on the balls of your feet and toes the ratio increases, because the lever arm from the ankle to where the force is applied to the ground becomes longer. In effect, you are shifting to a higher gear ratio, allowing the calf muscles to contract more slowly and generate more power. Without toes we would be limited to one gear.

The human ancestral heel bone was also an adaptation to life in the trees. It was part of a lever enabling the body to be kept

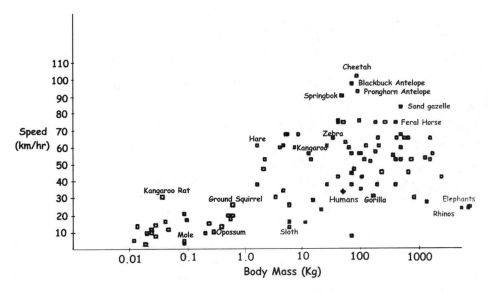

*Illustration 2:* Maximum running speeds of various animals (plotted by author using data from Theodore Garland, 1982).

upright in climbing and was also helpful in moving the body forward. In modern humans, the heel bone is still part of the propelling lever of the foot and provides balance for standing.

## How Human Running Speed Compares with Other Mammals

Illustration 2 shows the maximum speeds of approximately 100 species of mammals. Some of the speeds shown are questionable owing to the difficulties of measuring an animal's speed in the wild. Still, the data show that maximum running speed changes with weight. Note that humans are right in the middle.

Both very small and very large animals are slower than those of medium weight. Interestingly, very small mammals such as mice normally run when they move about. Very large ones—elephants, for example—cannot run at all. They do not have a phase in their stride when all four feet are off the ground.

A predatory animal's success at catching prey is strongly correlated with its speed of pursuit. Since humans are only average sprinters, it is unlikely that our ancestors were able to catch many animals by outsprinting them. The big cats are the true sprinters of the animal kingdom with the "world's fastest animal" title going to the cheetah, whose top speed is about 62 mph (100 km/hr). Cheetahs are "pure sprinters," in that they can run for only very short distances. They evolved without efficient cooling systems and after running 600 meters or less, their body temperatures reach 106 degrees F. (41 deg C.) and they must stop to cool themselves.

The best middle-distance runners among four-legged animals are pronghorn antelope. Pronghorns can run 6.2 miles (10 km) in nine minutes—an average speed of 41 mph (66 km/hr).

Three to four-million-year-old fossil footprints prove that prehumans walked and ran on two legs—although probably not as well as we do today. These footprints, discovered in 1977 in northern Tanzania, also proved that a large brain was not required for

*Illustration 3:* A 3.5-million-year-old pre-human made the footprint on the left. The creature walked upright, but the curved toes were not as efficient for running as the modern human foot on the right (drawing by author).

bipedal walking and running since prehumans at this time still had ape-sized brains. Although they were fully bipedal, these creatures kept some of their tree-dwelling characteristics. Their arms were longer than ours in proportion to their height, and their fingers and toes were curved. They were also stocky with large potbellies containing a long digestive track necessary for processing plant food. Their bodies were unsuited for long-distance running and they may have still spent considerable time in the trees. They probably sprinted to nearby trees when approached by predators.

Modern humans can sprint for only short distances. Champion sprinters reach their top speed of about 27 mph (44 km/hr) at 50–60 meters, but by 75 meters they have already begun to slow. Novice runners in a race longer than about 300 meters almost always run the first part of the race too fast. This tendency is known as "suicidal pacing" and most beginning runners have to be taught to overcome it to become competitive. This may be related to the "flight-response" mechanism, useful for escaping predators.

Humans are not only slow but, compared to most mammals, run inefficiently. Running efficiency is related to size and studies have shown that the energy required per body weight for running is greater for small animals than large ones. Small animals must develop forces with their muscles at higher rates than large animals when moving at equivalent speeds. Contracting muscles at high rates is less efficient than contracting them at slow rates.

Compared to most four-legged mammals of comparable size, humans are inefficient runners. They need about twice the energy to run at any given speed as most four-legged animals of similar weight. The reason for this is not well understood. It is not because people run on two legs rather than four. In 1973, C. Richard Taylor and V. J. Rowntree from Harvard University found that there was no measurable difference in the amount of energy consumed by a chimpanzee or monkey when running on two or four legs. Experiments have also shown that ponies and ostriches of equal weight use about the same energy for running at equal speeds.

In 1987, the British biologist R. McNeill Alexander calculated the energy a typical human runner loses and regains in each step. He found that a 154-pound (70 kg) runner at 10 mph (4.5 m/sec) requires about 100 joules of metabolic energy. Of this energy, 48 joules are wasted as heat which must be dissipated by the body's cooling system. About 35 joules go to stretch the Achilles tendon and 17 to flatten the foot's arch. This stored energy in the Achilles tendon and arch is returned by their elastic recoil. These "springs" in our legs and feet allow us to run with a moderate degree of efficiency.

## Running and Breathing

Almost all medium-to-large-sized mammals pant to lose heat when they run.

Panting cools by forcing air across evaporative surfaces in the nose and mouth. By panting, an animal can cool itself yet still have a thick furry coat for protection from cold and from the direct heat of the sun. A fur coat also offers protection from briars, insects and other hazards of a harsh environment. Other than pigs, humans are the only mammals our size that do not have a furry coat. The fact that we have so little hair has to be telling us something important.

Except for sprinting, the major part of the energy required to run is supplied by burning glycogens and fats. This "aerobic" running, whether by both humans or four legged animals, requires large amounts of oxygen. But running also generates large amounts of heat. A running four-legged animal has the conflicting needs of taking in large amounts of oxygen to burn fuel and at the same time using its respiratory cycle for panting to cool itself.

Bramble and Carrier found in 1983 that all four-legged animals have a serious limitation when they run fast (gallop). They can take only one breath per stride. As a four-legged animal gallops, its thoracic cavity, housing its heart and lungs, is compressed by the contracting muscular diaphragm so strongly that the animal is forced to breathe in synchronization with its stride. The more rapid the stride, the faster the animal must breathe. Breathing faster does not necessarily mean increased oxygen to the lungs however, because rapid breathing is usually shallow. This one-to-one coupling between breaths and strides constrains the respiratory frequency and makes it more difficult for the animal to cool itself. Conflicting needs of air for cooling and taking in enough oxygen to burn fuel for metabolic energy limit a panting animal's distance running performance, especially in the heat.

Because humans run upright on two legs, the lungs and diaphragm are not subject to direct impact loading and the one-breath-per-stride restriction does not apply.

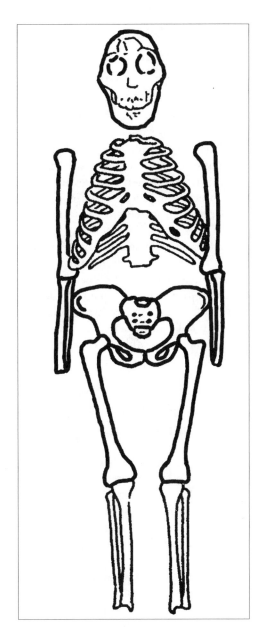

*Illustration 4:* "Lucy," a 3-million-year-old prehuman (drawing by author).

Bramble and Carrier found that, like four-legged mammals, a trained distance runner's breathing is synchronized with his or her stride. Humans, however, have a much more flexible respiratory system that can use at least five different breaths-to-strides ratios:

| Breaths | Strides |
|:-------:|:-------:|
| 1 | 4 |
| 1 | 3 |
| 2 | 5 |
| 1 | 2 |
| 2 | 3 |

These synchronized, variable-ratio, breathing patterns require no conscious effort. Synchronization becomes automatic with practice, and experienced distance runners synchronize their breathing with their strides within the first five strides. For trained distance runners, one breath for two strides is the most common ratio, but during slow running the ratio changes to one breath in four strides. Humans do not use a ratio of one breath per stride except for going up hills. Shifts between ratios occur quickly and smoothly over just a few strides.

## The Best Cooling System on the Planet

Most mammals, whether hunters or prey, can run for only relatively short distances. Exceptions are humans, horses, wolves and wolf descendants— dogs. A respiratory system that can adapt to variable strides per breath gives human runners ample oxygen to run at a wide range of speeds, but cooling by sweating is the key to human superiority at long distance running. Sweating, which provides about 95 percent of human cooling, depends on evaporation of moisture from glands found beneath the skin. Humans have from two to five million sweat glands— far more than any other mammal. These glands are also under the precise control of the central nervous system. The capillary system carries heat from the muscles through an under-skin fat layer to the skin. As air moves across sweaty skin, the moisture evaporates, cooling the skin and the blood flowing through the capillary system in the skin. Rapid air movement across the skin from a breeze or running enhances this cooling effect.

Sweating does not depend on the respiratory cycle and allows humans to use the whole skin surface to get rid of heat. A big drawback of efficient sweating is the reduced amount of hair growing on the body. This means that the relatively hairless prehumans were unprotected from both cold and direct sunlight. This was a lot to give up for the sole purpose of staying cool while doing heavy exercise in a hot environment.

By walking and running upright, however, prehumans were able to reduce their exposure to solar radiation during midday when the sun was at its hottest. The area receiving the most solar radiation during midday is the top of the head and shoulders. Prehumans did not give up their hair on these areas of their bodies.

## Prehuman Endurance Hunting

In his 1984 paper "The Energetic Paradox of Human Running and Hominid Evolution" published in *Current Anthropology*, David Carrier made a strong case that prehumans were daytime endurance hunters. He argued that their unique cooling, breathing and energy use pattern gave them an advantage over most four-legged animals for running long distances in hot weather.

The energy needed for a four-legged animal to run changes with speed. The minimum energy required occurs at an intermediate speed within each gait. When allowed to select their own speeds, most four-legged animals choose speeds requiring the least effort within that gait. There are ranges of speeds four-legged animals never use for any sustained periods.

Because humans are not required to take one breath per stride, there is no optimal or preferred human running speed.

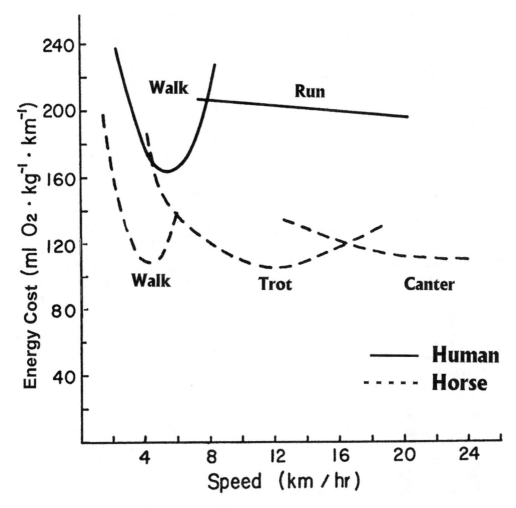

*Illustration 5:* Energy cost vs. speed of walking and running for humans and horses. Humans have an optimum speed for walking but not for running (from David R. Carrier, 1984).

The energy required for humans to run increases almost linearly with speed over the five to 12.5 mph (8 to 20 km/hr) range of speeds used by most distance runners. This means that, except for sprinting, the energy used for a human to run a given distance is nearly constant, regardless of the speed. Carrier postulated that prehumans, who could run at any speed in the five to 12.5 mph ranges, could have forced a prey animal to run at a speed where it had to use more energy than normal.

The human species is hundreds of thousands of years old (the human family

several millions of years old), and spent most of that time as a hunter-gatherer. Humans have led a semi-sedentary existence — based on farming and domestication of animals — for only the last 10,000 years or about three percent of the total. In the first 97 percent of human time on Earth, almost everything that defined humans came into being. One way to infer what those times might have been like is to observe the few hunter-gatherer societies that still exist and have not been corrupted by civilization.

There are many documented examples

of hunter-gatherers using the "run-down" hunting method. This hunting technique requires constant pursuit of a prey animal until it eventually becomes exhausted and can be easily taken. Although energetically inefficient, it is the ultimate in simplicity. It was ideally suited to prehumans who had a brain capacity of only a few hundred cubic centimeters.

## Running Down Animals

The run-down method requires only that the hunter be willing and able to run long distances and the animal have no place to hide. The following examples illustrate the technique.

American Indian:

Deer hunting of the Indians consists of chasing the deer for two days—never less than one day. The Tarahumara keeps the deer constantly on the move. Only occasionally does he get a glimpse of his quarry, but follows it unerringly through his own uncanny ability to read the tracks. The Indian chases the deer until the creature falls from exhaustion, often with its hoofs completely worn away.—Bennett and Zingg, *The Tarahumara* (1935, p. 113)

The Kanaka of the Philippines were noted for running down wild goats:

The goat hunter follows a flock on foot. As he approaches, they gallop away over the rocks, leaving the pursuer far behind. But they soon halt, tired and blown by their exertions, while the Kanaka keeps on. It becomes a question of endurance between the steady dog trot of the pursuer and the alternate halts and spasmodic efforts of the pursued. The Kanaka wins every time. In the course of a couple of hours the animals are too weary and too much discouraged to flee further. Reaching the first laggard, the hunter breaks its hind legs across his knee, and the remainder of the flock are treated in like manner.—C. E. Dutton, *Hawaiian Volcanoes* (1882, p. 137)

Several authors describe the run-down method as used by African hunters. Here is one example:

Another hunting technique was simply to wear the game out by pursuit, a method adopted in open country where the hunters had no chance to sneak up on the animals. The Bushmen have fantastic staying power, and can keep up the chase of an antelope for a long distance. They have been known to pursue the quarry for 30–40 km, not necessarily at a fast pace but at a steady, remorseless one. The fleeing animal tires itself out by running desperately and irregularly, by stopping to turn around and then dashing off again. When it gets hot and exhausted the Bushmen deliberately hold back and beguile the beast into lying down for a rest. It cools down, its muscles stiffen, and then the hunter chases after it suddenly so that the animal can often scarcely rise and becomes an easy victim of their spears.... When I visited the Auen Bushmen later on in the southerly Kalahari I procured skin from them and wondered why there was no hole in the skin from an arrow or a spear. They explained that they had run the animal off its feet and killed it with a club.—Bjerre, *Kalahari* (1958, p. 120)

In Australia, the favorite target of running hunters is the kangaroo:

[The kangaroo] is circumvented and captured in a variety of ways, but the noblest sport is the hunt pure and simple, practiced after the same fashion as the pursuit of the wild goat by the Hawaiians. The hunter follows the animal, and performs what seems at first sight the incredible feat of running it down; of course the kangaroo, like the wild goat, is much swifter afoot than the hunter, but it has not the same staying power, and so by keeping it constantly on the run it becomes, at length, completely "blown" and exhausted. It is only men of exceptional endurance, however, who can run down the kangaroo.— Sollas, *Ancient Hunters and Their Modern Representatives* (1924, p. 275)

Surprisingly, both the speedy cheetah and the mighty pronghorn have fallen prey to distance-running humans. Reports of humans running down animals often lack details, but typically, the length of the chase was from an hour to more than a day. The pursuer normally ran at a slow but steady pace while trying to force the prey animal to run in spurts. Usually the hunter killed the animal with his hands, a club or a spear.

The fossil evidence represented by "Lucy" implies that prehumans of three to four million years ago were primarily plant eaters and scavengers. Later, a dietary shift occurred when they began to obtain a larger proportion of their food from animals. One line of reasoning suggests that prehumans evolved the ability to chase down young, injured, or old animals. Finally, natural selection favored those who could run longer in the heat as they began to pursue the more plentiful healthy animals. A run-down hunter would not have had to perform an extended chase every day. He could have supplied himself and two or three others with an adequate meat supply by catching one medium-sized animal a week.

Early prehumans did not have efficient hunting weapons—not even sharp teeth. They began using primitive tools about 2.5 million years ago, but for butchering and crushing bone for marrow, not for hunting. In 1997 the earliest hunting weapons yet found were discovered in Germany. They were three six-to-seven foot (1.8-2.1 m) long wooden spears made of spruce. Apparently used to kill horses, the spears were dated at 400,000 years old. The sizes of the spears suggest their users were far stronger than modern humans. Bows and arrows are even more recent inventions, with the earliest direct evidence again coming from Germany about 10,500 years ago.

Although many prehuman females may have been occupied by taking care of their children, both sexes evolved the ability to run in the heat. By two million years ago, females were about as large in relation to males as they are today. If anything, women seem to tolerate running in hot weather slightly better than men. Their approximately 10 percent slower running speed compared to men would have made little difference in running down an animal. It was dogged determination rather than speed that counted.

Killing the animal would not have been a problem for either sex. Many animals suffer "chase myopathy"—the tendency to collapse from exhaustion and heat after an extended chase. They frequently die or become helpless—a serious problem in capturing wild animals for zoos or research. Run-down hunters may have hunted in groups, but hunting alone would have provided the greatest area coverage per hunter.

Prehumans could have chased animals at any speed between 8–20 km/hr as long as they kept the animal in sight or were able to track it. They could have forced the animal to waste energy by constantly stopping when it thought it was out of danger and starting again when it detected its pursuer. Stop-and-go running would have kept the animal from running long distances at its most energy-efficient speed. Intermittent running is especially inefficient if the running part is done anaerobically, which tends to add large amounts of lactic acid to the blood.

## A Runner from 1.6 Million Years Ago

In 1984, a member of Richard Leaky's team found the fossil skeleton of a 1.6 million-year-old early human boy near the Nariokotome sand river in northern Kenya.

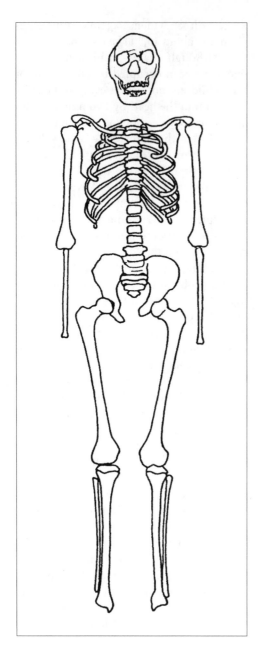

*Illustration 6:* 1.6 million-year-old skeleton of Nariokatome boy (drawing by author).

This remarkable discovery known as KNM-WT 1500 or the "Nariokotome Homo Erectus Skeleton" suggests that by this time early humans had lost their apelike proportions. This 12-year-old boy was slender with a narrow pelvis that may have been more

efficient for running than that of modern humans. His slender waist implies that he had lost the potbelly of the earlier pre-humans who were primarily plant eaters and that he probably ate more meat than "Lucy" did. Had he lived to adulthood, he would have weighed about 150 lb. (68 kg) and stood about 6 feet 1 inch (1.8 m) tall. This is close to the two pounds of body weight per inch of height considered to be ideal for a long distance runner.

Alan Walker and Richard Leakey in *The Nariokotome Homo Erectus Skeleton* (1993) believed this new body type supports Carrier's hypothesis:

> And finally, Carrier (1984) put forward an argument based on energetic principles that early hominids had a physiology that allowed endurance running at speeds which forced prey to avoid them in an inefficient way. This, he hypothesized, made them effective predators who could run down prey without succumbing to overheating. What we have learned from the Nariokotome skeleton can be taken to support Carrier.

The boy had long arms and legs, suggesting that he was well adapted to a hot environment. He was also incredibly strong. Elevations of dense bone develop where muscle tendons attach to bones. The sizes of these muscle attachment points are indicators of the forces generated by the attached muscles. The Nariokotome boy had big muscle attachment points and thick long bones, suggesting he had much greater strength than the average person of today.

A possible evolutionary enhancement to human distance running is known as "the second wind" or "runner's high." In the 1970s researchers found naturally occurring pain-reducing chemicals in the human brain, pituitary and adrenal glands. Running stimulates the production of these "endorphins." The amount produced varies with the individual. Most runners produce enough to feel their effects after running at a moderate to fast pace for from 30 minutes to two hours. A distance-running hunter would have met these requirements. Endorphins could have provided the extra incentive needed not to abandon the chase — to run a little farther.

California physician Walter Bortz, in a 1985 paper "Physical Exercise as an Evolutionary Force," argued that running down animals influenced the human body's response to training. He observed that to achieve a high level of fitness it is necessary to exercise strenuously and repetitively about three times a week for at least a half hour. This corresponds roughly with the observed hunting pattern of African Bushmen. Dr. Bortz believes that the modern human body's response to training evolved as a result of prehuman hunting using the run-down method.

Current human runners differ from early human runners of 1.5 million years ago in three important ways:

(1) Early humans were stronger and more heavily muscled than we are today.

(2) Early humans ran barefoot.

(3) Early humans ran in warm climates on relatively soft surfaces.

It is impossible to say whether this stronger, heavily muscled early human had fewer running injuries than modern runners. Some studies have suggested that in societies where people commonly go barefoot, running injuries are not as frequent as in our society. Shoes came late in human evolution, with the oldest ever found being discovered in 1934 in a cave in Oregon. These almost perfectly preserved shoes were carbon-dated at about 10,000 years old. They were made of twisted sagebrush fiber that had been knotted repeatedly across the soles, suggesting the shoes were used more for traction then protection.

Early humans, whether running from a predator or chasing down their dinner, would not have had time to warm up or stretch before running. These modern day rituals were apparently unnecessary for early humans running barefoot on the warm, grassy Savannah. This does not necessarily mean that warming up and stretching are a waste of time for the modern runner. Warming up, in particular, might compensate for the fact that most of us run in a cooler environment than early humans did.

Some modern humans run on the fronts of their feet and cannot bring their heel down to the ground normally — suggesting a trend toward faster running on the front of the foot. Other runners, however, suffer from "Morton's toe" or "Morton's foot," a condition in which the big toe is shorter than the second toe. This was useful in the apelike ancestral foot which grasped branches with the four outer toes, and used the first toe for completing the grasp in the other direction, something like a pincer. Morton's toe may be a partial "throwback" to the grasping big toe of our tree dwelling ancestors.

To summarize, humans have several characteristics that may be related to selection for endurance running: lack of body hair, enhanced sweating capacity, flexibility in lung ventilation due to bipedal posture, long legs, reduced length and mass of arms and narrow pelvic girdles. These characteristics separate modern humans from our apelike ancestors and are best explained by evolutionary selection for long-distance running.

Virtually all healthy humans possess the ability to run long distances whether they make use of it or not — a legacy from prehuman runners of long ago.

# II

---

# Running in the
# Ancient World
# (2650 B.C.–A.D. 500)

---

*Whoever wins your shining prize, Olympia, wears glory always.*
— Pindar (ca. 518–438 B.C.)

### Ritual Running
### by Egyptian Kings

With the beginning of agriculture about 10,000 years ago, the nature of human running changed. In many parts of the world it was no longer necessary to run to obtain food or escape predators. Humans found new uses for running — religious ceremonies, delivering messages, military purposes and sport.

The earliest evidence of a running course comes from the Old Kingdom in Egypt over 4,000 years ago. Ancient Egyptian kings celebrated a series of festivals that involved ceremonial running. During a king's coronation ceremony he made a run that symbolized laying claim to his domain

and proved that he was fit enough for the demands of his position.

After the king had reigned for 30 years, he was required to repeat his run to prove his physical powers had not deserted him. A feeble king was considered a danger to his kingdom. If the king successfully completed the run, he then had to repeat it every three years after that. The run was believed to magically renew the king's might and power.

### King Djoser's
### Running Course

Around 2600 B.C. King Djoser of the Third Dynasty had a massive stone temple

**King Djoser during a ceremonial run, about 2600 B.C. (drawing by author).**

designed for himself, known today as "The Step Pyramid of King Djoser." Part of this complex of buildings has been identified as a ceremonial running course. The course is broad and flat with two large B-shaped stones about 60 yards (55 meters) apart. The stones are believed to be turning posts. King Djoser ran alone on his magnificent running course since a king could have no rival. We do not know how many circuits he made.

## King Shulgi's Magnificent Run

Samuel Kramer in *History Begins at Sumer* (1981), describes the first written evidence of distance running. King Shulgi, the second king of the dynasty of Ur, ruled ancient Sumer in the Tigris-Euphrates valley from 2094 to 2047 B.C. He was a great monarch and an outstanding distance run-

ner. A hymn composed in his honor describes a remarkable run he made from Nippur to Ur:

> I the runner, rose in my strength, all set for the course, from Nippur to Ur. I resolved to traverse as if it were (but a distance) of one "double hour." Like a lion that wearies not of its virility I arose, put a girdle about my loins, swung my arms like a dove feverishly fleeing a snake, spread wide the knees like an Anzu bird with eyes lifted toward the mountain...

The "crow's-flight" distance between the ancient cities of Nippur and Ur is about 96 miles (154 km). The running distance may have been much longer. A run from Nippur to Ur and back would have been at least 200 miles (320 km). According to the hymn, the first half of the run was southward to Ur, where Shulgi arrived before dark. He feasted, bathed and rested that night. The next morning he rose early and ran back to Nippur encountering heavy rain and hail along the way. Shulgi's run was not across the desert but on well-maintained roads. In addition to proving his running powers, he wanted to celebrate religious festivals in the two cities that occurred on successive days.

The hymn doesn't say at what time of day Shulgi started his run, but the maximum amount of daylight in Sumer could not have been more than 15–16 hours. Currently, the world record for 100 miles is 11 hr, 30 min. Since he repeated his run in reverse the next day, an estimate of his total running time would be 30–32 hours. The modern record for 200 miles is 27 hr, 48 min. Poems written about kings of this era were sometimes used to maintain or bolster the royal image, gain respect from friends, and instill fear in enemies. If Shulgi actually made the run as described, he ranks as a formidable ultra-runner. Based on what modern ultra runners can do, his run was an outstanding performance.

Queen Hatshepsut, who ruled as if she

front of the town's religious center. The participants were probably Sumerian palace couriers. We know almost nothing about the runners except that they oiled themselves as the Greek runners would do over a thousand years later.

## Running in the Old Testament

In the Old Testament, there are several suggestions that running ability was highly regarded. In II Samuel, David gives thanks for his running ability: "For thee I have run through a troop, and by my God have I leaped over a wall…. He maketh my feet like hinds' feet … thou has enlarged my steps under me, that my feet did not slip."

In Psalm 19, David compares the sun to a man running on a race course: "He Rejoiceth as a strong man to run a race. His going forth is from the end of the heaven, and his circuit unto the ends of it." II Samuel 2:18 describes David's nephew Asahel as being "light of foot as a wild roe." Asahel's fondness for running may have led to his downfall. After twice refusing to stop following David's cousin Abner, he was killed by a wayward spear thrust.

Another athletic simile is contained in Jeremiah's warnings (Jeremiah 12:5): "If thou has run with the footmen and they have wearied thee, then how canst thou contend with horses?"

Queen Hatshepsut making a ritual run with the bull god Apis between 1490 and 1468 B.C. (from a block from the Temple of Karnak, 18th Dynasty).

were a man, was another "royal runner." An image of her running is shown on a 1480 B.C. stone relief from the 18th Dynasty of the New Kingdom in Egypt. She also had to prove her fitness with the time-honored ceremonial run. The stone relief shows her in the middle of the ceremony, accompanied by the bull-god Apis.*

Foot-racing is the oldest and most universal of all sports. The earliest known foot-races were the "city races" held in ancient Sumer. Dating from about 2035 B.C., these races concluded with animal sacrifices in

Finally, there are two interesting long-distance runs recorded in the Old Testament. These two runs were both to announce the outcome of battles and predated Pheidippides' legendary run from Marathon to Athens by over five centuries. I Samuel 4:12 describes a 1080 B.C. run by a man of the tribe of Benjamin. He ran 26 miles (42 km) from Aphek to Shiloh to

*Early artists had problems drawing correct running form from memory. Sometimes Greek artists drew a runner with both the right leg and right arm forward. Even in the 19th century illustrators were still having trouble depicting correct running form as can be seen by the illustration of "The Great Race" in Chapter IV where the runners still have both feet on the ground.

inform Eli, the Greek priest, of Israel's defeat by the Philistines. "And there ran a man of Benjamin out of the army, and came to Shiloh the same day, with his clothes rent, and with earth upon his head."

At about the same time (II Samuel 18) Ahimaaz outran a Cushite messenger to deliver the news of an Israeli victory. This run was about 36 miles (57 km) from Emphrain to Mahanaim. When Ahimaaz neared his destination, the watchman on the roof of the gate said, "I think the running of the foremost is like the running of Ahimaaz the son of Zadok." That he was recognized by his running form suggests Ahimaaz was already a well-known runner.

## Running in Greek Mythology

Running contests were popular in Greek mythology. At Olympia, in mythical times, Apollo beat Hermes at running. Odysseus won Penelope in a suitor's race staged by her father Icarius. Danaus of Argos needed help finding husbands for his daughters. It seems all but one of his 50 daughters (the Danaids) had slain their husbands on their wedding night. Danaus solved the problem by staging a suitor's race and letting the winner have the first choice for a wife. The second place finisher chose next and so on. The daughters who were left had to wait for a new batch of suitors and another race.

## Atalanta—Racing for Golden Apples

The two greatest runners in Greek mythology were Atalanta and Achilles. Atalanta was a woman who excelled at hunting, wrestling and running — activities usually dominated by men. Although the legend of Atalanta is a tale from classical (4th or 5th century B.C.) Greek mythology, the Roman writer Ovid (42 B.C.–A.D. 17) gives the best account of her running in *Metamorphoses*.

Atalanta doggedly repulsed a throng of suitors until her father finally insisted that she must marry. She agreed, but confident that no one could outrun her, made the condition that whomever she married must first beat her in a race. And should the unfortunate suitor lose the race he would also lose his life. Hippomones, who was not much of a runner, at first couldn't understand why the suitors were willing to meet their doom in futile races with Atalanta. When he got a glimpse of Atalanta ridding herself of superfluous clothing before a race, he changed his mind. He had not understood the value of the prize. Knowing he had no chance in a fair race with Atalanta, Hippomones asked the goddess Venus to help make up for his lack of speed and conditioning. In this excerpt from *Metamorphoses*, Venus described how she helped Hippomones win the race:

> The trumpet sounded the start: The pair, each crouching low, shot forward, skimming the sand with flying feet, so lightly they could run on waves and never wet their sandals, they could run on fields of grain and never bend them. He heard them cheering: "Go Hippomenes, lean to the work, use all your strength: go, go, you are sure to win!"
> I could not tell you whether the cheering pleased him more, or Atalanta. How many times, when she could have passed, she lingered, slowed to see his face, and most unwilling, sprinted ahead! And now his breath labored, came in great sobbing gasps, and the finish line was a long way off, and he tossed one golden apple, the first one, down. She looked at it with wonder, eager to have the shining fruit, she darted out of the course, and picked it up, still rolling, the golden thing. He gained the lead again as all the people roared applause. She passed him again, and once again lost ground to follow the toss of the second apple, and once more caught up and sprinted past him.

**Atalanta and Hippomones race (from the painting by Poynter) (from C. M. Gayley, *The Classic Myths in English Literature and in Art*, Ginn and Co., 1911).**

"O be near me, gift-bringing Goddess, help me now!" he cried, and this time threw the third apple farther, angling it off the course, way to one side. She hesitated, only for a moment, whether to chase it, but I made her do it, and made the fruit weigh more, so she was hindered both by the burden of her own delay. To run my story quickly, as the race was run, the girl was beaten, and the winner led off the prize.

Later, Venus was angry with Hippomenes for not showing the proper gratitude for his victory. She caused the couple to make love in a temple, an indiscretion that prompted the gods to turn them into lions. Before they were changed into lions, Atalanta and Hippomones had a son, Parthenopeus, who was a great runner and raced in the first Nemean Games.

## The Iliad—Achilles and Odysseus

Running was of special importance to the ancient Greeks. The philosopher Xenophanes considered swiftness of foot to be the most highly prized quality a man could have. Homer also thought running ability was man's most important physical trait. In the Iliad he consistently refers to the "fleet-footed," or in some translations, "the great runner" Achilles.

Throughout the *Iliad* (written about 750 B.C.), running plays a major role. Achilles, greatest of the Greek heroes, was given a choice. He could have either a heroic life and an early death, or a long life without honor. He chose the first option, as might many elite runners of today. This is born out by a poll Dr. Gabe Mirkin described in *The Sport Medicine Book* (1978). He asked 100 top runners: "If I could give you a pill that would make you an Olympic champion — and kills you in a year — would you take it?" More than half said they would.

The first account of running is in Book 22 of the *Iliad*. After Hector slew Achilles' lifelong friend Patroklos, an enraged Achilles chased Hector around the walls of Troy. Since Hector was a brave and honorable man, his running from Achilles is probably to prove Achilles' superiority at running rather than that Hector was a coward.

Fear fell upon Hector as he beheld him, and he dared not stay longer where he was but fled in dismay from before the gates, while Achilles darted after him at his utmost speed. As a mountain falcon, swiftest of all birds, swoops down upon some cowering dove — the dove flies before him but the falcon with a shrill scream follows close after, resolved to have her — even so did Achilles make straight for Hector with all his might, while Hector fled under the Trojan wall as fast as his limbs could take him.

On they flew along the wagon-road that ran hard by under the wall, past the lookout station, and past the weather-beaten wild fig-tree, till they came to two fair springs which feed the river Scamander. Past these did they fly, the one in front and the other giving chase behind him: good was the man that fled, but better far was he that followed after, and swiftly indeed did they run, for the prize was no mere beast for sacrifice or bullock's hide, as it might be for a common foot-race, but they ran for the life of Hector. As horses in a chariot race speed round the turning-posts when they are running for some great prize — a tripod or woman — at the games in honor of some dead hero, so did these two run full speed three times round the city of Priam.

Achilles continued the chase, keeping to the inside to prevent Hector from reaching the shelter of the walls. Apollo gave Hector a last burst of speed, but when they reached the springs for the fourth time Zeus weighed their fates:

...Then, at last, as they were nearing the fountains for the fourth time, the father of all balanced his golden scales and placed a doom in each of them, one for Achilles and the other for Hector. As he held the scales by the middle, the doom of Hector fell down deep into the house of Hades.

...and when the two were now close to one another great Hector was first to speak. "I will–no longer fly you, son of Peleus," said he, "as I have been doing hitherto. Three times have I fled round the mighty city of Priam, without daring to withstand you, but now, let me either slay or be slain, for I am in the mind to face you."

Hector, realizing he was doomed, bravely attacked, but Achilles dispatched him with a spear thrust and dragged his body around the walls of Troy behind his chariot.

We don't know how far they ran in their suits of bronze armor, but it may have been about 1.5 miles (2.4 km). Heinrich Schliemann, a German archaeologist, excavated what he thought was Troy in 1868. The walls were about a half mile (.8 km) in circumference. The Greeks would later have a race in armor in their athletic festivals, but the longest was only about a half mile. Even the great runner Achilles was taxed by the run as he complained of sore muscles the next day.

In Book 23 of the *Iliad*, Achilles held funeral games for his friend Patroklos. The ancient Greeks believed that the dead continued to exist in a sort of shadow world below the earth, but they were slow moving and without strength. Athletic competitions, they believed, would allow the dead to somehow absorb some of the energy of the athletes. Patroklos had been cremated and the crowd at the funeral was about to disperse when Achilles brought prizes from his ships and held seven athletic contests, one of them a foot-race:

The son of Peleus then offered prizes for speed in running — a mixing-bowl beautifully wrought, of pure silver... and Achilles now offered it as a prize in honor of his comrade to him who should be the swiftest runner. For the second prize he offered a large ox, well fattened, while for the last there was to be half a talent of gold. He then rose and said among the Argives, "Stand forward, you who will essay this contest."

Forthwith uprose fleet Ajax son of Oileus, with cunning Odysseus, and Nestor's son Antilochus, the fastest runner among all the youth of his time. They stood side by side and Achilles showed them the goal. The course was set out for them from the starting-post, and the son of Oileus took the lead at once, with Odysseus as close behind him as the shuttle is to a woman's bosom when she throws the woof across the warp and holds it close up to her; even so close behind him was Odysseus — treading in his footprints before the dust could settle there, and Ajax could feel his breath on the back of his head as he ran swiftly on.

The Achaeans all shouted applause as they saw him straining his utmost, and cheered him as he shot past them; but when they were, now nearing the end of the course Odysseus prayed inwardly to Athena. "Hear me," he cried, "and help my feet, O goddess." Thus did he pray, and Athena heard his prayer; she made his hands and his feet feel light, and when the runners were at the point of pouncing upon the prize, Ajax, through Athena's spite slipped upon some offal that was lying there from the cattle which Achilles had slaughtered in honor of Patroclus, and his mouth and nostrils were all filled with cow dung.

Odysseus therefore carried off the mixing-bowl, for he got before Ajax and came in first. But Ajax took the ox and stood with his hand on one of its horns, spitting the dung out of his mouth. Then he said to the Argives, "Alas, the goddess has spoiled my running; she watches over Odysseus and stands by him as though she were his own mother." Thus did he speak and they all of them laughed heartily.

The length of the race is uncertain but the "goal" referred to was probably a turning post. The race started and finished near the altar and was probably on an out-and-back course of perhaps 400 meters. Only three runners—all Greek heroes—competed. The prizes were not wreaths, as at Olympia, but expensive treasures for all three runners. In the last and decisive stage of the race Athena made doubly certain Odysseus would win by giving him a burst of speed and by causing Ajax to slip in ox dung. An observer would not have known that there was divine intervention although, somehow, Ajax does.

In Book eight of the *Odyssey*, Homer briefly describes a foot-race on the island of Phaeacia. Odysseus had been cast ashore on the island and befriended by the princess Nausikaa. The Phaeacians held a feast in Odysseus's honor and invited him to participate in their athletic contests, one of which was a foot-race.

> All lined up tense; then Go! and down the track they raised the dust in a flying bunch, strung out longer and longer behind Prince Klytoneus. By just so far as a mule team, breaking ground, will distance oxen, he left all behind and came up to the crowd, an easy winner.

This seemingly odd description of the winner's victory margin illustrates some of the difficulties the Greeks had measuring distance.

Later authors of epics shamelessly copied Homer's funeral-games race. Some of these were written over a thousand years after the Iliad. Each is different and gives a glimpse of running in the ancient world. It is difficult to tell if the author is describing foot-racing of his own time or an earlier time when the story took place.

## The Aeneid

In the *Aeneid* by Virgil (29–19 B. C.) the runners were young men and the field was huge.

> …at a sudden signal the runners from their places started forth and scattered like a cloud, eyes fixed on goal. Before them all by far ran Nisus, flashing and swifter than the wings of wind or lightning. Next to him but at a long interval Salius followed. Then with a space between came Euryalus, third. Helymus followed him, and at his heels flew Diores, his shoulder thrusting forward so closely that if they had raced a longer distance, he would have crossed the finish line a winner, or have tied.
>
> Now in the home stretch came the weary runners, when Nisus, unlucky, slipped on a bit of ground where bulls were slaughtered and their spilled blood had soaked the grass around. Here the young victor as he reached the spot, already triumphing, staggered and fell face

down in filthy and sacred gore. Yet not forgetful of Euryalus, his love, he rose from the slippery ground and blocked Salius: he in turn rolled over on the hard-packed sand. Euryalus flashed ahead to win first place, thanks to his friend, as if flying amidst applause. Helymus came in second and Diores third.

In this version there was no divine intervention. When Salius protested that he was tripped, the race director settled the dispute by giving prizes to all the runners.

## Thebaid

The next retelling is by the Roman poet Statius, in the *Thebaid*, written near the end of the first century A.D. He gave a fascinating account of the first Nemean Games held in 573 B.C. Among the runners in this race were Idas, a recent Olympic victor and Parthenopeus, son of Atalanta.

The champion runners then he bade compete for ample prizes, theirs a light-foot sport of frailest valor, a pursuit of peace when sacred games invite, of some use too in war, if strong hands shrink.

First of them all Idas sprang forth, whose brow Olympian wreaths had lately shaded, welcomed by the cheers of Elis' youth and Pisa's. After him Alcon of Sicyon and Phaedimus, twice acclaimed victor on the Isthmus' sands, and Dymas who had once outraced swift steeds but now age slowed him and he lagged behind, and many more unknown to the mixed crowd came forth, here, there, in silence.

But a roar rolled through the packed circles for Parthenopeus of Arcadia. His mother's speed was famous. Who does not know Atalanta's glory and those strides no suitor could outstrip? That fame of hers burdened her son and he, far-famed himself, in high Lycaeus' glades was said to catch defenseless hinds on foot and outrace a javelin. At last across the rows he vaulted flashing past,

and loosed the clasp of twisted gold that held his cloak. His body shone, the whole joy of his limbs displayed, his splendid shoulders, chest as fine as beardless cheeks, and valor plain to see. But he scorned the praise and held himself aloof from his admirers. Then he stooped and smeared, no novice, Pallas' oil and browned his skin with the rich ointment.

…then they all started limbering up in varied exercise, well-trained confusion, squatting with knees bent, slapping oiled chests and flexing firey legs in short-lived sprints that reach a sudden end.

The barrier dropped, the starting-line was clear, and down the course they sped, a lightfoot group, bare bodies gleaming.

Down the same furlongs the steeds that had just raced seemed not so fast; you'd think them arrows flying from the bows of Cretans or retreating Parthians, swift as the stags that course Hyrcanian wilds when from afar they hear or think they hear the roar of hungry lions; Terrified, they bunch together in blind flight and long the crash of clashing horns is audible.

Faster than racing winds the Arcadian lad outstripped the watching eye, and close behind grim Idas clung and breathed upon his back, his breath and body's shadow pressing hard; next Phaedimus and Dymas, side by side and Alcon on their heels. His golden hair hung down unshorn, from childhood nourished for Diana, daring promise vowed in vain to grace his father's altar, when from war with Thebes he should return victorious. Unbanded then and flowing wide behind it streamed back in the breeze, both hindering him and hampering his rival Idas too. So Idas meant to cheat and took his chance. The finish now was near. Parthenopeus, winning, was almost on the line when he pulled him back by his hair and took his place and breasting the long ribbon won the race.

From a running point-of-view, this is the most interesting version of the funeral games. Except for the oil and chest-beating, the way runners prepare for a race hasn't changed much in the last two thousand years. The phrase "the barrier dropped" is a reference to the starting-gate used at the Nemean Games. The tape at the finish is not shown in any Greek vase paintings.

Idas's grabbing Parthenopeus by the hair is probably the most blatant foul in running history. It's hard to imagine why he was not disqualified. Parthenopeus threw a tantrum and prayed to the goddess Diana, complaining that it was her fault he lost because he grew his hair long because of a vow he made to her. The race director — at first uncertain what to do—finally decided to rerun the race. In the rerun, he warned the two runners about cheating and put them in lanes on opposite sides of the track. Parthenopeus won easily — justice prevailed.

## The Greek Olympic Games—Model for the Modern Olympics

The Greek Olympic Games were inspired by religious festivals and funeral games and emerged from the mists of antiquity in 776 B.C. The Games, which were open to all free, male Greeks, were held in high regard and continued for over a thousand years without interruption. Each participant swore to Zeus that he would abide by the rules of the Games and the decisions of the judges. Winning an Olympic crown made of branches from a sacred olive tree was an act of worship to honor Zeus and to appease the spirits of dead heroes. Olympic winners received more than just an olive crown. They were allowed statues of themselves in the sanctuary at Olympia. After three victories they were entitled portrait statues instead of generic ones. The winner's native city often gave him a magnificent victory celebration, large cash awards and free meals for life. An Olympic victor might also have a victory hymn composed by a famous poet such as Pindar.

Although the Olympic Games were the most important of the Greek games, most of the other major city-states also had athletic games. By the middle of the 6th century B.C., three other "crown-games" were in existence. These four festivals were distinguished from the more local festivals in that they offered no prize money. Like today's Olympics they depended on their prestige to attract participants. The crown-games made up the "Circuit" which stood apart from the other festivals in the quality of athletic competition. The circuit consisted of the festivals in the table below.

The Circuit was arranged so that at least one of the Games was held every year. This allowed an athlete to compete against top competition from one Olympic festival to the next.

Greek foot-races were held on a rectangular space approximately 230 meters long and 30 meters wide called a stade or stadion. The length of the race took its name from this word — so did the place where the race was held (the stadium). On the sides, gently sloping embankments provided room for 20,000 to 40,000 spectators to stand or sit on the ground. At Olympia — grandest

| Festival | Site | First Held | In Honor of | Crown | Interval between |
|----------|------|------------|-------------|-------|------------------|
| Olympic | Olympia | 776 B.C. | Zeus | Olive | 4 yr. |
| Pythian | Delphi | 586 B.C. | Apollo | Laurel | 4 yr. |
| Isthmian | Corinth | 580 B.C. | Poseidon | Pine | 2 yr. |
| Nemean | Nemea | 573 B.C. | Zeus | Celery | 2 yr. |

of the crown games— the stade had 20 lanes and a 192-meter straightaway of clay covered with a thin layer of sand. Races longer than 192 meters (one stade) required abrupt 180-degree turns around turning-posts at each end of the race course.

The stadia at Olympia, Delphi, Nemea and Isthmia have all been excavated, but we still don't know for certain how the runners started, turned around the posts, or finished. Nor do we know much about their tactics or training, which probably varied from stadium to stadium and changed over the 12 centuries the Olympic Games lasted.

Throughout history, the problem of providing a fair start for short-distance races has challenged the ingenuity of those putting on races. The tension at the start of an important sprint race is extreme. The temptation to "jump the gun" or obtain an edge somehow is enormous. The Greeks developed some interesting ways to deal with this problem.

Runners at Olympia originally started from a line drawn in the sand. In the 5th century B.C. a stone slab was placed across the track with two parallel grooves perpendicular to the track and about six inches (15 cm) apart. The distance between the grooves varied from stadium to stadium but was commonly one half "foot." The barefoot runners used the grooves as simple starting blocks, pressing their heels against the lip of the rear groove and gripping the front groove with their toes. At Corinth, where the Isthmian Games were held, the grooves were replaced by two separate depressions in each of the 16 lanes. The front depression was for the left foot and the rear for the right. These depressions were 0.63 meters apart— much farther than the grooves at Olympia. The starting line at the Stadia at Isthmus and on Delos had only one groove.

If a Greek runner false-started, he was whipped with a forked stick. More serious offenses, such as trying to bribe opponents or officials, resulted in severe fines. The Greeks used these fines to build bronze stat-

ues of Zeus near the stadium entrance. At the base of each statue was an inscription warning against cheating. This method of punishment must have been effective because only 14 statues were erected.

Greek race officials went to great lengths to ensure fairness. Officials from Elis (the city-state that staged the Olympic Games) once sent ambassadors to ask the Egyptians if there was any way they could make the Olympic Games more fair. The Egyptians asked if the Eleans allowed their own citizens to compete. The Eleans answered proudly that the games were open to all Greeks, whether they belonged to Elis or not. But the Egyptians replied that if this were true, it was impossible for them not to favor their own countrymen and if they really wanted fairness, they should confine the contests to strangers.

Vases and statues show that the runners at Olympia — even the sprinters— started from upright positions. The closely-spaced double grooves in the starting slab made this starting position necessary. The grooves were not ideal for fast starts but they assured an equal length racecourse for each runner and kept the length of the racecourse the same.

## Starting Gates— a 400 B.C. Innovation

The need to guarantee a fair start was of paramount importance to the Greeks since the direction of the games reflected on the authority, reputation and prestige of the host. Archeologists have found evidence of starting gates in several Greek stadia. Oscar Broneer unearthed a starting gate at Isthmia in the 1950s which he called a "balbides" sill. It was dated at about 400 B.C. and consisted of a gate for each runner with grooves running along the ground for cords leading to the starter's pit behind the runners.

The starter released all the cords at the same time, allowing the barriers to fall and

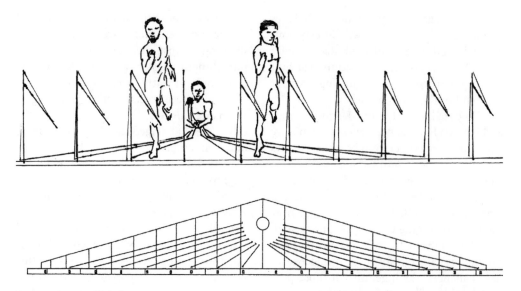

**Reconstruction of the balbides starting system. The system did not insure a fair start and was replaced by the more advanced hysplex (drawing by author).**

freeing each runner to start. This mechanism had two serious problems. With so many strings, it would have been easy for some to get snarled, leaving runners stranded on their marks. Because the cords were of different lengths, the gates would also not have all opened at the same time. David Romano, in *Athletics and Mathematics in Archaic Corinth: the Origins of the Greek Stadion* (1993), computed that the starting mechanism gave an unfair advantage of up to .1 second to the runners in the middle of the track. This may have been recognized quite quickly, since this type of starting gate was soon abandoned and the Greeks came up with a much more successful type called a *hysplex*. Until recently no one understood how it worked. The 1970 discovery of a broken Greek vase with an illustration of two runners starting behind two parallel ropes provided Greek Panos Valavanis and American Dr. Stephen G. Miller with enough information to reconstruct the device.

The *hysplex* consisted of two taut ropes stretched in front of the runners. One rope was about knee high and the other waist high. The ropes were attached to poles on each end. The poles and ropes were lowered

suddenly by twisted-rope springs at the bases of the poles. This is similar technology to that used in ancient catapults, but instead of hurling a stone the mechanism snapped the poles and ropes to the ground with an action like that of a mousetrap. From ancient writings we know that this was accompanied by a loud noise. Like today's starter's gun, the device announced to everyone in the stadium that the race had started.

When lowered, the ropes were flat on the ground in front of the runners; Dr. Miller was concerned that the runners might have tripped over them. He and Valavanis reconstructed the mechanism in 1993. Many tests, first with students and then in the revised Nemean Games, showed that tripping was not a problem. When the ropes were on the ground, they were in the midflight phase of the runners' strides.

Hysplex installations were also used at Isthmia, Corinth and Epidauros from roughly 300 B.C. According to Dr. Miller, it is possible that a Corinthian named Philon set up all four of them. Other types of starting gates were used elsewhere: Monumental versions with fancy pulleys and metallic springs were used at Priene and

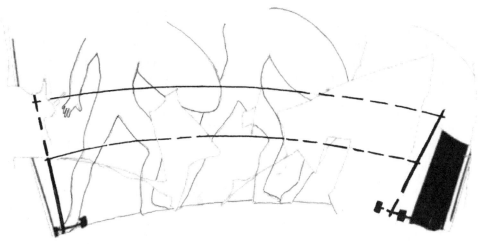

*Top:* Rope starting mechanism (hysplex). The two ropes were attached to spring-loaded poles that snapped down in front of the runners allowing them to start (Third Ephorate of Antiquities Collection A 6374, Athens, Greece). *Bottom:* Operation of hysplex system at Nemea (drawing by author).

Miletus from about 150 B.C. At Olympia, the part of the starting line that is preserved is from the Roman period (after 146 B.C.). The starting gate used there was lighter in construction than those at Priene and Miletus, and used metallic instead of twisted-rope springs. Starting gates have been tried in modern times. They were used at Madison Square Garden for indoor meets in the 1940s, but never caught on.

## Stadion Race (200 meters)

The winner of the Stadion race could justifiably be called the fastest man in the Greek world. According to legend, Herakles, whose feet were 0.32 meters (12.7 inches) long, stepped-off the Stadion at Olympia. Since he chose a distance of 600 "feet," this made the race at Olympia 192 meters. Herakles staged a race for his brothers, the Kouretes, and crowned the victor with a branch of wild olive. Although the Greek Stadion race was always 600 feet, other Greek gods had "feet" of different lengths. This caused the length of the Stadion race to vary slightly from stadium to stadium. The list of Olympic victors compiled by Hippias in about 400 B.C. lists the Stadion race as the only event in the first 13 Olympic Games. Coreobus of Elis, a cook, was the victor in the Stadion race in 776 B.C. and thus the first recorded Olympic victor.

According to another tradition, the Stadion race originated as a way of deciding who had the honor of lighting the sacrificial fire at the altar. The priest laid the sacrificial offerings ready on the altar at the finish, but did not light the fire. He stood waiting with a torch while the runners started from one Stadion away. The winner got to kindle the offering and was crowned Olympic victor. Based on this tradition early Greek racecourses were designed with their finishes near the altar.

Lots were drawn for lanes and heats

were run much as in modern races. The winner of each heat went on to the finals. It was therefore necessary to win twice to receive the olive crown for winning the Stadion. Beginning at the 37th Olympic festival (632 B.C.), there was a boys' (ages 17 through 20) Stadion race as well as men's. Interestingly, very few of the winning boys repeated their victories in later years in the men's races.

In about 300 B.C. Greek historians began using a calendar based on four-year periods called Olympiads. The festival itself wasn't an Olympiad, although the term is now commonly used to refer to the modern Olympic festival. Each Olympiad took the name of the winner of the Stadion race of the festival that began that period. Thus, the Stadion winner won a sort of immortality.

## Diaulos Race

The Diaulos or double Stadion (384 meters) race was added to the program at the 14th Olympic festival in 724 B.C. It differed from the 400-meter race of today in that it was necessary to turn around the posts at the end of the stadium. There is some uncertainty as to how the Greek runners made these turns. The most logical arrangement would have been for each runner to have a post at the edge of his lane. He then could turn without interference into the adjacent empty lane. This would have prevented collisions and interference but would have required an empty lane on each runner's left. Such an arrangement was possible since the stadium at Olympia had 20 lanes—enough for ten runners. As in indoor races of today which have tight turns, a small, light runner would have had an advantage at the turn. His momentum would have been less, making rounding the post easier. We know from vase painting that the Greeks turned counterclockwise around the posts.

Hercules chasing the Stag of Carynea. It took him a year to finally wear the animal down and catch it. Prehumans were able to do much better (from F. R. Niglutsch, *Greatest Nations and World Famous Events*, Axillary Education League, NY, 1913, 1914, 1921).

## Hippos Race

This race was four lengths of the stadium (a total distance of from 710–760 meters). It was named Hippos or "horsey" because it was the same length as the hippodrome used for the chariot races. Hippos races were run at Isthmia, Nemea and at various local festivals but not at Olympia.

## Dolichos Race (4,600 meters)

The Dolichos, or long race, was added to the Olympic program in 720 B.C. According to the Greek writer Philostratos, who wrote a training manual called *Gymnasticus* in A.D. 230, the race originated to provide a means for couriers or *Hemerodromos* (one who ran all day) to show their skills. Although the longest of the Greek races, it was more of a middle-distance race by today's standards. Its length varied from

seven to 24 stadia (1.3 to 4.6 km). At Olympia it was probably 4.6 km. A single turning-post near the center of each end of the racecourse was probably used for the turns. Runners were (and still are) normally strung out in a race of this length and multiple turning-posts at each end of the course would have been unnecessary.

A unique curved starting line used for the long race and dating from about 500 B.C. has been excavated in Corinth. Scholars believe the Greeks chose a curved starting line to provide an equal running distance for each runner. The focus of this curved starting line is about one-third of the way to the turning-post. This approximately 61-meter (200 ft.) distance was apparently the point where the Dolichos runners converged into a single wide lane in the center of the track. The curved starting line accounted for only about two feet (.6 m) and shows the extremes to which the Greeks would go to ensure fairness.

***Top:*** Greek Stadion runners of the fourth century B.C. (from Edward Norman Gardiner, ***Greek Athletic Sports and Festivals***, 1910). ***Bottom:*** Greek Dolichos or distance runners of 333 B.C. (from Edward Norman Gardiner, ***Greek Athletic Sports and Festivals***, 1910).

## Hoplitodromos (Racing in Armor)

The race in armor was the last running event to be added to the Olympic program. It was introduced in the 65th festival in 520 B.C. and was the last event on the program. It seems to have been one of the most popular races and was a common subject for vase painters of the time. At Olympia, the race was two stadia long, and the runners wore helmets and shin guards and carried bronze shields. Around 478 B.C. the shin guards were abandoned and the following

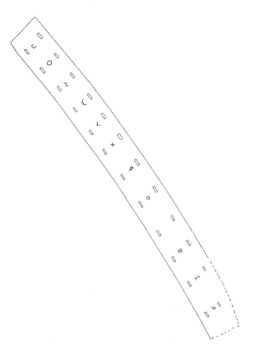

**Curved starting line at Corinth with painted lane numbers (drawing by author).**

century the helmets were discarded also. The runners carried the shield as long as the event was held. This race must have been a sight to behold, with the armed runners trying to retain their running form while rounding the turning posts carrying bulky shields. Greek vase paintings show several incidences of falls and collisions in this race.

According to Philostratos, the best of the armed races was held at Plataea. The race there was longer than at Olympia and the competitors raced in true battle armor. At Plataea there was also a strange custom that if the winner of the race entered a second time and lost, he was put to death. It would have taken a lot of courage to try to repeat as Hoplit champion at Plataea.

E. Norman Gardiner in 1903 arranged paintings from several vases to show how he thought the armed runners started, approached the turning-pole and turned.

## Lampadadromia (Relay Race with Torches)

There was no custom of relaying a torch to light the Olympic flame in the ancient games. Carl Diem, organizer of the 1936 Berlin Olympics, staged the first lighting of the Olympic flame. The torch race or *Lampadadromia* was a popular pastime

Race in armor, ancient Olympic Games (from Edward Norman Gardiner, *Greek Athletic Sports and Festivals*, 1910).

Edward Norman Gardiner's reconstruction of the armed race, showing the start (right) and turn (left) (from Edward Normal Gardiner, "Notes on the Greek Foot-race," *Journal of Hellenic Studies* 23, 1903).

among young Greeks. These were relay races run at night using lighted torches. Typically, six to eight runners made a team. The races not only required skill in exchanging the torches but also in keeping them lighted, for if the torch went out, that team lost. If the wind was blowing, the runners sometimes had to run in a comical, stooped attitude to protect the flame.

## Outstanding Runners in the Ancient World

The Greeks had two ways of measuring the passage of time — the sundial and the water clock. Neither of these was suitable for timing races. The use of a "foot" that varied from stadium to stadium would have made records meaningless in any case. Victories were what counted. There was no recognition for second or third place. In addition to seeking victories, runners tried to become the first to accomplish various feats, which if noteworthy enough, might earn them special recognition.

Alexander the Great (356–323 B.C.), in addition to conquering most of the known world, reportedly excelled at running. He was once asked if he would run in the Olympic Games. His answer suggests he was not sure he could win: "I would gladly run there, if I could run with kings, for if I should race with a private person, our victories would not be equal."

We have no way of knowing how running performances of the ancient Greeks would compare with those of today. We do have information on some memorable runs and runners, however. Polymnestor, a shepherd boy from Miletus and victor in the boys' Stadion race at the 46th Olympic festival, was credited with catching a hare by fleetness of foot. Lasthenes, the Theban, outraced a horse from Choroneus to Thebes, a distance of about 20 miles (32 km). Ageus of Argos won the Olympic Dolichos race (4.6 km) in 328 B.C., and ran the 60 miles (97 km) to his home the same day to announce his victory. Drymos of Epidauros also ran home the same day he won at Olympia, covering about 80 miles (130 km). The Spartan runner Anystis and Alexander the Great's courier Philonides both ran 148 miles (238 km) from Sicyon to Elis in a day. The modern record for running 24 hours was set in 1997 by Yiannis Kouros, a Greek-born Australian, when he ran 188.6 miles (303 km). Anystis and Philonides were quite respectable ultra-distance runners even by today's standards.

Ladas, a Dolichos runner of the fifth century B.C., was the most famous distance runner in the Greek Olympic Games. It was said that "after he had run over the sand, where all the other athletes left a deep imprint, there was no sign to show he had passed." On his way home from one of his Olympic victories, Ladas fell ill and died. In modern times the phrase "to pull a Ladas," has been used to describe a runner dropping dead, figuratively or otherwise, at the end of a race. There is no evidence, however, that Ladas died because of his running.

Leonidas of Rhodes, said to have had

The death of Ladas (19th century illustration). He actually died on his way home from the Olympic Games (from F. R. Niglutsch, *Greatest Nations and World Famous Events*, Axillary Education League, NY, 1913, 1914, 1921).

"the speed of a god," was the most famous sprinter in the Greek Olympic Games. Although he appeared late in the history of the games when the quality of competition may have been on the decline, his feat of winning the three short races in four Olympiads has never been equaled. Leonidas was eventually made a minor deity for his running achievements—probably the greatest honor a runner can obtain.

| Olympic Victories | | | | | |
|---|---|---|---|---|---|
| Leonidas of Rhodes | | | | Carl Lewis | |
| Olympic Festival | Date (B.C.) | Event | Olympic Festival | Date (A.D.) | Event |
| 154th | 164 | Stadion (200 m) Diaulos (400 m) Race in Armor (400 m) | 23rd | 1984 | 100 m 200 m 4 × 100 Relay Long Jump |
| 155th | 160 | Stadion Diaulos Race in Armor | 24th | 1988 | 100 m Long Jump |
| 156th | 156 | Stadion Diaulos Race in Armor | 25th | 1992 | 4 × 100 Relay Long Jump |
| 157th | 152 | Stadion Diaulos Race in Armor | 26th | 1996 | Long Jump |

It is interesting to compare Leonidas's Olympic victories with those of perhaps the greatest modern Olympic sprinter. It should be noted that Leonidas did not have to contend with a boycott as Carl Lewis did in 1980.

Who would have won a race between Leonidas and Lewis at 200 meters, a distance at which both won Olympic victories? Without a time machine, we will never know, but the odds would favor Lewis. Leonidas was the fastest runner in the Pan-Hellenic world, with a population of perhaps four million. Lewis was the fastest man on earth, when the earth's population was over five billion.

## Training for the Ancient Olympic Games

Philostratos in *On Gymnastics* (about A.D. 230) describes the optimum builds for the various races:

The best candidate for the *Dolichos* [4.6 km] should have a powerful neck and shoulders like the candidate for the pentathlon, but should have light, slender legs like the runners of the *Stadion* [200 meters]. The latter stir their legs into the sprint by using their hands as if they were wings. The runners in the *Dolichos* do this near the end of the race, but the rest of the time they move almost as if they were walking, holding up their hands in front of them, and because of this they need stronger shoulders....

Candidates for the *Diaulos* [400 meters] should be stronger than those for the *Stadion*, but lighter than those in the *Hoplitodromos* [400 meter race in armor]. Those who compete in all three races should be put together from qualifications which are needed in each single race. Do not think that this is impossible, for there have been such runners even in our day.

Except for the "powerful neck and shoulders" of the 4.6 km runners, Philostratos could be describing runners of today. The Olympic rules required that all those entered train for at least ten months before the festival and spend the last month at Olympia undergoing final preparations. Little is known of the ancients' actual training methods. Each Olympian had a coach or trainer who is usually shown on vase paintings holding a forked stick ready to strike the athlete. Training also included massage, walking and running exercises, as well as practicing starting and turning.

The Greeks believed that a special diet was needed to run well. Until the fifth century B.C. their diet included barley bread, wheat porridge, dried figs, nuts and fresh cheese. Later meat was added, mostly pork or beef. According to Pausanias, Dromeus of Stymphalus won the Olympic Dolichos in 484 and 480 B.C. on a diet of meat. The Greeks were not averse to trying to find "the racer's edge." The Greek physician Galen (about A.D. 180) reported Greek Olympians of the third century B.C. ate herbs and mushrooms in an effort to enhance performance.

Olympia, as well as many Greek cities, had an indoor running track for use during bad weather. These were long halls 10–12 meters wide and approximately the same length as the actual Olympic track. Many of them had provisions for practicing starts and making turns. Even today 200-meter indoor tracks are rare. Building and maintaining them would have been expensive for the ancient Greeks and illustrates their deep commitment to running.

Sprinters sometimes practiced in heavy sand and distance runners chased animals and ran up hills holding their breath. Distance runners were sometimes paced by men on horseback. Philostratos described a training method called "tetrads" which consisted of a four-day training cycle: "On the first day the athlete is prepared; on the second intensively engaged; on the third, given over to recreation; and on the fourth, moderately exerted."

The cycle was apparently repeated endlessly. Philostratos was critical of the method because he believed it deprived the athlete of an "intelligent understanding" of what he was doing.

It is unfortunate that we do not know more about the training methods of the ancient Greeks. Modern training methods for running date from Captain Barclay in the early 1800s and are still largely based on runners' or coaches' intuition and trial and error. Although we have had 200 years to develop these methods, the ancient Greeks had almost 1,200 years of Olympic experience in developing theirs.

## Letting All Things Be Uncovered—Running Naked

There are two major differences between the way the Greeks ran at Olympia and the way we run today. They ran both barefoot and *gymnos* (naked). Scholars of today, as well as the ancient Greeks themselves, agree that the custom of running naked was started in the Olympic Games but disagree on the date and the individual responsible for the innovation. Pausanias credits Orsippos of Megara, who was, according to tradition, the first Greek to race nude:

> Near the tomb of Koroibos is buried Orsippos, who won the *Stadion* at Olympia [720 B.C.]. While the other athletes in the competition wore loincloths in accordance with the ancient practice, he ran naked.... I think that the loincloth slipped off deliberately at Olympia, for he recognized that a nude man can run more easily than one who is girt.

This is the most famous legend explaining the origin of Greek nude racing, but other accounts claim that a Spartan was first. Isidore of Seville (seventh century A.D.) also has an interesting account:

> For earlier, when the contestants were covered so that they should not be nude, a certain runner was suddenly thrown and killed when his loincloth slipped. Therefore, the archon Hippomenes allowed the competitors to exercise nude from then on.

Pausanias's explanation of being able to run faster naked seems strange. Unless a loincloth was too tight or otherwise ill-fitted, it is hard to see how it would offer much hindrance to running. The second explanation is even stranger. How could a runner get tangled up in his loincloth and fall on a sand- covered track and kill himself? Lucian, in *Solon and Anacharsis* (2nd century A.D.), has a slightly more believable explanation — nudity as a training aid:

> ...for this reason, expecting to appear unclothed before so many people, they try to attain good physical condition so that they may not be ashamed of themselves when they are stripped, and each makes himself as fit to win as he can.

Plato (427–344 B.C.) in *The Republic* attributes the Cretans with originating the custom and suggests that even during their own time, the Greeks were scorned for running naked:

> Not long ago, as we shall remind them, the Hellenes were of the opinion, which is still generally received among the barbarians, that the sight of a naked man was ridiculous and improper; and when first the Cretans and then the Spartans introduced the custom, the wits of that day might equally have ridiculed the innovation. But when experience showed that to let all things be uncovered was far better than to cover them up, and the ludicrous effect to the outward eye vanished before the better principle which reason asserted, then the man was perceived to be a fool who directs the shafts of his ridicule at any other sight but that of folly and vice or seriously inclines to weigh the beautiful by any other standard but that of the very good.

Despite all these colorful explanations, many scholars believe the Greeks ran naked for ritual or religious reasons. Throughout history many people have preferred to do their running wearing little or nothing. Even in the 20th century the custom has not entirely vanished. Percy Cerutty, coach of the great Australian miler Herb Elliott, had his charges run naked along the deserted beach at their training camp at Portsea. Cerutty believed that "the only evil in nakedness was in the unclean minds of prudes." In any event, the Greeks were proud of their physiques, spent considerable time oiling and sunbathing, and considered running naked to be more civilized than wearing clothes.

## Women Runners in the Ancient World

Women were not allowed to compete in any of the Olympic races. According to Pausanias, the priestess of Demeter and unmarried women were allowed to watch the men and boys perform at Olympia. Other sources say that women were thrown off a cliff if they were found at the Olympic Games. The reason for excluding women spectators was probably for religious reasons rather than any sense of modesty.

Every fourth year, approximately a month before the men's Olympic Games, there was a separate festival at Olympia for unmarried women. This festival, called the *Heraia* in honor of Zeus's wife Hera, included a Stadion length race for three different age groups. These races were all ⅚ the length of the men's race. Greek women ran in short tunics with one breast bare, possibly to prove that they were really women. Winners received crowns of olives and portions of a sacrificed cow. The winners also had the right to dedicate images (probably paintings) in honor of their victories. We do not know if men were allowed to watch the women compete.

Women runners of Sparta sometimes trained with the men, and women's races were held at the Artemis festival in Sparta and at other Greek festivals. A first-century A.D. inscription found at Delphi says that Hermesianax of Tralles in Asia Minor

**Greek woman runner. The position of her feet (close together) suggests she may be getting ready to start (from Jakob von Falke,** *Greece and Rome,* **1882).**

## Running Stela of Taharqa—Egyptian Distance Runners

The Greeks were not the only outstanding runners of the ancient world. In 1977, a limestone monument known as the "Running Stela of Taharqa" was discovered along Egypt's ancient road of Dahshur. The inscription on the monument, dated about 685 B.C., tells of King Taharqa's admiration for his army and describes a memorable long-distance run. King Taharqa staged a foot-race for a group of his soldiers from the capital city of Memphis through the desert to Fayum and back — a total distance of about 62 miles (100 km). King Taharqa accompanied the runners on horseback and actually ran with them for part of the race. In order to avoid the heat, the Egyptians ran the first half of the race at night. After a rest of two hours the runners returned to Memphis. King Taharqa held a banquet for all those who ran well and praised all those who finished.

The fastest of the soldiers ran the 31 miles (50 km) from Memphis to Fayum in about four hours. No time is given for the return trip. The modern record for 50 km is 2 hr 48 min. The 62-mile (100 km) run was made by a group of soldiers, not elite ultra-distance runners and was on desert roads. This suggests that the ancient Egyptians were quite creditable distance runners.

## Chinese Runners

In ancient China, when dukes and princes went out in horse carts, their bodyguards ran behind. These bodyguards, called "brave warriors," were selected from running contests and enjoyed high esteem.

Long-distance running was a major part of military training down through the dynasties. In 513 B.C., Emperor Wu made his warriors run long distances in full battle gear until they reached their place of encampment. Each runner wore armor made

erected statues for his three daughters who were outstanding runners. Tryphosa won the Stadion race at both the Pythian Games and Isthmian Games. She was said to be the first woman to win the latter race. One of Tryphosa's sisters, Hedea, won the Stadion race at Nemea and at Sycion in Italy. Tryphosa's other sister, Dionysia, won the Stadion race at the Aescleperia near Epidaurus.

of rhinoceros hide and carried a sword in his belt, a bow in his hand, 50 arrows and a halberd on his back — as well as enough rations for three days. He had to cover 31 miles (50 km) every day before noon, covering a total of 93 miles (150 km) in three days. Only those who had attained this standard were allowed to demobilize and go home with awards of land and housing.

## The Origin of the Marathon—Fact and Fable

The marathon race was created for the first modern Olympic Games held in Athens in 1896 to provide a link between the ancient and modern games. Its roots can be traced to a curious combination of poetry and history. Herodotus, in *The Histories*, written about 60 years after the 490 B.C. battle of Marathon, describes the events leading up to the pivotal battle:

> Before leaving Athens for Marathon, the generals sent a messenger to Sparta, one Pheidippides, an Athenian who was by profession a trained runner. According to the account he gave to the Athenians on his return, when he was near Mount Parthenium, above Tegea, he fell in with the god Pan who called him by name and ordered him to ask the Athenians why they paid no honors to Pan, even though he was well-intentioned toward them and had helped them many times in the past and would do so again in the future. The Athenians believed this story and, when their affairs were settled once more they established a shrine to Pan at the foot of the Acropolis, and they have appeased him from the time of his message with annual sacrifices and a torch-race.

> Pheidippides arrived in Sparta on the day after he left Athens. The Spartans wished to help the Athenians but were unable to do so because of a law which required them to wait for the full moon.

Pheidippides (some sources say Philippides), was an *Hemerodromes*, a profes-

sional running-courier. Herodotus describes Pheidippides's 140 mile (225 km) run from Athens to Sparta before the battle, but says nothing of a 25-mile (40 km) run from Marathon to Athens after the battle. Apparently, the only thing Herodotus considered unusual about the run was the meeting with Pan.

Herodotus's account of the Athenian charge during the battle describes an interesting and quite practical reason for the Greeks practicing running:

> …the ranks of the center were diminished, and it became the weakest part of the line, while the wings were both made strong with a depth of many ranks.

> So when the battle was set in array, and the victims showed themselves favorable, instantly the Athenians, so soon as they were let go, charged the barbarians at a run. Now the distance between the two armies was little short of eight-Stade [about 1500 meters]. The Persians, therefore, when they saw the Greeks coming on at speed, made ready to receive them, although it seemed to them that the Athenians were bereft of their senses, and bent upon their own destruction; for they saw a mere handful of men coming on at a run without either horsemen or archers. Such was the opinion of the barbarians; but the Athenians in close array fell upon them, and fought in a manner worthy of being recorded. They were the first of the Greeks, so far as I know, who introduced the custom of charging the enemy at a run….

The combination of weakening their own lines at the center and the running charge at the Persians allowed the Greeks to rout the much larger Persian force. Some scholars have expressed doubts that the Greeks would have been able to run that far in full armor and still have the energy to fight.

The next we hear of Pheidippides is some 500 years later from the Roman historian Pliny the Elder (A.D. 23–79) in *Natural History*:

Pheidippides's running the 140 miles from Athens to Sparta in two days was a mighty feat, until Spartan runner Anystis and Alexander the Great's courier Philonides ran 148 miles (238 km) from Sicyon to Elis in one day.

This interesting account is the first written record of one runner's feat surpassing that of a runner of earlier times. According to Pliny, Anystis and Philonides broke Pheidippides' record, but there is still no mention of a run from Marathon to Athens.

The first mention of the famous Marathon-to-Athens run celebrated in the modern Olympics is by the later Greek Philosopher Plutarch (A.D. 46–120) in *Moralia*:

As Herakleides of Pontos states, Thersippos of Erchia announced the battle of Marathon. But most say that it was Eucles who— running with his armor and hot from the battle and bursting in at the doors of the first men of the state —could only say "Be Happy! We have won!" and immediately expired.

Here a runner dies after running from Marathon to Athens, to deliver news of the victory, but there seems to be some confusion as to his name. The authority Plutarch gives is Herakleides of Pontos, who flourished about 150 years after the battle and was notoriously inclined to myth.

Plutarch, in *Life of Aristides*, describes another Greek runner's death. Euchidas, after a Greek victory over the Persians at the battle of Platea in 479 B.C., ran to Delphi and back:

After all fire had been extinguished on the instructions of the Pythia, a Platean called Euchidas ran from Platea to Delphi to bring the sacred fire. On his arrival he purified himself with water and crowned himself with laurel, and then ran back to Platea, arriving before sunset, having accomplished a thousand

stades [112 miles/180 km] in the same day. He greeted his fellow citizens, gave them the fire, then immediately collapsed and after a short time expired. In admiration of him, the Plateans buried him in the sanctuary of Artemis Eucleia, and inscribed as epitaph this tetrameter:
"Euchidas ran to Delphi and back again in one day."

It seems a huge coincidence that two Greek runners would drop dead at the end of runs following Greek military victories. Perhaps the Greeks were trying to outdo each other in recounting their battles. Interestingly Euchidas' epitaph doesn't say he died after the run.

The earliest reference to Pheidippides running from Marathon to Athens to announce the victory is from Lucian's (2nd century A.D.) *A Slip of the Tongue in Greeting*:

It is said that the long-distance runner Philippides first used the word ["rejoice" or "be happy"] in this context when, announcing the victory after Marathon, said to the magistrates back in Athens "Be Happy! We have won!" and having said that he died....

In 1878 Robert Browning wrote the famous poem "Pheidippides," which combined Herodotus's account of Pheidippides's run to Sparta for aid with the later stories by Plutarch and Lucian of a runner carrying news of the victory at Marathon to Athens. Browning had Pheidippides do an incredible amount of running:

1. From Athens to Sparta (about 140 mi.)
2. From Sparta to Athens, meeting Pan on the way (140 mi.)
3. Athens to Marathon (25 mi.)
4. Take part in the battle (at least 1 mi.)
5. Marathon to Athens to announce the victory (25 mi.)

No wonder poor Pheidippides died! First Browning's account of the trip to Sparta:

> "Run, Pheidippides, run and race, reach Sparta for aid!
>
> Persia has come, we are here, where is She?" Your command I obeyed,
>
> Ran and raced: like stubble, some field which a fire runs through,
>
> Was the space between city and city: two days, two nights did I burn
>
> Over the hills, under the dales, down pits and up peaks.

The poem ends with Pheidippides' fatal run from Marathon to Athens.

> Unforeseeing one! Yes, he fought on the Marathon day:
>
> So, when Persia was dust, all cried, "To Acropolis!
>
> Run, Pheidippides, one race more the meed is thy due!
>
> 'Athens is saved, thank Pan,' go shout." He flung down his shield,
>
> Ran like fire once more: and the space 'twixt the Fennel-field
>
> And Athens was stubble again, a field which a fire runs through
>
> Till in he broke: "Rejoice, we conquer!" Like wine through clay,
>
> Joy in his blood bursting his heart, he died — the bliss!

Pheidippides's run from Athens to Sparta and back is historically sound and is a much more challenging feat than running from Marathon to Athens. Perhaps if the founders of the modern Olympics had been influenced by history instead of poetry and had better understood human ultra-running potential, the marathon race would have been 140 miles (226 km) — the distance from Athens to Sparta — rather than 26.2 (42 km). Races of 140 miles and longer had been common in the 1880s but no great poet had connected them with the ancient Greeks.

A race from Athens to Sparta, the Spartathlon, was initiated in 1983. This race is very difficult even for elite ultra-runners. It has heat, hills and cutoff times the runners must meet at various points along the way — a true test of human ultra-running. The record for the race (20 hr 25 min) is held by the amazing Greek runner Yiannis Kouros.

## The End of the Greek Olympics

With the Roman conquest of the Greeks in 146 B.C. the Olympic Games began to decline. Although some Romans were intrigued by the Greek festivals, most saw little practical value in any physical conditioning that didn't fill military needs. For entertainment they preferred "blood sports" — boxing, wrestling, and contests between gladiators or between men and beasts. Many Romans were also offended by the nudity that was part of the Greek games.

Pliny the Elder in the first century A.D. tells of a runner completing 147 miles (236 km) on the chariot racing course of the Roman Circus. Whether this was a race or an effort to see how far the runner could go is unclear. The Romans did use runners for messengers. These were usually slaves who might be severely punished if their messages were late. Fronto in the 2nd century A.D. reports the words of a runaway messenger: "I have run sixty miles for my master, I will run a hundred, for myself, to escape."

Running was not a part of the new religion Christianity, although Christian writers used running metaphors in their writing. In I Corinthians 9:24, Paul, who probably attended some of the Greek crown games, compares the Christian life to a race: "Know ye not that they which run in a race run all, but one receiveth the prize? So run that ye may obtain."

In Hebrews 12:1 he exhorts his followers: "Let us also lay aside every weight, and sin which clings so closely, and let us run with perseverance the race that is set before us."

Finally, in II Timothy 4:7, when Paul realizes he is near death: "I have fought the good fight, I have finished the race, I have kept the faith."

After nearly 1,200 years the age of the Greek Olympic Games finally sputtered to a close. The list of Olympic victors stops in A.D. 267 only to be resumed in A.D. 361. Many writers have attributed the demise of the Greek Olympics to popular "evils" of the writers' times such as greed and profes-sionalism. But the real reasons were more diverse. Invasions, economic decline and earthquakes all played a part.

The games, identified with the Olympian gods, were also opposed by followers of Christianity. In A.D. 394 Emperor Theodosius stopped the reckoning of time in Olympiads and banned all pagan festivals. This would make the 293rd Olympic festival which occurred in A.D. 393 the last to be held. With the death of the Olympics, along with the spirit they had kept alive, the Dark Ages set in.

# III

# From Running Footmen to Pedestrianism (A.D. 500–1800)

*Our destiny is to run to the edge of the world and beyond, off into the darkness.*

— Thomas Aquinas (1225–1274)

By the sixth century A.D. Greek style athletic festivals had died out and running on an Olympic scale would not reappear until the revival of the modern Olympic Games in 1896. We know little of running in the Dark Ages. Running is such a common human activity that most historians of the time did not bother recording it. The running that took place from A.D. 500–1800 was mostly local with people running for amusement or to deliver messages. A few, recognizing the health benefits, ran to stay fit.

In the Middle Ages we occasionally hear of a famous person who was also a runner. St. Cuthbert (7th century A.D.) was noted for his running, as was Harold I "Harefoot" (A.D. 1035–1040). King Henry V (1387–1422), along with two of his lords, was praised for running down a wild deer in a large park. James Scott, the Duke of Monmouth (1649–1685), won footraces wearing boots, competing with fast runners wearing shoes.

Foot races were popular in carnivals and festivals beginning in the Middle Ages and continuing into the 19th century. The carnival season began in January or late December, with excitement mounting as Lent approached. Carnivals were usually held in the open air near the center of the city. Foot-races were mostly for the entertainment of the crowds and the runners were often from the fringe of society. Variations on the foot-race in the medieval carnivals included sack-races, wheelbarrow-races and foot-races in which men wore bells around their legs. The Roman Carnival included races for young men, Jews and old men, as well as for prostitutes.

Several other Italian cities had foot-races for prostitutes. After the siege of Arezzo in 1335 the victorious Perugians staged a foot-race for prostitutes who followed the army. In 1501, Pope Alexander VI hosted a prostitutes' race at Saint Peter's Basilica in Rome. When Castruccio Castracani of Lucca wished to humiliate the besieged citizens of Florence, he staged a series of sports events, including a race for prostitutes, before the walls of the city. After his death, the Florentines repaid the insult and sent their city's prostitutes to race before the gates of Lucca.

Even less is known of running during the Middle Ages in non–European countries. During the Yuan Dynasty in China (1279–1368), however, the imperial guards ran long-distance races. In 1287 Kublai Khan, emperor of Yuan, organized a contingent of Royal Guards called the "Gui Chi Guards." Every year these guards, fully armed, ran 56–62 miles (90–100 km) from Beijing to Luanjing or the other way around. They started at dawn, lined up in order behind a rope which was lowered for the start. Some reportedly covered the distance in about six hours, which is close to the six-hour 10 minute current world record for 100 km, set by Don Richie in 1978.

## Scottish Highland Games — The McGregor Brothers

According to *The Book of Leinster* (A.D. 1150) which is a blend of legend and fact, the most ancient of all sports festivals were the Tailteann Games, dating back to 1829 B.C. They were held in County Meath, Ireland, and for 30 days men ran, jumped, wrestled, fenced and performed other athletic feats. These games lasted until the Norman invasion in A.D. 1168.

One of the first nationwide festivals emphasizing athletic events was the Scottish Highland Games. These games date back to the 13th century, but even earlier in the 11th century the clan chiefs held competitions to pick the strongest men for bodyguards and the fastest for messengers. In 1040, according to tradition, King Malcolm of the Big Head held such a competition to choose a messenger. In order to select a suitable candidate and at the same time provide entertainment for his subjects, the king organized a race to the summit of Craig Choinich. Many of Malcolm's loyal subjects turned out to run the race. The winner was to receive, in addition to the messenger's job, a fine sword and a purse of gold.

Two of the McGregor brothers from Ballochbuie were favored to win. King Malcolm, acting as starter, gave a rap on his shield and the runners were off. A short time later a late entrant arrived. The lad, a younger brother of the two McGregors who were already leading the race, pleaded with the king to be allowed to compete. His enthusiasm and sincerity impressed the king, who gave him permission, but warned that with such a late start he had little chance of winning. The young McGregor tore off with great speed and soon caught up with the plodders in the race. Up the hill the runners sped, scrambling, running, climbing. The youth gradually overtook the leaders and soon was in third place with only his brothers ahead of him. Nearing his two brothers, he yelled an offer to share the prize.

"No, every man for himself," gasped the brother in front as he tried to increase his lead.

The reply spurred the youngest McGregor on and he soon passed the brother in second place who, by this time, was too tired to fight him off. Overtaking his eldest brother, the youngest repeated his offer. "Split the pot and I'll let you win."

"Never," replied his brother.

As they approached the finish they pressed even harder and the youngest Mc-Gregor put on a final burst of speed. His brother, falling, desperately grabbed at him and managed to seize his kilt. The younger McGregor struggled to free himself but couldn't. Finally he shed the kilt and streaked on to the finish. Reaching the winning-post he yanked the stick from the ground and collapsed. Victory over a brother is twice as sweet.

## Dante's Runners from Hell

It was impossible to accurately time races in the Middle Ages and most references to running are very brief and contain little description of the races or runners. Some interesting accounts of running are contained in the literature of the period. Dante, in his book *Inferno* (A.D. 1300) described running in hell. In Canto III Dante and Virgil entered the Gates of Hell and immediately heard cries of anguish:

> I saw a banner there upon the mist.
> Circling and circling, it seemed to scorn all pause.
> So it ran on, and still behind it pressed
> A never-ending rout of souls in pain.
> I had not thought death had undone so many
> as passed before me in the mournful train.
> …These wretches never born and never dead
> ran naked in a swarm of wasps and hornets
> that goaded them the more they fled.

The 1544 illustration resembles the start of a modern "mega-race" such as the Peach Tree 10K in Atlanta. Like some coaches, Dante is using the carrot and stick approach to running. He probably has the runners chasing a banner because he was familiar with the *Palio* race in Verona where the prize for winning was a green banner. The hellish part is that these runners never get to stop and rest but are eternally goaded on by stinging insects.

In Canto XV there is another reference to the *Palio* foot-race:

> Away he turned and with no further word
> Across the wasteland scampered with such speed
> As to seem one who runs Verona's course
> For the green pallium, nay, such was his stride
> As would become the winner of that race.

The Italian word *palio* is a corruption of the Latin *pallium* or a rectangular piece of cloth. *Palio* came to mean a flag or banner. Originally one spoke of running to win the palio, later of running the palio. These races, which originated in Italy in the 13th century, could be either foot-races or horse-races.

The Palio of Verona commemorated a battle fought there in A.D. 1208. The race took place on the first Sunday of Lent on a wide plain outside the city. It was held until the 19th century. In addition to the green pallium which went to the winner, the last place runner received a rooster which he had to carry into the city. Another prize was a pair of gloves. Curiously, although the race was part of a Christian celebration, the runners ran naked. It was thought that, for fear of being embarrassed, no one would enter the race unless he considered himself a very fast runner. At the end of the 14th century Verona added a women's race for the Palio. No one seems to have recorded what, if anything, they wore.

In Canto XXI of *The Inferno,* the devil himself is described as a swift runner:

> Then did I turn as one who longs to see
> What he must flee from yet whom sudden fear
> Dismays so he lingers not to look.

"The Lukewarm Chasing Banner," from Dante's *Inferno*. This version is an 1865 pen drawing by Francesco Scaramuzza. Library of Congress Collection.

And back of us I saw a devil come
All black and running up the craggy bank
With outstretched wings and fleet upon
  his feet.

Ah, how ferocious was his evil grin!

...He spoke and hurled the hapless victim in
And hastened up the bank again; no
  hound
Unleashed to set on thief more swiftly
  sprang.

This devil flapped his wings as he ran, perhaps like a large bird trying to take off.

In book two of Milton's *Paradise Lost* (1667), the fallen angels stage races to occupy their time while waiting for the devil to return:

By false presumptuous hope, the ranged
  powers

Disbanded, and wandering each his sev-
  eral way
Pursues, as inclination or sad choice
Leads him perplexed, where he may like-
  liest find
Truce to his restless thoughts and enter-
  tain
The irksome hours, till his great chief re-
  turn.
Part on the plain, or in the air sublime
Upon the wing or in swift race contend,
As at th' Olympian games or Pythian
  fields;...

The fallen angels seem to have held flying-races as well as foot-races. Unfortunately Milton doesn't give us more details.

William Shakespeare, who wrote around A. D. 1600, no doubt saw the running matches of his day and mentioned running in several of his plays. In *Henry IV* he had Falstaff offer to race Poins: "I could give a thousand pounds I could run as fast as thou canst," said the stout knight. In *Henry VI*, there is another allusion to footracing: "Forspent with toil as runners with a race, I lay me down a little while to breathe." And only someone who had experienced the exhilaration of running could write:

Jog on, jog on, the footpath way,
And merrily hent the stile-a:
A merry heart goes all the day,
Your sad tires in a mile-a
                              (*Winter's Tale*)

## Running Footmen— Long-distance Runners of the 17th Century

Guillaume Depping's interesting book *Wonders of Bodily Strength and Skill* (1871) described Turkish couriers of the 16th century who were famous for their running. The Grand Turk always maintained 80 to 100 runners, called *peirles* (lackeys or footmen), who were generally natives of Persia and very willing and swift messengers. They ran on before their master when he traveled, and "capered with wonderful agility without apparently finding it necessary to stop and take breath." To amuse the Sultan, as soon as the procession had reached the open country they returned to the side of the Grand Seigneur, and ran backwards before him, bowing their heads with many antics and flourishes.

The Turkish couriers always ran with bare feet, which, after much running, became hard and devoid of feeling. Imaginative journalists reported that the couriers had themselves shod with "light iron shoes like horses." In addition, the couriers carried in their mouths silver balls pierced with holes and champed these as a horse would a bit. Their belts and garters were furnished with little bells, which tinkled as they ran. Near the end of the 16th century they stopped carrying the balls of silver in their mouths, and began to wear shoes.

Besides their pay, they received two complete suits of clothes every year. Their costume consisted of an Albanian cassock or damask of many colors and a large silk belt enriched with gold. The belt held a sheath containing an ivory-handled dagger. They also wore very long stockings, as well as coarse shoes. On their heads were high bonnets covered with silver leaf, from which waved enormous plumes of ostrich feathers. In one hand each carried his hatchet, with blade and hammer on opposite sides, and in the other hand a bag full of comfits, with which they kept their mouths moist as they ran. Depping tells of Turkish messengers running the 120 miles (193 km) from Constantinople to Adrianople. One of these runners made a bet he could cover the distance in 24 hours, and accomplished the feat, although he had to contend with the heat of August.

Fifteenth century Turkish messenger. The bells on his belt signaled his arrival (from Guillaume Depping, *Wonders of Bodily Strength and Skill*, 1871).

Running footmen were a special class of servants that first appeared in Western Europe in the 15th century. They were the forerunners of "pedestrians" or professional long distance runners or walkers. In those days, roads were very poorly maintained. The running footman's job was to run ahead of or beside coaches, steering the horses around hazards, and helping to stabilize and free the coach if it got stuck. Footmen also ran ahead to prepare for their masters' arrival at the next inn. Bad roads and clumsy coaches prevented traveling faster than about five miles an hour even with the assistance of footmen.

With the coming of hard-surfaced country roads and cobblestoned city streets, coach speeds increased to more than seven miles an hour. The footmen now had to be able to run for up to 20 miles (32 km) without stopping and up to 62 miles (100 km) in a day. Rest stops were infrequent and brief, consisting of pit stops at coaching inns for the horses to be watered and sometimes changed.

One of the actors in *A Mad World My Masters*, a 1608 play by Thomas Middleton, refers to a running footman as "you lousy seven-miles-an-hour," "you progressive roundabout rascal," and "linen stockings and three-score-a-day." Sir Thomas Overbury, an essayist (1614), had more to say about the running footman: "Let him never be so well made, yet his legs are not matches.... He is very long winded. He lives more by his owne heat than the warmth of cloathes. Tis impossible to draw his picture to the life, cause a man must take it as he's running."

In *Recollections of the Life of John O'Keeffe*, who was born in 1747, the author gives another interesting description of a running footman:

"My Lord's," or "the Squire's" was called the Big House, and it had its privileged fool or satirist, its piper and its running footman: the latter I have often seen skimming or flying across the road; one of them I particularly remember, his dress, a white jacket, blue silk sash round his waist, light black-velvet cap, with a silver tassel on the crown, round his neck a frill with a ribbon, and in his hand a staff about seven feet high with a silver top. He looked so agile, and seemed all air like a Mercury: he never minded roads, but took the shortest cut, and by the help of his pole absolutely seemed to fly over hedge, ditch and small river. His use was to carry a letter, message, or despatch; or, on a journey, to run before and prepare the inn, or baiting-place, for his family or master, who came the regular road in coach and two, or coach and four, or coach and six: his qualifications were fidelity, strength, and agility.

The running footmen's dress varied but they often wore a light black cap, a jockey coat and white linen trousers and thin-soled shoes. In the early part of the 1700s they had worn kilts, but these were replaced by breeches, possibly because, as a 1725 writer put it: "Our Village Maids delight to see the Running Footman fly bare-ars'd o'er the dusty Road."

On the end of the two-meter long pole the footman carried was a hollow silver ball containing a hard-boiled egg or a little white wine for nourishment. Running with a long pole is awkward for most of us. It must have required much practice to develop a smooth stride carrying one. If the coach had to travel at night the running footman might carry a torch instead of his pole.

Running footmen were sometimes rascally fellows. Several sources tell the story of the Duke of Queensberry, "Old Q," interviewing a man for a job as a running footman. Every candidate for the job was required to dress in a fancy footman's uniform and was given a staff to carry. He had to prove his skill by running back and forth in front of the Duke's house. One unusually hot day the Duke reclined on a balcony of his mansion overlooking Piccadilly as he timed a candidate. The prospect was running

I AM THE ONLY RUNNING FOOTMAN

**This running footman carried his lunch in the head of his long staff (from *Chambers Book of Days*, 1864).**

so well that the Duke made him run on and on in the heat just for the pleasure of watching him run. Finally the Duke shouted from the balcony, "You will do for me." "Yes," replied the footman, who had by this time decided he didn't want the job, "and this" (pointing to the gold-laced uniform) "will do for me," and he raced away giving the Duke one final glimpse of his running form.

Running footmen also served as messengers. The postal service in Europe in the 16th and 17th centuries was no better than the roads. A good running footman prided himself on his ability to outrun a horse on a long journey. In 1583, Langham, an Irish running footman, ran 148 miles (239 km) to get medicine for his master's wife, Lady Berkeley, who had become seriously ill. The journey took less than 42 hours, including an overnight stay at an apothecary's shop. Lady Berkeley rewarded Langham with a new suit of clothes.

We know little of the training methods of the running footman. It is possible they trained by running with dogs. "Old Choates," a retired running footman, trained his master's hounds by taking them out for runs. A 1625 play by John Webster contains another training method: "I have heard of cunning footmen that have Shooes made of lead some ten days fore a race to give them nimble and more active feet."

## Removing the Spleen to Run Faster

Runners of this era sometimes went to great lengths to improve their running. One method was to get rid of the spleen, or at least reduce its size. This curious procedure dates from the time of the ancient Greeks who were baffled by the spleen's purpose and believed it was a hindrance to fast running. Herbs were sometimes used to try to dissolve it. Pliny (A.D. 23–79) in *Natural History* describes a plant used for this purpose: "...*equisaetium*, called *hippuris* by the Greeks ... resembling horse hair, reduces the spleen of runners if as much as a pot will hold is boiled down and taken in drink for three days."

Depping tells of the German physician Godfrey Maebius, who lived in the 17th century, performing an operation to rid a runner of this offensive organ:

He had seen in the town of Halberstadt a courier in the service of Count Tilly,

who attributed his surprising speed solely to the operation which a surgeon had performed upon him in the region of the spleen. According to this courier's account he was first put to sleep by means of a narcotic, and the operator having made an incision in his side, then burned the spleen with a red-hot iron. Moebius saw the cicatrices [scar] which still marked the seat of the wound. Five other individuals had been treated in the same manner, at the same time as the courier, and only in one case did the operation result in the death of the patient.

The surgeon apparently considered a survival rate of 83 percent for the operation to be quite acceptable.

## Runners in Pepys's Diary

In the 17th and 18th centuries rich noblemen kept running footmen and raced them much as rich people of today might keep stables of racehorses. The English diarist Samuel Pepys recorded some of these contests. He has an entry for August 10, 1660, about watching a race in Hyde park:

I went by water to White-hall to the Privy Seale; and that done, with Mr. Moore and Creed to Hideparke by coach and saw a fine foot-race, three times around the park, between an Irishman and Crow that was once my Lord Claypoole's footman. Crow beat the other above two miles.

Although Hyde Park was larger in those days than it is now, two miles seems to be a rather large victory margin. Three years later on July 30, 1663, Pepys gives another account of a foot-race:

The town talk of this day is of nothing but the great foot-race run this day on Banstead Downes, between Lee, the Duke of Richmond's footman, and a Tyler, a famous runner. And Lee hath beat him; though the King and Duke of York and all men almost did bet three or four to one upon the Tyler's head.

Pepys's August 11, 1664, diary entry describes the familiar "run down" hunting method: "This day, for a wager before the King, my Lords of Castlehaven and Arran (a son of my Lord of Ormond's) they two alone did run down and kill a stoute bucke in St. James's parke."

Pepys gives no times for the races nor even precise distances. If this information was known to him, he apparently didn't consider it worth recording. All three of these events involved wagering, which has had a long and colorful history in Britain; running provided one of its prime outlets. Wealthy bettors sometimes made wagers of as much as £1,000 on these races. In 1664 a law was passed under Charles II, that limited bets to £100. Queen Anne, in 1711, further reduced the amount to £10.

Reportedly, a sizable number of running footmen died of consumption (tuberculosis) after three or four years of service. Running doesn't cause tuberculosis but breathing the germ-laden air on the dusty roads might have. This could explain why many doctors and much of the public in the 18th and 19th centuries thought distance running was harmful to one's health. By 1800, with improved roads, running footmen had a hard time keeping up with coaches and were no longer needed. The last English nobleman who employed one was the infamous Duke of Queensbury, who died in 1810.

Running footmen were not the only runners of this time. With the Restoration in 1660, and the revulsion against Puritanism, came a great burst of athletic enthusiasm. Both men's and women's running contests became more frequent and popular. Still, sports participation in England continued to be hampered throughout the 17th and much of the 18th centuries by the Puritan insistence that Sunday sports be forbidden.

Preston, the "Flying Butcher of Leeds," was a well-known runner of the late 1600s. He was able to earn more from his running than from his butcher-shop. In 1688, with 6,000 spectators watching, he defeated the king's favorite runner. Betting was so heavy on the king's runner that part of the crowd, having bet their horses on the match, had to walk home. Unfortunately, having vanquished all his competition, Preston could no longer persuade anyone to race against him. Later runners would try to solve this problem by offering incentives like handicaps or high odds. Preston's solution was to have himself disfigured so no one would recognize him. Claiming to be a miller, he was able to live under a false name in London for a long time before he was discovered. Most runners didn't go to the extent of disfiguring themselves, but running "black" or using an assumed name has a long history among professional runners. The custom continued at various times and for various reasons all the way up to the late 19th century.

## Women Who Ran for Smocks, She-shirts and Husbands

The second half of the 18th century was the first Golden Age for women's running. Women had not yet been deemed biologically unsuited for running. In 1765 a young woman ran 72 miles (116 km) from Bleneago Scotland to Newcastle in one day. Peter Radford, a 1960s British sprinter and historian, made an extensive study of British diaries, newspaper and magazine accounts of the period. In an analysis of 50 published running accounts from the 1790s, he found that at sporting events of the period less than a third had races for men and boys, but 80 percent had races for women or girls.

Women ran against other women, occasionally against men, or against time. There was usually wagering on the outcome, but sometimes the winning runner had to depend on a collection taken up by the spectators for her reward. By far the most popular races for women in the 17th and 18th centuries were smock or "she-shirt" races. These races were usually for young country "wenches" and were common at festivals, weddings and as additional attractions at cricket matches. They were held in England, Germany and even Colonial America. The number of runners was typically three to six. A common racing distance was half a mile and it was often necessary to win multiple "starts" to get the prize.

The poem "The Smock-Race at Finglas," from *Poetical Miscellanies*, published by John Steele in 1714, describes a smock-race on Ascension Day. The prize for winning was a fine Holland chemise decorated with ribbons, but the winner also received a bonus of sorts:

...When, lo, old Arbiter, amid the
    crowd,
Prince of the annual games, proclaim'd
    aloud,
'Ye Virgins, that intend to try the race,
The swiftest wins a smock enrich'd with
    lace:
A cambrick kerchuff shall the next adorn,
And kidden gloves shall by the third be
    worn.'
This said, he high in air display'd each
    prize;
All view the waving smock with longing
    eyes.

Fair Oonah at the barrier first appears,
Pride of the neighb'ring mill, in bloom of
    years
Her native brightness burrows not one
    grace,
Uncultivated charms adorn her face,
Her rosie cheeks with modest blushes
    glow,
At once her innocence and beauty show:
Oonah the eyes of each spectator draws,
What busom beats not in fair Oonah's
    cause.

Tall as a pine majestick Nora stood,

Her youthful veins were swell'd with
    sprightly blood
Inur'd to toyls, in wholesom gardens
    breed,
Exact in ev'ry limb, and form'd for speed.

To thee, O Shevan, next what praise is
    due?
Thy youth and beauty doubly strike the
    view,
Fresh as the plum that keeps the virgin
    blue!
Each well deserves the smock, — but fates
    decree,
But one must wear it, tho deserved by
    three.

Now side by side the panting rivals stand,
And fix their eyes upon th' appointed
    hand;
The signal giv'n, spring forward to the
    race,
No fam'd Camilla ran with fleeter pace.
Nora, as lightning swift, the rest o'er-
    pass'd,
While Shevan fleetly ran, yet ran the last.
But, Oonah, thou hadst Venus on thy
    side;
At Nora's petticoat the goddess ply'd,

And in a trice the fatal string unty'd.
Quick stop'd the maid, nor wou'd, to win
    the prize,
Expose her hidden charms to vulgar eyes.
But while to tye the treach'rous knot she
    staid,
Both her glad rivals pass the weeping
    maid.

Now in despair she plies the race again,
Not winged winds dart swifter o'er the
    plain:
Loud shouts and acclamation fill the
    place,
Tho' chance on Oonah had bestow'd the
    race;
Like Felim none rejoyc'd — a lovelier
    swain
Ne'er fed a flock on the Fingalian plain.
Long he with secret passion lov'd the
    maid,
Now his encreasing fame itself betray'd.
Strip for the race how bright did she ap-
    pear!
No cov'ring hid her feet, her bosom bare,

And to the wind she gave her flowing
    hair.
A thousand charms he saw, conceal'd be-
    fore,
Those yet conceal'd he fancy'd still were
    more.
Felim as night came on, young Oonah
    woo'd
Soon willing beauty was by truth sub-
    du'd.
No jarring settlement their bliss annoys,
No license need to defer their joys.
Oonah e'er morn the sweets of wedlock
    try'd,
The smock she won a virgin, wore a
    bride.

Oonah, like the ancient Greeks, found
that it often paid to race wearing the least
you could get by with. Winning a husband
along with the smock wasn't uncommon.
Men competed in similar races for hats.
They too could win a mate if they were fast
and looked good in someone's eyes.

In Germany women's racing was a bit
rougher. Depping describes a shepherdess's
race held in Wutemberg, Germany, on St.
Bartholomew's day. Contestants ran barefoot and wore short petticoats. These races
were so hotly contested that the town clerk
had to follow the runners on horseback to
break up fights:

> Each wishes of course to win the prize,
> and in endeavoring to obtain it all means
> are considered fair. One shoves her com-
> panion to make her fall, and will even
> roll upon the ground with her. Another
> strikes her neighbor in the side that she
> may thus, for a time, stop the breath of
> a dangerous rival.

In Markt-Groningen Germany, the
young women ran carrying a pitcher filled
with water in one hand. The object was to
reach the finish without spilling the water.
If the runner made one false step she was
drenched from head to toe.

Caricature of an 1811 smock race in England. One runner has tripped over a dog (from *The Caricature Magazine*, London; "Rural Sports. Smock Racing" by Thomas Rowlandson. Yale Center for British Art, Paul Mellon Collection).

Wutemberg Shepherdesses' Race. The rider is along to break up fights (from Sir Montague Shearman, *Athletics and Football*, 1888).

## Improvements in Timekeeping Make Running Records Possible

A revolution in time measurement took place in the second half of the 17th century. Before this time, clocks and watches were incapable of keeping time more closely than about 15 minutes per day. Most didn't have a minute or second hand and would have been useless for timing any but the longest races. In 1670 the pendulum-spring was invented and soon clocks and watches became available that could measure time to less than 10 seconds per day. With accurate and fairly dependable watches available it became worthwhile — for the first time in history — to record the times and distances for noteworthy running events. A runner could now race against time or, in a sense, any runner who ran the same or similar-length course.

The following table gives examples of how precisely watches of various periods could display time:

| Date | Precision (sec) | Source |
|------|-----------------|--------|
| 1712 | 60 | Celia Fiennes' diary |
| 1791 | ½ | Guts Muths |
| 1844–1866 | ¼ | *Spirit of the Times* |
| 1867–1924 | ⅕ | Oxford vs. Cambridge matches |
| 1924–1932 | ¹⁄₁₀ | (Newspaper Accounts) |
| 1932–2000 | ¹⁄₁₀₀ | (Olympic photo timers) |

The table provides an upper limit on timing accuracy because a race can't be timed more accurately than the timer can read his watch. In many cases the technology for greater timing precision was available long before it was commonly used to time races. For example, an ad in *Spirit of the Times* for 1844 lists a Swiss stopwatch capable of timing to ⅕ second, although it would be over 20 years before most races were timed with this precision.

Timing short races was still a problem,

however. It was well into the 1800s before races such as 100 yards could be reliably timed. Accurate timing means nothing unless the distance run is accurately measured. Until the 16th century there was no standard measurement of distance in Europe. In 1588 Queen Elizabeth standardized the length of the mile at its present distance of 5,280 feet. According to Andy Milroy in *The Long Distance Record Book* (1988), a 17th century Englishman named Gunter invented a 66 foot-long (20 m) iron measuring chain for accurately establishing milestones on the English turnpike roads. These markers were ideally suited for laying out racecourses on these roads. These improvements in measuring time and distance added a new dimension to running. A runner could now set a record that runners of a later time could try to beat.

Celia Fiennes, in *The Illustrated Journeys of Celia Fiennes*, edited by C. Morris (1947), describes a 22-mile (35.4 km) race that took place in Windsor Park near London in 1712. This is one of the earliest descriptions of a race where the time is given. Fiennes, an astute observer, also has some interesting things to say about the runners:

I drove through another part of the Forrest of Windsor to see a race by two footemen an English and Scot. The former a taller, bigger man than the other; the ground measur'd and cut even in a round was almost four mile, they were to run it round so often as to make up 22 mile, which was the distance between Chareing Cross and Windsor Cross; that was five times quite round and so farre as made up the odd miles and measure; they ran a round in 25 minutes; I saw them run the first three rounds and halfe another in an hour and seventeen minutes, and they finish'd it in two hours and a halfe, the English gain'd the second round the start and kept it at the same distance the five rounds and then the Scotch-man came up to him and got before him to the post; the Englishman fell down within a few yards of the post;

many hundred pounds were won and lost about it, they ran both veary neately but my judgement gave it the Scotch man because he seem'd to save himself to the last push.

This race was timed to the nearest minute — accurate enough for this distance. A time of 2:30 for 22 miles is equivalent to just under a three-hour marathon. Most races of this period were between two landmarks. The race Fiennes observed was different in that it was on a measured course that simulated the distance between two landmarks.

## Freak Races—Bizarre Running for Wagers

In the 17th and 18th centuries most running feats could be divided into three categories: 1) foot-races at fairs, wakes and festivals; 2) "freak runs"; and 3) feats of running and walking (pedestrianism) which would, in time, be considered as legitimate a sport as was boxing and horse racing.

In "freak runs" one or more of the runners either were ridiculous or had a ridiculous handicap imposed on them. The more bizarre the contest the more excited the British public became. One of the earliest known "freak races," described in the *Loyal Protestant* in 1660, was between two lame men on Newmarket Heath and witnessed by the king himself:

At 3 of the clock in the afternoon there was a foot-race between 2 cripples, each having a wooden leg. They started fair and hobbled a good pace, which caused great admiration and laughter among the beholders, but the taller of the two won by 2 or 3 yards.

In 1763, Thomas Dudley, a smith, and Isaac Voiterse, a noted runner, raced for a wager of 10 guineas on Kennington Common. Dudly ran 100 yards on stilts, while

Race in which each runner has a wooden leg. Such races were popular in the 17th and 18th centuries (from Sir Montague Shearman, *Athletics and Football*, 1888).

Voiterse ran 120 yards on foot. Dudly, on stilts, won with ease.

In 1763, a fishmonger also attempted a run from Hyde Park Corner to the seven-mile stone in Brentford carrying 56 pounds (25.4 kg) of fish on his head. To win the bet he needed to complete the run in one hour. He finished in 45 minutes.

In 1788, a young gentleman with a jockey booted and spurred on his back ran a match against an elderly fat man named Bullock. The winner wasn't specified.

Another method for handicapping a "freak race" was for the faster runner to wear a pair of boots and the slower to either run barefoot or wear light shoes.

On a more serious note were pedestrian feats. Up until about 1700, runners and walkers were known as footmen. In the 18th century when running footmen ceased to exist, the term pedestrian came into use. Pedestrianism referred to a running or walking contest between two or more men or between a man and time, or a jumping contest between two or more men. The occasional women who participated in these contests were called female pedestrians or, less commonly, pedestriennes. Almost all these contests involved betting.

Pedestrianism not only provided a vehicle for betting but also helped satisfy human curiosity as to how far and how fast

Runner on stilts vs. runner on foot. The runner on stilts was given a head start (from Sir Montague Shearman, *Athletics and Football*, 1888).

we are capable of going on foot. Early pedestrians usually performed against the clock or even the calendar with races making up only a few of their contests. Running or walking feats longer than 10 miles were the most popular with the public.

## Foster Powell—Father of English Pedestrians

The most highly regarded pedestrian of the 18th century was Foster Powell, who was born in 1734 near Leeds in Yorkshire, England. Powell, a law clerk, discovered his unusual ability for going long distances while making his rounds delivering legal papers. For 25 years the slender, 5-foot, 8-inch (1.7 m) Powell amazed the public by quickly covering distances from one to 400 miles.

In 1764 when he was 30, Powell ran 50 miles (80.5 km) on the Bath road in seven hours, reportedly doing the first 10 miles in an hour. He also covered 112 miles (180 km) in 24 hours in 1784, but he is best known for his 396-mile (638 km) trips from London to York and back. When he was 57 he made the last of these journeys in a personal best time of five days, 15 hours and 45 minutes. After completing this feat he wagered that he could walk one mile and run another in a total time of 15 minutes. He walked the first mile in 9:20, then ran the other in 5:23 to win the bet by 17 seconds. Powell died penniless in 1793 after a short illness. Despite his fame and success as a pedestrian, £40 was the most he ever made from any of his wagers.

Powell's pedestrian feats created enormous interest. Because of his great popularity, Astley's Amphitheater once hired him for 12 nights to display his form. Byng's *Torrington Diaries* reproduced the Sept. 4, 1790, announcement for the occasion:

> This famous Englishman will be crowned with laurels upon the Theater which is purposely prepared for the occasion, as is the Scenery, Machinery, Dances, Songs, Chorus, etc....
>
> Mr. Powell will appear in the dress he wore on the road on his last journey to York, and give spectators a specimen of the pace he commonly keeps on the road which is superior to that of any horse for a continuance of time.

Pierce Egan, an early 19th century sportswriter, wrote in *Sporting Anecdotes* (1825), "Powell was a pattern to all pedestrians for unblemished integrity; in no one instance was he ever challenged with making a cross." If more of the pedestrians who were to follow Powell had his integrity,

**Race between an obese elderly man and a man with a jockey (from Sir Montague Shearman,** *Athletics and Football,* **1888).**

perhaps the sport of pedestrianism would still be with us.

Powell's performances all involved wagering. Setting up a successful wager was difficult. Most pedestrians were not wealthy, which meant they had to find themselves backers. Even if they won their bets, the most they could hope for was a portion of the winnings and this often depended on how generous the backers happened to be. The pedestrian also had to choose a running or walking feat that others thought impossible yet was within his capabilities.

Usually he would try the feat in private before wagering he could do it. Still, it was easy to miscalculate. For example, in 1778 at age 44, Powell bet he could run two miles in 10 minutes but lost his wager when he could only manage 10 minutes 30 seconds for the distance.

## Running in Colonial America

In America the first runners we have a record of were the Inca messengers. Several other Empires, such as the Chinese and the Mogul empire in India, also developed message delivery systems using relays of runners. With no horses available, the Incas developed one of the best of these message-delivery systems. The messengers were stationed on the royal roads to rapidly convey the Inca king's orders and deliver reports to him from his kingdoms and provinces. They were called *chasquis*, and lived in groups of four or six in thatched huts, placed about three quarters of a mile apart along these roads. They were all young men who were especially good runners. It was their duty to keep permanent watch of the road, in both directions, in order to catch sight of messengers from the other relays, then hurry out to meet them. The huts were built on high ground, in sight of one another.

When a messenger arrived in view of the next hut, he began to call out and repeated the message three or four times to the one who was running out to meet him. In this way messages could be transmitted 1,000 miles (1610 km) in three or four days under prime conditions.

In Colonial America foot-races occurred only on a local scale and no reliable times for them are available. These races took place wherever people got together — at the courthouse, at taverns and at country stores. Running was also included in the contests of the semiannual fairs where, in addition to normal foot-races, sack races, obstacle races and chasing a goose or a greased pig were all popular. These contests were open to everyone; however, in 1691 Sir Francis Nicholson started a series of athletic games which included running but required that only "the better sort of Virginians who were bachelors" could compete.

In 1757 a visitor to Detroit described a race held there. At that time, Detroit was a remote French outpost. The French and the Pottawatami Indians held a 1.5-mile race each spring from Detroit to the Pottawa-

FOSTER POWELL.

**Foster Powell, the greatest pedestrian of the 18th century (author's collection).**

tami village and back. The Indians wagered furs against merchandise put up by the French.

Most of what we know about running from A.D. 500–1800 comes from Britain with some information from Italy, Germany and America. The development of foot-racing (especially track and cross country) was greatly influenced by 17th and 18th century running by the British. The reason for this is not obvious. Good roads, accurately measured courses and accurate and cheap watches all played a part; however, these were also available in other parts of the world. British people love to gamble. This may have been the key since much of their early running was done to satisfy wagers.

# IV

## The Origin of Modern Running (1800–1850)

*Never back anything as can talk.*
— Fred Swindles

In the 19th century, public interest in running ranged from intense to almost none, both in the United States and Britain. Enthusiasm was created by exceptional runners and running rivalries. Public apathy was caused by a lack of outstanding runners and by the running fans becoming fed up with the race "fixing" which plagued professional running.

Running standards in England in 1800 were: a quarter mile in a minute or a second or two less; a half mile in 2:07; a mile in five minutes; two miles in 10:10; four miles in 21:30; and 10 miles in an hour. Runners able to beat any of these times were difficult to find.

### Captain Barclay— A Gentleman Pedestrian

The first outstanding pedestrian of the 19th century was Robert Barclay Allardyce (1779–1854), a Scottish nobleman better known as "Captain Barclay." He surpassed Foster Powell's performances and made the sport respectable for "gentlemen." In addition, his training methods were widely adopted by English and American runners and walkers for most of the 19th century.

Barclay was a powerful man whose father and grandfather had also been noted strong men. He was most famous for walking long distances, but he was also a respectable runner for his day, running the quarter mile in 56 seconds and the mile in 4:50. Although he was known for his honesty and integrity, some of his rivals were not. In July 1807, Barclay, the best long-distance walker of his day, faced Abraham Wood, the best long-distance runner of the early 1800s in a 24 hour race. Barclay was to walk as far as he could in the 24-hours while Wood was to "go-as-he-pleased," either running or walking as he saw fit. Because he was restricted to walking, Barclay received a 20-mile (32 km) handicap.

Interest in the match was great. According to one observer, it attracted "the greatest concourse of people ever assembled at Newmarket." The course was a carefully measured, rolled-and-lined mile on the side of the turnpike road from Newmarket to London. When the race started, Wood quickly took the lead and ran the first two miles in 15 minutes and reached eight miles in an hour. He continued at a "lounging run," covering 20 miles in 2:41. By running 22 miles (35.4 km) in the first three hours he made up four of the 20 miles he had given Barclay.

After 24 miles (38.6 km), which he covered in 3 hr 16 min, Wood went to his tent where he ate and rested for five minutes. At 32 miles (51.5 km) he lay down for another 10 minutes, appearing tired. His handlers rubbed his ankles and body, and took off his shoes. He ran the next four miles barefoot — slowing noticeably and taking over 20 minutes to go the last two miles. Although he had run barefoot in other races, the sharp stones cut his feet and he had to stop and put his shoes back on. He covered 40 miles (64.4 km) in 6:22, then stopped and went into his tent. A short time later, Wood's backers announced that he had resigned the match.

Meanwhile Barclay, unperturbed by Wood's early speed, walked a steady six miles an hour — not varying a minute. When he reached 18 miles (28.9 km), he paused briefly to eat some warm fowl. At 36 miles

(58 km) he stopped again and as he rested he learned that Wood had quit.

The unexpected end to the race shocked the spectators who had thought highly of Wood. He had previously been credited with four miles in 20:21, and had run 40 miles (64.4 km) in 4:56. Several of those who had bet on him refused to pay, suspecting something unfair had taken place. Barclay had been suspicious of Wood all along and had refused the match until a "Gentleman" agreed to back Wood. It was finally discovered that Wood's handlers had given him liquid laudanum (a tincture of opium) at 22 miles (35.4 km). Two doctors examined Wood after the match and concluded that he was feverish and could not have gone much farther. One correspondent believed Wood's handlers had given him the drug after secretly betting against him.

Wood went on to win many races. His best performances included 440 yards (54 seconds); 880 yards (2:06); the mile (4:34); and four miles (20:21). In 1816 when he was in the twilight of his career, he made a wager that showed what pedestrianism of his day was all about. After a three-day-and-night drinking bout, he bet that in an hour he could: catch a duck on the turnpike road, pluck it, roast it, eat it, then run a five-minute mile. He won the bet, devouring the duck (washed down with a quart of ale) then running a 4:56 mile, all within the hour.

In July 1809, Barclay undertook a task that would make him a legend. He bet he could walk 1,000 miles (1,610 km) with one mile being covered in each of 1,000 consecutive hours. The money riding on the attempt was enormous. Barclay bet £16,000 on himself and over 10,000 spectators were on hand to witness the attempt.

Walking a mile in each of 1,000 consecutive hours is not a test of speed and possibly not even a test of athletic ability. The real difficulty is going 41 days with very little sleep. Barclay devised a system of walking the first mile at the end of each hour

Captain Barclay performing the feat of walking 1,000 miles in 1,000 hours, July 1809 (*Illustrated Sporting News*, June 27, 1863).

## Mensen Ernst—"To Move Is to Live, to Stand Still Is to Die"

I chose a calling that, however strange and fruitless most people may find it, did bring me much honor and much money in addition to a rich harvest of all the pleasures of traveling. Though I must admit, also some of its sorrows and hardships.—Mensen Ernst (1838)

In the 1830s Norwegian Mensen Ernst reportedly performed long-distance running feats that have never been equaled. Although three books and dozens of articles have been written on Ernst, the truth about him remains as elusive as his feats were spectacular.

The origin of many of the details of Ernst's life is the 1838 biography *Des Stauermannes Mensen Ernst* by German author Gustav Rieck. This book is based on interviews with Ernst, his diaries and, to an unknown extent, Rieck's imagination. For example, Rieck wrote that Ernst was born in Bergen, Norway, in 1799, the son of a British sea captain and a Norwegian mother descended from the Viking Eric the Red. Rieck also wrote that Ernst's parents died in a gale on the North Sea. After researching Ernst's early life, Norwegian Bredo Berntsen, author of *Løperkongen (The King of Running): The Adventurous Life of the Norwegian Mensen Ernst* (1986) found that these details of Ernst's early life were pure fiction. This makes it difficult to accept the rest of Rieck's book without substantiating evidence. But we can't dismiss Ernst outright, because other sources written in his time confirm that he was at the very least a popular and very colorful long-distance pedestrian.

Berntsen found that Ernst—whose given name was Mons Monsen Øyri—was born in 1795 in Fresvik, Norway. His father, a poor tenant farmer, died that same year, and the family scraped by on their tiny farm with the aid of charity. When he was a

then immediately starting a second mile at the beginning of the next hour. This provided uninterrupted rest periods of almost 1.5 hours.

He battled dust, high winds, rain, soreness in his legs and feet and a toothache. An eyewitness reported that "so overpowering was the drowsiness which affected Barclay during the last days of the walk that he could be kept awake only by sticking needles into him, and by firing pistols close to his ears. His legs also swelled prodigiously."

After completing the 1,000th mile, Barclay collected his £16,000, took a warm bath, and went to sleep, giving strict orders to be awakened after eight hours. He was worried that because of his extreme fatigue and sleepiness he might not wake up. Fortunately, he need not have worried; he awoke the next day "without pain and in perfect health."

teenager, young Øyri moved to Bergen where he soon shipped out as a sailor. He never returned to his homeland and spent his early life at sea in the British merchant marine (on the ship *Caledonia* according to Rieck). While at sea, he semi-anglicized his name to Mensen Ernst.

In 1818 Ernst left the sea and went to London to become a long-distance pedestrian—a career that lasted 25 years. According to Rieck, Ernst's first notable run was in 1819 when he ran the 72 miles (116 km) from London to Portsmouth in nine hours. A short time later he ran from London to Liverpool, which Rieck reported as 150 miles (241 km), in 32 hours.* Pedestrian events were popular in England in Ernst's time and these feats, if they took place, were impressive enough to have been headline news. Strangely, British newspapers of the time made no mention of either of them.

Ernst performed more than 60 pedestrian feats between 1824 and 1832 in such cities as Paris, Istanbul, Rome and Venice. These were mostly against time rather than other runners, and he usually won his wagers, although he admitted that he occasionally performed poorly in order to encourage future betting against him. Rieck's descriptions of Ernst's performances are vague and do not provide enough information to accurately assess them.

In 1826 Ernst was mentioned for the first time in a Norwegian newspaper. The Oslo *Morgenbladet* reported that the people in Rendsburg in Denmark (now Germany) "have in large numbers been lured out through the gates to see a runner by the name of Ernst from Bergen." In Copenhagen the newspapers reported in February and March of 1826 that the crowds were so large that Ernst was almost unable to perform.

Ernst is most noted for three ultralong "journey" runs made between 1832 and

Mensen Ernst, whose navigational experience later proved useful in his long runs (from Bredo Berntsen, *The King of Running: The Adventurous Life of the Norwegian Mensen Ernst*, 1986. Courtesy of Bredo Berntsen).

1836. Unfortunately, we must depend on Rieck for most of what we know of these runs. He wrote that in 1832, Ernst went to Paris and began publicizing an upcoming run from Paris to Moscow. Ernst was to receive 3,800 francs if he could cover the distance in 15 days. Wearing a loose white tunic over tight black trousers, accented by a wide belt and a derby with a large feathered plume, he left the Palace Vendome in Paris at four a.m. on June 11. He reportedly reached the Kremlin in Moscow at 10 A.M. on June 25, almost two days early. According to Rieck, the commander there had been expecting him but because Ernst arrived early and in rags, he was mistaken for a beggar. When Ernst showed his identification, the Russians apologized and ordered a lavish celebration.

Whether he actually made this 13-day,

*The actual distance from London to Liverpool is 205 to 207 miles (330–333 km).*

eight-hour run as Rieck reported is uncertain. If he did, it was a prodigious feat. The "as-the-crow-flies" distance from Paris to Moscow is about 1,500 miles (2,414 km). Ernst would have had to cover at least 112 miles (180 km) a day. For comparison, when George Littlewood set the 19th-century six-day record of 623 miles (1,003.8 km) in 1888 (see section five), he averaged just under 104 miles (167 km) a day. Littlewood's record was made on a carefully prepared indoor track, and he had ample support from his trainers. It is almost inconceivable that Ernst, running alone on poor to nonexistent roads, could have covered more than twice Littlewood's distance and at a faster speed. In 1999 Norwegian Trond Olav Svendsen and a colleague made an extensive search of 1832 Moscow newspapers but found no mention of Ernst's feat. Whether valid or not, stories of the run secured Ernst's reputation, and he then traveled from city to city all over Europe, a one-man circus and folk hero.

Ernst began his second great run on June 6, 1833, when he left Munich at one p.m. carrying letters from the Bavarian king to his son Otto, King of Greece, in Nauplion. The run was 1,577 miles (2,538 km), and the territory was far more rugged than that between Paris and Moscow. Rieck reported that Ernst was robbed of his money, maps, and compass and later arrested as a spy and jailed for two days. He still managed to complete the run in just over 24 days and delivered the messages seven days sooner than if they had been sent by regular mail. Allowing about four days for delay and various mishaps, his running time would have been 20 days, with an average of about 79 miles (127 km) a day. This run is supported by some evidence from Ernst's time. Berntsen found newspapers that told how Ernst left Munich, came to Fuynem and returned to Trieste (where he stayed in quarantine), then returned to Munich and was greeted by the royal family.

According to Rieck, Ernst undertook his greatest run on July 28, 1836, from Constantinople through central Asia to Calcutta and back. He crossed the mountain wilderness of Asia Minor, the deserts of Syria, the plains of Persia, the mountains and canyons of Afghanistan, and the Himalayas (where he sometimes had to use snowshoes). He arrived in Calcutta 30 days later in one-third the time of the swiftest caravan. After a four-day rest he ran back to Constantinople, arriving on September 23. Despite being shot at, robbed, and bitten by snakes, he reportedly covered the approximately 5,000-mile (8,047 km) route in 59 days, averaging at least 85 miles (137 km) a day. During the run, he had to make his way across deserts and uninhabited salt swamps that went on for hundreds of miles. Some of the countries he ran through were in a state of continuous war and infested with robbers.

Less than a year later, on March 24, 1837, the London Times gave brief accounts of the three runs and added: "This latter performance [Calcutta to Constantinople] would be incredible, but that it is attested by unquestionable certificates." This article loses some of its credibility when it goes on to tell how in 1827 Ernst had served with distinction on the British ship the Bukarest at the battle of Navarino against the Turkish-Egyptian fleet (this incident is also described in Rieck's book). Careful checking by British ultrarunning historian Andy Milroy failed to turn up any ship in the British Navy named Bukarest.

Ernst was a short (barely 5 ft. 7 in., or 1.7 m), muscular pedestrian who led a Spartan existence, preferring to eat cold food and sleep outside on the ground. According to Rieck, Ernst seldom slept more than three or four hours a day, and when he was running, he slept only 10 to 15 minutes twice a day—leaning against a tree with a cloth over his eyes. While on his runs, he avoided towns and cities where inquisitive crowds might slow him, but gave little heed to obstacles like mountains or streams. He seldom walked, but preferred to run with a long, swinging lope. For food, he carried biscuits and raspberry syrup and drank large amounts of wine, sometimes as he ran.

In 1842 he made plans for what was to be his crowning achievement — a run across Africa from Cairo to Cape Town, in the process of which he would find the mysterious White Nile. Count Hermann von Pückler-Muskau, a famous German author and adventurer who had traveled extensively in Egypt, wrote to a friend on February 11, 1842: "Nothing to report except that I have hired the runner Mensen Ernst as two-legged trotting horse in Turkish costume." The count offered to sponsor Ernst's run across Africa and provide him with references.

On May 11, 1842, Ernst set off from Muskau in Poland. He passed Constantinople and reached Jerusalem in 30 days, then ran the 320 miles (515 km) to Cairo. After some months in Cairo he headed south along the Nile. On the morning of January 22, 1843, he stopped to rest near the present Egypt-Sudan border. He leaned against a palm tree, covered his face with a handkerchief and went to sleep. Later, a group of tourists tried to wake him, but he was dead, apparently a victim of dysentery. He had fulfilled his motto of "To move is to live, to stand still is to die." He was buried under some stones at a spot now submerged by the Aswan Dam. Count Von Pückler-Muskau reportedly had the following epitaph carved on a stone above Ernst's grave: "Swift as the deer, restless as the swallow. Earth, his arena, never saw his like."

Was Ernst the greatest ultrarunner ever or just a clever self-promoter who exaggerated or invented his most spectacular feats? There is a maxim that claims of extraordinary deeds require extraordinary proof. Unfortunately the only source for much of Ernst's career (especially his three most important runs) comes from his biographer Rieck, who we know invented the details of Ernst's early life. Despite the efforts that have been made so far, separating what Ernst really did from Rieck's questionable account remains a thorny challenge for running historians.

## The Rise of Professional Runners

Prior to the early 1800s, foot-races for wagers were mostly between people of higher class, or their servants (footmen). With the urbanization of Britain a new class of runners from the working class arose who made, or at least attempted to make, a living from the sport. As this new sport of professional running or pedestrianism emerged, the center of running activity shifted from the gentlemen's clubs to public houses or taverns in the major cities. Where runners like Barclay had been essentially self-motivated and independent, the new class of runners depended on backers for financial support and trainers to help them prepare for their matches.

In 1838 the leading British sporting publication *Bell's Life* gave pedestrianism a section of its own and actively began promoting running matches. It provided a calendar of matches, acted as stakeholder, provided a forum for issuing and answering challenges and wrote detailed and usually favorable accounts of the matches. Between 1840 and 1850, pedestrianism underwent a boom period in England that spilled over to America. By 1850 the public houses were beginning to have their own "cinder paths" or tracks. Most races involved only two runners and were for small stakes, usually £5 per side, but this could rise to £100 or more for a championship match which might draw a huge crowd.

## The Origin of Modern Training Methods for Running

British pedestrian fans adored Captain Barclay. Many pedestrians, hoping to equal or surpass his feats, adopted his training methods. The first book written specifically on running and walking was Walter Thom's *Pedestrianism*, published in 1813. In the preface Thom acknowledged that Barclay furnished the chapter on training and revised "the greater part of the work." The book, sometimes referred to as *Barclay's Pedestrianism*, contains details of Barclay's training methods. He took most of them from Sir John Sinclair's *A Collection of Papers on the Subject of Athletic Exercises* (1806). Sinclair's training methods were based mainly on those of John Jackson, known as "Gentleman" Jackson, a famous pugilist and one of the great trainers of the early 19th century. Up to the time of Sinclair's book, athletic training methods were often considered the livelihood of a trainer, kept a closely guarded secret, and orally passed on to the next generation. Here are the training methods described by Thom:

The pedestrian, who may be supposed to be in tolerable condition, enters upon his training with a regular course of physic, which consists of three doses. Glauber salts are generally preferred, and from one ounce and a half to two ounces, are taken each time, with an interval of four days, between each dose. After having gone through the course of physic, he commences his regular exercise, which is gradually increased as he proceeds in the training. When the object in view is the accomplishment of a pedestrian match, his regular exercise may be from 20–24 miles a day. He must rise at 5 in the morning:

1. Run ½ mi. at top speed up a hill.
2. Walk six miles at a moderate pace.
3. Breakfast at about seven A.M. (beefsteaks, muttonchops, underdone with stale bread and old beer.)
4. Walk six miles at a moderate pace.
5. Lie in bed without clothes for ½ hour.
6. Walk four miles
7. Dinner at four P.M. (beefsteaks, muttonchops with bread and beer as at breakfast.)
8. Immediately after dinner, run ½ mile at top speed.
9. Walk six miles at a moderate pace.
10. Bed at eight and repeat the next day.

Avoid liquids as much as possible only enough to quench the thirst. Milk is never allowed, as it curdles on the stomach. Soups are not used. It is impossible to fix a precise period for the completion of the training process, as it depends on the condition of the pedestrian. From two to three months of training will, in most cases, be sufficient, especially if he is in tolerable shape to begin with.

Both walkers and runners used "Barclay's method" well into the second half of the 19th century. Trainers thought a pedestrian's system had to be cleansed before training could begin. Professional runners, walkers and boxers of the time came mostly from the working classes and may have had poor diets and unhealthy life styles. A medicine that caused vomiting (an emetic) was given to cleanse the system from the stomach up and a laxative from the stomach down. Artificial sweating was used as a quick method of weight reduction since runners didn't train continuously but, like boxers, went through a new training cycle for each important match. Barclay was well known for training boxers and this is reflected in his training methods which are quite general.

Training for sprinters was similar. According to an unknown contributor to C. A. Wheeler's *Sportascrapiana* (1866), the sprinter in training was encouraged to:

1. Use a "strong physic," for the first two days.
2. Wear heavy shoes for all exercises.
3. Walk a couple of miles before breakfast.
4. Shower and be rubbed for twenty minutes.
5. Walk ten miles after breakfast
6. Practice starting for one hour.
7. Walk two or three miles after dinner.

8. Every third day run the race distance at top speed.

By the mid–19th century some trainers had begun to doubt Barclay's training methods. One wrote: "Such training if carried into effect is calculated to send a man to his grave rather than to the cinder path." Barclay's methods were harsh and the purging, sweating and restriction of fluids may have done more harm than good. Another weakness of his methods, especially for runners, was that they called for large amounts of walking but relatively little running. Most runners and trainers of the time believed the majority of a runner's training should consist of walking. Training runs longer than the race distance would make a pedestrian "dead legged," they believed.

Although some questioned aspects of Barclay's training methods such as violent exercise just after eating and artificial sweating, his methods were repeated in most British and American books on training until late in the 19th century. The great contribution to running by Jackson, Sinclair and Barclay was that they were willing to share and write down athletic training methods—flawed as they were — and make them widely available for examination, discussion and verification.

## Jem Wantling—First Sprinter to "Break Evens"

The first accounts of sprint races in England date from the late 17th century, but no times were recorded. Detailed accounts of sprint races, some including times, begin to appear in the late 18th century. These races were usually run on turnpike roads. The first sprinter who could be considered a national champion was James "Jem" Wantling, a potter born in about 1801 in Derby. Wantling was noted for always wrapping his calves and thighs tightly with leather straps before he raced — probably to keep from pulling a muscle. The public at first laughed at this strange habit, but the laughing stopped when Wantling began beating every sprinter in sight.

By 1822 he had defeated all the sprinters in Derby and Nottinghamshire. He then raced the well-known sprinter, Shaw of Lane-end, and twice defeated him easily. The first race was at 120 yards with Wantling running 12½ seconds (at this time watches could only time to the nearest half second), and the second at 300 yards. Shaw's friends had backed him to such an extent that many didn't have money enough to return home. Afterward Shaw sent word to his father, "that he [Wantling] was no man, but the devil."

By 1824 Wantling had proven to be the fastest sprinter in England. The distinguished sports writer Pierce Egan in *Sporting Anecdotes* (1825) describes how highly Wantling was regarded in his day:

No man can run with Wantling level handed.... By his conduct he gained the esteem of all his friends, and made an impression on their affectations that will never be forgotten. He defeated Own at Newcastle and wishing him well through life, handsomely gave him something more substantial than wishes: the same he did to Shaw and to his other opponents. This is noble, and is a conduct worthy of Jem Wantling ... Wantling owes his swiftness to his peculiar formation; he is almost a mass of muscle; he is firm and compact, and has a heart that shows no fear; he has the utmost presence of mind, and it is next to impossible to get the start of him; his times are incredible to old runners; he runs close as possible, and as far as we can tell from anything on record, or oral tradition, sets at a great distance all former runners. In civilized life there is nothing equal to him.

Wantling's brother, a Coventry bookbinder, stated in 1843 that Jem had run 200 yards several times in 19 seconds. He is most noted, however, for reportedly running 100 yards in nine seconds on a turnpike road. If this claim could be proven — considering the date and primitive conditions he must have run under — Wantling would have to be considered one of the fastest sprinters ever.

Unfortunately, according to British sport historian David Terry, the sporting publications of the time reported neither the 19 second 200 yards nor the nine-second 100 yards. *Bell's Life*, however, does credit Wantling with running 500 yards in 61 seconds on December 14, 1826. Wantling, in all probability, was the first sprinter we know of who was capable of running 100 yards in less than 10 seconds.

## A Notable Picking Up Stones Contest

An interesting variation on pedestrian racing of the early 1800s was "Picking Up Stones." These were matches where runners picked up small stones spaced every yard along a straight line and placed them in a basket at one end. The formula for calculating the total distance (D) covered in this type of race is $D = N(N + 1)$, where N is the number of stones. The race distance quickly gets large. For example, if the stones are a meter apart:

| Number of Stones | Race Distance (km) |
| --- | --- |
| 100 | 10.1 |
| 200 | 40.2 |
| 300 | 90.3 |

Abrupt turns and stooping to pick up the stones add to the difficulty. A shortened version of this race, the "potato race," using potatoes rather than stones, was popular in late 19th century American club and college track meets.

*Bell's Life* for May 14, 1837, described a race to pick up 300 stones a yard apart. John Phipps Townsend, who had won the first 52-mile (84 km) London to Brighton race in eight hours, 37 minutes in January of that year, was one competitor. Townsend, born in 1792, was unusually robust at 154 pounds (70 kg) and standing five feet five inches (1.65 m) tall. He had won 289 professional matches out of a total of 295 in his 30-year career and called himself "The Champion of Living Pedestrians." His rival was a lesser known Lancashire runner named Edward Drinkwater "Temperance," who was considered faster than Townsend up to 10 miles but was an unknown quantity at this distance (51.3 mi./82.7 km). To make things more interesting, Townsend agreed to pick up his stones with his mouth while Drinkwater was allowed to use his hands.

The ground's owner had taken great pains to prepare the course. It was swept clean with brushes, measured and remeasured. The day of the contest was gloomy with showers which kept the crowd small and gate receipts — divided equally between the two runners and the ground's owner — to about £50. Drinkwater's stones were small round pebbles, about the size of a pigeon's egg. The cagey Townsend, however, had scoured Brighton Beach for rather long stones he positioned on end to make it easier to pick them up with his mouth. He had also prepared himself for kneeling by sewing a leather pad in his pants at the knee.

Drinkwater started at a very fast pace and picked up his stones in order, the nearer ones first, but Townsend started slower and chose a quite different plan. After picking up a few stones near his basket Townsend started off, still fresh, for the more distant ones. He pursued this plan for several stones in succession. He then picked up stones at various points near home, "as his wind appeared to serve him," and again went for the outsiders. By this method he varied his efforts according to how he felt. His pace was rapid and steady, sometimes running, sometimes walking.

At the end of three hours Townsend

had picked up 103 stones at various distances and Drinkwater had retrieved nearly 200 of the nearby stones. When five and a quarter hours had passed Townsend still lagged, having retrieved 212 stones to Drinkwater's 260. Townsend's remaining stones were close in however, while Drinkwater's were outsiders. After eight hours Drinkwater gave up and was carried into his room "completely worn out and incapable of further effort."

Townsend picked up his last stone at 8:19. "With enthusiastic cheers, he was carried to the Pavilion where he received the congratulations of his wife and sons, only blaming the former for not selling his pigs as he had desired her in order that he might have laid out their value on the match."

Later that night at his victory party Townsend ate a hearty dinner of cold roast-beef and then offered to back himself to stand on one leg for an hour. In 1821 he had set a record by standing on one leg for seven hours and three minutes. This time, his friends wisely talked him out of making the attempt.

Townsend was forced to retire in 1842. In 1843 he lost the use of one of his legs, possibly as a result of the one-legged feat he had performed so many times during his 30-year career. Drinkwater, after his running days were over, operated a popular tavern aptly named "Temperance's." Many British pedestrians, when they became too old to compete, worked in taverns. If they had been successful at their running, they might even own their own sporting house. Like retired professional athletes of today, they were still "drawing cards" and most had spent large amounts of time in taverns during their running days. It was there that races were arranged, backers found and running news exchanged. Unfortunately many were better runners than businessmen and failed in the business and fell into poverty.

## The Origin of Cross Country Running

Running after a pack of hunting beagles is a form of exercise that probably dates back to the Middle Ages. This was such great fun that the beagles were eventually dispensed with and British schoolboys, as early as the 16th century, amused themselves by playing "Hunt the Fox," or "Hunt the Hare."

The sport we know as cross country evolved along two lines—steeple chasing and "hare and hounds." *Bell's Life* for April 20, 1834, gives an account of a "steeple-chase on foot," that took place at Rugby School. The race was patterned after the 18th-century sport of steeple chasing (a race to a church steeple on horseback). It started in a field about a mile from town without the approval of the school masters who would have put a stop to it had they known about it,

> …but luckily they heard of it too late, and thirty of the best runners in the school started at half-past three at full speed for Baily Hill, a distance of about four miles which was accomplished by the winner in the space of 24 minutes. The fencing was stiff and frequent, the most difficult of which was a tremendous hedge and brook, was cleared in fine style by most of the gentlemen whilst others, ignorant of the existence of the brook, found themselves suddenly immersed in a cold bath….

The only problem noted was that because the race had been run on the sly, no flags or markers could be used to mark the course and some of the runners got lost.

These "steeplechases on foot" as well as "hare and hounds" were eventually approved of by the school masters and became popular in the 1830s at Rugby and Shrewsbury. Hare and hounds became known to the world from Thomas Hughes's 1857 novel *Tom Brown's School Days*. A chapter in the book gives an insightful account of an 1830s hare and hounds contest — the famous "Barby hill run" at Rugby School.

The "hares" usually started 10 to 15 minutes before the "hounds" — an interval known as "law." After laying false trails that led nowhere and getting rid of all their "scent" (strips of paper used to mark the course) they left their bags and ran straight to their destination. The hounds could do the same when they either spotted the hares or came upon the empty bags. This was where the real racing began. The hounds seldom caught the hares, especially if the hares were good at laying false trails.

Hare and hounds had a charm lacking in more intense racing. It was a battle of wits between the hares and hounds, calling for cooperation among the hounds. Even if one was not a fast runner one could plod to the finish with the rest of the duffers, conscious of a couple of hours well spent, with lungs full of fresh air and many pleasant memories. After the run it was customary to have a big meal and socialize.

In 1838, Rugby School held its first "Crick" run. This 12.5-mile (20.1 km) race has been held nearly every year since and is probably the oldest foot-race still in existence. Among the dozen or so hare and hound courses used at Rugby School, the Crick run established itself as the most prestigious from 1865 on, whereas the Barby Hill course was used only occasionally after 1857. To this day cross country runners are still known as harriers (hare-hunters).

## Running in America

By the 1820s running in North America had begun to take on a national flavor. Prior to this time, foot-racing had attracted little public interest except on a local scale. Following the examples set by Barclay and other British pedestrians, Americans began to find their own running heroes. By the late 1830s running was second only to horse racing as a spectator sport in America. The public began to marvel at the skill and endurance of pedestrians. Neighborhoods and towns backed their "fast man" in local races, and foot-racing took on a regional and sometimes national character. For example, in Augusta, Georgia, on Dec. 17, 1836, Henry Perrit of Georgia raced John Day of Kentucky for $3,000 a side. Day was heavily favored but Perritt won the race easily, beating Day by 6½ feet in 50 yards.

Foot-races were initially through city streets, but in order to charge admission, they were moved to horse tracks. By the late 1830s horse tracks in Philadelphia and Hoboken, N.J., had regular programs of foot-races. Their distances varied. Four, five and 10 miles were popular, as were occasional longer races of 15 or 20 miles. Shorter "spins" such as 100 and 200 yards were also common.

### The First National Race in America

The first race of national importance in the United States took place on April 24, 1835. John C. Stevens, a wealthy horse owner from New York and a liberal patron of sports, bet Samuel L. Gouverneur that somewhere in America he could find a man able to run 10 miles in an hour.

Covering 10 miles in an hour doesn't take great running talent. According to Thom in *Pedestrianism*, the feat was fairly commonplace in Britain by 1813. "Ten miles in an hour has frequently been performed," he wrote, and listed Charles Orton as the first to do it, when he ran 10 miles in 57 minutes in 1771. Others claimed that Preston, "the Flying Butcher of Leeds," ran 10 miles within the hour in 1690. In any case, as of 1835, there was no record of anyone accomplishing the feat in America. Stevens offered a $1,000 purse and promised to add another $300 if several ran and only one finished within the hour.

The novelty of the experience, the

money and the sporting reputations of the sponsors produced much interest in the contest. Nine men started the race on the Union Course before a crowd of nearly 30,000. The runners, a diverse group, wore colorful jockey outfits. One was an Indian, two were foreign-born (Prussian and Irish) and a couple were farmers from upstate New York and Connecticut.

Three finished the race, but only one within an hour. Henry Stannard, a Connecticut farmer who had "been in training for a month," was accompanied on horseback by Stevens, the sponsor. Stevens, watch in hand, kept Stannard on an even pace. He ran a 5:36 first mile and a 5:54 last mile, on his way to a 59:44 victory. Celebrating with a flourish, Stannard climbed upon a box, made a short speech, then jumped on a horse and galloped around the course.

Stannard's covering 10 miles in less than an hour created wide interest in footracing in America and gave aspiring pedestrians a clear idea of the performances required to be considered first-rate. America's first running champion won several other races in the following years but never improved on his 59:44 10 mile. According to John Cumming in *Runners and Walkers* (1981), Stannard earned enough money from running to purchase a restaurant in Killingsworth, Connecticut which he renamed the Pedestrian Hotel.

## THE BRITISH INVASION

Built at a cost of more than $60,000, the Beacon Race Course in Hoboken, N.J., was the first luxurious race track in North America. It opened in 1837, and in 1844 the course was the site of three major pedestrian races that helped establish the sport in America. The proprietors of the course, offering substantial prize money, advertised widely both in America and Britain and attracted outstanding runners from both countries.

On Oct. 14, a one-hour race for $1,000,

billed as "between England and America," was held on the Beacon Course. According to *The American Turf Register*, "after the stands were packed with 10,000 persons, a dense multitude of 'Oliver Twists' crashed the gate and encircled the entire course." Included in the field of 17 runners were Stannard; a New Yorker—John Gildersleeve; an Indian—John Steeprock; and three Englishmen—John Barlow, Tom Greenhalgh and Ambrose Jackson. The British runners' lack of clothing shocked the American press. Unlike the Americans who wore modified jockey outfits, the British runners were "quite naked," except for linen drawers with the legs and waists cut off.

Stannard, by this time 33 years old, was the only proven American performer. Although the British runners were mostly unknown in the United States, because of the British tradition of excellence at running, the crowd bet heavily on Barlow and Greenhalgh. Steeprock, who spoke no English and ran with a wild bounding gait, was the crowd favorite. In order to let the runners know if they had slipped to a slower than six-minute-per-mile pace, a bell was to be struck once three minutes after the start and three times at six minutes. This pattern was repeated throughout the race.

Steeprock led the pack through the first mile in 5:16 before his trainer told him to fall back. Going into the 10th mile, Greenhalgh overtook Barlow, who had been leading most of the race. Gildersleeve and Steeprock were 40 yards back. At the 10-mile mark, which Greenhalgh and Barlow passed in 57:01, both the runners and the crowd became confused. Many of the crowd, thinking the race was over, poured onto the course. Gildersleeve passed Barlow, who had slowed to a trot, and took off after Greenhalgh. When passed, Greenhalgh also slowed to a walk. The winner, Gildersleeve, kept going and had covered 10 miles, 955 yards when the official gave the signal that one hour had passed.

The first five runners had covered more than 10 miles within the hour in what one newspaper called "one of the greatest foot-races that ever took place in America or England." Barlow, who came in third after leading most of the race, would later be accused of sandbagging in this race to improve the betting odds on later races.

The second race in the "England vs. America" series took place on November 19, 1844, at the Beacon course. The race produced the first "world's best" running performance on American soil. At least 30,000 assembled on the muddy, damp course. The entries, except for Stannard who didn't run, were basically the same as for the October 14 race.

Gildersleeve was in even better condition than in the previous race, but was suffering from a cold. Steeprock, the Indian, was still a crowd favorite. One correspondent wrote "Place Steeprock in the hands of a first-rate English trainer, and we doubt if there is a man alive who can beat him at 10 miles." Steeprock had the habit of "shoeing" (behaving like a horse kept in a dark stable) when he approached the stands, and was nicknamed the "werry fast crab." Betting was almost even on Gildersleeve and Barlow against the field.

The two Englishmen had devised a strategy whereby Barlow was to set a blistering pace to draw out and exhaust Steeprock while Greenhalgh stayed back and took on Gildersleeve. After a false start Barlow jumped into the lead and covered the first mile in 5:10. The railing and both sides of the course were densely packed with spectators and, even at the start, the runners had to "run the gauntlet." A *Spirit of the Times* reporter wrote: "Nearly every one of the pedestrians was more than once thrown off his stride by the obstructions of the horses, or the crowding upon them of the spectators."

By the second mile, which he covered in 5:15, Barlow had established a sizable lead over everyone but Steeprock. During the

third mile he increased his lead over Steeprock to 50 yards followed by Gildersleeve and Greenhalgh. As the race went on Barlow continued to increase the distance between himself and the others. By the start of the 10th mile Barlow — "strong, steady and precise as a steam engine" — had the race in hand leading Steeprock by about 250 yards. Greenhalgh, who had been following Gildersleeve, turned to his rival and said "Goodby, Gilder!" and spurted ahead covering the last mile in 4:48 to take third place and almost overtake Steeprock.

Pierce Egan's *The Fancy* (1826) listed the fastest time ever run for 10 miles as 54:53 by a British runner named Miles in 1821. Barlow's record-breaking time was 54:21, followed by Steeprock in 54:53, Greenhalgh in 55:10 and Gildersleeve in 55:51. The prize money was substantial for the period, with Barlow receiving $700, Steeprock $250, Greenhalgh $150 and Gildersleeve $75.

Barlow, known as "Tallick" in England, took his winnings and sailed for Liverpool. On arriving home, his description of racing in America was quite different from that he had given to the New York newspapers. He reported that in his last race in America plans were underway for a lot of "barbarians" to be planted along the track to impede his progress. His backer, Sullivan, heard of the plan and placed a number of burly men around the track who took turns running with Barlow and fending off the mob.

Gildersleeve and Greenhalgh ran the final race of the series on December 15, 1844. The 12-mile (19.3 km) race turned out to be perhaps the best of the whole series. The weather was extremely cold with a piercing wind and falling snow. Greenhalgh again ran "nearly nude," with just a yellow cap and shorts. It was "cold enough to have frozen any other man as stiff as Lot's wife in 5 minutes," wrote one reporter. A smaller-than-usual crowd of about 2,000 jammed the track, stamping and dancing to try to

The great foot-race at the Beacon Course, Hoboken, N.J., October 14, 1844. John Gildersleeve, who has just taken the lead, won the one-hour race with 10 miles, 955 yards (*Illustrated London News*, January 11, 1845).

stay warm. The odds were 10 to 6 on Greenhalgh. So feverish was the betting that it was said that "one could not ask the time without being answered '10 to 6' and if you only looked a man in the face he roared out 'Done, Sir!'"

From the start it was a tactical race between two evenly matched runners, both of them fit and mentally prepared. Gildersleeve took the lead from the start, running at just under five minutes per mile for the first five miles, with the shirtless Greenhalgh a stride behind. On the sixth mile Gildersleeve surged to a 5:33 mile, but could not shake his rival. They passed 10 miles in 57:52 — a good performance under the circumstances. Both were perspiring heavily despite the near-blizzard conditions.

As they began the last mile, both accelerated, running the last lap stride-for-stride with Gildersleeve still a step ahead. Within a few yards of the finish, Greenhalgh sprinted past Gildersleeve to score a narrow victory, then nearly collapsed from exhaustion. He had covered the last mile in 5:18 and the 12 miles in 68:48. Greenhalgh recovered his breath, put on warm clothes and

made a grateful speech, praising American hospitality and sportsmanship. He then rode away in a carriage amidst the cheers of thousands of newly acquired friends. Gildersleeve, after his running days, moved to California when gold fever broke out in 1849 and died in Roseberg, Oregon, in 1895 at the age of 83.

### WILLIAM JACKSON— "THE AMERICAN DEER"

On Jan 6, 1845, William Howitt became the first man to run 11 miles (17.7 km) in an hour and live to tell about it. Previously a runner named Bettridge had accomplished the feat but died of "over-exertion" shortly afterward.

Out of deference to his brother, who worked for *Bell's Life*, Howitt ran under the name of William Jackson. Why he chose that name is uncertain, but there had been an earlier celebrated British pedestrian who competed in the 1820s with the same name. The five foot three inch 105-pound Jackson also called himself "The American Deer," although he was born in Norwich, Britain, on February 14, 1821. He adopted the "American Deer" name after making a short trip to America to visit his brother. Howitt's choice of names has led to much confusion. Some writers have referred to him as an American, others have confused him with the American Indian, Louis Bennett "Deerfoot," who ran in the 1860s. He has also been confused with the earlier William Jackson.

For his historic 11-miles-in-an-hour run, Jackson was matched with William Sheppard, "the Birmingham Pet." Sheppard was an outstanding 27-year-old runner who, up to this time, had tried to keep his best performances "dark" or secret. A *Bell's Life* reporter believed Sheppard was capable of running 10 miles in about 54 minutes although he had officially been clocked in only 56:30. The race took place between two mileposts on the Hatfield turnpike road two miles from Barnet.* A man stood at each milepost holding a handkerchief which the runners touched before turning around. An immense number of spectators lined the mile of road making up the race course.

Sheppard, noted for his graceful stride, jumped into the lead with Jackson a step behind, covering the first two miles in 10:15. They went by four miles in 20:35, with Sheppard still a foot ahead. At eight miles (42:30) Sheppard was four seconds in the lead. After the turn at the ninth mile Jackson ran up alongside Sheppard and looked him in the eyes—hoping to find signs of fatigue. When Sheppard was within about 400 yards of the 10-mile mark he seemed to gather himself and began running faster than at in any part of the race. On nearing the handkerchiefs, Sheppard thrust out his hand, grabbed one of them, and fell on his hands and knees completely exhausted. He had covered 10 miles in 53:35, a new world record — unfortunately for him, the race wasn't over.

Jackson, not far behind, touched the handkerchief and ran out the hour at a "sur-

prising speed," finishing with a total of 11 miles, 40 yards, two feet and four inches. The reason for Sheppard's stopping at 10 miles is unclear. Some were of the opinion that he was confused and thought the race was over. Others firmly believed he was "run to earth," falling from exhaustion. Sheppard definitely ran with a handicap. It was later discovered that he had carried 150 pounds during the race —150 pounds sterling in his money belt.

## GEORGE SEWARD—
### THE AMERICAN WONDER

You won't find the name of George Seward on any Track & Field Hall of Fame list, nor on any other list of famous American sports heroes. The reason for Seward's obscurity may be that he did his best running as an expatriate living in England. He was also a professional and his running was done so long ago and was so extraordinary that many have dismissed him out of hand without checking carefully into what the sports writers of his own time thought of him.

Seward was born on October 16, 1817, in New Haven, Connecticut, and as a youth excelled at running and jumping. He liked to wager small amounts that he could take a short run and jump over a horse. Once, taking a run of about 15 feet, young Seward jumped across a 21-foot-wide stream. He learned the trade of silver-plating, but his real love was running.

His first professional race was with Henry Ainsworth in New Haven on October 18, 1841. The distance was 100 yards and the stakes $50. Seward won with ease, as he did a second match with Ainsworth over the same distance a month later, winning $250. In December of that year he defeated William Belden in a 100-yard race winning $500 on Long Island's Centerville Course. Belden had been considered the

---

*Tracks or "running-paths" did not become plentiful in England until about 1850.

William Sheppard leads Jackson, "The American Deer," in their one-hour race in 1845. Jackson won and became the first man to exceed 11 miles in an hour. His total distance was 11 miles, 40 yards, 2 feet, 4 inches (*Illustrated London Times*, January 11, 1845).

best American sprinter until that race. All who saw the race agreed that a truly phenomenal sprinter had emerged. For the next two years Seward searched the Northeast in vain trying to find another sprinter willing to race him. In the spring of 1843, frustrated because all the Americans considered him unbeatable, he quietly embarked as a seaman on a ship bound for England.

As soon as he arrived in Liverpool he went to a leading sporting-house kept by a well-known pugilist named Jem Ward. There he asked about making a match with Jack Fowler, a noted Liverpool sprinter. The race was to be 100 yards and Seward, pretending to be a novice, insisted on a head-start. Fowler's backers jumped at the chance to take the young sailor's money and the match was set for the next day.

The race grounds were crowded when Seward arrived wearing his sailor's cap, worsted over-shirt, and boots. As he strolled around surveying the course, the crowd laughed and taunted the young stranger with the odd New England accent. The betting was 10 to 1 on Fowler and even at these odds the only person willing to bet on Seward was the American himself.

Seward bet his last £10 and got ready to start. Sitting on his haunches, he kicked off his boots and pulled his worsted shirt over his head, revealing silk flesh-colored racing tights and shirt. A hush came over the crowd and someone yelled "flyer" as he put on his running shoes and took a few warm-up strides. Still, Fowler was confident of victory, and with Seward starting a few feet ahead, they were off. Fowler gradually drew even, then, suddenly the American opened up and Fowler found himself a badly beaten pedestrian.

There were no more matches to be had

in Liverpool, but Seward found a backer and began to ply his trade as a Connecticut Yankee sprinter in Queen Victoria's England. At first he challenged only the second and third rate sprinters, always winning by just enough to ensure a second and sometimes a third match. This worked for a while, but the exploits of a really fast sprinter could not be kept secret for long in a country where pedestrianism rivaled horse racing and boxing as the country's national sport.

In February 1844, a *Bell's Life* correspondent wrote: "Seward, commonly called the Cockfield Putter, is a very superior runner, and does not wish his victories to be published, that he may have greater opportunities of making matches with second and third rate men." The correspondent added that it would be more manly for Seward to challenge a first rate sprinter like William Robinson.

By the fall of that year Seward had met and defeated all the best sprinters in England, as he described in a letter to the November 30, 1844, *Spirit of the Times* in New York:

*Letter of a Yankee Pedestrian*

The present champion of England, Durham, England, Nov. 1, 1844

Sir: You will oblige me by inserting a few lines in your paper which I think will be relayed to the American Sporting World, as coming from a countryman in a foreign land. There are comparatively few who are fond of Pedestrianism in the USA but knows or has heard of me.... My name is Seward; I am from New Haven, Conn.

After I defeated William Belden of NY, and Ainsworth I thought I would try my luck among the English peds. I landed in Liverpool on the 26th of June 1843 and got a match on at that place the second day after I landed, which I won. I should have given an account of my races before, for I presume there are very few of my sporting friends in NY who knew

where I am; they may have seen some of my races in "Bell's Life in London."... I have won some *sixteen of seventeen races* since I have been in this country, and now have the honor to stand *Champion of England.*

You will see an account of my last race in "Bell's Life" of Oct. 6th or "The Era." It was with a man of the name of Robinson, considered by his countrymen to be the best man in the world; he went by the name of "the *Wonder of the World.*" I ran him for 50 pounds; there were thousands to see the race from all parts of the country, and a good deal of money changed hands. I won it by two yards. I likewise challenged, in the same paper, to give any man one yard start in 100 yards, or two yards start in 120 yards, for 50 or 100 pounds; as yet no one has accepted.

I have had fair play in every respect, in every race I have run, and have done very well since I have been here. I likewise won a beautiful silver cup, open to all England, to run 410 yards and leap six hurdles.

By inserting these few lines in your paper, you will very much oblige.

Your obedient servant,
George Seward

After defeating Robinson and becoming the champion of England, Seward began to call himself "the American Wonder." His victory over Robinson in 9¼ seconds on September 30, 1844, was probably the fastest 100-yard race of the 19th century. The race was held on a turnpike road near the Seven Stars Inn in Hammersmith. Robinson's backers brought their man to the race in a "four-in-hand" carriage and when he arrived, a band struck up "See the conquering hero comes." Seward, more modestly, walked to the race with little fanfare. The October 6, 1844, *Bell's Life* described the race:

After nearly a dozen false starts they bounded away together, and a more even "go off" could not have been effected. The pace was a "splitting" one, and they ran as nearly abreast as possible for about 60 yards, when Seward made one of the most splendid rushes ever witnessed, and in a few strides left the Lancashire Clipper at least two yards in the rear. Robinson seemed thunder-struck at the circumstance, but he brought all his energies into action and endeavored to overhaul the leading man, but without success, for Seward went in a most gallant winner by about two yards. The referee stated that it was not more than a yard and a half, while others asserted it was a full three yards. The distance was run in *less than ten seconds* but the American Deer said that by his first rate watch the time was *nine and a quarter seconds.*

It was not until 1961 that anyone recorded a legitimate time for 100 yards faster than 9¼ seconds. Not surprisingly, Seward's performance has been questioned many times over the years. During 1874 and 1875, T. Griffith, the pedestrian editor of *Bell's Life,* and J. Jenn, "a living encyclopedia of records," wrote a series of articles on British running records for the London journal *Land and Water.* Neither of these men witnessed Seward's race, but their careful analysis of the performance is probably as close to the facts as we are likely to get.

The questions they asked were: Was the time taken by a reliable person? Was the distance accurately measured? Did the runner ever before or since show similar form? Were there any circumstances likely to qualify the performance? Was the start valid?

They found that all the above conditions were met except for the method of starting. The normal way to start a sprint race in Seward's time was by "mutual consent." Both runners stood at the "scratch," and either could start whenever he felt like it. If both men did not go over the line, it was not a valid start. This sometimes led to many false starts—there were nearly a dozen in Seward's race with Robinson. The timer of a "mutual consent" race started his watch on the "bend of the knee." Griffith and Jenn believed this gave Seward about

2.5 yards or a quarter second advantage over a runner timed from the flash of a pistol—the starting method which replaced mutual consent starting in about 1860.

They estimated that Seward would have run about 9½ seconds had he been timed starting with a pistol and concluded:

> All these matters tend to prove that Seward, without doubt, was a long way ahead of any one of his day, and although it is almost too much to expect anyone to credit that a pedestrian could cover 100 yards in 9¼ seconds under any circumstances whatever, it certainly is within the range of probability that, on the occasion alluded to, it was closely approached.

No wind measurements were made at 19th century sprint races but the effects of winds on sprint times were understood and George Cook, Seward's trainer and attendant, stated that the wind "was not in favor of the runners."

Seward's reputation doesn't rest solely on his 9¼-second 100 yards. His best public performances are listed below:

| | |
|---|---|
| 100 yards | 9¼ (Best time on Record), also 9½ twice |
| 120 yards | 11½ (Best time on Record) |
| 200 yards | 19½ (Best time on Record) |
| 440 yards | 49 |
| One mile | 4:30 |

On March 23, 1845, a notice appeared in *Bell's Life* announcing a series of races to be run on the Beacon Course in New Jersey offering $4000–$5000 prize money. A month later Seward and his friend William Jackson "the American Deer" were on their way to America.

They arrived in Philadelphia in late June and on July 7, Jackson won a five-mile race on the Beacon Course in 27:39. A reporter remarked, "Jackson could easily have won by half a mile. He has no more muscular development than an eel—but the

George Seward, "The American Wonder," was best known for running 100 yards in 9¼ seconds in 1844. He spent most of his life in England and was the first runner to be undisputed champion of England and America (*New York Clipper*, 1880).

way he can sling himself would have raised Atalanta out of her boots—if she wore any!"

The two champion runners spent the rest of 1845 and half of 1846 touring America, racing all comers. This was the first nationwide athletic tour in America and was made possible by improved travel. In all, they toured 23 states and Canada, offering to run "any man that could be produced" from 100 yards to 20 miles. Seward offered to give starts of five feet in 100 yards, eight feet in 150 yards, and 10 feet in 200 yards. Jackson offered 100 yards in four miles, 200 yards in six, a quarter mile in 10, and a half mile in 20.

Despite these generous handicaps, the two men were so far in advance of American runners of the time they had great difficulty finding anyone willing to race them. Jackson had the opportunity to earn more money than Seward because race promoters offered purses of as much as $1,000 for the hour's entertainment provided by a 10-mile race. The most they would offer the winner of a sprint race was about $50, so Seward had to depend on betting to earn most of his money.

After winning a quarter-mile hurdle race on the Beacon course on July 28, 1845, Seward offered to repeat the performance against a champion hurdle-racing horse appropriately named Hops. Seward received no handicap and led over the first seven of 12 hurdles. But Hops finally got up to speed and came home an easy winner.

Jackson's only serious opposition came at two miles from 19-year-old William Freestone, alias "Billy Barlow." Young Barlow (no relation to John Barlow) was from New York and had previously run a 4:36 mile. On September 22, 1845, Barlow and Jackson met in a two-mile race on the Beacon Course. Barlow out-sprinted Jackson on the last lap, finishing in 9:44.

During their visit to Canada in November 1845, Jackson easily won all his races and Seward at last found a two-legged rival. He gave a five-yard start to a relatively unknown runner named Leakdigger in a 100-yard race and lost. Whether Seward lost the race intentionally is unknown but Leakdigger refused a rematch. In December they traveled to New Orleans and on February 8, 1846, Jackson ran in a 15-mile (24.1 km) race on the Metairie Course. Although he allowed all the other runners a 600-yard start, he was still a heavy favorite. He easily worked his way through the field and at six miles caught Gildersleeve, his strongest opponent. Strangely, he never passed Gildersleeve, but stayed just behind him for the next eight miles and lost the race by a step. It was widely believed that Jackson threw the race at the direction of his backers. On February 15, 1846, "the American Wonder" defeated a sprinter from Alabama named Collins in a 100-yard match race on the Metairie Course for $500 a side.

Jackson twice tried to repeat the 11-miles-in-an-hour feat he had performed in England, but fate was against him. His first attempt was on February 25, 1846, in New Orleans for a bet of $1,000. He was on pace until 10 miles (53:30) when one of his spikes penetrated his shoe sole. Painfully, he hobbled the last mile in 6:40 and lost the bet by 10 seconds.

Seward and Jackson continued their tour, racing in South Carolina, Kentucky and other states. Jackson was still confident he could accomplish his 11-miles-in-an-hour feat and tried again on June 16 in Philadelphia — betting $700 against $1,000 that he could do it. Jackson made sure the course was accurately measured by competent engineers under his supervision. He led off with a 4:55 mile but again he failed, this time by 28 seconds. Jackson angrily wrote to *The Spirit of the Times* complaining of "the scandalous treatment he received while running." An immense crowd had poured onto the race course and on several occasions the 105-pound Jackson had to shove his way through. Jackson felt the interference was deliberate and had cost him the bet.

On August 8, in Washington, D.C., Seward raced G. W. Morgan, the best American sprinter of the time, for $250 a side. Morgan, at six feet two inches (1.9 m) was noted for his prodigious strength and speed but possessed an awkward style. Seward gave his opponent a three-yard start and when they came to the starting line offered to bet Morgan $10 to $50 that he would beat him by an additional six feet, but Morgan declined. Morgan led by a yard at 75 yards but Seward, running just fast enough to win, beat him by two feet.

Jackson was unable to come to terms with Barlow for another two-mile race and with no more Americans willing to race them, the two champions sailed for England in October. Both men resumed their racing in England but Seward intended to return to America with his wife in late 1848. Before he was to leave, he and Jackson signed

"William Howitt (better known by the name of Jackson the American Deer)," mezzotint by William Bromley III. Howitt won 138 races in England and America during his long career (Yale Center for British Art, Paul Mellon Collection).

articles to run a one-mile race for the rather large stakes of £200 a side. Although a mile was far beyond Seward's best distance, it was short for Jackson, so the two men were considered fairly evenly matched.

Before the race could take place, Seward was seized by a crippling attack of rheumatism and, unable to race, had to forfeit £265 to Jackson. With the American Wonder still on his sickbed, his backer handed the stakes over to Jackson in early November 1848, at Spring's Sporting House. Jackson gave a short speech saying he would be glad to run Seward when he recovered and left £10 for his ailing friend. He pocketed the rest of the money and left. His irate backer found out later that "The Deer" had "bolted" with the stakes and returned to America. Seward resumed racing in July 1849, but according to *Bell's Life*, his bout with rheumatism had left him "only a shadow of his former self."

Seward was described as a "particularly muscular and fine made young man with a display of muscle that excited the attention and admiration of all beholders." His racing colors were "American"—white trimmed in blue—and he wore a pair of cordovan spikes that were custom-made for him by his backer George Colpitts.

Although his favorite distance was 100 yards, in the latter part of his career Seward competed successfully in races up to two miles. He did little training for his short races, but when he moved up to longer distances, he sometimes took several weeks to prepare for an important race. While in training his favorite dish was boiled pig's head and cabbage, washed down with milk. A reporter stated that after a breakfast of a pint and a half of milk and four pancakes, Seward could easily run 100 yards in 9½ seconds.

Though a foreigner, Seward became something of a legend in the British sporting world. When he suffered his first major defeat in 1849, the city of Manchester, where he was a great favorite, went into shock. It took a magnificent performance to beat Seward—a 48.5-second quarter mile by H. A. Reed. But the unbeatable American had finally been defeated. Seward ran his last race, a 100-yard sprint, on February 24, 1866, when he was in his 50th year. In this race he proved that he still had "fire in his legs" by vanquishing Joe Horrocks, about 40, for £25 a side.

Seward sometimes gave athletic exhibitions to entertain the large crowds that came to watch him run. One of his favorite stunts was jumping over three horses standing side-by-side. Seward also liked to race a series of opponents in quick succession. In 1848 he beat eight sprinters (running each separately) over 80 yards at the Albion Tavern, Wolverhampton, in less than 16½ minutes and on another occasion defeated 10 over 80 yards within 29 minutes. On October 2, 1848, he attempted to race 10 men separately for 100 yards in 60 minutes but

An 1863 illustration of George Seward at age 46. His dog Venture had just killed 100 barn rats in 7 minutes, 16 seconds (*Illustrated Sporting and Dramatic News*, October 17, 1863).

in the sixth race he was obstructed by the crowd and lost.

After his running days, Seward took up his old trade of silver-plating and sank into obscurity. He died of heart disease in 1883 at age 66, leaving a wife, Ann, and six children, three of them under age 10. His obituary provided a short description of the great sprinter:

Seward was a thickset and very muscular man, stood 5'8½" and weighed 159 pounds. He was peculiar in his habits, and trained but little for his undertakings; he lived widely different in those days to other pedestrians, and partook very sparingly of animal food.... He was particularly well behaved, very intellectual, and a great reader.

A year after his death *Bell's Life* contained a moving tribute to the former champion, along with a plea for assistance to his widow who was "in reduced circumstances and sadly in need of pecuniary assistance."

It has been the fashion of late amongst the present class of writers on athletic subjects to sneer at the performances of the "giants of old." Probably they do not know that when Seward was the recognized sprint champion he not only offered long starts to all the best men of his day but would even allow some runners to start in the ordinary way, whilst he remained on the mark in a kneeling position. He also frequently undertook the task of beating several at intervals of a few minutes each with the provision that he was to receive nothing unless successful in every instance. Of all the champions we ever had he was perhaps the most unassuming....

In England, Seward's 9¼ second 100-yard record was dropped from the record books in 1880. No reason was given, but there was a tendency at the time to mistrust old records, especially if the current runners couldn't come close to them. In 1889 M. J. Finn, writing for *The New York Clipper,* interviewed an unnamed Englishman who claimed to have seen Seward's race 45 years earlier. The "eyewitness" said the race was started with a pistol and that Seward took a running start on a downhill course with a tail wind. Although none of this agreed with the 1844 *Bell's Life* account, Finn's story was used as justification to expunge Seward's 100-yard record from the record books in America.

It was inconceivable to late 19th century sports writers that with the "modern training methods, superior tracks and better athletes of the 1890's" that no sprinter could approach a record that was half a century old. Seward's other records were surpassed in the 19th century. His 120-yard record of 11½ seconds was tied by Australian Tom Malone in April 1888 and later bettered by both Harry Hutchens and Bernie Wefers when they ran the distance in 11²⁄₅ seconds.

During his best years (1844–1849) Seward repeatedly issued the following challenges through *Bell's Life:*

1. — To give any man in England five yards start in 100 or six in 120 for £50 or £100.
2. — To carry ten pounds weight and run any man level for £50.
3. — To give any man 10 yards start in 160 yards for £50
4. — To run 4 of the best men in England 100 yards inside 30 minutes, to run each man separately and run the best man last for £50 or £100.
5. — To jump on ice on skates against any man jumping on land.
6. — To run 100 yards in 9¼ sec, 120 yards in 11½ sec, 150 yards in 14½ sec, 200 yards in 19½ sec, and 300 yards in 30 sec, for £50.

To give any man in England, some of whom were capable of "even-time" (10.0 seconds for 100 yards), five yards in a 100-yard race suggests Seward had extraordinary speed. In 1847, when he was 29 years old, and probably at his peak, a frustrated Seward wrote to *Bell's Life:* "Mr. Editor: As I have challenged so frequently without success, I will now try against 'Old Time,' if anyone will stake £100 to £50 against my running 200 yards inside 19½ seconds, or 120 yards in 11 seconds, or 100 yards inside 9¼ seconds."

With watches timing to the nearest quarter second, running inside 9¼ meant running nine flat. Professional runners of Seward's day didn't make matches they had no chance to win. His willingness to wager a substantial sum that he could beat his best public performances probably meant he had done so in trials.* It is a testament to Seward's greatness that of his six challenges,

*The following appeared in the November 24, 1850, Bell's Life: "Three years ago Seward was the fastest runner in the world; he could run 100 yards in 9 seconds, 200 yards in 19 seconds, and 300 yards in 29 seconds."

only his offer to race several opponents in quick succession was ever accepted. He was truly an American wonder.

While Seward and Jackson were on their way to America in 1845, Mr. Bragg, the proprietor of the North Star Inn in Slough, made a bet that he could produce a man who could run 20 miles within two hours. It had been rumored that a couple of runners had already accomplished the feat in private, but many doubted this. Bragg chose a 26-year-old runner named Thomas Maxfield, "the North Star," to make the attempt. Maxfield was so confident that before the effort he was seen wearing a shirt with a star in the center and the words "20 Miles in Two Hours, May 16, 1845."

On the day of the attempt, the odds were 6 to 4 in favor of his opponent, the "old scythe bearer" (time). Maxfield ran the first two miles in 10:12 and went by 10 miles in 55:16. Although he needed 13:09 to cover the last two miles, he finished in 1:58:30 and became the first runner to cover 20 miles in less than two hours. Later attempts at running 20 miles in less than two hours would be known as the "Maxfield feat," and the grounds where he accomplished the feat, "Star's Mile."

After bolting with the forfeited £265 stakes he received from Seward's backer in November 1848, William Jackson returned to America. His first performance was a 10.5-mile race at the Saratoga Trotting Course in New York, which he won. He ran many races during this stay in America, mostly against Native Americans. Although the Indians he raced greatly admired him, he wasn't always appreciated by pedestrian fans who had become suspicious of professional foot-racing. On May 23, 1850, Jackson ran a five-mile race in Cincinnati, Ohio, against a Native American named Coffee. The *Cincinnati Enquirer* described the outcome of the race:

By the fourth mile, Jackson had a 350-yard lead, and half way round on the fifth mile he was 300 yards ahead, but, wonderful to relate, Coffee beat him. That part of the crowd in attendance who had put up their dimes on Jackson, were quite indignant at the result, and there was some talk of a lynching.

It seems strange that Jackson should lose in this manner. He was an intelligent, resourceful runner and if he were going to "throw" the race, surely he would have been more subtle in doing so. In his defense, he was bothered throughout much of his career with a bad ankle which more than once forced him to stop or back off in the midst of a race. Fortunately, he escaped from the Cincinnati crowd without injury.

Outstanding British runners racing in America and Americans crossing the Atlantic to race in Britain enriched running in both countries. Initially the crowds wanted to see the foreigners defeated but in time came to appreciate and admire great runners, no matter what their nationality. This trend would continue throughout the 19th century.

After the initial flurry of interest in professional running in the United States in 1844, the sport was unable to sustain the large crowds that turned out to see the Americans vs. the English. This was partly because no American besides Seward was capable of competing with their rivals from across the sea. The British had a running tradition that included the hare-and-hounds contests in the schools as well as professional contests going back to the 18th century and earlier. They were hardened by frequent, high-quality competition at a level not seen in the rest of the world in the 1800–1850 period.

# V

# The Golden Age of
# the Pros and the Rise of
# the Amateurs (1850–1900)

Until the middle of the 19th century, British and American runners were called "pedestrians" and prizes for races were invariably money. As the British roads became more heavily traveled, the long-standing custom of racing between mile markers on a turnpike road proved a hindrance to traffic and in 1850 these races were banned in and around London. Runners were forced to turn to private grounds. Enclosed race courses, usually operated by taverns, sprang up all over Britain. These "cinder paths" ranged from one-eighth to one-half mile in circumference and may have had sharp corners and changes in elevation. Each of the large cities had its own running grounds. These included such venues as the Copenhagen House in Islington, Hackney Wick in London, and the Royal Oak in Manchester. While races on the turnpike roads had been free to the public, enclosed grounds allowed the proprietor to charge

entrance fees. He either divided the entrance money with the pedestrians or provided some other incentive, such as prizes, for luring professionals to race on his course.

Running also became popular in the public schools, then the universities and clubs. The first school to promote interclass athletics was Eton in 1837. Exeter College, Oxford, followed in 1850. The earliest intercollegiate athletic meets were held at Cambridge in 1857 and Oxford in 1860. There were also regular athletic meets in the British army, at the military academies of Sandhurst and Woolwith, and later the Civil Service. Many of these nonprofessional runners were reluctant to compete with the lower classes and professionals. This led to the concept of the "amateur." Although the definition an of amateur changed many times, one of the earliest and most accepted was as follows:

Any gentleman who has never competed in an open competition, or for public money, or for admission money, or with professionals for a prize, or admission money; nor has at any period of his life, taught, or assisted in the pursuit of athletic exercises as a means of a livelihood; nor is a mechanic, artisan, or laborer.

Not everyone in England agreed with the "gentleman" and the "mechanic, artisan, or laborer" restrictions and by the 1870s some enlightened promoters of amateur races dropped these requirements for competing in their races. Between 1866 and 1868, middle- and upper-class men organized the New York Athletic Club and brought amateurism to the United States. Other clubs soon followed. At first, the U.S. clubs were restricted to the upper classes, but the urge to win soon caused them to enlist superior athletes from the lower classes. Competing for money prizes and against professionals was forbidden in both countries. Running by nonprofessionals became known as "athletic sports" or "athletics" and its participants were called "athletes."

Gambling was initially allowed at amateur athletic meets, both in England and America. Later, it was considered undesirable and banned. With gambling eliminated, the amateur system went a long way toward solving the "race-fixing" of the pros but it had problems of its own. According to A. R. Downer in *Running Recollections* (1908), many late 19th century race promoters routinely made "under-the-table" payments to top amateurs to entice them to run in their meets. If amateurs were caught taking "excessive" money, they sometimes lost their amateur status. There was no effective way to punish the race promoters, however, and the custom went on for a hundred years.

Professional runners and walkers continued to be known as pedestrians. For the most part, 19th century pedestrians outperformed the amateurs, yet a complete account of pedestrianism has never been written. Many writers have taken a "purist" view of running history, concentrating on the "more noble" amateurs with little or no mention of the professionals. Other writers unjustly dismissed the pedestrians with blanket statements such as "pro sprinters all used running starts."

Efforts to write about pedestrianism have also been thwarted by the lack of times for professional races. In the first half of the 19th century, extremely few timings were reported in events up to 440 yards. Although early watches were quite accurate, timing was difficult because many watches did not have "flyback" mechanisms to give them the capability of being quickly reset. In addition, a large percentage of sprint races were handicapped, which made accurate timing for everyone but the scratch runner nearly impossible since only the scratch runner ran the full distance.

Times were also kept secret to avoid the betting odds or handicapping being stacked against a promising runner. Even at longer distances where timing was easier, many reports simply gave the name of the winner. Although the historical record is less than complete, 19th century professional runners achieved some remarkable feats and many were fascinating men and women as well.

## Sprinting for Fame and Fortune

*To those who do not know, I will say that, in a sprint, very much depends on the start; that a contestant must be off with the pistol, or steal on it if he can.* — William Lindsey (1895)

Besides George Seward, who was covered in the previous section, the fastest sprinters in England in the mid–19th century were Charles Westhall, John Howard and Henry Allen Reed. Westhall, born in

**Charles Westhall, an outstanding sprinter, miler and walker (*Illustrated Sporting & Dramatic News*, September 27, 1862).**

1823, was an outstanding sprinter, a champion long-distance walker, and the first man to break 4:30 for the mile on a track.

On February 4, 1851, Westhall ran a remarkable 150-yard race against William Hayes, "the Ruddington Hero," at Bellevue in Manchester. It was a cold, raw day and the track was covered with snow. After 32 false starts, which took nearly an hour, the two sprinters finally got underway. Westhall slipped on the icy track and Hayes took a two-yard lead and increased it to three at 80 yards. There he turned his head, and looking back at Westhall, put his thumb to his nose in a mocking gesture. This acted like magic on Westhall. With a grim smile and running with "deer-like bounds," he caught Hayes at 120 yards, and won by 2½ yards. Crossing the finish line, Westhall pressed his hands on his "nether end," retaliating for Hayes's slight. Westhall's winning time

was 15 seconds flat—the fastest time on record for 150 yards.

Like Westhall, John Howard, born in 1824, was a versatile performer. In a race with Robert Law in February 1850, Howard ran 100 yards in 9¾ seconds on a course that was reported to be slightly uphill. Howard was even more famous for his long-jumping and crowds of up to 25,000 marveled at his feats. He used dumbbells, which he threw behind him as he sprang from a block of wood two feet long that rose to about four inches high at the front. His best jump using this method was 29 feet, 7 inches, in 1856. On several occasions he bet he could clear 30 feet, but never attempted the distance in public.

Although Howard was a great athlete, he was unable to beat George Seward "the American Wonder" at sprinting. They met on June 10, 1850, in a 100-yard race at the Flora Grounds in Bayswater. Seward ran just fast enough to win by half a yard in 9½ seconds. The two men also raced each other at 200 and 440 yards. Seward won at 200 yards but gave Howard a ten-yard start in the 440-yard race and lost. The two men sometimes teamed up and took on all comers at sprinting and jumping.

Henry Allen Reed is best known for his 440 and 880 yard performances, but was also credited with running "inside evens," covering 120 yards in 11¾ seconds in 1852. He was reported to have covered the distance in 11½ in a trial.

### JOHN WESTLEY COZAD— A PERVERSE PEDESTRIAN

Shortly after the Civil War in America, John Westley Cozad from Iowa came to New York to try his sprinting ability against the Easterners. On November 23, 1868, at the Fashion Course on Long Island, Cozad, the "California Plow-Boy," ran a 125-yard race against Edward Depew Davis, the "Flying Boy of Kingston," from Kingston, New York. The race was billed as the "Foot race

John Howard, a fast sprinter who was better known for his long jumping. He cleared 29 feet, 7 inches, using weights (*Illustrated Sporting & Dramatic News*, May 10, 1862).

for the championship of America." Davis was a heavy favorite, having won races against 25 competitors. His backers were willing to bet $2,500 against $2,000 that their man could defeat the relatively unknown Westerner. Davis showed his confidence by betting his diamonds, two watches and a ring on himself.

The course was measured, then remeasured, and at about 2:00 P.M. both men appeared. The runners used a "scratch start," with each man starting 15 feet behind the starting-line. According to the rules both had to cross the line for a valid start to occur.

After four false starts, Cozad went over the line for the fifth time. Davis had not intended to follow, but accidently stepped over and the race was on. He gradually made up the two feet he lost at the start and the men were even at 50 yards. Cozad, with his

head erect, but his body moving from side to side, gradually left Davis. He broke the winning string of handkerchiefs eight feet ahead in a best-on-record time of 12½ seconds. Two weeks later, on the same course, Cozad easily defeated "Poke" Perry from Trenton, New Jersey, at 70 yards in 7¼ seconds for another record.

Now the champion American sprinter, Cozad challenged all comers, but found few takers and had to be content with exhibitions and offering handicaps in the form of starts to rivals. He raced for several years with many of his races reportedly "not on the square." In November 1880 at the fair grounds in Denver, Colorado, he ran 125 yards against Austin Banks and Court Thompson. The purse was $75 with $35 to go to the first man at 50 yards, $15 to the first at 100 yards and the remainder to the winner. Banks won in 13½ seconds, but it was obvious that Cozad was not trying. The judge declared the race off and refused to award the purse.

A short time later, an article in the newspaper *The Pacific Life* described an 80-yard race that Cozad had "thrown." The article stated that Cozad's backer, irate because he had lost $18,000 on the match, gunned down the double-crossing champion. Without verifying the story, the *National Police Gazette* printed it with an illustration. Like many of the *Gazette's* illustrations it was entirely imaginary.

*Wilkes Spirit of the Times* for December 25, 1880, published a tongue-in-cheek editorial about the incident. The article suggested that the editor knew all along Cozad had not really been killed:

The prompt punishment of perverse pedestrians is a branch of industry sadly neglected this side of the Mississippi, though our fields are ripe for such a harvest. If this gentleman [Cozad's backer] will come to NY City — and bring his pistol with him — we will guarantee him permanent employment and good wages. The moral of this incident is twofold:

John Westly Cozad defeating E. D. Davis at 125 yards on November 23, 1868. Cozad's time of 12½ seconds was a record (*Harper's Weekly*, December 12, 1868).

Pedestrians should be honest, and their backers should carry a gun.

Cozad wrote a letter to *Wilkes Spirit of the Times*, protesting his "death" and the paper's harsh criticism of him. "Every word of the story was false," he insisted. The report of Cozad's death, although premature, proved strangely prophetic. In Salida, Colorado, on April 24, 1882, he was found in his room dying, robbed of his money and watch. Although poisoning was suspected, a Coroner's jury found no satisfactory explanation for his death.

The mark of an outstanding sprinter in the 19th century was someone who could do "even time." In an even time race the average time for each yard is ¹⁄₁₀ of a second and one can substitute yards for tenths of seconds. For example, 9⅘ (9.8) seconds for 100 yards is two yards "inside even time." With a much smaller world population, poor running surfaces and standing starts, sprinters who could run "inside evens" were a rare breed.

Accurately timing a sprint race was difficult in the 19th century and incorrect times were fairly common. A strong tailwind, a downhill or short course, or a watch with sticking hands all could make a mediocre sprinter appear exceedingly fast. Some sprinters were also adept at beating the gun. Finding out who the "fast men" really were is difficult, and one must consider the sprinter's entire career as well as his competition instead of a one-time performance.

Three 19th century sprinters stand out above the rest — Jem Wantling, George Seward and Harry Hutchens. Jem Wantling was the fastest sprinter we know of in the early 1800s. In his day, watches could time no better than to the nearest half second. This and the lack of documentation of his performances, including his claimed 100 yards in nine seconds in the mid–1820s, prevent a good assessment of his career.

*Bell's Life* was the most authoritative sporting journal in England until it folded in the 1880s. Its September 22, 1841, "Answers to Correspondents" column gave the

Illustration from the *National Police Gazette* for December 1880 showing Cozad being killed by an irate backer. The magazine's story of Cozad's death was untrue. He actually died of poisoning two years later.

"best on record" time for 100 yards as Wantling's nine seconds. This answer was continued until April 4, 1858, when the editors apparently began to doubt Wantling's performance and the following appeared: "Seward ran 100 yards in 9½ seconds. Wantling is said to have been faster." Finally, by December 8, 1861, Seward was listed as the best on record with 9¼ seconds and Wantling was no longer mentioned. From then until the journal folded, *Bell's Life* considered Seward's 9¼ seconds the fastest 100 yards on record.

The two most important British venues for sprint races were at Sheffield and the Powderhall Grounds in Edinburgh, Scot-

land. Sheffield began to exert itself as the center of pedestrianism in 1857 when the first major sprint handicap was held there. This burgeoning industrial city with many public houses and sports grounds hosted sprint races at several venues. Harry Hutchens became the great star at Sheffield and professional sprinting continued there until 1899.

Powderhall Stadium, named for the gunpowder factory nearby, held its first race in 1870 and professional races were run there until the 1980s. One of the most brilliant of the early sprinters at Powderhall was Don Wight of Jedburgh. Wight was an exceptional sprinter from boyhood, and in

1877, starting from scratch, tied for first place in a 150-yard handicap with a remarkable 14¼ seconds. In his career, Wight won more than 100 races at distances from 100 to 880 yards. He was invited back to Powderhall in 1920 and the 70-year-old runner was cheered wildly as he made his way to the starting line for one last race.

### HARRY HUTCHENS—
### FASTEST RUNNER ON EARTH

George Seward would have a clear claim to being the fastest sprinter of the 19th century if it were not for Londoner Harry Hutchens who was born in 1858 in Putney (London). Hutchens discovered that he was a fast runner when he was 14 and working as a messenger at Putney Station. His first professional race was in 1876 when he entered a 125-yard Breads handicap along with 149 other runners. From a 10-yard start Hutchens won the final with ease and earned £13 for his efforts. The victory drew the attention of a Mr. Hobson who became Hutchens's backer and invited him to Sheffield to train for the world-famous Sheffield Handicap.

Hutchens trained during 1877 using the still popular methods of Captain Barclay, which emphasized purgatives and sweating. An important lesson Hutchens learned early was that extravagant public displays of speed could do more harm than good to the career of a professional sprinter. The 20-year-old sprinter entered his first Sheffield Handicap on March 5, 1878. He received a 5¼-yard start over the scratch runner and champion, George Wallace, a six-foot two-inch coal miner. Hutchens won the approximately 130-yard race by a foot.

The following year when Hutchens returned to Sheffield the handicapper had reduced his start to only 1¾ yards over Wallace. Before he had gone 70 yards Hutchens had passed all the runners, including Wallace, and won the race "in fine style" by two yards. He now offered to run Wallace or any other man in the world for £500, but found no takers.

In 1882 Hutchens entered another Sheffield Handicap. This time, running from scratch in the 131¼-yard race,* he showed the phenomenal speed that would become his trademark. In a desperate finish, he lost by inches to two runners who started 6¾ and 3½ yards ahead of him. Although he lost, Hutchens finished in 12⅕ seconds— the equivalent of 100 yards in about 9½ seconds or 100 meters in about 10.3.

In an interview when he was 70, Hutchens considered this his best performance and believed he would have won had it not been for a prank played on him by some of his "friends." Between the semifinals and final they took him for a ride in a cab and made him walk back. The route back to the stadium was uphill and Hutchens believed the walk tired his legs.

Lon Myers, America's best middle distance runner of the 19th century, visited England in 1881 and Hutchens graciously helped the young American with his training. Myers had run 10 seconds flat for 100 yards and was confident he could beat Hutchens. James S. Mitchel in *Outing Magazine* for May 1901 described a practice race between the two "cracks":

So one day he [Myers] challenged the ex-Sheffielder to run him a 100 level for a basket of wine. "All right Yank," said Hutchens, "but in order to make it more interesting, I'll give you four yards start. You'll want it badly long before you finish." Of course, Myers scouted the proposition, saying he did not need a yard from the best man on earth. After

*Using the "Sheffield" system, the handicapper based all handicaps on a fixed standard, not on the fastest man entered. Each runner was given a handicap based on the number of yards he was estimated to be slower than that standard. This resulted in the best runner usually not starting from scratch but some yards from the line and running an odd distance like 131¼ yards.

some persuasion, however, Myers accepted the handicap. They started, and to Myers' consternation, Hutchens, running in his straight-leg style like a pacer, drew level at the 60-yard mark, and for the remaining 40 yards the Englishman gained two additional yards on the American.

Hutchens is probably best known for running 300 yards around a turn on a narrow, uneven, track at the January 2, 1884, "New Year's Handicap" at Powderhall. Despite the cold and a soft, sloppy track from a snowfall the previous night, Hutchens won his heat easily in a record 30⅖ seconds. An hour later, after a full meal of roast beef and potatoes, he ran the final. Starting from scratch, with his nearest opponent 18 yards ahead of him, he got away to a good start. He swept around the first curve well on the outside and with a "beautiful raking stride," ran through the field like a deer through a flock of frightened sheep. He caught the last runner with 12 yards to go, then dropped his arms as he won the race with ease in 30.0 seconds. An eyewitness said that Hutchens must have run at least seven or eight yards more than the specified distance. This record lasted well into the 20th century.* According to an article by Peter Lovesey in the Dec. 25, 1982, *Athletics Weekly*, on the night before the race Hutchens had downed either 26 or 27 beers.

Hutchens visited America in October 1884. At the time there were some good American professional sprinters, including H. M. Johnson, Harry Bethune and Mike Kittleman. One of these men might have tested Hutchens, if given a small start. It was not to be, however. On November 1, Hutchens ran in America's most prestigious professional sprint race, Acton & Taylor's 135-yard handicap at Pastime Park in Philadelphia. Because of the large handicaps—19 and 21 yards—he had no chance and lost his heat by a foot. There was a dispute over the

Harry Hutchens using the "Sheffield Start." Hutchens is generally believed to be the fastest sprinter of the second half of the 19th century (from Alfred R. Downer, *Running Recollections*, 1908).

gate receipts and Acton, one of the racetrack owners, had William Squires, Hutchens's backer and trainer, arrested for embezzlement. Hutchens ran no more races in America but took the next ship back to England. His only trip to the United States had lasted but a week.

Like George Seward, Hutchens was bothered by rheumatism. He left in late 1886 on a tour of Australia where he hoped a change in the climate would ease his aching joints. Since its settlement, Australia had enjoyed a rich tradition of professional running. Centered in Victoria, professional running was at its peak from 1870 to 1912. Many pros from all over the world made the long trip to Australia to try their hands in match races and the "Gifts." The "Gifts" were patterned after the Sheffield Handicaps and named for the tradition of wealthy

*In preparing for the race, Hutchens was timed in 29½ seconds in a trial at Axwell Park, finishing with a smile.

gold mine owners donating a gold nugget for the winner's prize. The famous Stawell Gift, first run in 1878, lives on as one of the few 19th century professional races still in existence.

In January 1887, Hutchens ran a series of races with Charlie Samuels, a Queensland Aborigine known as "the prince of black pedestrians." Samuels, who was said to have trained on a box of cigars, tobacco pipe and plenty of sherry, had distinguished himself by winning a 136-yard Botany handicap in 13⅕ seconds. The Australian defeated Hutchens twice, but Hutchens later admitted that in these races, he was running "under orders" to lose in order to build interest for a betting "coup." Hutchens finally showed Samuels what he could do when unleashed. In the 150-yard last race of the series, with large sums of money riding on the outcome, Hutchens ran 14½ seconds to defeat Samuels by such a mar-

gin that the Australian retired from running.

Later on the tour, Hutchens ran a series of races with "Peerless" Tom Malone, an outstanding Irish runner. Thomas Michael Malone was an all-around athlete who competed as both an amateur and professional in Ireland and England. The lure of big prize money in Australia tempted him to emigrate and he arrived there in November 1882. In 1884 Malone was at his peak, running some very fast times in his adopted country: 9⅘ for 100 yards, 11½ for 120, 21½ for 220, 47⅗ for 440, and 1:53½ for 880. Unfortunately, in November 1886 he injured his hamstring in a race with William Clarke and the injury had not completely healed when he raced Hutchens in January 1887.

Hutchens later said he "took Malone very seriously," and considered him the

**Charlie Samuels from Queensland, Australia, twice defeated Harry Hutchens in 1887 (*National Police Gazette*, April 30, 1887).**

**Tom Malone ran many fast times in Australia (from William Dooley, *Champions of the Athletic Arena*, 1946).**

finest sprinter he ever faced. With Malone injured, Hutchens won the first two races easily and there was no need for a third. Before leaving for home Hutchens received a special award for running 50 yards with a running or "flying start" in 4½ seconds.

When Hutchens returned to England in the summer of 1887, he found a rival waiting to challenge him for the title of "Champion" sprinter of England. The new sprint sensation was 26-year-old Harry Gent, a Darlington cabby. On May 31, 1887, Gent had won the Sheffield Handicap by running 122 yards in 11³/₅ seconds — equivalent to 100 yards in about 9.7 seconds. Promoters for the two men arranged a 120-yard race at Lillie Bridge for the "Championship of the World" and £200. On Sept 19, 1887, 15,500 fans paid a shilling each to watch the two men race.

A rumor was circulating that Hutchens was "hog fat" and not fit to run a good race. Hutchens did nothing to dispel the rumor and his erratic training led many to believe he planned to lose the race. Gent's backers bet heavily on their man, and Hutchens and his backers snapped up the bets. When Hutchens appeared, fit and ready to run the race of his life, Gent's backers panicked. In order to keep from losing the money they had bet, they forcibly abducted Gent from his dressing room and spirited him off the grounds by way of an underground passage. Hutchens's backers, sensing an impending riot, removed their man from the grounds also.

When the crowd discovered the runners were missing, they demanded their admission money back. Unfortunately, the money-taker had already left with the money. The enraged crowd decided to get their shilling's worth of entertainment by destroying the stadium. They demolished two grandstands and used the debris to make six bonfires. Then they set fire to the wooden railings along the railway before looting nearby liquor stores. Firemen summoned to the scene were pelted with empty bottles

and to make matters worse, low water pressure made fighting the fire almost impossible. The majority of buildings on the grounds were destroyed and a station-master with a weak heart died of a heart attack from the excitement.

Professional sprinting in London ended with the destruction of the Lillie Bridge grounds. Except for a few isolated locations in Scotland, South Africa and Australia, the sport never regained its lost popularity. When the two sprinters finally raced on October 29, 1887, at Gateshead, Hutchens lost, but his career was not over. In 1891 he won his fourth Sheffield Handicap and at age 38 was still scratch man at Sheffield.

A master of winning by the least margin possible, Hutchens cared little for fast times or breaking records. Big and strong (five feet 10½ inches/1.8 m, 177 pounds/80.4 kg), he ran with a 7½ foot stride that grew to nine feet at the end of a race. He admitted that he "ran to the book," but insisted that "when the real money was down he ran to win."

Hutchens used the upright start known as the "dab" or "Sheffield." To the end of his days he insisted it was faster than the crouch start. He believed he was the best runner on earth and thought training was but a grind. After a race, Hutchens liked a good massage for his stiff muscles with a little whiskey rubbed in with a towel. But he warned, "keep watch on the coach, as on one occasion, when he was having his legs rubbed the coach drank the whisky and rubbed in water." Hutchens died in 1939 at age 81, poor and in obscurity.

A notable British amateur sprinter of the late 19th century was Arthur "Darkie" Wharton from Ghana, who attended Darlington College and was Britain's first black sprint champion. In 1886 he became the first British amateur to cover 100 yards in 10 seconds flat in a championship meet. He did it in two successive heats at the Amateur Athletic Association (AAA) meet at Stamford Bridge Grounds, London. Wharton went on to win the Sheffield Handicap as a professional in 1888.

Alfred R. Downer, born in Jamaica in 1873, was the best of the 19th century British sprinters who came after Hutchens and Gent. Downer moved to Edinburgh with his mother in 1880. As an amateur, he had

Alfred R. Downer, world champion professional sprinter in the late 1890s (from Alfred R. Downer, *Running Recollections*, 1908).

many duels with Charlie Bradley, the champion amateur sprinter of England in the mid 1890s. Bradley had nearly 50 straight wins against the best sprinters in Great Britain and was a reliable 10-second 100-yard runner. In most of their races, Bradley would be slightly in front at 50 yards, but Downer would usually reel him in and nip him at the tape.

In 1896, Downer was declared a professional by the AAA which charged him with taking under-the-table payments from meet-promoters. He continued his running as a professional and in his book *Running Recollections* (1908), described the greatest race he ever ran—a 130-yard handicap at Powderhall in 1898. He conceded 8½ yards to a sprinter named Ducan in a heat of the world-famous New Year's Handicap and lost by 1½ yards. In losing, he finished 4½ yards inside even time, a brilliant performance. Downer, who lived life to the fullest, died at age 39.

## The Best of the American Professional Sprinters

In America in the 1880s there were a number of professional sprinters who, although probably not as fast as Hutchens, were nevertheless outstanding. Mostly because they were professionals, their deeds have been pretty much forgotten.

George H. Smith of Pittsburgh was one of the few professional sprinters of the time who would have nothing to do with crooked races. Smith traveled to England in 1881 and won the Sheffield Whitsuntide 208-yard Handicap beating 62 competitors. Smith was credited with running 125 yards in 12¼ seconds in December 1886 in Pittsburgh.

Harry M. Johnson was born in England in 1863 but moved to New York as a youth. He turned pro in 1882 and in August of 1883 entered Acton & Taylor's 135-yard handicap at Pastime Park, Philadelphia. He won easily, running 123 yards in 12⅕ sec-

George H. Smith, an American professional sprinter known for his honesty (*National Police Gazette*, June 25, 1881).

onds. The race promoter was astounded, stating "Such running has never been shown in any other foot-handicap in America," and at first refused to award the first place prize to Johnson thinking he must be a "ringer."

On August 16, 1884, Johnson started from scratch in Acton & Taylor's 130-yard handicap at Pastime Park. His intention was to beat the American professional 100-yard record. He was timed at the 100-yard mark by N. Jutson and Arthur Chambers, two experienced timers. Both men timed Johnson in 9¾ seconds.

Johnson won the famous 120-yard Shrovetide Handicap in Sheffield, England, on March 8, 1886. Hutchens was scratch man but didn't make it to the final. The final was unusual in that it was run twice with Johnson winning both times. On the first start, the cartridge in the starter's pistol didn't fire but the men were away at the snap of the gun and couldn't be recalled. Johnson won by two yards, but the race was declared a "no start." On the rerun, Johnson won again, this time by a yard.

On July 31, 1886, at the summer meeting of the Cleveland Athletic Club, Johnson won a 100-yard race by six yards in 9⅘. Five

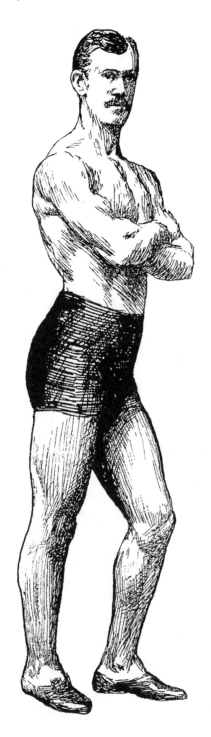

H. M. Johnson, champion professional sprinter of the United States in the mid–1880s. He was credited with 9⅘ seconds for 100 yards (*Outing*, May 1881).

watches were held on him, and the track, when surveyed, was found to be two inches over the stated distance. Three watches caught him in 9⅗ and two in 9⅘. He was later credited with 50 yards in 5⅖ , and 130 yards in 12½. Johnson was a big man (six feet, ½ inch/1.8 m) and weighed 186 pounds (84.5 kg). He died in 1890 in San Francisco at age 27.

Mike K. Kittleman of Harper, Kansas, was another "fast man" of this era. On August 18, 1884, he defeated H. M. Johnson in a 125-yard open race in Pittsburgh, in 12¼ seconds for each of two heats. Kittleman was reported to have won several races in England disguised as an amateur. This was considered a criminal offense at the time and, had he been caught, he could have received six months of hard labor.

Harry Bethune was said to be "the fastest runner that ever ran in spiked shoes for 75 or 100 yards." Bethune, a shadowy figure who was variously reported to hail from Canada, California, and New Philadelphia, Ohio, was perhaps the best of the American professionals of this era. He was credited with tying George Seward's 200-yard record with 19½ seconds at Plattsburg New York on September 1, 1887. He also ran 100 yards in 9⅘ seconds at the "Olympic Games," of the Olympic Club of San Francisco on February 23, 1888.

Bethune and his partner Boyd often used their speed to outrun angry bettors they had swindled. In 1890, Bethune inherited a large fortune from an uncle in Scotland and retired from running.

## Tricks of the Pros

Nineteenth century pedestrians sometimes won by guile rather than swiftness of foot. One common ploy was to try to fool the handicapper. Both amateur and professional meets in the United States and Britain featured handicap races. Sprint handicaps ranged from one or two yards to as many as

Marley K. Kittleman, an American professional sprinter who ran 125 yards in 12¼ seconds in 1884 (*National Police Gazette*, June 6, 1885).

12. Sixty or more runners participated, so the problems of calculating appropriate handicaps were considerable. Handicappers, who kept books of performances of large numbers of runners, were the forerunners of modern track statisticians. A good handicapper took pride in being able to spot a runner attempting to fatten his handicap by "running dead" (not trying). Examples of tricks used to fool the handicapper included wearing lead insoles or running very hard the day before a race. Some runners even tried to fake their identity. The January 6, 1883, *Bell's Life* humor-

**Harry Bethune was one of the best American professional sprinters in the late 1880s. He is shown here gripping his "corks" (*National Police Gazette*, January 29, 1887).**

ously described such an effort at the Powderhall New Year's Handicap: "150-yard handicap — Second round ... Moore Hill (6 yards start) was also in the heat, but turned out to be Cameron of Liverpool, and when his wig slipped off he was glad to follow suit."

Tricks were sometimes used in nonhandicap races to improve the betting odds. A. R. Downer in *Running Recollections* describes his method:

My backers were well pleased with the results of my trial, unfortunately the time leaked out, and the odds went from 6 to 4 to 2 to 1. A "Downey" trick to get a better price was now attempted. It transpired that I was going to run a trial

at a certain time one day. In consequence, there were about 30 or 40 people on the ground "seeking information." I gave my trial horse, W. Williams, 12 yards, and carrying three quarters-of-a-pound of lead in either hand, was just beaten to the worsted. The time was a full second slower than in my genuine trial, and so well did the ruse succeed, that the odds went back to 6 to 4.

The *New York Times* for January 16, 1888, reported a scam almost as old as running itself, worked to perfection by two American sprinters. William Boyd from Iowa could run "evens" for 100 yards whenever he chose and compared with the average sprinter of the time looked unbeatable. His partner, Harry Bethune, was one of the fastest sprinters of the 19th century. In 1887, shortly after they had separated a wealthy Montreal man from $8,000, the two men and their backer came to Brooklyn looking for prey.

Boyd, with his excellent dress and demeanor, sought out three wealthy brothers who owned a large milling operation. The brothers were sporting admirers and always willing to back a good thing. Using a false name, Boyd obtained an introduction and soon brought up the topic of fast running. He casually remarked that he could "outrun anything but a locomotive or a first-class race horse." The mill owners became interested at once and took their new friend to the Brooklyn Athletic Association track for a trial at 100 yards. Boyd carefully measured off the distance, but unknown to his potential backers, drew the start and finish lines only 95 yards apart. The brothers were astonished when their expensive split-second watches caught Boyd in 9⅖ seconds. Sure they had a winner, the men longed for a sprinter with a wealthy backer for their man to race.

Bethune, also using a false name, soon made his appearance, accompanied by his backer. The three brothers agreed to back Boyd against Bethune at 100 yards for a large wager. A dozen persons showed up at the Brooklyn Athletic Association track to witness the race.

Just before the race, Bethune's backer drew his pistol and remarked that "somebody's head would be blown off his shoulders if anything crooked was attempted." The brothers, walking arsenals themselves, agreed and declared that unless the race was run in less than 10 seconds they would do some shooting themselves and Boyd would be the target. The start was by "mutual consent" and the men were timed from the "bend of the knee." Those that saw the race agreed it was the finest they had ever witnessed. Although it was plain to everybody present that Boyd gave his best effort, Bethune won by two feet in 9⅗ seconds. Seeing their man fairly beaten, the brothers took the loss philosophically. The winners collected the stakes and the entire party adjourned to a bar for a drink.

## Amateur Sprinters Break "Evens"

*Sprinting is something that every man ought to learn, because in learning how to run one acquires the faculty of quick thinking and physical control.* — Michael C. Murphy (1895)

Near the end of the 19th century, American athletic clubs and universities began producing outstanding amateur sprinters in abundance. This new breed of fast men would eventually replace the professionals. By 1890 at least a dozen amateurs in America and England had run "even time" for 100 yards. Some claimed to have beaten 10 seconds, but usually it turned out that the track was short or downhill, or a tail-wind was blowing, or the runner had beaten the gun.

The two most notable early claims of amateurs running under 10 seconds for 100 yards were by Irishman Tom Malone and American Victor Schifferstein. For some reason Malone's 9⅘ performance in Limer-

ick, Ireland, on June 15, 1882, was not considered a record by statisticians of his time although he was later credited with 9⅘ as a professional in Australia. Schifferstein's 9⅘ on September 9, 1888, at the Western AAU championships in St. Louis, was not considered a record either. It may have been because it was run far away from the Northeast, the center of American sprinting at the time. Schifferstein had earlier raced professional Harry Bethune, which may also have been a factor in his performance not being considered an amateur record.

John Owen, Jr., of the Detroit Athletic Club became the first amateur to officially run inside even time for 100 yards on October 11, 1890. Owen, slender, and a bundle of nerves, was 28 years old when he took up sprinting in 1889. His coach was Michael Murphy, a former professional sprinter, who would become one of America's greatest track coaches. Owen's historic race took place at the AAU championships on Analostan Island (now called Theodore Roosevelt Island), a pear-shaped island in the Potomac river, opposite Georgetown and almost in the shadow of the Washington Monument. The field was loaded. Luther Cary of Princeton, the fastest collegian, and Fred Westing of the New York Athletic Club, the fastest of the club sprinters, had both previously run 10 flat. Also in the final were Remington and William Robinson, two 10⅕-second men.

Using the Sheffield Start, Owen got away to a three-foot lead over Cary. Although Cary nearly made up the lost ground, Owen broke the red woolen yarn at the finish a foot ahead. All four timers caught him in 9⅘ seconds and soon the telegraphs were wiring the news to the world: "Owen of Detroit has broken the world's record for 100 yards." There was no opposition to admitting the time as a record as it was in a championship meet, into a headwind and on a level track. When the course was remeasured, it was found to be 100 yards and one inch.

A week later the astounding news came from Princeton that Luther Cary had been timed in 9½ seconds for 100 yards. At first the performance was looked on favorably, but later the *New York Times* reported that Cary had "retired to a lonely Jersey by-road near Princeton, and, accompanied by two alleged timekeepers, made up the record."

Cary was not to be denied his place in running history, however. In the Intercollegiate Association of Amateur Athletes of America (IC4A) championship meet of 1891 he ran 220 yards in 21⅕ for an amateur record and added the record for 100 meters in Paris on July 4, 1891. His Paris time of 10¾ seconds made him the first man to break 11 seconds for the metric 100.

John Owen was the first amateur sprinter to run under 10 seconds for 100 yards (*Outing*, July 1902).

Luther Cary from Princeton ran the 100 meters in 10¾ seconds in Paris in 1891, becoming the first runner to break 11 seconds. He also held the amateur record for 220 yards (21⅕) (*Harper's Weekly*, May 30, 1891).

Bernard Joseph "Bernie" Wefers, who ran for Georgetown, was even more brilliant than Owen or Cary. Up until 1895, Wefers was a fast, but not great, sprinter. That year he went to Travers Island to train with the New York Athletic Club for the upcoming games with the London Athletic Club. After a few weeks under coach Mike Murphy, Wefers emerged an awesome sprinter.

On May 30, 1896, at Manhattan Field, Wefers not only ran a 9⅘ hundred but also won the 220 (run on a straight course) by 11 yards in 21⅕ seconds. This was the best 220 up to that time by either amateur or professional. A tall, powerful man, Wefers resembled Hutchens in both physique and competitive ability. He was nervous, and always ready for a race. He ran with a succession of great, space-covering bounds. Wefers was equal to the best 19th century amateurs at 100 yards and at the 220, he was the best. His records of 150 yards in 14⅗, 220 yards in 21⅕, and 300 yards in 30⅗ seconds all stood for many years. After his running days he coached track & field successfully for 45 years. Although Wefers never broke the amateur record of 9⅘ seconds* for 100 yards, he equaled it many times.

**Bernard Wefers, probably the best amateur sprinter of the 19th century (*Outing*, July 1902).**

## Origin of the Crouch Start

The biggest innovation to come along in sprinting since the starting gates of ancient Greece was the "crouch start." But even near the time of its first use, no one seems to have been quite sure where it came from. As early as the 1840s, George Seward sometimes started from a kneeling position as a method of handicapping himself. Later, some traveling pros, starting from a lying position, could beat novices. The novice used his normal standing start, but the pro would lie flat on his back, with his head pointed toward the finish. Using a snap-roll into the crouch position, he was usually off the line no more than half a second (about five yards) behind the novice. This was about half the distance a pro could beat a novice in 100 yards and the pro was usually in the lead by 75 yards.

Until the adoption of the crouch, the most common type of standing start was called the "Sheffield." A runner using this start held both the right arm and right leg, or left arm and left leg forward. The other arm was held at shoulder level or higher behind him. At the gun, he made a very fast poking stroke a short distance beyond the scratch with his leading foot and at the same time swung his opposite arm sharply forward.

Although many late 19th century runners claimed to have originated the crouch start, two claims deserve serious consideration. Michael Murphy, a former profes-

*Wefers claimed that in 1895 he was timed (on five watches) in 9⅖ seconds for 100 yards. William "Father Bill" Curtis, founder and head of the AAU, stared at the timers' watches and shook his head. "No man can run that fast," he said, and disallowed the record.

**C. H. Sherrill of Yale using the crouch start at Long Island, New York, May 12, 1888. This was the first use of the crouch start in America (Hawn, *How to Sprint*, 1923. Courtesy of Spalding Sports Worldwide, Inc.).**

sional sprinter, wrote in *How to Become a Sprinter* (1913):

> The crouching start was first used by me in professional work in 1880, and introduced in 1887 when C. H. Sherrill, of Yale, the intercollegiate champion, showed it. Needless to say, he was laughed at when he got down on all fours, but today no good sprinter ever thinks of trying any other start.

Murphy was the world's most famous coach in the late 19th and early 20th centuries. His claim that he used the "crouch" in 1880 is plausible, but has not been verified. He said that he hit upon this method of starting almost by accident through his habit of falling forward on his hands to avoid going over the line. Murphy claimed to have experimented with the start for several years before he taught it to Sherrill, who was an "even time" sprinter but very unsteady with the standing start.

James E. Sullivan, in his pamphlet, *How to Become an Athlete* (1921), argued for

the crouch start originating in Australia, writing: "The 'crouch,' which should be called the 'Kangaroo' or 'Australian' start, is the perfect and up-to-date method of starting."

It was a bitterly cold night at the Carrington Ground in Sydney in 1887 when Aborigine Bobby McDonald surprised everyone by starting from a crouch. McDonald, a better-than-average sprinter, wrote a letter to the July 1913, *Referee*, an Australian sporting journal, describing his claim. The letter is reproduced in Colin Tatz's *Obstacle Race: Aborigines in Sport* (1995):

> I first got the idea of the sitting style of start (as I always called it) to dodge the strong winds, which made me feel cold and miserable while waiting for the starter to send us away. One day while sitting down, almost, the starter sent us away, and I found that I could get off the mark much quicker sitting than ever I could standing, and afterwards I always used the sitting or crouch start. I never saw anyone using what is known as the crouch start before I did.

**C. H. Sherrill using the Sheffield Start in 1889 (courtesy of Yale University).**

Whether Murphy came up with the crouch independently will probably never be known. All we know for sure is that he introduced it in America. Thomas L. Nicholas, in late 1888, was the first British sprinter to use the crouch start.

Regardless of who invented it, by 1890–1891 the crouch had gained a foothold among American colleges and rapidly spread to the club runners. Initially, sprinters adopted the crouch, not because they thought it made for a faster start, but because it allowed them to start from a more stable position. Using the crouch, they were less likely to either "jump the gun" or be left on their marks. The crouch was soon held in such high regard that not only sprinters, but also runners in distances of two and even three miles sometimes used it.

When the crouch start first came into use there was some confusion as to where the runner should place his hands. Notice that in the picture of Sherrill starting, he is on the line as are the other runners. Some starters, particularly in Britain, allowed runners to place their hands across the line as long as their feet were behind it. This gave the user of the crouch a considerable advantage. Eventually a rule was passed that required that runners place both hands behind the line.

## Bygone Foot-races— Sacks, Potatoes, Fire-Hoses and Men vs. Horses

Some forms of foot-racing that were popular in the 19th century never survived. In addition to normal running, sack races, three-legged races and wheelbarrow races were common in 19th century America. The sack race, which dates from the Middle Ages, was normally run strictly for laughs. In the late 1800s, however, the race was taken seriously in America, at least by some. College track teams had sack-racing specialists who trained as diligently as any other member of the team.

There was no fixed distance for the race but it was usually from 50 to 150 yards. The sack had a drawstring which was drawn around the athlete's neck. It enveloped him, leaving nothing but his head visible. He was allowed to grasp the sides of the sack with his hands and could either make a series of jumps, or take very small steps. Most sack racers seemed to do better jumping. Falls were frequent as it was easy to trip, or get bumped by a competitor and go down. The moment the athlete was aware he was about to fall, he tried to allow his body to fall in the direction he was going. When he hit the ground, instead of getting up immediately, he rolled over in such a way that he could get quickly to his feet again. With sufficient practice he lost practically nothing from a fall.

Before starting, the sack-racer put the toes of each foot into a corner of the sack to keep his feet from getting tangled. It required good pace judgment and endurance to jump from 50 to 100 times in a sack without becoming exhausted. Sometimes the race was made even more difficult by the addition of 18-inch hurdles.

In addition to the "potato race," which was a shortened form of the "picking up stones" race described in Section Four, hose-team races were popular in America in the 1880s. Much of the 19th century firefighting equipment was hand-drawn. Firemen, having a lot of time on their hands between fires, formed hose teams and practiced diligently. The 16-man team typically pulled a

Sack Race at the New York Caledonian Games in 1884. The runner is clearing an 18-inch hurdle (*Illustrated Sporting & Dramatic Journal*, September 20, 1884).

two-wheeled 700-pound (318 kg) hose-cart 200 yards, unwound 300 feet of hose, coupled it to a hydrant, and attached the nozzle. These races drew huge crowds and the better hose-teams actively recruited outstanding sprinters. A team with Steve Farrell, "Pooch" Donovan, "Piper" Donovan, Keene Fitzpatrick, and Mike Murphy was virtually unbeatable.

The ancient Greeks, as well as running footmen of the 16th and 17th centuries, ran against horses. This form of racing was still popular in the 19th century. A horse can run at over twice the speed of a human and no man has a chance in an "even-up" race of less than 100 miles (161 km) against a well-trained horse. Race promoters, however, found a multitude of ways to even the odds and create a race whose outcome was in doubt. A popular match-up was for the man to run 100 yards while the horse ran 150. For longer races the man might run five to five-and-a-quarter miles while one or more horses ran or trotted 10.

## Quarter and Half Milers

*Next season I am going to alter all of the records from one hundred yards to the mile.*—L. E. "Lon" Myers (1879)

Early 19th century runners such as Captain Barclay in 1803 and Abraham Wood in 1809 ran the quarter mile in about 55 seconds. Wood ran the half mile in 2:06.

### H. A. REED—FIRST GREAT MIDDLE-DISTANCE RUNNER

The first great quarter/half miler was Henry Allen Reed. Known as "the Great H.A.," he was born in High Wycombe, Buckinghamshire, in 1825 and began his running career in 1847. Reed was five feet eight inches and weighed 126 lbs. with a "greyhound-like" build. He had a broad chest, slender waist, and muscular thighs— very long from the hip to the knee. His long,

**Three-legged races were popular at many 19th century track meets (*The Prize*, 1896).**

bounding stride—once measured at nine feet four inches—was most suited to the straight courses laid out on turnpike roads. When running tracks became common in England in the early 1850s Reed still preferred to race on turnpike roads, admitting that he had a "slovenly" style of getting around corners.

Reed ran his greatest race on June 25, 1849, on the turnpike road near the Magpies Inn about three miles from Hounslow. His opponent was George Seward, "the American Wonder." Both men were eager to see who was best at a quarter mile and the stakes were £200, a large amount of money at the time. Reed hurt his leg in training for

Hose race teams recruited the fastest sprinters they could get (*Frank Leslie's Illustrated Newspaper*, September 4, 1878).

the race and asked for a postponement. Instead of claiming forfeit, Seward graciously agreed to Reed's request. Seward even trained for the race, which was almost unheard of for the "American Wonder." Reed too, trained carefully and by race date was "as fine as a star," having trained down from 154 pounds (70 kg) to little more than 126 (57.3 kg).

Tom Oliver carefully measured the course and roped off the last 200 yards to prevent the runners from interfering with each other. The race was scheduled for 3:00 P.M. and despite it being the hottest day of the summer, 6,000 spectators showed up. Because of the heat, the runners agreed to postpone the match until 5:00 P.M., but it was 7:00 P.M. before they finally came to the scratch. Seward was the favorite, but Reed was confident of victory and bet his last £20 on himself. A *Bell's Life* reporter described the race as follows:

There were at least five and twenty false starts, and Reed, imagining that Seward

had received the "office" to ruffle his temper, assured him that the attempts would prove futile; he had got Seward there that day and did not mind waiting as long as he pleased, for he was sure to prove victorious when they did run. A smile beamed on the good-looking countenance of Seward, who on the question being put to him, "Do you mean to go now, George?" replied in the affirmative, and away they went at a clipping pace, rarely if ever equaled.

Both got well off together, but Reed, determined to "do or die," put on the steam to such an extent at the onset that we thought it would prove a "burster" ere half the distance had been accomplished. Seward, who had won the toss for choice of sides, stuck well to his man on the left side for about 100 yards, when he fell a trifle in the rear. At 150 yards Reed, who was still going at the same flying rate, increased his lead to nearly two yards and on approaching the Magpies it was evident that Seward could not live the pace, and Reed from this time gradually left him, ultimately winning by about 14 or 15 yards, once turning his head slightly to ascertain the precise position of his opponent. Loud cheers greeted the winner as he passed the goal, but he was evidently "done up" and could hardly make a walk of it to his quarters, having run from end to end at the top of his speed, accomplishing the distance in the unprecedented short time of *forty-eight and a half seconds!*

Although Reed's performance was not on a track, it was the first well-documented sub–50 second quarter mile.* He ran the distance in 49.0 the following February in defeating Edward Roberts (the Welshman) who had a five-yard start. There is little doubt that Reed could have run under 50 seconds on a track.† He broke down in an 880-yard race with Thomas Horspool in September 1858, and vowed to never run another match. Upon retirement he became a sports reporter and ended his life in sad circumstances. He died in what was known then as a lunatic asylum at the age of 48.

On October 4, 1873, Dick Buttery, "the Sheffield Blade," broke Reed's record. Running from scratch on a track at Gateshead Borough Ground, Buttery won a 440-yard handicap by a yard in 48¼ Buttery's performance made him the first to break 50 seconds for the quarter mile on a track.

Reed was also the first man to run the half mile in less than two minutes. He accomplished the feat in an April 11, 1854, duel with Tom Horspool on a track at Westhill Park, Halifax. With 150 yards to go, the inside of the track, which was raised ground, gave way under Horspool's foot allowing Reed to win by two yards in 1:58.

Reed's half mile record was surpassed on May 20, 1865, by Robert McInstray of Glasgow. McInstray accomplished the feat at the Royal Oak Grounds in a race with two other outstanding half-milers, William

Richards "the Welshman" and John Heywood, who was but four feet 7½ inches tall. McInstray led all the way and after looking back twice, won easily by five yards in 1:56½.

Described as "compact, agile and powerful of limb," James Nuttall was one of the best sprinters and quarter milers in England in the 1860s. His favorite distances were from 600 yards to half a mile and he had easily won all his races at these distances. In 1864, he had defeated Siah Albison in Manchester at 600 yards with a fast 1:13. On August 31, 1867, at the Copenhagen Grounds, Nuttall lowered McInstray's half-mile record. Nuttall's opponent was five foot 4½" John Fleet from Manchester. Earlier, on February 28, 1867, the aptly named Fleet had won a 1.5-mile (2.4 km) race in a world's best time of 6:50. After this race, Fleet, training on the turnpike road, was assaulted by ruffians and severely beaten. On recovering, he managed to use his loss of training to wrangle a 10-yard start from Nuttall.

The race course was crowded and the betting fast and furious. Nuttall made up a yard and a half of the handicap when Fleet got off to a slow start. Using his long strides, Nuttall steadily ate into Fleet's lead and passed him with 140 yards to go. Fleet struggled gamely but couldn't stay with Nuttall who finished three yards ahead in a remarkable 1:55½.

Frank "Scurry" Hewitt, who had emigrated from Ireland to New Zealand, became the next half-mile record holder on August 23, 1871. Hewitt had bet £25 to £50 that he could, on a level road, without a tailwind, beat Nuttall's record of 1:55½. The course on the Riccarton Road, near Lyttelton, was not selected until the morning of the race in order to avoid a head wind. Hewitt chose a stretch of road that, while

---

*Bell's Life *for August 17, 1851, stated that William Robinson, who lost the famous 9¼ second 100-yard race to Seward in 1844, had run 440 yards in 49 seconds at some time in his career, but gave no details.*

†*According to the January 2, 1875,* Bell's Life, *Reed twice ran 440-yard trials on the turnpike road inside 47 seconds.*

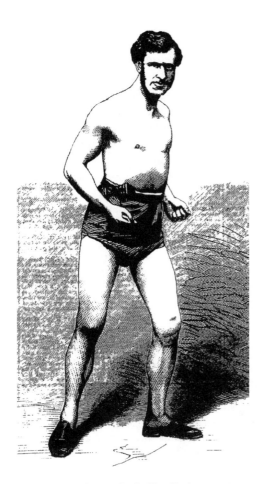

James Nuttall ran the half-mile in 1:55½ on August 31, 1867, at the Copenhagen House Grounds in London (*Illustrated Sporting News*, January 3, 1866).

not level, Mr. Stead, the "backer of time," agreed was not downhill. It was carefully measured with a surveyor's chain, then cleared of loose stones. By race time a large crowd had gathered to watch the attempt. The weather was beautiful with a gentle crosswind. Based on his trials, Hewitt believed that he could get his best time by "running himself out," (going out very fast right from the start).

Starting alone, he was off at the crack of the pistol and covered the first quarter mile in 51¼—an amazing split for 1871. At that point, a pacesetter, J. G. Harris, joined him. Hewitt ran about three feet behind Harris and slowed so much near the end that the crowd began to shout "He'll not do it; he'll lose." But the official timers gave him 1:53½—two seconds under Nuttall's record. Hewitt's performance was scoffed at by some because it was not in a race and was on a road rather than a track, but it would be considered the best half mile on record until 1895.

The first amateur to break two minutes was A. L. Pelham, of Cambridge, who ran the half mile in 1:59⅗ at Fenner's on March 26, 1873. On October 7, 1876, Pelham raced three other outstanding half milers in a memorable race in London. After several lead changes, all four finished under two minutes—Frederick Elborough 1:57½, Henry Hill 1:58, and Walter Slade and Pelham a shade inside 1:59 and 2:00 respectively.

## LON MYERS— WORLD'S GREATEST RUNNER

Until the 1870s, running records made in America were suspect. Both competitors and spectators were usually satisfied to know who won a race without being overly concerned with whether the course was accurately measured or the time accurately taken. American timing and course measurement gradually improved, but as late as 1880 the British were justifiably suspicious of fast times run in America. Laurence Eugene "Lon" Myers changed all that. He brought credibility to American runners and their records by rewriting the record books in both America and England.

Myers was born on February 15, 1858, in Richmond, Virginia. Although he was a sickly youth, he was noted for his running and jumping. When he graduated from high school, his family moved to New York City. There he worked for a wholesale drug firm for four years before taking up running to try to improve his health. In need of a coach, he sought out John Fraser, a well-known Scottish athletic shoemaker and trainer. Because Myers had a bad cough and delicate appearance, Fraser was reluctant to coach him. Fraser's wife was sure that Myers had consumption and that training would kill him. Although Myers's mother had died of the dreaded disease when he was a baby, he never contracted it.

Myers ran his first race at the New York Athletic Club games on November 5, 1878. Aided by an 18-yard handicap, he won the 440 in a slow 55 seconds. The following year he was troubled, as he would be most of his short life, with bouts of malaria and other illnesses. He was also fond of gambling and couldn't resist a poker game, sometimes playing all night. Still, he made remarkable progress as a runner and on Sept 20, 1879, set his first record. Competing for the Manhattan Athletic Club, he ran the 440 in an "unprecedented" 49⅕ seconds despite losing his right shoe with 120 yards to go. The timekeepers were astounded and at first refused to show their watches, thinking something had gone wrong with them.

No amateur had run that fast before. E. J. Colbeck, from England, had almost broken 50 seconds back in 1868. Unfortunately a sheep had wandered onto the track and Colbeck ran into it, breaking his stride and the sheep's leg. Colbeck finished in 50⅖. On March 7, 1871, at the Corpus Christi College Sports at Fenners, Robert Philpot nosed out his teammate Abbot Upcher by a yard in 49¾. The time was not accepted as a record because the 576-yard track had a six-foot slope that favored the runners. When the English press heard of Myers' performance, they were unconvinced, believing the track was short or the timekeepers had erred.

Myers set out to prove that not only could he break 50 seconds for the quarter any time he wished, he could beat any American at any distance from 100 yards to the mile. Once Myers got going in 1880, American track records fell like drops of sweat from a man waiting to be executed. He broke the 100-yard record with 10.0, the

220 with 22¾, the 440 with 49⅕, the 880 with 1:56⅛, the 1000 with 2:18¼ and the mile with 4:29½. At the national championships in 1880 he won national titles in the 100, 220, 440, and 880 all on the same day. Three days later at the Canadian Championships in Montreal, Myers repeated his victories and became undisputed champion of American middle distance runners.

Since the British press had commented frequently on the inaccuracy of American timing, Myers was anxious to go to England and try to duplicate his performances there. He later commented on the disparity between American and British records in "Confessions of a Champion Athlete," in *Lippincott's Monthly Magazine* in 1886:

> It was generally conceded that, owing to atmospheric influences, it was impossible to repeat in this country the performances credited to English athletes. I took a different view of the matter — attributing the fact that our standards were so much below the English either to the disposition on the part of our men to let well enough alone or to their not training properly.

The Manhattan Athletic club helped raise money for the trip and Myers sailed for England in the summer of 1881. He ran his first race there in early July, winning the 440 in 49⅘ seconds and a week later lowered his time for the distance to 49.0.

On July 16, before a crowd of 20,000 at Birmingham's Aston Lower Grounds, Myers suffered his only non-handicapped defeat on English soil. He was easy to spot as he warmed up for the 100 yards in knee-length pants, a head-scarf, and the "cherry diamond" of the Manhattan Athletic Club emblazoned on his chest. The five-foot seven-inch (1.7 m), 115-pound (52.3 kg) American was dwarfed by six-foot two-inch (1.9 m) William Phillips, the amateur 100-yard champion of England, who limbered up beside him.

As the gun sounded for his heat of the

100-yard race, Myers stumbled. Regaining his form, he managed to catch the other runners, but the effort had cost him too much energy and he faded to fourth at the finish. The great Myers had been eliminated in the heats!

When the 440 started, Phillips jumped into a four-yard lead. Myers, despite his loss in the 100, was not worried. He fell back into third place until half the distance had been covered, then suddenly cut loose, and before anyone knew what was happening, was 10 yards in front. Running at his best speed, he soon had the field strung out like telegraph poles. Several times he turned and playfully beckoned for Phillips to come on and make a race of it. Myers finished in a walk in 48⅗—a sensational performance. The spectators were amazed at the skinny American who appeared to be all legs. They were also astonished by his odd running style with his arms hanging loosely at his sides as his long legs did all the work.

Myers was disappointed when the En-

Lon Myers winning his first race in England in 1881 (*Illustrated Sporting and Dramatic News*, July 2, 1881).

glish amateur champion Walter George complained of illness and refused to race him. George, however, recovered enough to set a new amateur record of 2:18 for the 1,000 yards the day Myers arrived back in New York. On leaving the ship, Myers received a tumultuous welcome and a few days later, to show his appreciation, lowered the American record for 300 yards to 31½ seconds.

On October 8, 1881, at the Manhattan Polo Association grounds he ran his greatest race ever. Rested and running on a fast 640-yard track, he made an assault on George's 1,000-yard record. Aware that the British would probably question the record, the officials—20 experts with carefully regulated watches—were on hand. Myers was too eager and false started. On the restart he quickly took the lead and left the other five runners far behind. When he heard 1:55⅗ announced at the half mile, he knew he had the record. Near the end he appeared exhausted, but still ran several yards past the tape.

The three official watches all caught him in 2:13. Of all his records, this was Myers's best performance, but he was undoubtedly capable of more. Because of the false start, he was overcautious and got off late. He had no "rabbits" or opposition to push him, and he ran an extra 18–20 feet to avoid soft spots and ruts in the track. Still, he had not only broken George's amateur 1,000-yard record by five seconds, he was also four seconds under William Cummings's professional record. The performance brought forth no complaints from British journalists of short courses or shoddy timing. They had become believers in Myers.

Running was not all glory for Myers. Bothered by poor health in 1884, his problems were compounded when he was accused by one of his rivals of being a professional. He eventually cleared himself of the charges and returned to England hoping to run in the English championships of

1884 and face Walter George. The promoters refused to allow him to run in the championships that year and George avoided him. But the British fans loved him, and he responded by lowering his 880 record to 1:55⅖.

In 1885 he made his last trip to England where he was again warmly received by the knowledgeable fans and won a satchel full of medals and the English Championships at 440 and 880 yards. During his three trips to England, Myers won nearly a hundred prizes and lost only one non-handicapped race. When he returned home from his last trip to England, he announced his retirement from running.

His career was not over, however. In January 1886 Walter George, who had turned professional in 1884, arrived in New York and challenged Myers. As amateurs in 1882, the two men had run three races with Myers winning the half mile and George the three-quarter mile and mile. Myers was eager to avenge his losses. The two men, both now professionals, signed an agreement for three races in Madison Square Garden at 1,000 yards, three quarters of a mile and mile. In all three races Myers let the methodical George set the pace, stayed with him, and used his superior speed to sprint past the Englishman near the end.

After trying unsuccessfully to arrange races with both William Cummings and Harry Hutchens in England, Myers left for Australia in 1887 where professional running had long been popular. Myers stayed in Australia for 18 months, racing with some success but setting no more records.

Myers raced his old foe Walter George three times in Australia and won twice. This gave him a lifetime record of six wins and three losses in races with George. The match-ups created much interest and drew huge crowds but never brought out the best in either man. The races were mismatches in that the two men's best distances didn't overlap. George was the better runner at three quarters of a mile and above, but

was no match for Myers below this distance.

At distances shorter than 300 yards, Myers didn't have the speed to contend with Hutchens, but from 300 to 1,000 yards he had no equal in his time. Lack of anyone close to his ability and his tendency to run many different races kept him from running faster than he did. On his return from Australia he retired from running for good and became a bookmaker and race horse owner. In 1888, at Oxford, Francis J. K. Cross lowered Myers's amateur half-mile record to 1:54⅗. Myers's 1,000 yard record of 2:13 was not broken until 1910 when Mel Sheppard ran 2:12⅖.

A relapse of pneumonia in 1899 ended Myers's short life, within a day of his 41st birthday. Thomas I. Lee in *Muncey's Magazine* for July 1901 summed up Myers best:

> In build Myers was a freak. Of medium height and very slender, with long legs all out of proportion to his upper body, thin and sallow faced, he looked anything but an athlete. Stripped ready to race, he was a powerful pair of legs carrying a small trunk of concentrated nerve force, topped off with a wise, quick thinking head. He ran like a machine, with a big, bounding space eating stride that lengthened and quickened without apparent effort. His judgement of pace was astounding and he won many wagers by running 440 yards in exactly the number of seconds he chose. What Myers could have done had he trained properly will always be a problem; for when in his prime, he never took care of himself. He played poker all one night and, without sleep, rest, or food, except two apples and a cup of coffee, he went forth and broke a world's record.

Myers was noted for his generosity and honesty, giving away more than 200 of his prizes and frequently skipping races to give his teammates a chance to win. There were similarities between Myers in America and George in England. They were honorable men whose careers illustrated both the strengths and weaknesses of the amateur system. They proved that amateurs could equal or exceed the best performances of the professionals of their day. But both had to earn a living and the only way they could do that and continue to run was to become professionals.

Four runners in the 19th century ran the 440 in less than 48 seconds. All but one of these performances were made on straight or nearly straight courses. Tom Malone ran 47⅗ seconds in 1884 at Ballarat, Australia, but little information about the performance is available. On July 1, 1886, Wendell Baker from Harvard traveled to Beacon Park in New York, hoping to run a fast 440 on a straight section of the carefully prepared horse track.

As a tune-up, Baker equaled the world record of 10.0 for 100 yards, but ripped his left shoe in the process. After the wind was checked and deemed not to be favoring, Baker got off to a good start and sprinted the first 220 alone in 23⅕ seconds. Then a pacemaker led him over the rest of the distance. Although he was staggering at the end and had run the last 150 yards without his left shoe, he finished in 47¾ seconds.

Walter George (sitting) and Lon Myers in 1882. They were great rivals, but also friends (*Frank Leslie's Illustrated Newspaper*, November 11, 1882).

Baker later admitted that on that track Myers would probably have run 45½. Myers, surprised that his record was broken so soon after he left the amateur ranks, maintained that he had always been able to give Baker several yards and beat him. He vowed to go to Beacon Park in October 1886 and lower all the professional records from 250 to 1,000 yards, but instead decided in September to go to Australia to race George.

Walter C. Downs of Harvard made a record attempt on the same track on July 9, 1890, and did 47⅖ under similar conditions. But because of a dispute over the location of the finish line, his mark was never accepted as a record.

Thomas E. Burke, of Boston, became the first 400-meter Olympic champion by winning in 1896 at Athens in 54⅕ seconds. The slow time was caused by the loose cinders and hairpin turns on the track at Athens. Burke ran the distance in 48⅘ in winning the AAU title that year. He also won the first Olympic 100-meter championship at Athens and was an outstanding half miler with a best time of 1:56.

Maxwell W. "Maxey" Long, a powerful, awkward runner, with a punishing finish, closed out 19th century quarter-miling. After winning the 1900 Olympic 400 meters in 49²/₅, on a primitive track in Paris, Long ran the two fastest quarter miles run up to that time. The first was in a Sept. 29, 1900, handicap race at the New York Athletic Club's annual games on Travers Island. Long started from scratch against eight other runners with handicaps ranging from 10 to 24 yards. He got off to a fast start on the 352-yard track and caught the field in the first 200 yards. The Columbia University star went through the pack with ease and came down the stretch 10 yards in the lead, gathering speed at every step. His winning time of 47⁴/₅ was the only 440 run inside 48 seconds on a non-straightaway track in the 19th century.

Maxwell Long ran 47.0 for 440 yards on a straight track in 1900 (*Outing*, June 1902).

Wendell Baker from Harvard broke Lon Myers's 440 yard record by running the 440 in 47¾ seconds on a straight horse track at Beacon Park, New Jersey, on July 1, 1886 (*Outing*, May 18, 1891).

A week later at the Guttenberg race track in New Jersey, Long went after Baker's straight-course record. A straightaway had been improvised by sprinkling and rolling the loose gravels and top dressing of the old horse track into a smooth, hard surface. Several sprinters jumped in and set the pace at various points along the course. Long ran with his head thrown back, his face set and drawn and his fists clenched. He finished in an impressive 47.0 seconds, beating all records, amateur or professional.

Since the days of Jackson and Seward in the mid–1840s, Americans had raced in Britain and British runners had crossed the Atlantic to race in America. But not until the 1880s were American track and field teams strong enough to compete with those in England. In 1891 the Manhattan Athletic club sent a team that competed successfully in England and France. In July of 1894, Yale, the intercollegiate champion in the United

States, traveled to England to face Oxford, winner of the Oxford-Cambridge meet. Oxford won the meet with 5½ points to Yale's 3½.

A year later on September 21, 1895, the best athletes from both countries met at Manhattan Field in New York. This meet between the New York Athletic Club and the London Athletic Club marked a coming-of-age for American track and field. Although American B. J. Wefers tied the amateur 100-yard record with 9⅘ seconds and set a world record for the 220 in 21⅗ seconds, the highlight of the meet was the half mile.

Charles H. Kilpatrick, running for the American team, was the best half miler in the world but a poor judge of pace, sometimes losing when he ran the first lap too slowly. Before the race, Mike Murphy, coach of the American team, gave Kilpatrick a brief talking-to that showed how well Murphy knew his athletes. Putting his hands on Kilpatrick's shoulders and looking him squarely in the eyes, Murphy spoke with a voice trembling with excitement: "Charlie, there's no man in the world that can beat you today. If he [F. S. Horan] should be on your shoulder when you come into the stretch, just squeeze on your corks* and think of your mother." Murphy gave his star half miler a reassuring pat on the shoulder and gripped his hand hard before scurrying away to inspire the other team members.

Murphy had instructed Lyons, Kilpatrick's teammate, to run the first quarter in 54½ seconds and Kilpatrick was to stay with him. Lewin, of the English team, evidently had similar instructions, as he ran with Lyons. The two real contenders, Kilpatrick and F. S. Horan, captain of the London team, made no attempt to take the lead until the end of the first lap, which was run

on schedule. Kilpatrick then moved to the front with Horan at his heels—the real race had begun. Slowly Kilpatrick drew away over the next 200 yards. Horan made a gallant effort and closed the gap a little, but Kilpatrick responded with a burst of speed and won by about 16 yards in 1:53⅖. He had run the fastest 880 of the 19th century, amateur or professional.

C. H. Kilpatrick, fastest half-miler of the 19th century. He ran 1:53⅖ in 1895 (*Outing*, June 1902).

---

*Corks were about four inches long and one inch thick and spindle shaped. They were hollowed out to allow the passage of a rubber band that slipped over the hand to hold them firmly in the palms. When the runner wanted to bear down he squeezed his corks. They were popular in the late 19th century but were discarded in the 1920s.

The British team was missing two of its stars. Both E. C. Bredin, who had run 49⅗ for the quarter and 1:55⅕ for the half and F. E. Bacon who had run the mile in 4:17, declined to make the trip. In addition Downer was injured. The one-sidedness of the meet was still a surprise. The Americans won all the events and became the world leader at track and field.

## The Mile—Origin of a Classic Foot-Race

*I have run five and ten miles so often in practice and in races that a mile or two is nothing for me to do, even if the pace is a little stiff.* — Walter George (1886)

The roots of the mile race can be traced to the roads of 18th-century England where mile races were common. While two men sometimes raced each other, races against time were more common. Times were usually in the five-minute range although, occasionally, contemporary newspapers reported faster performances.

In 1770, an unnamed runner was reported to have run a mile through the streets between Charter House Wall and Shereditch Church gates in four minutes! In 1787, Walpole, a butcher from Newgate Market, ran a mile against a well-known pedestrian named Pope along the city road. Walpole won in 4:30. Since 19th century writers doubted these times, perhaps we should also, especially the four-minute mile. Women occasionally ran also. According to *Sporting Magazine* (1801) an unnamed 15-year-old girl ran a mile in 5:28 in 1796.

In the early 1800s a five-minute mile was still thought remarkable. One of the first notable mile performances believed to be valid was by Captain Barclay, of 1,000 miles in 1,000 hours fame. Barclay, a wealthy Scotch landowner, bet 500 guineas that he could beat John Ireland, who was

regarded as one of the swiftest runners in the Manchester area. The race took place on October 12, 1804, with Barclay running Ireland to a standstill by three-quarters of a mile. Barclay kept on and finished in the then unprecedented time of 4:50.

For 21 years, no one could beat Barclay's time, although mile races were common and sometimes run for large stakes. On June 28, 1825, James Metcalf, a "tailor by trade, but a pedestrian by profession," conceded a 20-yard start in a mile race to J. Halton, another celebrated runner. The 22-year-old Metcalf won easily in 4:30. Metcalf and Halton's race on the Knavesmire road was for a bet of 1,000 guineas.

To improve his wind and speed, Metcalf trained by running after the king's stag hounds. On one training run, about 10 days before a match, he became ill from heat exhaustion and his backers thought they would have to forfeit the stakes. According to sports writer Pierce Egan, "Bleeding and due care brought him around and after keeping to bed a day the confidence of his friends was restored." Some trainers used bleeding "to clear the poisons from a pedestrian's system" and the custom continued for much of the 19th century.

Metcalf's time remained the best on record until July 2, 1849, when William Matthews and Charles Westhall raced a mile on the turnpike road at Lansdown, near Bath. After a good race for three-quarters of the way, Matthews moved ahead, and won by 30 yards. The timers didn't agree and reported 4:38, 4:28, and 4:27. *Bell's Life* believed one of the latter times was correct.

Westhall ran a remarkable mile race on July 26, 1852, against the two most celebrated runners of his day, George Seward "the American Wonder" and William Jackson "the American Deer." The race was held on the Copenhagen House Grounds one-third-of-a-mile (537 meter) track in north London. An hour's torrential downpour just before the start had turned the track into a sea of mud. Seward was the favorite and since the distance was thought short for Jackson, he was allowed a 10-yard start. Westhall, who started from scratch with Seward, was given almost no chance against the two world famous runners.

Seward made up Jackson's 10-yard lead by the first corner, but Jackson refused to let him pass. Jackson, knowing he had no chance in a sprint for the finish with Seward, kept the pace very "hot," although the mud caused the men's feet to sink over their shoe-tops for 200 yards of each lap. On the last lap Seward made a final surge, but the fast early pace had left him without a finishing kick. Locked in their struggle, the two men completely forgot about Westhall, who came from 30 yards behind and sprinted past to win by 10 yards. Again the timers disagreed, recording 4:26½, 4:27, and 4:28. The last time was taken by H. A. Reed and considered official, although the other two times were recorded by equally reliable men.

On July 12, 1858, at the Copenhagen House Grounds, Tom Horspool of Basford ran perhaps the first mile worthy of being called a "world's best." The five-foot five-inch (1.65 m) 111-pound (50.4 kg) Horspool, carefully prepared by the famous trainer Leggy Graves of Sheffield, had given Job Smith of Manchester a 10-yard start for this race. On the first lap Horspool, running easily, gained a couple of yards, but was unable to decrease Smith's lead any further on the second lap. Smith spurted on the last lap, and gained four yards, but Horspool fought back and at the last corner came within two yards of Smith. In the straight Horspool drew even and as they passed the stands, took the lead and won by 10 yards. His time of 4:23 was deemed "an unsurpassable display of celerity."

Interest in the mile race increased in August 1860 when the proprietor of the Copenhagen House grounds offered a splendid mile "champion's" belt valued at 60 guineas. When Siah Albison of Bowlee saw the belt, he immediately vowed that he would own it. The first running for the belt was on August 11, 1860, on a muddy track at the Copenhagen Grounds. The runners were Albison, William Lang "the Crowcatcher," Jack White "the Gateshead Clipper" and two others. Lang wasn't in top form and was not a contender in this race. Albison came from 30 yards behind to beat White by four yards and take possession of the belt, as he had promised, in a non-record 4:24.

Lang, not happy with his third place finish, challenged Albison to a rematch which took place on October 27, 1860, on the same course before a crowd of 4,000. This time both the runners and the course were in excellent condition. At the start Lang set a killing pace, attempting to exhaust or "cut down" Albison. By the end of the first lap he was 10 yards ahead but could increase the lead no farther. A hundred yards from the tape Albison drew even and the two men sprinted for the finish. In spite of all that the Crowcatcher could do, Albison won by a yard in a record 4:22¼.

On October 30, 1861, Lang ran his famous "downhill" mile. Although never considered a record, it was still a memorable performance. Lang had made a wager that he could run a mile in 4:15. Allowed to choose the course, he selected a downhill stretch of road between Cambridge and Newmarket. According to *Sporting Life*, the first half mile of the course was dead flat, then downhill for a quarter mile, the next 250 yards a steep descent, and the last run in was level. In spite of a head wind, Lang almost broke four minutes, covering the mile in 4:02.*

Albison's legitimate 4:22¼ mile, run in

---

*Running downhill to achieve a fast time for the mile has also been tried in modern times. In the early 1980s a downhill mile, the "Queens Street Mile" was held in Auckland, New Zealand. Mike Boit of Kenya won the 1983 race with 3:28, probably the fastest mile yet run.*

1860, remained unbeaten until 1863. That year Lang, who had been steadily improving, became the record holder by defeating James Sanderson, "Treacle," by eight yards at the City Grounds, Manchester. Lang's time was 4:21¾.

The next record holder was Cockney Edward Mills, of Bethnal Green, known as "Young England." He broke the old record on April 23, 1864, in a match with Patrick Stapleton of Mossley at the Royal Oak Grounds. A good race was expected as the 30-year-old Stapleton had previously run a 4:25 mile in "almost a tornado of wind and rain."

The race started with Mills taking a yard-and-a-half lead which he increased to three yards, covering the quarter in 60 seconds. Mills continued to lead, passing the half mile in 2:08 and the three-quarter flag in 3:16. On the last bend about 220 yards from the finish Stapleton passed Mills and took a four-yard lead, "looking very like a

Edward Mills "Young England" set a mile record of 4:20½ in 1864 (The Old Print Shop, New York).

winner." Mills, however, "screwing his courage to the sticking point," succeeded in regaining the lead. Stapleton gave up 80 yards from the finish, and Mills continued to lower the mile record to 4:20½, which one reporter described as a "feat without parallel."

### WILLIAM LANG AND WILLIAM RICHARDS — FIRST WORLD CHAMPION MILERS

It was a beautiful afternoon on August 19, 1865, when the greatest field of milers yet assembled met at the Royal Oak Grounds in Manchester. England, Scotland and Ireland were all represented in this contest for the Mile Championship Cup, £30 and the title of "Champion Miler of the World." Outside the grounds, anxious spectators filled every available spot for watching the race — treetops, rooftops and second-story windows. Inside 15,000 paying fans eagerly awaited the race. Covering a mile at the "Oak" grounds required two laps plus 458 yards on the superbly prepared 651-yard track. The entry list included the seven best milers of the day:

*Edward Mills*, "Young England," the mile record holder (4:20½ set in 1864).

*William Lang*, "the Crowcatcher," former mile record holder (4:21¾ set in 1863).

*Siah Albison*, former mile record holder (4:22¼ in 1860).

*William Richards*, "the Welshman," 29-year-old Welsh champion.

*Robert McInstray*, champion pedestrian of Scotland, who was very fast up to ¾ mile and holder of the 880 yd. world record of 1:56½ set three months earlier.

*James Sanderson*, "Treacle," who had run a 4:21½ mile in 1863.

*James Nuttall*, who was beyond his best distance. A week after this race he would break McInstray's half-mile record. He would serve as a rabbit.

When it was discovered that Mills was injured and couldn't run, Lang became the favorite. The race got off to an uneven start and Nuttall, with his half-miler speed, led through the first 440 in 60 seconds. Sanderson and McInstray were just behind, followed by Richards. Lang, who had drawn the undesirable outside position, was fighting his way through the pack. Nuttall continued to lead and passed the 880 flag in 2:05, but dropped out a short time later. On the third 440, McInstray took the lead, but Sanderson passed him and increased the already fast pace. McInstray regained the lead and went by three quarters of a mile in 3:14.

On the last 440 Sanderson faded and only Richards, Lang and McInstray, running in a group, were left with a chance to win. Just before the final turn McInstray, who didn't have the "bottom" of the other two runners, began to fall back. Lang and Richards, knowing the race was now between just them, became locked in a brilliant struggle over the last 150 yards. As the immense crowd roared its approval, the two men crossed the finish in a blur, five yards ahead of McInstray. The referee, unable to separate Lang and Richards, ruled a dead heat. Their time of 4:17¼ was a world record that would stand for 16 years.

The 19th century history of the mile is almost entirely British, although there is the possibility that a great American miler ran in the late 1870s. Big Hawk Chief, born in about 1853, was widely acclaimed as the greatest runner among the Pawnee, a nation known for its runners. According to a military physician who examined him at Fort Sidney, Nebraska, Big Hawk Chief was "the most perfect specimen of man" he had ever seen.

In 1876 or '77 Big Hawk Chief ran from the Pawnee Agency, Nebraska, to the Wichitas, a distance of about 120 miles (193 km) in 24 hours. On the return trip the "Hawk" outran a Wichita chief who raced him on horseback using a relay of two horses. Big Hawk Chief completed the return trip in about 20 hours.

In April 1877 Captain Luther North, leader of a group of Pawnee Scouts, had 24-year-old Big Hawk Chief display his running ability for some friends. North chose a half-mile horse track near Fort Sidney, which is 4,000+ feet above sea level. Here he and gambler Hughey Bean timed Big Hawk Chief for a mile. The fleet-footed Pawnee astounded the men by covering the first half mile in 2:00 and the second in 1:58. North and his friends were amazed and had the track remeasured with a steel tape. They found it to be exactly one-half mile. Big Hawk Chief had apparently run a 3:58 mile!

To analyze this claim, we must ask the same questions as in the case of Seward's 100 yards in 9¼ seconds. Was the time taken by a reliable person? Was the distance accurately measured? Did the runner ever before or since show similar form? Were there any circumstances likely to qualify the performance?

Although Luther North was known for his honesty, we know nothing of his ability at timing races. There is also no mention of whether his watch agreed with Bean's. Years later North had this to say of Big Hawk Chief: "Within my personal observation — the West of the '60's and 70's — he had no equal; I would like to have seen him matched against the best runners in this or any other country."

North's statement is probably the strongest argument against taking the performance seriously. There is no record of Big Hawk Chief running in any other race. To be fair, we can't say with certainty that Captain North was in error. Given the number of sub-four-minute milers living today, it seems possible that there were also men in the 19th century capable of running a mile in under four minutes. What they lacked were today's training methods, the knowledge that a sub-four-minute mile was possible, and the opportunity to compete against other sub four-minute milers.

Nothing else is known of Big Hawk Chief except that he died in Oklahoma in 1893 when he was about 40 years old.

In England, professional milers Lang, Mills and Richards faded from the scene without improving the Lang-Richards 1865 mile record of 4:17¼. By this time, the mile had also become a popular event in amateur track and field meets. Although 4:30 had been beaten by a number of pros, it was considered a barrier for amateurs. Walter Chinnery broke the barrier in a race at Corpus Christi, Cambridge, on March 14, 1868. He won by 20 yards in 4:29¾. A dedicated club runner, Chinnery was a founder of the London Athletic club.

Chinnery's amateur record was short lived. On April 3 of the same year Walter C. Gibbs from Cambridge ran 4:28⅘ in a match with Oxford. In 1874 Walter Slade lowered the amateur mile record to 4:26 when he won the open mile from scratch at the Civil Service Sports. A year later, Slade eclipsed his previous performance, running

Walter Slade won the English Amateur Mile Championship five years in a row from 1873 to 1877. His best time was 4:24½ (*Illustrated Sporting News*, May 5, 1877).

a 4:24½ mile at a London Athletic Club meet at Stamford Bridge. Slade, a "natural" runner who trained very little, won the English mile championship title five years in a row from 1873 to 1877.

After this flurry of record setting by the amateurs, the stage was set for the arrival of perhaps the two greatest milers of the 19th century.

William J. Cummings was born on

Walter Chinnery — the first amateur miler to break 4:30 (*Illustrated Sporting News*, August 1, 1868).

June 10, 1858, in Paisley, Scotland. He was a pro from the beginning, starting his career in 1876. By March 24, 1877, Cummings had begun to show his potential, winning a special one-mile handicap at Powderhall from a start of 80 yards. He improved rapidly using a light training program of an easy mile once a day, faster runs once or twice a week and occasional 10-mile walks. A big part of his training consisted of frequent racing.

On July 1, 1878, at Lillie Bridge the 20-year-old Cummings won the Mile Championship Belt in 4:28 and became the professional mile Champion of England. He ran much faster a month later when, starting from scratch in a one mile handicap at Springfield Grounds, Glasgow, he improved his mile time to 4:18½. Three years later on April 30, 1881, he raced William Duddle at 1,000 yards at Preston and won by six yards in world's-best time of 2:17.

Cummings faced Duddle again at the Borough Grounds in Preston on May 14, 1881, and this time he got the mile record. Running on a 603-yard track in a steady rain, Duddle forced the pace for the first two laps with Cummings sticking to his left shoulder. With about 220 yards to go Cummings took the lead and Duddle couldn't respond. Cummings turned his head a half-dozen times before cantering across the finish-line, winning by eight yards. His time of 4:16⅕ beat Lang and Richards's 16-year-old professional record by just over a second. The easy manner in which Cummings won caused a sensation, for many had thought the previous record would never be beaten. Described as "one of the prettiest runners who ever put on a running pump," the five-foot six-inch, 124-pound (56.4 kg) Cummings was a shrewd, level-headed runner admired by both fans and fellow runners.

### WALTER GEORGE—FATHER OF THE MILE FOOT-RACE

A threat to Cummings's domination of the mile appeared when Walter G. George,

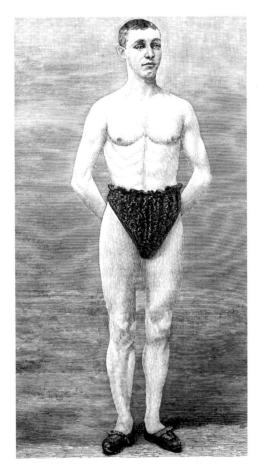

William Cummings lowered the mile record to 4:16⅕ (*National Police Gazette*, July 7, 1883).

a willowy 19 year old, began his career in 1878. George wrote in *Training for Athletics* (1908) of his early plans to become the world's greatest miler:

> In 1878 I was apprentice to chemistry at Worcester, and I made up my mind to try and run a mile. First, I figured out the time I thought the mile should be run in. Secondly, I started testing my theories *and particularly* my own constitution and capabilities; the result of this study soon convinced me that the then existing records at the distance were by no means good. Having formed these ideas, I prepared a schedule and at once started to try and demonstrate that my suppositions were correct.

I have a very vivid recollection of reading aloud (for the first time) this prepared schedule to a few of my club mates, and how they laughed and ridiculed the idea of any such record as therein laid down ever being established; nevertheless, I believed in my schedule and stuck to my guns, and as I still possess the original, I here append a copy of it in its entirety.

| Distance (mi) | Total Time | Lap Time (sec) |
|---|---|---|
| ¼ | 0:59 | 59 |
| ½ | 2:02 | 63 |
| ¾ | 3:08 | 66 |
| 1.0 | 4:12 | 64 |

This sequence of fast-medium-slow-medium laps is similar to the pacing used by Lang and Richards in their classic record-producing duel in 1865 and was used by both amateur and professional milers until the 1920s. George's dream of a 4:12 mile and his rivalry with Cummings would eventually lead to the fastest mile of the 19th century.

George, at five feet 11 inches and 136 lbs., had unusual stamina and speed for a middle-distance runner. Much of his training for the first five or six years of his career was an indoor exercise he called the "100-Up." This exercise, which George thrived on, consisted of dancing up and down on his toes to exercise his running muscles. Using this as his primary training method, George improved his running steadily and on August 16, 1880, he set a world amateur mile record of 4:23½ seconds.

As he matured, George's training became more sophisticated but still light according to today's standards. By 1882 he was running every day except Sunday, doing two-a-day workouts that included slow, medium and three-quarter-speed drills along with many time trials and long walks. He also retained his "100-Up." His favorite training diet was bread and cheese with a glass of beer.

By 1884 he had surpassed all other amateur runners at distances from three quarters of a mile to more than 10 miles. The London Athletic club held a series of races that year which showcased George's running. In these races he improved his mile time to 4:18⅘, two miles to 9:17¼ and three miles (4,831 meters) to 14:39. In a 10-mile handicap race in April 1884, he broke all the amateur records from 4¼ to 10 miles. His 10-mile time of 51:20 was six seconds quicker than the by then legendary Deerfoot had run 21 years earlier.

Looking for still more challenges, George went after Deerfoot's one-hour record,

Walter George, the best miler of the 19th century. His record of 4:12¾ set on August 23, 1886, was not broken for 29 years by either amateur or professional (from J. H. Hardwick, *Distance and Cross-Country Running*, 1912).

making the attempt at Stamford Bridge on July 28, 1884. Although he did his utmost and beat the amateur records for five, six, seven, eight, and 11 miles, he failed, finishing 38 yards short of Deerfoot's 11 miles, 970 yards.

George wanted badly to race Cummings to settle once and for all who was the best miler in the world. In 1883 he had approached the Amateur Athletic Association (AAA) of England for permission to run against Cummings. Even though George was deeply in debt, he was willing to give his half of the gate money to the Worcester Infirmary. The AAA refused to sanction the race and George was left with but one option if he wanted to race Cummings — to turn professional.

By the end of 1884 George had little left to accomplish as an amateur, having won countless prizes and set many amateur records. He had pursued running at the expense of his education as a druggist and was £1,000 in debt. Cummings, too, was anxious to race George. During 1883 Cummings had made a trip to the United States where he had raced William Steele, another noted Scottish runner who had emigrated to Pennsylvania. Cummings defeated Steele easily in a five-mile race at the Polo Grounds on June 16 but withdrew half way through a 10-mile race at Blossburg, Pennsylvania on August 18. An irate fan who had lost money on the contest entered Cummings's dressing room and began beating him, shouting "Take that, you Scotch thief, for selling out!" On his return to England, Cummings found running with little competition boring and went into semi-retirement.

George announced his decision to turn pro late in 1884 and the following year Cummings agreed to run a series of three races at one, four, and 10 miles. The first race took place at Lillie Bridge on August 31, 1885. Although it was a miserably wet evening, an enormous crowd of 25,000 showed up. Since the promoters had expected a maximum of 10,000, the stadium was soon

jammed. An hour before the race, the officials unwisely announced that the grounds were full and the gates would be closed. This set off a near riot as enraged fans, fearful of missing the race, stormed the fences and smashed their way into the stadium. George, caught outside, had great difficulty in reaching his dressing room. Finally, using a ladder to climb above the crowd, he was able to dress and make his way to the track at the last minute.

Although Cummings had run the mile in 4:16⅓ compared to George's best of 4:18⅘, George was a slight favorite. Jack White, the famed "Gateshead Clipper," fired the gun at 6:15 P.M. and the men were off. George took the lead from the start with Cummings on his heels — too close on his heels. George felt something strike him on the heel as his foot came up behind. For an instant he thought Cummings was trying to spike him, but he quickly regained his composure and ran his laps according to the 4:12 mile schedule he had mapped out seven years earlier — the first quarter mile in 58 seconds, half in 2:02, and three quarters in 3:09. On the last lap Cummings got within a yard, but with 350 yards to go, George made a "grand effort" which Cummings couldn't match. Unpressed at the end George won by 65 yards in 4:20⅕. After the race George spoke to Cummings about the spiking incident. Cummings grinned and replied:

Ah did not try t'spike thee, lad. What Ah did do was ti try and frighten thee by just tappun' tha heels wi' ma finger tips as tha brought foot oop behind. Ah think Ah did scare thee, but not enough to beat thee. More's t' pity.

George later wrote that he believed he could have run 4:12 on that day had Cummings been able to push him.

Cummings won the second race in the series at three miles when George gave up. The third race on Sept 28, 1885 at Lillie Bridge produced what the 20,000 spectators wanted — a new record. The time would undoubtedly have been faster except for a ponderously slow first mile. According to Peter Lovesey in *Kings of Distance* (1968), George was suffering from a mysterious illness. Two days before the race he had seven times collapsed into unconsciousness. He suspected he had been poisoned but had no proof.

Cummings knew that George ran to a rigid schedule of lap times and had decided to follow during the early part of the race. George made no effort to lead but instead looked as if he might drop in his tracks. After following George to a slow 5:21 mile, the baffled Cummings finally realized he couldn't depend on George to set the pace and spurted to a 20-yard lead. From that point the race was virtually over. An unpressed Cummings won by 430 yards, in 51:06⅗, beating George's 10-mile record by 13⅖ seconds.

George, disappointed with losing two out of the three races but much better off financially, left for New York. There he hoped to encourage the great American amateur middle-distance runner L. E. "Lon" Myers to turn professional and run a series of races with him. Myers, also in need of money, turned pro and defeated a sub-par George in all three of their races at half, three-quarters and a mile on the indoor one-eighth-mile (201 meter) track at Madison Square Garden. On his return to England, George arranged another series of races with Cummings over the same distances they had run in 1885.

The mile race took place on August 23, 1886, at Lillie Bridge, before 25,000 excited fans. The central quarter-mile bicycle track had been carefully leveled and measured and was in splendid condition. George looked well and confident but nervous. Cummings looked thin and drawn. He wore an elastic stocking that hinted of a bad ankle. Jack White again started the runners and as in their first match George set the pace, running to his 4:12 mile schedule. Cummings followed two yards behind ready to strike when he felt the time was ripe. George went through the first quarter in 58½ seconds, the half in 2:02.

On the third lap Cummings pulled alongside George, forcing him to increase the pace. Both runners reached the three-quarter mile mark in 3:07 — only a second off George's schedule. At the beginning of the last quarter mile George's face clearly showed the strain of the fast pace. Sensing his chance to put George away, Cummings made his move, intending to sprint to the finish or until one of them dropped from exhaustion. On the backstretch he forged an eight-yard lead with George trying desperately to hang on. But Cummings had overestimated how far he could sprint after a fast three-quarters of a mile. With 200 yards to go, he began to slow and with 150 remaining George was again on his shoulder. Seventy yards from the finish Cummings suddenly staggered and fell senseless. George, unaware of what had happened to Cummings, kept up the torrid pace. He crossed the finish line in 4:12¾ to the wild cheering of the crowd. George had achieved his life's ambition — becoming the greatest miler of his age.

The two men raced each other several more times but nothing could compare with this "Mile of the Century." One late 19th century sports writer described George's feat as "the finest performance in the authentic annals of athleticism, irrespective of distance or class of contest, in fact, a performance beside which the picked feats of cycling, swimming, and all other sports pale their ineffectual fires."*

Cummings, after a business life in England, returned to his native Scotland and

---

*George may have run an even faster mile in practice. According to a letter he wrote to Guy Butler in 1937, he ran a time trial in 4:10¼ in 1885 just prior to his first race with Cummings. He also said he ran 59:29 for 12 miles (19.3 km) and 49:29 for 10 miles in practice.

William Cummings (in white) and Walter George in their 10-mile race on September 28, 1885, when Cummings set a record of 51:06⅗. George was suffering from a mysterious illness (*The Graphic*, October 5, 1885).

died at Glasgow on July 13, 1919, at age 62. George wasn't as successful after his running days and suffered financial hardship in his old age. A group of Fleet Street journalists learned of his difficulties and saw that he and his wife lived their last days in relative comfort. He was often seen in his later years pacing the track on the *News of the World* grounds, perhaps reliving in his memory the glory days of his youth. Walter George died on June 4, 1943, at age 84.

George's mile record was not approached by amateurs or professionals until well into the 20th century. As the 19th century drew to a close, America moved into the lead in amateur track and field. The 1880s were the heyday of amateur athletic clubs in America and there was furious competition to field the strongest track and field team. The two biggest rivals were the famed New York and Manhattan athletic clubs. In 1885 champion English miler Edward C. Carter came to America and joined the New York Athletic Club. He won the amateur championships in 1886 and 1887 in both the mile and five miles (8 km), breaking the five-mile record. The Manhattan Athletic club, not to be outdone, recruited A. B. George, Walter George's younger brother, from England, and Thomas Patrick Conneff from Ireland.

These "imported" amateurs brought with them quality competition and increased interest in amateur distance running. Tommy Conneff was already famous when he came to America in 1888. He had defeated E. C. Carter at four miles in 1887 before a crowd of 20,000 in Dublin with a time of 19:44⅖. Conneff proved to be the best of the "adopted" amateurs and dominated the mile in America. In 1893 he broke George's amateur mile record by running 4:17⅘ but that same year Englishman Fred E. Bacon lowered the amateur record to 4:17. Bacon, as a professional in 1897, broke Deerfoot's record for one hour. Paced by a cyclist, he covered 11 miles, 1,243 yards.

Conneff disliked training and from 1893 to 1895 disappeared from the public eye. In 1895 the United States was preparing for the match between New York and London Athletic Clubs and the American coach Mike Murphy recruited Conneff and put him on a strict three-month course of training at Travers Island. The result was astonishing. On August 21, 1895, after working all night as a Pullman-car conductor, he ran a three-quarter-mile handicap race in Boston. He won the race in 3:02⅘, a time that wasn't bettered until 1931.

The United States held trials at Travers Island in the autumn of 1895 to pick its international team. In this meet Conneff ran the fastest amateur mile of the 19th century. George W. Orton, the intercollegiate mile champion, paced the first lap in 62⅗ and

then fell back. Conneff ran the second and third laps alone, both in 64⅕ seconds. E. C. Carter joined him on the last lap and set the pace as Conneff ran 64⅘ and finished in 4:15⅗.

For the first time, a fast mile had been run at almost even pace. Milers in the 19th century normally ran the first lap very fast, floated the middle part of the race and ended with a sprint. Unfortunately, Conneff's even pacing was probably an accident. Conneff later explained his approach to running the mile:

I have often thought that the secret of my success to a great extent lies in the fact that I punished myself more than other men. I go the first quarter on my speed. By the time I reach the half I am getting quite weary. At the three-quarter pole I feel dead to the world but I go another quarter because I have to and because I make myself do it.

His coach, Mike Murphy, discussed pacing the mile in *College Athletics* (1906):

In actual racing the first quarter should be run fast, for it is then that time can be made without unduly distressing the runner. The second and third quarters will naturally be slower, as the strain upon the heart, lungs and legs becomes greater. By the time the last quarter is reached a reaction should have set in and this, combined with the runner's determination to run fast and to win out, will make the last quarter fast.

From these statements it appears that neither Murphy nor Conneff believed even pacing was the best way to run a fast mile. Conneff's amateur mile record was not beaten until 16 years later by John Paul Jones of Cornell University.

In the International match, on September 21, 1895, Conneff won the mile with ease in 4:18⅕. It was evident to all present that he could have taken several seconds off this time but instead he saved himself for the three miles held later in the day, which he also won. By 1896 he was perhaps past his prime. He turned professional and ran a series of three races with British professional Fred E. Bacon. Unfortunately, Conneff was suffering from malaria and Bacon won all three races in times much slower than both men were capable of running.

On August 21, 1897, at Worcester, Massachusetts, Conneff met the fine Irish professional George "Gander" Tincler. Conneff again suffered a stinging defeat as Tincler set a fast pace of 61, 2:04½, and 3:08 and coasted home in 4:15⅕ which was the fastest mile run in America up to that time. Conneff asked for a rematch, but with a 25-yard start. Tincler agreed, and again won in 4:17. Conneff then retired from running and died tragically at the age of 46. He was found drowned near Manila, in the Philippine Islands, in October 1912, where he was a sergeant in the 7th United States Cavalry.

During a 25-year career, Tincler ran many races in Australia, Canada, South

George B. Tincler was the 19th century runner who came the closest to Walter George's mile record (from Alfred Downer, *Running Recollections*, 1908).

Africa and America. He defeated all the top milers of his day and was a crowd favorite. Although he never improved on his 4:15 1/5 mile,* he won 40 of 41 races in 1897-1898. Tincler competed successfully until 1916 when he was 41 years old.

Thomas P. Conneff lowered the amateur mile record to 4:15⅗ in 1895. His low arm carriage was typical of American middle-distance runners of the time (*Munsey's Magazine,* 1901).

---

*Tincler never ran faster than 4:15 in public but in a trial in 1898, he reportedly ran a mile in 4:09.

## Two and Three Miles

The first account of a runner breaking 10 minutes for two miles (3.22 km) is from 1777 when Englishman Joseph Headley ran two miles in 9:45 on the Knavesmire high road. Headley's performance had been forgotten or disregarded by most pedestrian fans in the spring of 1836 when James Metcalf attempted, for a bet of £100, to run two miles in 10 minutes on Sunbury Common. On the morning of the attempt, there was such a gale, that everyone agreed to wait until the afternoon. The wind finally died down and Metcalf, running at an even pace, finished in 9:41. This was considered an amazing performance. Abraham Wood, the speediest distance runner of his day, had twice failed in attempts to break 10 minutes.

James Pudney, on April 7, 1852, at the Copenhagen House Grounds, ran a 4:38 first mile then came back with 5:00 to record 9:38 in a tough race with James Byrom, whom he had given a 25-yard start. It was not until April 20, 1861, in a memorable race between Jack "the Gateshead Clipper" White and James "Treacle" Sanderson, that the record was lowered again. They met at the Copenhagen Grounds, and raced for a bet of £50. Sanderson received a 20-yard start, and a tough struggle was anticipated. To complete the distance, the men had to run 108 yards less than six laps.

On the first lap, White gained five yards, and on reaching the stands the second time had almost made up the 20 yards. Passing Sanderson on the third lap, White took a three-yard lead. Sanderson, however, was not to be shaken off, and drew even at the mile, which they covered in 4:28. White then took a four-yard lead and kept it until the last lap. Sanderson made another effort, but White had the most left and won by eight yards, in 9:20.

WILLIAM LANG
"THE CROWCATCHER"—
TWO MILES IN 9:11 IN 1863

On Saturday, August 1, 1863, an immense crowd at the City Ground in Manchester witnessed one of the greatest races of the 19th century. Both William Lang and his opponent Sanderson were in top shape. Less than a month earlier Lang had defeated Sanderson at one mile in 4:21½, a best-on-record time. The track was circular, and measured 800 yards, requiring the men to run four laps plus an additional 320 yards. Sanderson at once took a four-yard lead and the two stayed in this position for the first lap, both running in "splendid style."

On the back stretch of the second lap Sanderson began to leave Lang farther in the rear, amid the deafening shouts of the crowd. Lang gradually narrowed the gap, but on passing the stands the last time, both men began to feel the effects of their 4:28 first mile. Going down the back stretch, Lang gradually crept up on Sanderson and finally shot in front about 450 yards from the finish. Sanderson made a desperate effort and again caught Lang and they ran side by side, amid great cheering. But he couldn't match Lang's seven-foot stride. Entering the straight run home, Lang was five yards ahead which he improved to six at the finish. His winning time of 9:11½ wouldn't be bettered until 1903.

Lang, who was born in London on December 11, 1838, had many firsts to his credit. In 1863 he and Jack White had run a 29:50 six miles (9.7 km) in a memorable race with Deerfoot. At Manchester on July 18, 1863, Lang ran a world's best mile and a quarter in 5:35½. Lang competed throughout the 1860s.

In America during the 1860s and '70s some race courses were accurately measured with competent timers, but many were not. This makes it difficult to tell how good some of the American runners of this era really were. A prime example is William Edgar

William Lang "The Crowcatcher" is best known for his two-mile record of 9:11½ set in 1864, a mark not approached again in the 19th century (*Outing*, June 1901).

Harding from Toronto, Canada, who ran from 1863 to 1869. As a young man Harding moved to New York and the city claimed him as its own. His most notable races were with De Kelso "the Wonder," champion of Canada. De Kelso, his father an Indian and his mother a French Canadian, had run a 9:14 two miles over a course that was probably short.

In August of 1867 Harding traveled to Aurelia, Canada, to race De Kelso for stakes of $2,000. Harding appeared on the track wearing yellow silk tights and shirt, blue star-spangled trunks, a red belt with the word Champion and spikeless shoes. De Kelso wore white tights, blue shirt, brown trunks, the Union Jack around his loins and

spiked shoes. At the word "Go," both darted away. De Kelso got off first because of Harding's over-anxiety, but Harding caught up and took a slight lead at 30 yards. The partisan crowd cheered De Kelso and booed the American. Harding's first mile was reported as 4:14 to De Kelso's 4:20.

The second mile was timed in 4:30 and the third in 4:25. Harding won the three-mile race in the unbelievable time of 13:09. De Kelso's losing time was 13:19. These incredible times caused the *New York Clipper* to write: "We don't wish to distract in the least from Harding's merits, but the time is so extraordinarily fast that nobody posted in such matters will credit it until the proper test is made."

Harding's backer, a Mr. Davis, offered to wager $4,000 that Harding could run three miles in 13:10 on the accurately-measured Fashion Course on Long Island. There were no takers, although the *Clipper* thought that had a reasonable sum been named someone would have taken the bet. Harding ran other incredible times on what were in all probability short courses—a 9:06 two miles and a repeat victory over De Kelso on the same Aurelia course in 13:03.

In 1867, Harding sent a challenge to *Bell's Life* in London offering to run Fleet, Mills, Lang, Sanderson or any man in England a three mile race for $5,000. He also offered expenses for the race to be run in the United States. The prospects of such a match created a great deal of excitement. Although few believed Harding's three mile times, his victories over De Kelso gave him a legitimate claim to "Champion Three-Mile Runner of the U.S."

After a series of proposals and counter proposals with Edward Mills and his backer, the challenge was finally taken up in 1868 by 28-year-old William Lang "the Crow-catcher." Lang arrived in Philadelphia in October and offered to race Harding at any distance from a half mile upwards. By this time Harding hadn't raced for almost a year and had taken a job as sports editor of the

William Harding, "Three Mile Champion of America," in 1866. His best times were run on questionable-length courses (from William Edgar Harding, *The American Athlete*, ca. 1881).

*New York Daily News.* He promised to race Lang in the spring, but the match never took place and a disappointed Lang returned to England. Unfortunately, it is unlikely that we will ever know how fast Harding could actually run three miles.

A contemporary of George and Cummings was Scottish professional Peter "Paddy" Cannon. Cannon was almost unbeatable from two to four miles, and defeated Walter George in a two mile match at the old Victoria Running Grounds, Govan. At Glasgow on May 5, 1888, Cannon ran the three miles in 14:19½, beating Jack White's 1863 record of 14:36, and on November 8, 1888, surpassed Jack White's four-mile record by running 19:25⅖.

## Cross Country

*I doubt whether any man ever feels more thoroughly satisfied with his physical condition or more keenly anticipates the pleasures which such condition has fit him to enjoy, than a well-trained Cross-Country runner.*—Ernest Harold Baynes (1898)

In 1850, an undergraduate at Exter College named Halifax Wyatt complained to his friends that he would rather run the steeplechase course than ride it on a horse that had just thrown him in a race. This led to a steeplechase footrace at Blinsey, near Oxford, later that year. The first man to complete the two-mile course with 24 jumps was Wyatt himself. Rugby School started an annual steeplechase foot race in 1858 to honor Tom Hughes and his popular novel *Tom Brown's School Days*, published a year earlier. In December 1867, the Thames Rowing Club, also inspired by Hughes's novel, organized the Thames Handicap Steeplechase No. 1, the first of 44 such races. Although this race was "treated more as a joke than anything else," the second race attracted quality runners from the London Athletic Club. Hughes attended, acting as judge, and the event's success led to the formation of the Thames Hare and Hounds Club. By 1889, London had 30 more such clubs.

The first English Cross Country Championships were held in Epping Forest in 1876, but when all competitors went off course the race was declared void. The inaugural National Championship is therefore considered to have been the 1877 race over the 11.25-mile (18.1 km) course at Roehampton.

In the early days of cross country, race promoters sometimes experimented with various ways of scoring the race. Four, five and six-man teams were all tried. In some meets the team with the lowest average time was the winner, but the system of adding up finish places and taking the lowest score proved simpler.

On November 10, 1883, the Thames Hare and Hounds club tried a curious handicapping experiment. All the runners started together but were handicapped, horse-racing style, by carrying different amounts of weight. Each runner could carry his allotted weight (up to 28 pounds/12.7 kg) any way he chose. The majority carried their handicaps in knapsacks. One runner wrapped

A Paper Chase of Thames Hare and Hounds (*Frank Leslie's Illustrated Newspaper*, November 8, 1879).

metal bands around his waist but they kept falling off. E. M. Wilson, the winner, ran "splendidly and carried his 17 pounds (7.7 kg) easily." The promoters must have considered the experiment a failure as this method of handicapping never caught on.

The first U.S. Hare and Hounds club, the Westchester Hare and Hounds, was not formed until 1878. Getting a rule book from the Thames Hare and Hounds Club in England, the Westchester club held its first run on Thanksgiving Day, 1878. A hound's uniform included a scarlet jacket, with black buttons, black knickerbockers and stockings and a black cap with a visor. The hares wore black jerseys with the scarlet figure of a hare on the chest. As in England, the sport gradually changed and cross country races over measured courses replaced Hare and Hounds races.

The New York Athletic Club held the first important cross country race in the U.S. on November 6, 1883, at Mott Haven. Two dozen runners entered this "Cross Country Championship of America," including the great Lon Myers. The course, starting down a steep hill, was billed as five miles but was probably only about four. Although the race was far beyond his best distance, Myers took the lead at the bottom of the hill, bounding over a four-board fence. Many spectators on horseback and in carriages followed the race. Myers and Delaney shared the lead for the first three miles until Myers got stuck in a fence and faded badly after getting free. Delaney won with Myers finishing seventh. One runner managed to lose his trousers during the race and came in covered with "confusion and a horse blanket."

### THE STRANGE LIFE AND DEATH OF "WILLIE" DAY

Near the end of the 19th century, cross country had become popular with athletes in both Britain and the United States. Spectator interest, however, was usually slim,

*Top:* Hares scattering "scent" in an 1879 Westchester Hare and Hounds race. Their dress is rather formal by today's standards (*Frank Leslie's Illustrated Newspaper*, November 8, 1879). *Bottom:* First race for the Cross-Country Championship of America, November 6, 1883 (*Frank Leslie's Illustrated Newspaper*, November 17, 1883).

even at the big meets. Courses ranged from five to ten miles in length and were usually more difficult than modern ones.

Since it is nearly impossible to compare performances on different courses, to say nothing of different countries, rating 19th century cross country runners is very difficult. But if we cannot determine who was the best, we can at least acknowledge one of the strangest: American William D. "Willie" Day, who is probably unknown to most modern cross country runners. In some respects, his career foreshadowed that of the legendary Steve Prefontaine.

Day, who was 5 feet, 5 inches (1.65 m) tall and weighed 106 pounds (48 kg), began his career in 1889 when he joined the New Jersey Athletic Club in Bergen Point, New Jersey. He was a strange young man — slim, pale, small-limbed, with a flat chest and long body. Having no coach, he seldom trained but spent his time cavorting around the track or swimming and rowing, usually by himself. He appeared to live on pies, doughnuts, and sarsaparilla, smoked cigarettes and was said to be fond of strong drink. Despite all these faults, he displayed remarkable speed, courage, and endurance in his running.

Although Day was best known for cross country, his first great race was on a track. On October 26, 1889, at the Staten Island Athletic Club games, a dull, nasty fog hung close among the treetops, and the far end of the track was indistinct and blurry in the dampness and mist. Rain fell occasionally as the runners warmed up for the open handicapped ten-mile race. Day was offered a one-minute handicap but refused and started from scratch with the two favorites, Englishmen E. C. Carter and Sydney Thomas. Carter was the holder of the American record of 52 minutes 58 seconds for ten miles, and Thomas, a year earlier, had been the champion cross country runner of England. The New York Athletic Club had recruited both men.

By the ninth mile (14.5 km), Day had

passed these two men and was gaining on the three runners still ahead of him. Although he failed to overtake one runner who had started with a 3:25 handicap, Day ran the last mile in a remarkable 4:56 and finished in 52 minutes 38 seconds, an American record. This was over a minute slower than George's and Cummings's times for ten miles in England, but Day's youth and strong finish promised faster times to come.

Day's greatest race was on March 16, 1890 — an eight-mile cross country handicap at Morris Park, New York. A rain that had begun early Friday continued until Saturday morning. Then came a few hours of damp, sticky snow, followed by a raw cutting wind from the north. Nevertheless, more than 200 brave souls showed up to run the race, including Day's rival Sidney Thomas. The course consisted of two four-mile circuits where the runners had to twice cross a combined hedge and ditch and jump, climb, or crawl over ten fences. The first two miles had 12 miles of soft sloppy turf while the last two were bare dirt or plowed fields covered with ankle-deep to knee-deep mud.

Day started from scratch, giving Thomas 30 seconds and the rest of the field up to seven and a half minutes. As Day stood shivering in the cold, waiting for his turn to start, a stranger would have picked the frail young runner as one of the first to quit. Finally, with none of the other runners in sight, he got the word to go.

He caught Thomas at 2.5 miles (4 km) and worked his way through the pack, which was now strung out for nearly two miles. At the start of the last mile, two "limit-men" with handicaps of 6:30 and 6:45 were all that remained ahead of him. The run home was down a famous ¾-mile straight that had been a stumbling block for many outstanding runners. The rain had turned it into a sea of deep, clinging slime. Starting the straight, Day seemed to stagger and looked exhausted, but he gathered himself for a final effort. Giving it everything he had down the straight, he strode over the finish line, covered with mud and bruised from falls, but the winner of the race. After the race, the *New York Clipper* wrote: "If Day keeps his good health until a few added years shall mature his strength, he will eclipse the fame and wipe out the records of all his predecessors on either side of the Atlantic."

Two months later he won the National Cross Country Championships with ridiculous ease. He joked with the judges at each flag and jumped the hurdles that his pursuers climbed, crawled and rolled over. Finishing "as if he had been out for an easy jog," he vaulted a fence and ran up the hill to the dressing room, where he took a shower and was having a rubdown when the second-place runner finished.

In August 1894 — by which time he had won two five-mile national championships, two national individual cross country championships, and held most of the American records from two to ten miles — Day was arrested because he failed to account for $112 he had collected for the Manhattan Laundry where he worked. Being extremely shy, he was deeply troubled by the publicity. A friend posted bail and Day was allowed to go home, but he didn't tell his parents about being arrested.

The next morning he sauntered into the office of the New Jersey Athletic Club. On the wall was a large poster announcing the club's upcoming Labor Day games. In large letters, the poster read: TWO MILE SCRATCH RACE — W. D. DAY, NJAC CHAMPION OF AMERICA AND METROPOLITAN ASSOCIATION; GEORGE JARVIS NYAC; GEORGE ORTON OF NYAC; H. J. WALSH OF AAA; A. O. HOLLAN OF PAC .

Day glanced at the poster and laughingly remarked, "Well, boys, I guess I must run a hard and long race to win against such men as those, but I guess I will run, seeing that they have got my name printed in big letters like that."

Those were the last words anyone ever

heard him say. He picked up the New York morning papers and glanced through them. Five minutes later he left the room, and, although no one noticed it then, loungers at the club afterward remembered that Day's face was white and his features seemed hard and fixed. When someone picked up the papers Day had been reading they found them all folded, showing prominently the story of his arrest.

He dashed out of the clubhouse toward a strip of woods that he had run through many times before. When he tried to jump a ditch, he tumbled into the water. Two women saw him fall and one laughingly remarked, "Wille Day is a better runner than jumper." He sprang up, uninjured, and disappeared into a thicket. Nobody ever saw him alive after that. His body was found two days later hanging from the upper branches of a small wild cherry tree. The tree was in full view of the track where he had performed many of his most brilliant running feats.

Day's death was officially declared a suicide, but newspaper reports hinted of things they were unwilling to print. He had told a friend that he was "in trouble with a woman" and needed $150 at once. If he could not get the money he said he would leave town and not run in the Labor Day race. Reports also circulated that he had been hounded and fired at from ambush by a brother of the young woman. Two newspaper accounts said that his feet and one of his arms were securely tied when he was found. One reporter offered the hard-to-believe explanation that Day, a sailor, was an expert at tying knots and had tied himself up.

Whatever the reason for his death, he was not a thief. In a letter to the *New York Times* accompanying his obituary, the manager of the laundry admitted that a "grave error" had been made in charging Day — that he had never taken any money from the firm.

In 1890, the City College of New York,

William D. "Willie" Day (*Frank Leslie's Weekly*, September 21, 1893).

the University of Pennsylvania and Cornell took part in the first intercollegiate cross country race in the United States, with Pennsylvania winning. Michael C. Murphy explained the importance of cross country in his book *Athletic Training* (1914):

> Prior to the Olympic Games of 1908 the U.S. was distinctly inferior to England at all events from the half mile upward. Nearly all of our original ideas on training came from England. Upon this foundation the U.S. has made great improvement and has developed many ideas which England is now copying. England's superiority was due to the fact that Englishmen were taught to run distances from their youth up. Such games as the paper-chase and hare and hounds were almost a part of the English boy's education. With this as a foundation it was easy and natural for England to produce good distance runners. It was not until the U.S. began to foster Cross Country that we began to develop good distance runners.

# Ten Miles

## THE 10-MILE CHAMPION'S BELT— A CLASSIC RACE IN 1852

In 1852, John Garratt, proprietor of the Copenhagen House, offered a "Champion's Belt" for runners. The belt was worth about £25 and the owner earned the right to the title "Champion" of runners at the popular 10-mile distance. Whoever held the belt had to defend it against all challengers for a year before taking permanent possession. The struggle for the "Champion's Belt" led to an exciting series of races and a substantial lowering of the world's best time for 10 miles.

All the best distance runners in England showed up at the Copenhagen House track on January 12, 1852, to try to become the first holder of the belt. Despite heavy rains, 6,000 spectators came to see the race. George Frost, "the Suffolk Stag," took the lead on the fourth lap and won the 10-mile race on the muddy track in 54:09. Ireland's most heralded runner, John Levett, who had won all but two of his 31 professional matches, quickly challenged Frost for the belt. Nearly 25,000 spectators assembled at the "Cope" on March 22 to see the second race in the series.

The two men started cautiously with Frost taking a slight lead. On the third mile Levett put on a spurt, took the lead, and tried to pull away, but the "Stag" hung on gamely. The pace became faster and faster as the miles went by — each mile taking just more than five minutes. By the sixth mile Levett had struggled to a 30-yard lead, but Frost battled back in the next mile and moved ahead slightly. Frost kept the lead to the start of the backstretch of the last lap when Levett drew even and finally pulled ahead to win in an astonishing 52:35. The course was remeasured and owing to the corners having been widened for horse racing, turned out to be 250 yards long. This was a sure sign that even faster times were to come.

*Top:* George Frost leading the first race for the Ten-Mile Championship Belt at the Copenhagen House Grounds on January 12, 1852 (*Illustrated London Times,* January 16, 1852). *Bottom:* Another view of the race. Note the track's sharp corners and that the men are running shirtless in January (The Old Print Shop, New York).

William Jackson, "the American Deer," soon gave notice that he too, was ready to challenge for the belt. Jackson, now 31 years old, had just returned from his second racing trip to America and many thought his best running days were behind him. He proved his critics wrong on March 29, 1852, in a 20-mile (32.2 km), non-championship race with Levett and 10 others. The diminutive "Deer" took the lead in the third mile and, despite a painful ankle injury, went on to lap most of the field. Blazing the first 10 miles in 53:35, he put Levett 300 yards behind. He ran 11 miles in 59:20 — a distance no other runner had covered in an hour since the "Deer" himself had accomplished the feat in 1845. Despite his lameness he passed 15 miles in an hour and 22 minutes, a new record, before slowing to a walk because of his injury. Unable to shake off the effects of the injury, Jackson watched helplessly as Levett eventually trotted past for an easy win. Jackson, despite his injury, immediately challenged Levett for the belt.

This race took place on May 31, 1852, at the Copenhagen grounds. Jackson, running the race of his life, opened a 30-yard lead on Levett which he continued to increase until the end of the race. His mile splits as reported in *Bell's Life* and *Spirit of the Times* were phenomenal:

| Mile | Time (*Bell's Life*) | (*Spirit of the Times*) |
| --- | --- | --- |
| 1. | 4:52 | 4:52 — Jackson by 40 yds. |
| 2. | 9:54 | 9:54 — Jackson by 40 yds. |
| 3. | 14:52 | 14:54 — Jackson by 60 yds. |
| 4. | 19:56 | 19:58 — Jackson by 100 yds. |
| 5. | 24:57 | 24:59 — Jackson by 200 yds. |
| 6. | 30:04 | 30:06 — Jackson by 300 yds. |
| 7. | 35:13 | 35:15 — Jackson by 350 yds. |
| 8. | 40:20 | 40:22 |
| 9. | 45:21 | 45:23 — Jackson by ⅓ mile |
| 10. | About 52 min | 51:34 |

Levett, when lapped by Jackson near the end of the race, quit. Jackson continued running for two-thirds of the last lap then walked the last 200 yards. Confusion exists as to Jackson's time for the race. The *Bell's Life* reporter stopped timing when Levett quit and gave Jackson "about 52 minutes." The *Spirit of the Times* correspondent, however, gave Jackson 6:11 for the last mile (including his 200-yard walk) and recorded a total time of 51:34.

Had Jackson run the entire 10 miles, his time would have been about 50:45. It may seem strange that he should stop and walk when he was running the best race of his life, but in order to encourage future races, a professional could never show more of his running prowess than absolutely necessary. Records were worth little except perhaps bragging rights. In most cases, it was only when a pro was forced to go all out to win that the public saw his true potential.

A sub 51-minute 10 mile — something no runner achieved in public during the 19th century — was within Jackson's grasp. He was satisfied, however, with winning the match and regaining possession of the belt. He would never run this fast again and had he ran out the 10 miles perhaps he would have been considered the best distance runner of the 19th century. His eight and nine mile times were considered best-on-record performances. Levett immediately asked for a rematch and Jackson replied that he would abide by the terms of the belt. He added drily that he "thought he could run once, but had only one good leg now."

After the race, Jackson left London for a rest and it was a long time before he and Levett could agree on a new match. Levett conceded that he had taken Jackson too lightly and vowed to reclaim the belt. The race finally took place on October 11, 1852, and this time Levett was ready. Jackson took the lead and tried to pull away as before. Levett, however, never let Jackson get more than five yards ahead. At eight miles Levett seemed to weaken but still managed to hang with Jackson. With 80 yards to go they were even, but Levett had a slightly better finishing sprint than Jackson and won by two yards in 51:42. Jackson, before leaving the course, challenged Levett to yet another contest.

Unfortunately, the race never took place. Levett "went into business," becoming host and trainer at the Garrick Tavern in Sheffield. Despite the rules governing ownership of the belt, he ignored Jackson's challenges. Jackson was furious and wrote many angry letters to *Bell's Life* demanding that Levett give up the belt. After losing the belt to Frost in 1853, Levett eventually regained it and in 1854 surpassed Jackson's one-hour run record by covering 11 miles, 350 yards, in 59:20. Levett then retired and wrote a book about running, *How to Train* (1862).

Jackson made the first of many retirements from running in 1853. He used his winnings to open a nursery raising cucumbers. A disastrous fire in late 1854 destroyed the nursery and forced him out of retirement. He ran for many more years although he set no more records. Much later in 1892, Sir John Astley, the nearest thing to a patron saint 19th century runners ever had, put on a benefit 10-mile race for runners over 50 to raise money for Jackson. The "Deer," like many retired professional runners of the time, had become "short of coin" in his old age. Even at age 72, Jackson would have placed in this race for men with shrunken shanks had his old ankle injury not given him trouble. At a dinner afterward, Astley presented the £25 proceeds to the well-preserved relic. Jackson, in turn, gave each guest a portrait of himself in his glory days.

John Levett, champion runner of Ireland, ran 10 miles in 51:42 on October 11, 1852 (*Illustrated Sporting & Dramatic News*, June 7, 1862).

## DEERFOOT— GREATEST AMERICAN DISTANCE RUNNER OF THE 19TH CENTURY

Running has long been of special importance to Native Americans. Before the coming of the white man, Indians ran to deliver messages, to fight, to hunt and to recreate their myths. For the most part, the running feats of 19th century Indians are lost to us because few of them ran on the white man's tracks where they could be timed over accurate distances. The story of Louis Bennett, better known as Deerfoot, shows what a 19th century American Indian could achieve given proper incentives and first class coaching and training.

Like fellow American George Seward,

Deerfoot achieved greatness while running in England. Unlike Seward, Deerfoot was known for endurance rather than speed. He was a Seneca Indian, born on the Catarangus Reservation in Erie County, New York. Deerfoot's gravestone in Forest Lawn Cemetery in Buffalo says he was born in 1830 but other sources say 1828, 1826 or 1825.

The champion runner of the Eagle tribe, Deerfoot ran his first professional race in 1856 at a county fair in Fredonia, New York, not many miles from the Indian reserve. He received $50 for winning the five mile race in a sizzling time of 25 minutes flat. Because of lack of attention to course measuring and timing in the United States during this period the fast time caused few ripples in sporting circles. Later that year, John Grindell, champion of American long-distance runners, traveled to New York to race the Indian. To everyone's surprise, Deerfoot easily defeated Grindell.

In June 1861 a wily English promoter and trainer named George Martin brought three runners to New York to test their speed against the Americans. Among them was Jack White, the "Gateshead Clipper." Martin planned to enter White in races in the Northeastern United States, back him heavily, and make some money before the American pedestrian fans discovered how good White really was. White and a fellow Englishman named Mower raced Native Americans Deerfoot and Albert Smith at 10 miles on June 10, 1861, at the Fashion Course on Long Island. Deerfoot led through the first mile in 4:49 with White close behind. The second mile went by in 5:20 as Deerfoot and White left the others far behind.

Deerfoot's running wasn't pretty. The tall (almost six feet/1.8 m) 160 pound (72.7 kg) Indian had a long, powerful stride but ran with a peculiar rocking-rolling gait, swinging his body from side to side and rolling his head. In contrast, the much smaller White ran with an easy, catlike grace. At the end of six miles White fell 30 yards behind, but on the seventh he man-aged to catch up and took the lead by 15 yards. Deerfoot struggled gamely to over-take White and gained slightly, but with three miles to go slowed to a walk, conceding the race to White who jogged the rest of the 10 miles to finish in 59:56. Although Deerfoot lost the race, he impressed Martin who agreed to take him to England to race the top British pedestrians.

On September 9, 1861, a month after Deerfoot arrived, he ran his first race on English soil. This six-mile race on London's 260-yard Hackney Wick track was against 20-year-old Edward Mills. Mills was part of a trio of remarkable English long-distance runners of the early 1860s. When in top shape, any of these three pedestrians (Mills, White and William Lang) was capable of beating Deerfoot or anyone else.

Deerfoot made a dramatic appearance for his first race in England, shedding his wolf-skin cloak and parading around the grounds. On his head was a small red band trimmed in gold which held a single eagle's feather. Around his waist was a short red apron with a row of small brass bells that jingled as he ran. A bead necklace and earrings completed the outfit. He was offered a pair of spikes, but he sneered and tossed them aside, saying he preferred moccasins.

A pistol shot started the two runners on their 41-lap journey. The bare-chested Indian and the much smaller Mills in long-sleeved shirt, tights and scarlet shorts brought forth a roar from the 4,000 spectators that would last the entire race. Deerfoot was in poor condition. His long crossing had caused him to gain weight and reportedly his trainer had a hard time getting him to submit to the customary British training regime. Mills was also short of training because of a bad foot. Deerfoot managed to stay with Mills as they rounded the sharp turns of the small track. He even surged into the lead several times before Mills drew away on the last lap to win by about 10 yards in a respectable 32:31. Deerfoot had lost his

**Deerfoot the Seneca Indian running in England in 1862 (The Old Print Shop, New York).**

first race in England but had proven immensely popular with the spectators.

After the race Deerfoot and his backers were overwhelmed with challenges. During the rest of 1861 he traveled throughout England running 15 more races in 13 weeks against the best runners in England. Remarkably, he won all of these races except for tying the last. In addition, Deerfoot proved that he was a first-class showman. In one race his opponent, Mills, collapsed from exhaustion and the crowd came pouring onto the track. Having eight laps to go to win the race, Deerfoot gave a ringing war-whoop, grabbed a small flagpole and used it as a tomahawk to clear his way through the bewildered spectators. In an-

other race his opponent, Barker, was leading but developed a cramp and suddenly grabbed his side. The eagle-eyed Deerfoot spotted Barker's difficulty immediately and with a bound and a whoop, threw up his arms and dashed to the front, letting everyone know he had chalked up another victory.

Deerfoot's favorite tactic was surging or "spurting" at various points in the race. The top British runners usually ran the first mile of a four to 10-mile race in just less than five minutes. They then settled into a relatively even pace a bit slower than five minutes per mile until the sprint for the finish. Deerfoot's surging was devastating. The British runners quickly adopted it but, possibly because they didn't have his strength, it was not as effective for them. No one knows why Deerfoot ran as he did. He may have just been a naturally uninhibited runner who ran as he felt at the moment. On the other hand, George Martin — his trainer and running "wizard" — controlled the tempo of Deerfoot's exhibition races of 1862 and may have regulated the pace in at least some of his legitimate races also.

In November of 1861 the Prince of Wales — the future King Edward VII — invited Deerfoot to run in a six-mile race at Cambridge. Deerfoot won the race and the prince congratulated him afterward and presented him with a watch and two bank notes — mementos Deerfoot treasured to the end of his days. Later, the sports loving prince invited the American to dine with him and his party at the Red Lion hotel. Deerfoot, "after being liberally plied with champagne, treated the company to a war song and finished it off with his most powerful whoops."

One of the changes that Deerfoot brought to British pedestrianism was his popularity with British men and women of high society. Although few women attended pedestrian races of the time, many were intrigued by Deerfoot and wanted to see him

run. Obliging promoters fenced off reserved sections at many of his races allowing high society men and women to avoid mingling with the rowdy spectators common at these events. The promoters also had Deerfoot race in a "proper costume," consisting of a shirt and long pants in order not to offend the women's delicate Victorian sensibilities. Deerfoot also traded his moccasins for spiked running shoes for these races.

His last race of 1861 was an eight mile dead-heat with Mills at Hackney Wick on

*Left:* Deerfoot displaying mementos given to him by the Prince of Wales (*Illustrated Sporting & Dramatic News*, September 20, 1862). *Below:* Edward Mills leading Deerfoot in a six-mile race on December 26, 1862, at Hackney Wick. Deerfoot is racing in "English" costume including spikes. Mills won by 100 yards (*Illustrated Sporting and Dramatic News*, January 3, 1863).

December 16. This race, added to his grueling race schedule and endless travel, left him exhausted. He took a much needed month's rest in January of 1862, staying at the home of his trainer George Martin. Deerfoot's best race during 1861 had been on December 11, in a 10-mile race at Victoria grounds Yarmouth when he ran 52:31. This was an excellent performance but not fast enough to make him a legend.

While Deerfoot rested in early 1862, the ingenious Martin concocted a traveling "Deerfoot Circus." Sensing the public obsession with Deerfoot, Martin planned to exhibit him all over the British Isles. The planned tour required that Deerfoot compete nearly every day of the week except Sunday. In order to charge admission in towns with no enclosed race grounds, Martin had a portable race course enclosure of wood and canvas built. He also hired a group of runners to provide token opposition, the most notable of whom were the aging William Jackson and John Brighton, who was known as "the Norwich Milkboy" for running alongside milk-carts when he was a boy.

The usual race distance was four miles on the 220-yard enclosed track. Martin secretly orchestrated the races with subtle movements of his scoring book. These exhibitions were "fixed" since Martin thought it necessary for Deerfoot to always win in order to keep up interest. Yet Martin couldn't fool the knowledgeable pedestrian fans entirely. The "performers" had to run respectable times almost every day of the week.

The "Deerfoot running circus" wasn't as profitable as Martin had hoped and after visiting about 40 towns it ground to a halt when Martin was unable to pay the performers. William Jackson — still popular with pedestrian fans, but too old to win races— sued Martin for a week's salary (£4). Somehow Martin managed to continue the tour in July through Scotland and Ireland and by September had visited every major

city and dozens of smaller towns in the United Kingdom. According to Peter Lovesey in *Kings of Distance* (1968), Deerfoot "raced" more than 400 miles (644 km) and was seen by more than 150,000 people on this tour.

On October 23, 1862, Judge Frazer of the Wandsworth County court heard Jackson's suit against Martin. During the proceedings Jackson and Brighton admitted that the traveling Deerfoot Circus races were "fixed" for Deerfoot to win. This revelation created a storm of negative publicity that haunted Deerfoot the rest of his stay in England. Most of the public failed to understand the difference between the exhibitions of the Deerfoot Circus and Deerfoot's legitimate races.

Professional runners of Deerfoot's time normally ran only fast enough to win their races. But to restore Deerfoot's lost prestige, drastic measures were necessary. Regaining the public's confidence required proving, beyond any doubt, that Deerfoot was the best distance runner of his time. The only way he could do that was to run faster than anyone had ever run before and that's what Deerfoot set out to do.

On November 2, 1862, in his first race after the race-fixing news broke, Deerfoot ran a remarkable one-hour race at Brompton, setting his first world's best time. The early part of the race was like many others he had run, the first mile went by in 4:50, two in 9:57, three in 15:22, four in 20:40 and five in 25:55. Until the third lap of the sixth mile he and his opponent, Brighton, alternated leading. Suddenly Deerfoot, to the amazement of the spectators, "shot like a meteor ahead and finished the mile, amid vociferous cheering, between 50 and 60 yards ahead of Brighton." He continued to pour it on, finishing 10 miles in 52:22 and 11 in 57:51.

When the gun sounded to end the hour, Deerfoot had set a world's best for one hour by running 11 miles, 720 yards. Until this race only William Jackson, John

Levett and Jem Pudney had ever run 11 miles or more in an hour.*

Deerfoot improved his one-hour record slightly to 11 miles, 790 yards on January 12, 1863, at Hackney Wick, this time against Mills. He continued his record-breaking spree on February 28, at Brompton. Jones, Richards, John Brighton and White took turns as pacesetters for Deerfoot as he set out to run 11.5 miles (18.5 km) within the hour. He covered 10 miles in 51:57 and went on to perform the feat with relative ease, stopping with 16 seconds to spare when he reached 11.5 miles in 59:44. One reporter believed Deerfoot, "had it been required, could have done it in much less time."†

Deerfoot's record breaking improved his tarnished image considerably. *Bell's Life* for March 1, 1863, contained the following tribute:

> Of Deerfoot, it is but justice to say that, apart from any adventitious circumstances, he has, by his wonderful powers, immense stride, and speed, combined with endurance never equaled before, scattered any prejudice to the winds that may have been felt against him; and he is now acknowledged the most extraordinary pedestrian that has ever appeared in England.

Although he was setting records, Deerfoot's running became erratic during his last few months in England. When he lost, he was accused of drinking heavily and not

**Deerfoot and Lang at Brompton on April 3, 1863. Deerfoot set records at 10, 11, and 12 miles, as well as for the hour run (*Illustrated Sporting & Dramatic News*, April 11, 1863).**

*William Jackson ran 11 miles, 40 yards, two feet, four inches in January 1845 and 11 even in March 1852. John Levett ran 11 miles, 350 yards in 59:20 in August 1854. Jem Pudney ran 11 miles in 57:20 at Oxford on November 5, 1856.

†According to the August 23, 1884, Spirit of the Times, Deerfoot ran 12 miles (19.3 km) in 59:47 in a trial during his stay in England. This has not been confirmed, however.

training. In reality, he had been in England for a year and a half and was homesick. His grueling race schedule probably also contributed to his inconsistent performances.

On March 9, he lost a 10-mile race to Mills, who ran 53:24 but on Good Friday, April 3, 1863, he ran the race of his life — a classic 12-mile struggle with William "Crowcatcher" Lang at Hackney Wick. Lang was given a 100-yard start which turned out to be an ideal distance for him to act as a "rabbit."

As he started the race, Deerfoot reportedly gave a quick, defiant glance at the spectators, lifted his head high and "shot down the track with the fleetness of an arrow." Trying to overtake Lang, he ran the first three miles in 14:55 and covered six miles in 30:25, but at nine miles he was still 30 yards behind the fast-striding Lang. Deerfoot passed 10 miles in 51:26 — beating William Jackson's 1852 record of 51:34 — and managed to draw even with Lang.

Lang refused to concede and although Deerfoot passed 11 miles in 56:52 he couldn't put the "Crowcatcher" away. Halfway around the back stretch of the last lap Deerfoot again caught up and momentarily took the lead. Lang wouldn't give up and they ran abreast for the last 150 yards with Lang winning by half a yard. Deerfoot had lost the race, but few cared about that. What everyone would remember were his times. He finished the 12-mile race in a record 62:02½. Along the way he had set new records for the hour run (11 miles, 970 yards) and had also run the fastest times ever for 10 and 11 miles. The 10-mile record would last for 21 years, the one-hour record for 34.

Deerfoot competed for another month but won no more races in England. He ran his last race there on May 11, 1863, at Hackney Wick before 8,000 spectators. The crowd wanted to see the Indian run one last time. The stars of the race, however, were White and Lang. Both were in peak condition, and they believed that, despite his recent record breaking, Deerfoot was vulnerable if the early pace was fast enough. White set a "killing" pace, going past the mile in 4:40 and two miles in 9:39. He and Lang continued the torrid pace, covering three miles in 14:36.

Although Deerfoot ran the first three miles in less than 15 minutes, this wasn't his day. Between three and four miles he fell a lap (260 yds.) behind and, as was the custom on being lapped, stepped off the track. White and Lang went by four miles in 19:36, five in 24:49, and jointly became the first runners to break 30 minutes for six miles when they covered the distance in 29:50. Even after seven miles (34:45), White was still running at under a five-minutes-per-mile pace. Lang finally conceded first place and dropped back. With the race in hand, White also eased up, finishing the 10-mile race in 52:14. Both he and Lang had performed brilliantly. White — since he won the race — was given credit for world's-best times at three, four, five, six and seven miles. The crowd, however, had come to see Deerfoot and expressed great indignation at his career in England ending in this "most miserable failure."

On May 13, 1863, Deerfoot boarded the steamship *Great Eastern* and sailed for home, taking with him earnings of more than £1,000. When he reached the reservation, his Indian friends were astounded to see that the buttons on his coat were made of English sovereigns. Deerfoot used some of his winnings to buy a small farm where he lived the rest of his life. He had gained a measure of financial security from his trip to England, but the magic that for a brief time had made him the greatest distance runner the world had yet seen was gone. He never again approached the level of running he had done in England. Two years after his return to America he raced against horses in Chicago. He also competed in Buffalo and Cleveland before settling down in 1866 to spend the rest of his years on the Catarangus Reservation.

Not much is known of Deerfoot's

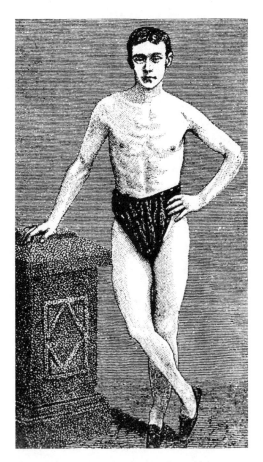

**Jack White, "The Gateshead Clipper," set records for 3 miles (14:36), 4 miles (19:36), 5 miles (24:49), 6 miles (29:50) and 7 miles on May 11, 1863, in a 10-mile race withi Deerfoot and Bill Lang (*Outing*, June 1901).**

training. According to some accounts he trained little if at all. The *Warren Centennial* (1895), written a year before Deerfoot died, gives a quite different account.

> When in training Deerfoot ran and walked at least 40 miles a day. His diet consisted of beer, mutton, chicken, vegetables, and at supper a glass of port wine or sherry. His trainer watched him with a watch in one hand and a whip in the other.... He trotted on a quarter-mile track some portion of the day, and walked the balance of his allotted 40-mile task.

The references to the use of a whip and 40 miles (64.4 km) a day training are almost surely exaggerations. The many quality races Deerfoot ran in 1861 and 1862 plus the almost daily exhibition races of the "Deerfoot Circus" tour probably contributed much to his high fitness level.

A year before his death, Deerfoot still had the competitive spirit and gift for showmanship that had thrilled the British pedestrian fans. In an interview that appeared in the *Oil City Derrick* in 1895, the 65-year-old Indian insisted that he was not a "has been," but was "ready to run any horse or man 10 miles, and bet his house and farm he could defeat them." He was honored (some accounts say exhibited) at the Chicago World's Fair in 1893 and died January 18, 1896.

George Martin, Deerfoot's trainer, was known as the "wizard of pedestrianism" for his innovative ideas and promotional abilities. He believed that all other sports sank into insignificance when compared with running. Despite some problems promoting Deerfoot, he had shown an uncanny sense of how to please running fans and many of the fastest races of the era had been run at his Royal Oak Grounds. White, Mills and Lang continued to race but concentrated on the mile as interest in pedestrianism in England declined. Martin's unexpected death two years after Deerfoot left England was a severe blow to the sport.

## The Great Six-Day Go-As-You-Please Races

*One good old gentleman at my club, pathetically besought me one day to abandon a [six-day Go-As-You-Please] competition that I was just starting; saying: "My dear Sir John, I feel sure you will some day be tried for manslaughter when one of your competitors dies on the track." I replied, "Worthy sir, I will bet you 'fifty' and leave it to our heirs and assigns to determine, that you die from want of exer-*

*cise before any one of the competitors dies from taking too much"; but, will you believe it? He would not book the bet, and quietly slipped into his grave (being short of exercise) some six months afterward.—* Sir John Astley

## THE STRUGGLE FOR
## THE ASTLEY BELT

From 1878 to 1889 the public, both in England and the United States, became captivated by six-day racing. Because of opposition to sporting events taking place on Sunday, the six days and nights from midnight Sunday to midnight Saturday became a popular time for long walking or running feats. The American Edward Payson Weston, sometimes called the "father of six-day racing," started the craze in the mid–1870s. Although an outstanding athlete, Weston was even more a showman. During some of his walking feats he was known to "jiggle, limp, hop, trot, and dance" to entertain the crowd. Some thought he was a "humbug" (cheat), others thought he was crazy, but it all just added to his popularity.

He became famous in 1861 by walking 442 miles (712 km) from Boston to Washington, D.C., in order to attend Lincoln's first inauguration. In 1867 he walked 1,326 miles (2,135 km) from Portland, Maine, to Chicago in 26 days. Finally, he hit upon the idea of being first to walk 500 miles (805 km) in six days. After three failures he succeeded in December 1874 at the Washington Street Rink in Newark New Jersey.

A rival to Weston soon appeared in the form of Daniel O'Leary, an Irish-American. He had emigrated to America in 1866 and discovered his long-distance walking ability while selling Bibles in the Chicago area. In April 1875 O'Leary completed a 500-mile walk in 6 days at the West Side Rink in Chicago and then challenged Weston to a match that would decide the "World Champion" of long distance walking. Each man put up $5,000 for the race, which took place from November 15–20, 1875, in Chicago.

O'Leary won, covering 501 miles in the six days to Weston's 450. A short time later, Weston, seeing his popularity fading in America, sailed for England. The British, with their tradition of long-distance running and walking, greeted him with open arms. At the time Britain had no long-distance walkers of Weston's caliber and he was initially quite successful in a series of matches with the best British walkers.

Sir John Astley, "the sporting baron," was impressed with Weston's performances and offered to back him against "any man breathing." Astley, a member of Parliament, had won and lost vast sums of money betting on horse races and other sports. When Astley won, he spent his winnings, but when he lost he borrowed money to cover his losses. Amazingly he made a good living for 25 years with this strategy before it finally crumbled. In his old age he would encounter financial hardship, but as long as he had money, he was a willing backer of pedestrians if he thought their cause worthy. Some of Astley's interest and support for runners undoubtedly stemmed from his own running career. He had been a notable "gentleman" sprinter in the 1850s, running 100 yards in a quite respectable 10¼ seconds and winning most of his matches.

O'Leary, reading of Weston's success, followed him to England, and took up Astley's challenge. Astley rented the Agricultural Hall at Islington, and the race took place there early in April 1877. Weston was confident he could walk 510 miles (821 km) and could beat O'Leary, who had never gone more than 505. More than 70,000 spectators witnessed the contest in which O'Leary, to both Astley and Weston's amazement, covered 519¾ miles (837 km) to Weston's 510 miles.

Although he lost a fortune (£20,000) backing Weston, Astley was so taken with six-day racing that he decided to do all he could to encourage the sport. He had a beautiful championship belt made and offered generous prize money. Since Astley

April 1887: The final day of the six-day walking match between Edward Payson Weston (on the inside track) and Dan O'Leary. The race was won by O'Leary, who covered 520 miles (*The Graphic*, April 14, 1877).

was famous in sporting circles and from the British upper class, his involvement with six-day racing gave it a badly needed measure of respectability. His efforts led to a series of races that became known as "Astley Belt Races" and represented the peak of six-day racing.

Astley wrote in his autobiography, *Fifty Years of My Life* (1894), "… but as the wobbling gait of Weston was open to objection as not being fair heel-and-toe walk-

ing I proposed that the competitors should 'go as they pleased.'"* O'Leary saw Astley's motivation differently, writing, "Satisfied that it was impossible to beat us at long distance walking, the Englishmen invented the style of progression called 'Go-As-You-Please.'"

Whatever his motivation, Astley's decision to open the contests up to running greatly increased the popularity of six-day racing.

*Judging walking matches has been a major problem since the beginning of the sport. If a walker has both feet off the ground at the same time he is "lifting" or running which is not allowed. The judge must watch the walker's feet very closely which is difficult or impossible in a long race. Currently, scientists are trying to develop "smart shoes" that automatically notify the judges when both feet are off the ground.

**Sir John Astley was a member of Parliament who invented the "go-as-you-please" format for six-day races (from Astley, *Fifty Years of My Life*).**

Like Astley, the public became intrigued with these bizarre contests. In England the entrance fee for spectators was usually only a shilling ($.25), in New York, either 50 cents or a dollar, depending on the popularity of the contest. Droves of people came just to have a peep, and were gripped with a fascination they couldn't resist. Footsore and weary, gaunt and grim, the pedestrians plodded along; walking, running, walking again; not stopping even to eat but snatching food from their trainers' hands as they endlessly circled the small indoor tracks. Many spectators stayed for hours and returned day after day to watch these struggles of courage and endurance against hunger, fatigue and physical distress. The fans seemed to sense that, despite their cheap and sordid element, there was something noble about these races—something magnificent and fine.

O'Leary won the first Astley Belt race in London in March 1878, beating 17 Englishmen and covering 520¼ miles (837.8 km). A short time later he left for Chicago, taking the already famous belt with him. He defended the belt in Gilmore's Madison Square Garden in the fall of 1878. His only opponent was John "The Leper" Hughes. Competing strictly to win, O'Leary covered a modest 403 miles (649 km) but took home $10,000 in prize money. Hughes, who was poorly trained, covered only 310 miles (499 km). He would do much better later in his career.

Sir John Astley and his sporting friends wanted the belt back on British soil and searched far and wide for a fellow countryman to challenge the American champion. They chose young Charles Rowell. Astley, in his autobiography, described his selection:

> Rowell took my fancy as he was a very clean-made, muscular young fellow, and had formerly been our boat-boy at the Guards' Club at Maidenhead. He had since that time run long distances well, and was real fond of the business, though he had not made any great score. However, I fancied he could, if properly looked after; so I posted 100 pounds for Rowell and entered him for a six days and nights' competition at Madison square gardens at New York; and I bid Rowell get himself fit, and I would pay expenses of himself and two friends (to look after him) in the land of Stars and Stripes.

The five-foot, six-inch (1.7 m), 140-pound (63.6 kg) Rowell proved to be one of

**The Astley Belt was the most coveted prize in six-day racing (courtesy Dahn Shaulis).**

the best and most popular of the six-day racers. His efficient "dogtrot" was well suited to the sport. He was not a good walker, having a short awkward walking stride, but seemingly never tired when running slowly. Rowell, along with three others, started the third Astley Belt race at the "Garden" in New York at 1:00 A.M., March 10, 1879. Even at this hour the Garden was jammed and the police had to restrain several thousand who were refused admission. O'Leary, now 31 years old, was favored, but was not in condition for the race. John Ennis, 37, who was often bothered by stomach problems, and handsome six-foot, one-inch Charles A. Harriman, rounded out the field.

Interest in the contest grew by the hour. The progress of the race was posted at hotels, in barrooms, cigar-stores, barbershops, corner groceries and every place where people congregated. By Friday evening, Rowell had accumulated 417 miles (671.5 km) to 390 (628 km) for Harriman and 387 (623 km) for Ennis. O'Leary had quit at 215 miles (346 km). On Saturday, a drunken Irishman suddenly stepped from the crowd onto the track and raised his clenched fist as if to strike Rowell. Two policemen seized the drunk and marched him away, as he cursed all Englishmen, and Rowell in particular. Ennis heard the disturbance and slowed his pace allowing Rowell to catch up. He shook his little competitor's hand then turned to the crowd and shouted:

"Gentlemen, I don't know whether you are friends of mine or not. If you are, you can best show your friendship by respecting this man." He pointed at Rowell and a loud cheer went up from the audience. When the applause had subsided, Ennis pointed at Rowell again and with his eyes flashing added:

"I want all of you to understand that if this man is injured I will leave the track and not walk another mile. He is an Englishman, and I'm an Irishman, but that

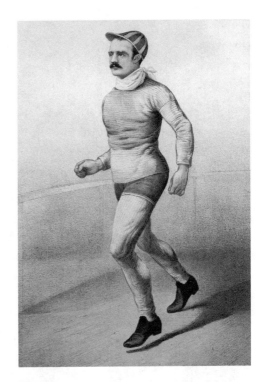

Charles Rowell, permanent holder of the Astley Belt (Currier & Ives, 1879, author's collection).

Englishman has done the square thing ever since the walk began. If he wins, it will be because he is the best man." The two men then clasped hands amidst thunderous applause and circled the track together. Rowell won the race with 500 miles (805 km) while Ennis finished second with 475 miles (765 km) and Harriman third with 450 (725 km). Rowell returned to England with the belt and $20,000.

Edward Weston, seeing that huge sums of money could be made from the Astley belt contests, quickly challenged Rowell. The 40-year-old Weston had concluded that a good runner could beat any walker at six-day racing and immediately began perfecting his running form.

The fourth Astley belt race took place in London in June 1879. Rowell was forced to skip the race, having run a nail into his right heel, and O'Leary had temporally retired. Although the odds were 10 to 1 against

**Ennis rebukes the mob and shakes hands with Rowell at Madison Square Garden on March 10, 1879 (*Frank Leslie's Illustrated Newspaper*, March 1879).**

Weston, the crafty veteran went all out to win. John Ennis said of Weston: "For the first time since I've known him, he went on the track to win and not to gain the admiration of the ladies." Alternately walking and running, Weston took the lead on the fourth day and won with a record 550 miles (886 km).

The fifth and last Astley belt race started shortly after midnight on Monday, Sept 22, 1879, in the "Garden" in New York. Among the 13 starters were Weston, Rowell, Frank Hart, and George Hazael. George Hazael was a 30-year-old Englishman noted for his ability at short (20–50 mile) races. Hazael was round-shouldered and power-

A sprint for the lead in the Fifth Astley Belt Race at Madison Square Garden, September 1879. Hazael is in the lead, followed by Harriman, Rowell and Hart. Rowell won the race with 530 miles (*Frank Leslie's Illustrated Newspaper*, March 29, 1879).

fully built and ran with the "lope of a deer." The other contender was six-foot-tall Sam Merritt of Bridgeport, Connecticut. At first, the race appeared to be another easy victory for Rowell. By Friday morning he had covered 419 miles (675 km) and was far in the lead. Hazael was second with 385 miles (620 km) and Merritt third with 384 (618 km).

Late Friday morning Rowell failed to leave his tent after a rest stop. Finally, after six hours, he appeared looking ill, his eyes dull and heavy, and his normally smooth running stride stiff and awkward. As Rowell shuffled slowly around the track, Merritt drew closer and closer. Although the cause of Rowell's breakdown was kept secret, Astley wrote years later that Rowell "had some poisonous stuff put in his food or drink."* The word that Rowell was in trouble and rapidly losing ground quickly spread throughout New York City and people came in droves.

All that day Rowell struggled to cling to his dwindling lead. At 8:58 P.M. Merritt, who had closed to within 8.5 miles (13.7 km), broke into a fast run. Rowell, realizing he could not let his lead shrink any farther, accepted the challenge. Despite his illness, he ran with Merritt and refused to let him gain any more. By 1:00 A.M. Saturday morning 6,000 enthusiasts were still watching the struggle. Rowell now led with 452 miles (728 km) to Merritt's 442. The little Englishman reached 500 miles at 1:02 P.M. and the band played "God Save the Queen." Public interest in the race was so great that the *New York Times* devoted its entire September 27, 1879, front page to coverage. The Garden was packed with a huge throng for the finish at 9:49 P.M. when Rowell completed his 530th mile (853 km). Merritt ended with 515 and Hazael covered an even 500.

Rowell won a record $30,000 and permanent possession of the Astley belt. In two six-day races in New York City, Rowell had made more money than he could have earned in several lifetimes at a trade in his own country. When he returned to England and retired the belt, public interest in six-day racing began to fade. From this time on only races in which the world record was threatened or races whose outcomes were in doubt to the end would hold the public's interest.

## To the Limits of Human Endurance— 623 Miles in Six Days

In February 1880, the English brickmaker Henry "Blower" Brown covered 553 miles (890 km) and broke Weston's record by three miles. Brown had distinguished himself by his swiftness in trundling his wheelbarrow of bricks to the kiln and back again. Like many brick-makers of his time, he was fond of beer. When his trainer "Old Jack" Smith wished to get an extra spurt out of his protégé, he would yell, "Well done, Blower! Go it, Blower! You have got 'em all beat, my beauty! Yes! Blower shall have a barrel of beer all to himself if he wins, go it, Blower!"

In New York City from April 5–10, 1880, Frank Hart ran and walked 565 miles (910 km) in six days. Hart, originally known as Fred Hichborn, was born in Haiti in 1859. He was also known as "Black Dan," because he was black and seemed to have as much potential as his mentor Daniel O'Leary. Though jokes were made that Hart was the "dark horse," he was a favorite with many of the fans, although he received taunting and racial slurs from others. He proved that a black American could rival the best endurance athletes in the world. Several other men of color followed Hart's lead and took up six-day racing.

Although not required to by the rules, Rowell defended the Astley belt on November 1–6, 1880, at the Agricultural Hall in London, against two Americans, William Pegram and John Dobler. Rowell won easily with a new record of 566 miles (911 km). His closest rival was a rising star, Englishman George Littlewood, who trailed him by nearly 100 miles.

American John Hughes was ahead of his time in that he raced with the name of his sponsor, the *National Police Gazette*, in

---

*There were other attempts, probably by gamblers, to put runners out of commission. For example in June 1879 a pedestrian's bed was saturated with chloroform requiring four hours for him to recover from the stupor.

large letters on his shirt. In January 1881, Hughes ran and walked 568 miles, 825 yards (915 km), in six days to win the O'Leary International Belt. Because Madison Square Garden was undergoing repairs, the race had to be held at the American Institute building, the only other available site large enough to hold an eighth-of-a-mile track.

Robert Vint, born in Ireland in 1846, was a bootmaker who lived in Brooklyn. He took up professional running to try to improve living conditions for his family. Usually the smallest man in the field at only five feet two inches, Vint was a crowd favorite. From May 23 to May 28, 1881, he set a record of 578 miles, 610 yards and over the Christmas holidays in 1881, Irish-American Patrick Fitzgerald, a former alderman from Long Island, increased the record to 582 miles.

On March 3, 1882, in New York, Rowell totaled a staggering 150 miles (241 km) in the first 24 hours of a six-day race. The now-wealthy Rowell was experimenting with the strategy of building an insurmountable

Frank Hart ("Black Dan") set a record of 565 miles in the second O'Leary Belt race in Madison Square Garden in April 1880 (*National Police Gazette*, March 12, 1881).

Henry "Blower" Brown covered a record 553 miles in six days in February 1880 (from Ed James, *Practical Training for Running, Walking, Rowing, Wrestling, Boxing, Jumping and All Kinds of Athletic Feats*, 1877).

John Hughes ("The Leper") covered 568 miles in a six-day race in January 1881 (from William Edgar Harding, *The American Athlete*, ca. 1881).

lead early in the race. On the third day, however, he mistakenly gulped down a cup of vinegar, became sick, and had to resign. Because of his prodigious early effort, it's doubtful that he would have won even if he hadn't become ill. He never tried this strategy again and his record of 150 miles in 24 hours lasted until 1953. George Hazael won the race. Pulled along by Rowell's fast early pace, he became the first man to cover 600 miles (966 km) in six days.

An especially gruesome demonstration of how far some men would go to win a six-day race took place May 3, 1884, at Madison Square Garden. In a race witnessed by 12,000, Patrick Fitzgerald had overtaken favorite Rowell and forged a sizable lead, but in the process had exhausted himself. On the beginning of the last day he looked "as if a twelve-story flat had fallen on him." He had changed his clothes during the night and was now wearing pink silk tights with white shorts. A red silk scarf that didn't quite cover the scar where he had been bled the evening before completed his outfit. The bleeding to "remove poisons from his blood" was a mild procedure compared to what was to come.

Saturday morning at 1:00 A.M. he was ahead of Rowell by 20 miles but by 7:00 A.M. the much fresher Rowell was only 10 miles back and by noon had cut the lead to four miles. Finally, midway through the afternoon, the fading Fitzgerald's legs became so stiff he could barely move. In desperation, a medical advisor, a Dr. Naylor, was summoned to try a new medical procedure on the spent pedestrian.

Fitzgerald was carried to his hut, a badly ventilated 6-by-12-foot room, lighted with an oil lamp. There he was stripped and placed on a cot while Naylor removed a "scarificator" from his medical bag. This rectangular bronze instrument had 16 retractable razor-sharp blades. Naylor placed the sinister device on Fitzgerald's left thigh and pulled the trigger, slashing 16 one-eighth inch deep incisions in Fitzgerald's

Robert Vint improved the six-day record to 578 miles in May 1881 (*National Police Gazette*, October 28, 1882).

George Hazael became the first man to cover 600 miles in six days on April 3, 1882 (*Frank Leslie's Illustrated Newspaper*, October 4, 1879).

thigh. Then he did the other thigh. It worked. With the pressure on his swollen legs eased Fitzgerald returned to the track and went on to set a world record of 610

Fitzgerald, with the help of a "Scarificator," covered 610 miles in six days in May 1884 (cigarette card, 1888, author's collection).

miles (982 km) to Rowell's 602 (969 km). The 39-year-old Fitzgerald won $9,600, retired, and used the money to buy a hotel and athletic grounds on Long Island.

On February 9, 1888, James Albert, "Cathcart," a Philadelphia alderman, faced a huge field of 69 men at Madison Square Garden. He had days of 130, 108, 110, 102, 95 and 76 miles on his way to a record 621 miles (1,000 km). Albert rested only 19 hours and 22 minutes during the six-day period. The Americans were overjoyed since one of their own now held the record.

Finally in November 1888 in Madison Square Garden, George Littlewood set the last of the 19th century six-day records. Littlewood had a smooth, efficient running stride and unusual persistence even for a six-day pedestrian. The light-haired, boyish looking Englishman started the race with a 5:02 mile, seemingly extravagant for someone with more than 600 more to go. He continued with days of 122, 95.6, 102.9, 110.2, 107.5 and 85.2 to cover 623.75 miles (1,004.4 km) in 139 hours and 59 minutes. Going into the last day, Littlewood was far ahead and moving easily. Knowledgeable observers felt he could have covered 650 miles (1,047 km) had he used his customary easy running stride on the last day. Instead, because it was customary for the male record breakers to receive a $1,000 bonus each time they broke the record, he chose to walk at a leisurely 4.5 mile/hr. pace. He would make it easy to break the record at a later date.

At 8:01 P.M., Littlewood finished 621¾ miles, (1,001 km) breaking Albert's record. Albert jumped on the track and ran with him on the next lap carrying his hat in one hand and a new broom, into which a couple of American flags had been thrust, in the other. The new broom signified sweeping away the old record. The crowd cheered and clapped frantically while the band played "Rule Britannia" and "Hail to the Chief." With his total of 623¾ miles Littlewood had set a record for six-day racing that would last nearly a century. Despite his great performance, the race barely broke even and he received only $4,824 of the $16,823 gate receipts.

Albert promptly challenged Littlewood and no one doubted that when the two giants of six-day racing met, the 623-mile record would fall. There was even talk of one of the men eventually pushing the record to more than 700 miles (1,127 km). But enthusiasm for the match soon faded. Because of declining public interest, the promoters found that the gate receipts from the six-day races had dropped precipitously. They could no longer count on making money or even breaking even and the great matches were at an end, although some of the lesser races continued for a time.

In February 1888, James Albert (inset) improved the six-day record to 621¾ miles (*Frank Leslie's Illustrated Weekly*, 1888).

### AMY HOWARD—THE BEST THE WORLD EVER PRODUCED

*Since 1878 I have been on the track over half the time and have been in every kind of pedestrian match, from a half-hour run to a 14-day walk, and I have won every one I ever entered in, either against men or women.* — Amy Howard (1880)

The first major six-day race for women began on March 26, 1879, in New York's Madison Square Garden. The *New York Times* called the race cruel and referred to the pedestriennes as "eighteen unfortunate women whose poverty has compelled them to undertake the six-day's walk." The *Times* also pointed out that many of the women were poorly prepared. Some wore sturdy laced boots, but many raced in low-cut dancing slippers that quickly filled with sawdust. To be considered decently attired, the women were required to wear heavy velvet dresses, which made running and walking difficult and undoubtedly shortened the mileage they were able to achieve. In addition, the unruly, mostly male audience often hurled insults at the contestants.

Many of the women were also under-

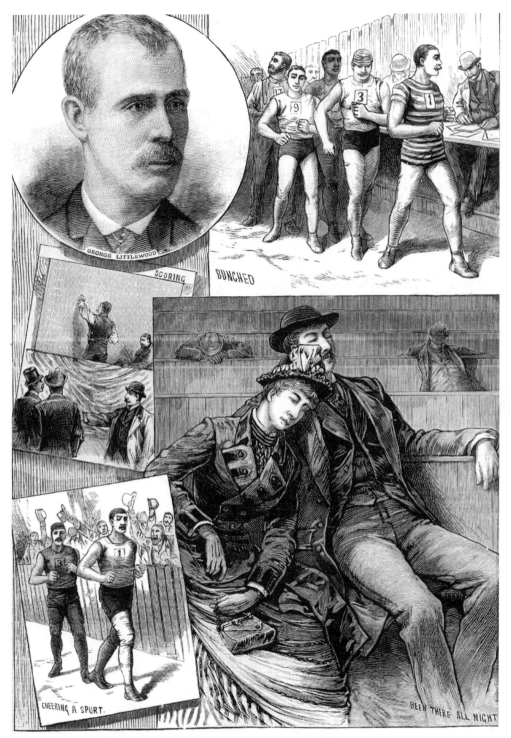

LITTLEWOOD BEATS THE RECORD.

Scenes from the last of the major six-day races held in November 1888 at Madison Square Garden. George Littlewood's final 19th-century record of 623¾ miles lasted for 96 years. The couple in the lower right are demonstrating that these races could be tiring to fans as well as the athletes (*National Police Gazette*, December 15, 1888).

trained for the hardships of a six-day race, and only five of the 18 starters managed to finish. Because so many broke down or dropped out, the contest became known as "the cripples' race." Yet the race was not a total disaster. The *New York Times* admitted that Bertha Von Berg, the winner, "was moving easily and steadily" at the end and "suffered no ill effects from six days and nights of running and walking." Von Berg covered 372 miles (599 km) and finished 20 miles ahead of second place Bella Killbury.

The women were better prepared for the second race in the Garden, which started on December 15, 1879. Twenty-five "pedestriennes" showed up to contend for the first-place prize of $1,000 and a championship belt valued at $500. The race was billed as the "Grand Ladies' International Tournament for the Championship of the World."

Most of the top pedestriennes were there. Among the favorites was Madame Exilda La Chappelle from Paris, holder of the California Diamond belt and a six-day best of 372 miles (599 km). Gray-haired May Marshall, "The Mother of Female Long-distance Pedestrianism," with a best of 350 miles (563 km) was also entered, as was Madame Sarah Tobias from Brooklyn with a best of 349 miles (562 km). Madame Ada Anderson from London, famous for walking 2,700 quarter miles in as many quarter hours the previous spring, was making her first and only attempt at a six-day race.

Because of a harassment incident in the previous women's six-day race in the Garden, the management imposed some curious new rules: "No quarreling, loud talking, profane or obscene language, no conversations with the audience, entrants must keep themselves perfectly neat and clean, no tights without a dress over same and hair must be neatly arranged."

At the word "Go," the women were off, but a man in women's clothing interrupted the contest. He had sneaked onto the track and joined the race without anyone noticing. The unamused police yanked him from

Bertha Von Berg won the first women's six-day race in Madison Square Garden in March 1879 with 372 miles (from Ed James, *Practical Training for Running, Walking, Rowing, Wrestling, Boxing, Jumping and All Kinds of Athletic Feats*, 1877).

the race and arrested him at the end of the first lap.

As the shouts and laughter subsided, unknown Amy Howard, a wispy 17-year-old blonde from Brooklyn, quickly moved to the front and finished the first mile in seven minutes. According to the *New York Sun*, Howard "skipped lightly over the track" as she continued to lead and cover a record 90 miles (145 km) in the first 24 hours. Madame Tobias finished the day in second place with 85 miles (137 km).

Because of construction work on the Garden, part of the roof and one wall section was missing. Only a large red, white, and blue curtain protected the athletes and audience from the elements. Two large cylinder stoves were kept red-hot but could not drive away the cold and damp from the huge building. To make matters worse, the air was made foul by the pipeless stoves and the tobacco smoke from the spectators.

At the start of the second day Howard felt bad and found it difficult to keep going. She changed to a blue silk dress with a short, stylish skirt, white lace at the neck, and sleeves cut off at the elbows. This helped for a while, but within an hour she lagged again and Tobias closed menacingly. Howard, feeling that something must be done, dashed into her tent, and when she emerged her skirt was pulled further back, her blonde hair had been dressed and a ribbon was tied neatly around her neck. These costume changes refreshed her and she increased her speed, but toward noon she was nearly overcome by weariness. Her slender form swayed from side to side, her face took on a gloomy expression and it seemed to the spectators that the wet spots on her cheeks were tears rather than perspiration. She retired again and added two curls to the hanging hair on her back, rearranged the lace on her throat, and put on gold bracelets, but it did no good. Tobias, closing steadily and surely, passed her and gradually left her behind.

At the end of the second day, Tobias was still in first place with 154.5 miles (249 km) to Howard's 153.3 miles (247 km). On the third day, however, Howard showed what she was made of. She stormed back into the lead and stubbornly refused to give it up the rest of the way.

Five thousand fans, many of them women, came to see the 19 finishers on the last day. The *New York Times* wrote: "Little Howard, with invincible courage and wonderful endurance, though having made the greatest distance of any, still strode around the circle with a strong elastic step and jaunty air." She finished with a world six-day record for women by covering 393⅛ miles (633 km). The first six finishers all completed more than 350 miles (563 km).

Madame Tobias, who came in second with 387 miles (623 km), challenged Howard to a rematch. But before another race could be scheduled in the Garden, the New York City Board of Aldermen, concerned about the "respectability" of women's long-distance running and walking, passed a resolution banning women's six-day races in New York City.

Unwilling to give up their new careers, many of the contestants made the long, arduous trek to the West Coast for the next major race which was held in San Francisco's Mechanic's Pavilion in May 1880. Howard and La Chappelle took a steamer around South America while Tobias crossed the continent by rail. During the two weeks prior to the race, the favorites practiced diligently, taking ten and twenty-mile runs every morning and afternoon at the Pavilion.

In a pre-race interview with the *San Francisco Chronicle*, Howard described her method of covering long distances:

> I go nearly all the time in long races on a dog trot, for I can run that way easier than I can walk. I cover about seven miles an hour without distressing myself in that way, and thus get a longer time to rest and sleep.

The race proved to be the greatest women's six-day race ever. Howard went straight to the front with what the *San Francisco Chronicle* called an "unusually springy and muscular as well as graceful run." She led the twenty-woman field through the first mile on the seven-laps-to-a-mile sawdust-covered track in 7:11. Howard held the lead for the first 24 hours and covered 95 miles (153 km) to Tobias's 92 (148 km). The other favorite, Madame La Chappelle, had not fully recovered from a respiratory illness she attributed to the polluted air in Madison Square Garden and eventually dropped out.

On the second day, Tobias, as she had done in New York, took over first place by resting less than Howard. By 11:00 P.M., however, Howard had passed her and taken a sizable seven-mile lead with a total of 165 miles (266 km) to Tobias' 158 (254 km). Howard's strategy now was to just stay even

Madame Tobias finished second to Amy Howard and covered 400 miles in a six-day race in San Francisco in May 1880 (from Ed James, **Practical Training for Running, Walking, Rowing, Wrestling, Boxing, Jumping and All Kinds of Athletic Feats**, 1877).

with Tobias and keep her lead. All the third day, the two leaders maintained an uneasy truce, conserving their energy. Neither did any running as they walked steadily and kept their places.

It was customary for the fans of a six-day race to show their appreciation by handing the pedestriennes bouquets. After carrying them for a lap, the women gave them to their trainers, who used them to decorate the pedestrienne's tents. Howard's tent was easily the most decorated, with three rows of closely spaced trophies. At the end of three days she still led with 230 miles (370 km) to 226 (364 km) for Tobias.

The Pavilion was packed on the fourth day. The audience had been expecting a struggle between the two leaders, and they were not disappointed. In the afternoon Howard suddenly broke into a run which

was immediately taken up by Tobias. At no time in the race had the women been more than ten miles apart. Usually there was only a four-mile difference. Every time Tobias closed the gap slightly, Howard would surge ahead. During the evening, the two leaders almost came to blows. Tobias, who was being dogged by the plucky Howard, turned and accused her rival of interference. The officials quickly separated the two.

On the last day, the *San Francisco Chronicle* reported that Howard, leading by seven miles, "looked as fresh and full of energy as when she had started." Madame Tobias made a valiant effort to cut into her lead but finally abandoned the task as hopeless. That evening, two bands played continuous music to urge on the tired pedestriennes as a large, appreciative crowd filled the Pavilion for the finish. Howard left the track for good at 10:10 P.M. with almost an hour left. Her 409 miles (658 km) were a new record that would last for 102 years. Tobias pushed on until 10:45 to complete 400 miles (644 km).

Howard went on to win every women's six-day race she entered. Madame Tobias, her greatest rival, could sometimes get close, but Howard was so superior to the other women of her time that they usually had little chance against her. In May 1881, in a six-day race in San Francisco, she agreed to give the rest of the field starts. Those from the Pacific Coast she gave 20 miles and her main rivals Millie Young, Madame La Chappelle, and Belle Sherman she allowed ten. Howard covered 364 miles (586 km), which was just enough to beat second place La Chappelle's 353 (568 km).

Howard's favorite tactic was to go to the front early and stay in the lead by just enough to ensure that, unless she had a major breakdown, she could not be caught. If there had been a bonus for setting women's six-day records, as there was for men, Howard's mileage totals would have undoubtedly been greater. In 1881, with the *National Police Gazette's* backing, she bet

Amy Howard was the Champion Pedestrienne of the World in 1880. Her record of 409 miles in May 1880 lasted for 102 years (*National Police Gazette*, August 7, 1881).

$1,000 she could cover 500 miles (805 km) in six days, but no one would take the bet. She was willing to race almost anyone under nearly any conditions. Once she entered a six-day race against two men pushing wheelbarrows, and on another occasion she entered a men's six-day race. Between races Howard teamed with her sister Alice and performed a song and dance routine in Vaudeville.

In 1882 Madame Dupree from Denver, Colorado, claimed to have broken Howard's six-day record by covering 456 miles (734 km), but her claim is dubious at best. While Howard set her six-day records in well-monitored races against the best women of her day, Dupree never raced the other top women. In addition, she performed in saloons, far from the eyes of impartial race judges or the press. One of Dupree's six-day performances was later found to have been short by 154 miles (248 km).

Amy Howard, noted for her cheerfulness and the graceful way she ran, died in childbirth on October 4, 1885, at age 23. Because women runners of the time were held in such low esteem, the death of the best female distance runner on the planet went unreported except for two sentences in the *New York Clipper*.

A short time after Howard's death, British long-distance champion Kate Brown challenged American women to a six-day race. William Harding, champion three-mile runner and sports editor for the *National Police Gazette*, recognized Howard's greatness when he wrote in his column for December 19, 1885: "If Amy Howard, the champion long-distance pedestrian, and the best the world ever produced, was living, there would be no delay in arranging a match."

Sadly, with Howard's death, America had no champion and the British challenge went unanswered.

Curiously, the fascination that pedestrians such as Hazael, Littlewood, Vint, Hart and Tobias had for six-day racing far outlasted that of the fickle public. For 10 years after Littlewood's 1888 record these men and women, unable to forget the golden age of the sport when $20,000 or more and instant worldwide fame went to the winner, continued to travel the country looking for races. Many of the races during the sport's dying days were poorly attended and often canceled in less than six days because of poor attendance. When this happened, the pedestrians got nothing for their efforts except sore muscles and blisters.

One thing the six-day pedestrians

proved was that outstanding runners can always beat outstanding walkers, no matter what the distance. Littlewood's six-day record was not broken until July 1984 when the Greek ultra running specialist Yiannis Kouros covered 635 miles 147 yards (1,022.7 km) at Randall's Island, New York. The current record holder is Jean-Gilles Boussiquet of France, who covered 640 miles (1,030 km) in November of 1992 at La Rochelle France.

Women never really cashed in on the six-day race mania. They were motivated by the money, as were the men. And perhaps some wanted to show that they were as tough and enduring as any man, which they did. The press, both in the United States and Britain, considered six-day racing unsuitable for women and if they reported on it at all it was to loudly condemn it. Although men's six-day racing was financially profitable for about 10 years, only a handful of women's races were money makers.

Amy Howard's record of 409 miles in 1880 lasted for 102 years, outliving her by 97 years. The modern women's six-day record is 548 miles 558 yards (883.6 km) by Sandra Barwick of New Zealand, set at Campbelltown in November of 1990.

Six-day racing in the 1800s was not for the faint-of-heart as was illustrated by the use of the scarificator on Fitzgerald. Tired and sleepy pedestrians were kept going with lively music, hot baths, plunging their heads into buckets of ice water, and electric shocks. Sometimes a trainer might put crushed walnut shells in a ped's shoes to keep him awake. There were no rules against doping and trainers freely dispensed champagne, brandy, minute doses of strychnine or belladonna and sponges soaked in ammonia for the pedestrians to hold to their noses. The greatest stimulant of all was the money to be had.

Training methods for six-day racing were closely guarded secrets. Barclay's methods, with some modifications, were still in use. Many six-day performers trained by covering from 40 to 75 miles a day for several weeks before a major race. According to Lawrence Robbins in "A Vanished Profession" (*Outing Magazine,* February 1923), a typical training day for the better six-day man was about 60 miles (97 km) running at a comfortable six to seven miles-per-hour pace.

The better six-day performers probably could have kept this up almost indefinitely, as suggested by a feat undertaken by George Noremac in the fall and winter of 1884. Noremac, who was a good six-day man but not among the best, attempted the feat of running 51 miles (82 km) daily for 100 days, Sundays excluded, on a small track in New York. He never completed the task, probably because the exhibitions were poorly attended, but a contemporary newspaper reported that he maintained his schedule for 37 days. He performed during the afternoons and evenings only and always ran the distance.

The six-day competitors were allowed to reverse direction — usually at the end of any lap — which helped even-out stresses on their knees and hips. In addition, the tracks (usually one-eighth mile per lap) were carefully prepared and surveyed. At Madison Square Garden, the most important American venue for six-day racing, the track was laid with a base of loam. Tanbark (shredded bark from which the tannin had been extracted) was added and the track rolled until it was well packed. Sawdust was sprinkled on top of this making a spongy surface about 3.5 inches thick. Special attention was paid to keeping the track clear of debris during the race. The track at the Agricultural Hall in London was covered with loam and fine gravel.

Six-day racers usually slept four to five hours each 24 hours but some managed to get by on less than three. They tried, at least early in the race, to keep to scheduled rest periods. The better performers ran during the first day. From then on the pedestrians gradually switched to a mix of running and walking, with walking at about four miles an hour used as a form of rest. When James Albert set his record of 621¾ miles, he used the simple strategy of running as far as possible each day before doing any walking.

With the possible exception of dogs or wolves, humans can cover a greater distance in six days than any other animal on land. In 1879, when six-day racing was at its peak, O'Leary and Weston had a disagreement on whether horses could defeat men at six-day racing. O'Leary thought the horses would win, but Weston disagreed. A human vs. horse six-day race was held in San Francisco beginning on October 15, with seven men racing 11 horses. No first-rate men were entered and a horse named Pinafore won with 557 miles (897 km).

Weston was still unconvinced, causing O'Leary to sponsor another men vs. horses race in Chicago starting on September 4, 1880. Five horses and 15 men entered the 6.5-day "test" go-as-you-please race. The $3,000 in prize money attracted some first-rate horses and men, including Robert Vint of Brooklyn. The horses led early, but on September 9, Michael J. Byrne from Buffalo, New York, took the lead. On the last day of the race tragedy struck. The horse Speculator, who had regained the lead, died while resting in his stable. Byrne scored a hollow victory covering 578 miles (931 km) and winning $2,000. Betsy Baker, one of the surviving horses, which were all "weary and sore," finished second with 563 miles (907 km), winning $1,000. The race didn't prove men could beat horses at multi-day racing, although it did show that horses were prone to dropping dead from exhaustion or overheating in long races, but humans were not.

Sir John Astley wrote in his autobiography: "I never knew of any man injuring his physique or constitution by a six-day's tramp." Astley's assessment of human endurance was nearly correct. John Howard, a 20 year old, started his first six-day race along with 64 other men on December 21, 1879, at Madison Square Garden. He cov-

ered 75 miles (121 km) on the first day but became sick and quit at 5:00 P.M. Howard died a week later at his home in Long Island of "prostration."

The April 12, 1879, *National Police Gazette* reported a death in the first major women's six-day race in Gillmore's Garden. The report was only a couple of sentences long. Although the incident should have been headline news it was not reported in any other newspapers, suggesting it was either hushed up or may have never happened.

Such a small number of incidents out of hundreds of races, instead of proving the dangers of six-day racing, argue that it is remarkably safe for a healthy human. Many veterans of dozens of six-day races lived to advanced old ages suggesting that the sport didn't shorten one's life as some had feared. According to Osler and Dodd in *Ultra-Marathoning* (1979), O'Leary began the custom of walking 100 miles in 24 hours on his birthday when he was 35. He was still doing it up until 1921 when he was 75! Weston,

Edward Weston still going strong in 1910 when, at age 71, he walked from Los Angeles to New York, approximately 3,600 miles, in 77 days (cigarette card, about 1910, author's collection).

likewise, was still going strong in his old age. In 1909 at age 70, he attempted a 4,000-mile (6,437 km) walk from New York to San Francisco in 100 days. He failed, but just barely, completing 3,900 miles (6,276 km) in 105 days.

At their best, six-day races were epic struggles in which men, and a few women, pushed themselves to the very limit of human endurance. As impressive as the 19th century mileage totals were, six-day racing for high stakes lasted only about 10 years—not nearly enough time for the record progression to have leveled out. It is safe to predict that we are nowhere near the limit of distance that a sufficiently motivated human can go on foot in six days.

## The Revival of the Olympic Games

The first modern Olympic Games, held in Athens in 1896, were of great significance in the history of running. Although loosely patterned after the ancient games, the new games were not to honor the gods as the ancient games had been. Frenchman Baron de Coubertin, founder of the new games, formulated many of his ideas during a visit to England's schools in 1883. He hoped the games would bring people together and contribute to world peace. As in ancient times, running proved to be the backbone and most popular part of the games.

The French started the modern games and chose to measure the Olympic races in metric units. As a result, metric race-distances slowly replaced their English equivalents even in non–Olympic races. The traditional 220, 440, 880 yards, three and six-mile distances all have near metric equivalents. Switching from English to metric units for these distances was a small change. Unfortunately, the most classic of

all English races, the 100 yards and the mile, didn't fare so well.

The 100-meter race is about 10 yards or nine percent longer than 100 yards, and 1,500 meters is 120 yards or seven percent shorter than the mile. These differences are significant and changed the character of these races. A "metric mile" of 1,600 meters would have been less than a one percent change and would have made an even four laps on a 400-meter track, but for some reason was not adopted.* By 1976 all English race distances except the mile had been replaced by their metric equivalents.

Many of the 19th century British tracks, where most of the world's running customs originated, were irregular in size and not always level. Races might be run either clockwise or slightly more commonly, counterclockwise. Race organizers often arranged their races to give the less-than-one-lap runners the benefit of a downhill stretch of the track. For example, quarter-mile races on the old one-third-mile track at Cambridge were arranged clockwise on a gentle descent.

Both Oxford and Cambridge ran clockwise until as recently as 1948. That was how they were able to produce outstanding middle distance runners, Roger Bannister wrote jokingly in *The Four-Minute Mile* (1955). "By running clockwise they strengthened the left leg more than the right. Assuming that the right leg is naturally stronger, this method should result in an even level stride — the secret of success!"

In the modern Olympic games in Athens in 1896 and 1906, and in Paris (1900), races were also run in the clockwise direction. But by 1906 there were complaints, as many countries had by then settled on the American custom of running in the counterclockwise direction. The Olympic Games from 1908 on have all been run counterclockwise. Illustrations of track races in

---

*According to one theory, the French chose 1,500 meters for the first "Olympic mile" because a Frenchman, Michel Soalhat, had run the best-on-record time of 4:16⅕ for 1,500 in 1895.*

Start of Olympic 100 meters in 1896. Tom Burke (second from left), who is using the crouch start, won the race in a slow time. The runner in the center lane is resting his hands on sticks (cigarette card, author's collection).

America before 1900 always show them being run counterclockwise. This may be because many of the early running matches in America were held on horse tracks and in the United States, the horses ran counterclockwise.

Times for the races at the first Olympic Games were slow. The track was made of loose cinders and had been squeezed to fit the narrow renovated ancient stadium. The only way to do this was to make the turns very sharp. It was almost like running around the ancient turning-posts.

### THE FIRST MARATHON

The highlight of the first modern games was the marathon which had been included to honor the ancient Greeks. The race had been proposed by professor Michel Breal, a French linguist and historian who donated a gold cup as a prize for the winner.

The Greeks were captivated by the race and made a special effort to win. Even though the Olympics were strictly for amateurs, any Greek who could win the race was promised a new suit of clothes, free shaves and two cups of coffee per day for life, a dinner a day for a year and free laundry for life. In addition, at least one woman had promised to marry the winner sight unseen as long as he was a Greek. In an effort to enhance their victory chances, the Greeks held two preliminary races of 25 miles (40 km) over the Olympic course on March 10, 1896, and again on March 24. These races were the first marathons.

The excitement at the first Olympic stadium on April 10, 1896, was extreme. Everywhere one heard the cry, "The other events to the Americans, the Marathon to a Greek." From the stadium entrance for as far as could be seen, people stood three and four deep on both sides of the road eager to catch sight of the marathon runners.

Twenty-one of the 25 starters were Greeks; however, the early leader was Albin Lermusiaux, a slim Frenchman who started at a terrific pace and at 10 miles was far in the lead. Edwin Flack from Australia, who had already won both the 800 and 1,500 meter runs, was second, and American Arthur Blake third. At about 12 miles (19 km) the steady uphill grade and dusty, gravel road began to take their toll. Near the halfway point Lermusiaux grew tired and paused for an alcohol rubdown. At 15 miles (24 km), the new leader, Blake, dropped out. A few miles farther Flack and Lermusiaux, who had reentered the race, dropped out. Then the Greeks, who had wisely set a slower pace, came to the front and fought it out among themselves.

A sudden silence fell over the stadium as the runners approached. Then a murmur arose in the long line of watchers outside the stadium. The murmur grew to a shout, and then to an immense roar — "A Greek! A Greek wins!" A moment later a panting, dusty, Spiridon Louis burst into the stadium seven minutes ahead of the next runner. Snow-white doves, decked with ribbons of blue and white, the Greek national colors, were set free. The crowd showered flowers, money and jewelry on the victor. On completing his lap on the track, with Prince Nicholas and Prince George on either side, Louis was borne away on the shoulders of his countrymen. The world's first Olympic marathon victor had completed the 25 mile course in 2:58:50, getting the new race off to a grand start.

Less than three months later, on July 19, Len Hurst, a 24-year-old British brick maker, won the first professional marathon in a time that was 17 minutes faster. Hurst, the best of the 19th century marathon runners, won the race from the western part of Paris to the city of Conflans (via Versailles) easily in 2:31. The distance was reported to be 40 km. Hurst repeated his victory two

**Spiron Louis, accompanied by Prince Nicholas and Prince George, wins the first Olympic marathon in Athens in 1896 (*Illustrated London News*, April 25, 1896).**

Len Hurst winning the first professional marathon race. This marathon was held on July 19, 1896, from the western part of Paris to the city of Conflans, via Versailles. The distance was reported to be 40km and Hurst's winning time was 2:31:30 (*La Petit Journal*, 1896).

more times, with his best performance being 2:26:48 in 1900.

Hurst also excelled at distances longer than the marathon (ultra-marathons). In 1900 he ran 31 miles (50 km) in 3:36:45 and 1903 won the London-to-Brighton 52¼-mile (84 km) race in 6:32. Hurst trained for his long races by walking five to six hours a day with six or more miles of steady running added. He took pride in being able to make 8,000 bricks and run 10 miles, all within 12 hours.

The 19th century produced some truly great runners. It is easy to imagine a Valhalla-like place where the best runners of all time might go to, as Milton put it, "in swift race contend." George Seward, Deerfoot, Harry Hutchens, Lon Myers and Walter George would surely all be there. Amy Howard and Willie Day might also have made it had they lived to reach their potential.

# VI

# Modern Running Goes Worldwide (1900–1950)

*There is no deeper or more thrilling joy in life than to take part in an athletic contest in which you have to strain every nerve, sinew, and even mind, in order to overcome. Under such conditions, you experience the joy of living to an extent which no other pursuit and amusement can afford you.*

— Arthur Duffey (1905)

## Technical Advances

Although "best-on-record" running performance lists had been kept since the 18th century, no worldwide authoritative body checked and approved them. In 1913 the International Amateur Athletic Federation (IAAF) was formed and the following year published an IAAF-approved list of world records. Indoor records and the marathon were excluded from the lists.

After World War I, stopwatches timing to ⅒ second began to replace the ⅕-second models that had been in use since the 1880s. The U.S.'s Amateur Athletic Union (AAU) adopted ⅒-second timing in 1922, but because the more conservative IAAF refused to go along, the AAU switched back to ⅕ second timing in 1927. In 1929 the IAAF finally approved ⅒-second timing and the AAU quickly followed suit.

Crude forms of "automatic" timing had been used in the 19th century. *Bell's Life* for March 28, 1874, reported: "The celebrated firm of Morris Benson, has erected a clock opposite the winning post at Lillie Bridge, which is to be set going by electricity at the start of a race and the action of breaking the tape is to stop it." Similar methods were used in Canada and the United States in the 1880s.

The 1912 Olympics in Stockholm were the first to use a form of automatic timing. In this system the winning runner broke a cord that caused a camera to take a photo of the finish line and a timing device. Similar systems were used to provide unofficial times up until the 1928 Olympics. In 1926, a Netherlands company developed a high-speed movie camera to aid in finish judging and timing. This system was used in 1928 at the Olympic Games in Amsterdam.

The first really successful fully automatic system, the "Kirby two-eyed camera," was used in the 1932 U.S. championships and Olympic trials, and later that year in the Olympic Games in Los Angeles. It was the brainchild of Gustavus T. Kirby, president emeritus of the U.S. Olympic Committee, who developed the system with the help of Bell Labs. It was a marvel for its day. One "eye" looked at a mechanical time display reading in hundredths of a second, the other looked at the finish line. Both images were recorded on each motion-picture frame at 128 frames-per-second.

The Kirby two-eye system was instrumental in picking Eddie Tolan as the winner of the controversial 100-meter final in the 1932 Olympics when he and Ralph Metcalfe hit the tape in what seemed to the finish judges to be a dead heat. For the 1936 Olympics in Berlin, Zeiss Ikon AG of Dresden designed a similar system filming at 100 frames-per-second. Race official were slow in relinquishing their control over race timing and insisted that the official times still be taken with stopwatches. This continued until the 1972 Olympics in Munich.

In 1927, Americans George Bresnahan and William Tuttle invented starting blocks; they were first used in Chicago in 1929. Like the crouch start, starting blocks were welcomed by sprinters and coaches, but it was many years before the IAAF approved them. For a time, separate records were kept for races with and without blocks. Tests showed that blocks improved a sprinter's time by about $\frac{1}{30}$ second compared to starting from the small holes that sprinters dug to keep their feet from slipping at the start. The IAAF finally approved starting blocks in 1937 and they were allowed in the next Olympic Games in 1948.

Race officials used a wind gauge in the 1936 Olympics, and in 1938 the IAAF decreed that no official sprint record would be ratified without a wind gauge reading. The maximum tailwind allowed was set at 2 m/sec (4.47 mi/hr). Studies showed that a 2 m/sec tailwind improved a 100-meter time by about .1 second. Since watches of this era read to .1 second, 2 m/sec was a reasonable limit.

## Sprints

*Sprinters, like poets, can only rise to the occasion when under the influence of great inspiration.* — Arthur Duffey (1904)

While running 100 yards in 10 seconds, a runner averages 10 yards per second or two yards (six feet) in $\frac{1}{5}$ second. With $\frac{1}{5}$-second reading watches, setting a record required that the old mark be broken by at least six feet. This created a logjam of co-record holders until finally a sprinter might emerge who could beat the old record decisively.

By 1902, a half-dozen amateur sprinters had tied John Owen's 1890 record of $9\frac{4}{5}$ seconds for 100 yards, but none could better it. Some sprinters even spoke of a "fast" $9\frac{4}{5}$ or a "slow" $9\frac{4}{5}$ and many who followed sprinting thought that in all the ages to follow no human would better Owen's marvelous record.

ARTHUR DUFFEY—
THE MAN WHO NEVER COMPETED

Usually, when a runner sets a world record it is his to keep until someone can break it, but not always. Arthur Francis Duffey (he sometimes signed his name Duffy) broke John Owen's 1890 record of 9⅘ for 100 yards, but then saw his record disappear as if it had only been a dream.

Born in 1879, Duffey began his athletic career in 1896 at Boston High School. He tried pole vaulting, but skinned his arms and legs so badly from falling into the sawdust pit that his parents made him quit. He then tried sprinting, and the following year at the New England Interscholastic championships became the first high-school sprinter to run 10 seconds flat for 100 yards. From then on the short and slender young man specialized in the 100 and depended on a fast start for much of his success. In 1898 at the AAU championships he ran 9⅘ in a heat, and went on to beat a declining Bernie Wefers in the final with 10 flat.

That fall he joined Wefers at Georgetown University but had to sit out the 1900 Inter-College Championships because the previous year he had run for an athletic club. Looking for competition, Duffey left for Europe. He won the English 100 yard championships in 10 flat, beating R. W. Wadsley, of the Highgate Harriers, who was considered the best English sprinter. At the 1900 Paris Olympics Duffey was the odds-on favorite in the 100 meters.

There was no track at the Paris Games. Instead the race was run on 100 meters of grass that "rose and fell like a roller coaster" and was littered with bumps and holes. Duffey won his heats easily, and in the final used his quick start to take a commanding lead and looked like an easy winner. But at 50 meters a tendon in his left leg gave way and he suddenly leaped into the air and crashed to the ground. "I felt a peculiar twitching after going twenty yards," he said after the race. "I then seemed to lose con-

trol of my leg, and suddenly it gave out, throwing me on my face. But that is the fortunes of sport, and I cannot complain. I do not think I can compete again here."

He ran his greatest race in the Intercollegiate Association of Amateur Athletes of America (IC4A) Championships, held at Berkeley Oval, in New York, on May 31, 1902. He had trained hard for the race, working out twice a day and practicing "bounding," or springing forward with his knees locked to develop his calves and thighs. Duffey's main rival for the championship was Bill Schick of Harvard, who had won the Yale-Harvard meet in a world-record-tying 9⅘ seconds and was in even better condition for the championships.

In the semifinals, Fay Moulton from Yale won the first heat in 10 flat, with Schick second. Duffey put the crowd on edge by winning his heat, beating Earl Cadogan of California in 9⅘. Just before the final, a strong breeze suddenly whipped up, but as the runners took their marks two members of the AAU records committee hoisted their pocket handkerchiefs as primitive wind gauges. While the race was underway there was not enough wind to sway the handkerchiefs.

Duffey described his record-breaking race in *Outing* magazine for July 1902:

I went to the mark all in a tremble. When we drew for positions, I got a bad lane. The man who had used it in the semifinal had dug holes like graves. I filled them, but that made loose cinders under my feet and was worse than ever. I do not remember much about the start; I never do. I get set, and think of nothing but the pistol. I suppose I must be in a sort of hypnotic state. The next thing I remember is that we were going down the track, probably twenty yards from the start, and Schick was leading. I have known Schick for a long time. We ran against each other in high school, and I had always beaten him off. Now I saw he had beaten me. I thought I must have got a bad start, and it came over me that if he beat me at the start he might win at the finish too.

Every runner has a different way of covering the course. Schick seems to go like a steam engine from start to finish. I go in two bursts, or beats. When I felt that my first burst was over, I could still hear Schick at my side. I thought at the time he must be about a foot ahead and I was never scared so badly before. I let out harder, and worked as I had never done in any other race. When a man is frightened and loses his senses he forgets form, throws back his head, and pumps with his arms high in the air. I felt just like doing that. It seemed as though something was pulling my head back and my arms up. But I knew I must hold myself and not let that happen. So I gripped my palms and shoved my head forward and tried to run harder than ever. I then pulled away.

Three of the four timers caught Duffey in 9⅗ and the other in 9⅖. The official time of 9⅗ was accepted as a world record.

Duffey excelled at starting and was probably the first sprinter to completely master the crouch start. In a race in Scotland in 1903, his start was a little too quick. Tired from running many heats and facing an opponent with a generous handicap, he realized he couldn't win unless he resorted to a "little strategy" with the starter:

> Cautiously I crouched and awaited my opportunity, and as the lingering sounds of "Get Ready" passed from the starter's lips and died away among the crowd, like a frightened animal scenting danger I sprang forward, catching the report of the pistol as I flew by my competitor at top speed. The sudden shock surprised everybody; but my rival, game to the end, went with me — neck and neck we ran. The result was inevitable; for with the start I received I managed to make up the handicap and broke the tape a scant yard in front.

News of Duffey's extraordinary start preceded him on the rest of his trip and at

**Duffey (far left) running 9⅗ for 100 yards at Berkeley Oval in New York on May 31, 1902 (*Outing*, July 1902).**

one race a no-nonsense starter brought out a double-barreled shotgun to start the race. He informed Duffey that the first barrel was loaded with a blank and was for starting the race. The second barrel was loaded with buckshot and Duffey could guess where he would get shot if he tried any "fliers."

By 1905, Duffey's speed had begun to leave him and after he and Alfred Shrubb toured Australia and New Zealand he considered retirement. The end of his career was hastened by a November 1905 article he wrote for Bernarr MacFadden's *Physical Culture* magazine. In his article, Duffey told how he had received more-than-generous expense money from race promoters since 1898 and insisted that most other top amateur athletes had done the same. Unfortunately, MacFadden's accompanying editorial outraged the AAU officials:

> He [Duffey] is not in any sense an amateur, in accordance with the definition of the AAU. He has not been an amateur for several years, and still he has been competing not only in this country, but in Australia and England, and in various other parts of the world, as a bona fide amateur athlete. He has supported himself by his ability as an "amateur" athlete since the year 1898...

Duffey, perhaps realizing he had gone too far, insisted he never told MacFadden he was a professional and even had MacFadden retract his statement in the December issue of *Physical Culture:*

> It appears that Mr. Duffey did not at any time accept direct financial recompense for his services as an athlete, but that in his case, as in the case of most "star" athletes, his "expenses" were allowed to him by the athletic managements, under whose auspices he contested.

MacFadden's retraction did little good. Instead of being grateful for Duffey's efforts to blow the whistle on abuses of the amateur system, James E. Sullivan, secretary of the AAU, called Duffey's article the "most startling ever made in athletics." Sullivan, for whom the prestigious Sullivan Award is named, vowed to prosecute Duffey as a

**Arthur Duffey (*Georgetown College Journal*, July 1902).**

criminal if possible. He expunged from the *Spalding Official Athletic Almanac*, which he edited, all of Duffey's achievements, including his world record of 9⅗ seconds for 100 yards and his records for 40, 50 and 60 yards.

Duffey went to court, without success, to have his records reinstated, and after a brief stint as a professional became a sports journalist for the Boston *Post*. Other outstanding times by Duffey were 5.0 seconds for 50 yards and 11⅖ for 120 yards. He ran 9⅕ seconds for 100 yards in Abergavenny, Wales, on a "slightly downhill" course and again in Furness, England, with a strong wind at his back. Neither of these was considered a record. His expunged record of 9⅗ was equaled "officially" in 1906 by Dan Kelly of Oregon University and again in 1913 by Howard Drew from the University of Southern California.

Archie Hahn was the next great sprinter after Duffey. Although he never ran 100 yards in 9⅗ seconds, he was more consistent than Duffey. He won several National Championships as well as four Olympic sprint titles—the 60, 100 and 200-meter races in St. Louis in 1904 and the 100-meter crown in the "Interim" Olympics at Athens in 1906. He also wrote *How to Sprint* (1923), a classic book on sprinting.

### Minoru Fujii—A Fast Man from Japan

America didn't have a monopoly on great sprinters in the early 1900s. In 1907, *The New York Times* printed a story about an extraordinary running performance by Minoru Fujii from Japan. Fujii had been electrically timed in an amazing 10.24 seconds for 100 meters. His November 10, 1902, performance at the "Annual Sports" at the University of Tokyo exceeded the best on record time for 100 meters by .36 seconds. News of it had taken almost five years to reach the west.

Fujii, who was born in 1880, was big and strong at five feet 10¾ inches (1.8 m),

**Minoru Fujii from Japan was timed in 10.24 for 100 meters in 1902 (*New York Times*, May 1907).**

and 157 pounds (71.4 kg). In 1906 he cleared 12 feet 9.5 inches (3.9 m) in the pole vault — five inches (13 cm) better than the listed world record. Officials in Japan sent letters to the AAU in America and its counterpart, the AAA in England, to try to get Fujii's marks recognized as world bests. These letters described in detail the electric timing apparatus used to time Fujii. The timing system was very similar to one designed by Professor C. H. McCloud at McGill University and first used at the Montreal Athletic Association Games in the fall of 1883. It consisted of a timing circuit that was started by a switch on the starter's pistol and stopped by the winner breaking a thin wire. The start and stop impulses were recorded on a strip chart that had been calibrated with a chronometer. In principle, the device should have been capable of timing with .01 second accuracy. Details on course measurement and winds were unfortunately lacking.

Fujii planned trips to America and England in 1907 and hoped to take part in the Olympic Games in London in 1908. He never made these trips, however, and the world never got to see him compete against the champion sprinters of other countries. Probably for this reason, his performances were never widely accepted as world bests.

### ARTHUR POSTLE AND JACK DONALDSON— BLAZING SPEED FROM DOWN UNDER

The 15 years before World War I were the golden age of professional running in the "land down under." Australia, however, had timing credibility problems similar to those that had faced America in the 1880s. Many sporting journalists from America and Britain refused to believe the fast sprint times recorded in the antipodes. It required a couple of great runners, racing on three continents, to make believers of them.

Arthur Postle, "The Crimson Flash" (from Alfred Shrubb, *Distance and Cross-Country Running*, 1908).

Australians Arthur Postle and Jack Donaldson had few peers among sprinters of their day, either amateur or professional. Postle, known as the "Crimson Flash" because of his red running singlet, turned pro in 1902 and was almost unbeatable up to 80 yards.

In 1906, before a crowd of 20,000 at the Kalgoorlie gold fields in Australia, he beat Irishman Beauchamp Day at 75 yards in a record 7⅕ seconds. At Durban, on February 15, 1908, Postle set a professional record for 50 yards in 5⅕ seconds, and in March of that year he added another record by running 60 yards in 6¹⁄₁₀ seconds. Postle also ran 80 yards in 7⅘ seconds three times in his career. His biggest asset was his quick start. In his heyday he claimed that he never met a sprinter to whom he couldn't give two yards and beat in a 40-yard race.

Jack Donaldson, the "Blue Streak," raced in all blue and was Australia's greatest sprinter, amateur or professional. This remarkable Australian raced in Australia, New Zealand, South Africa, England and Scotland. At Johannesburg, South Africa on February 12, 1910, he was challenged by Postle and the American pro champion C. E. "Bullet" Holway to race for the 100-yard pro championship of the world. Excitement was intense as they took their positions on their marks.

Postle, as expected, was quickest away and was out in front at 20 yards. At 50 yards his lead had grown to three yards and at 80 Postle was still in front, but the "Blue Streak" was closing fast. With 15 yards to go Donaldson caught and passed Postle and won by 2½ yards. Donaldson's time of 9⅜ seconds was actually recorded as 9⁶⁄₁₆ as it was taken on watches (which recorded in 16ths of a second) used for timing whippets. Johannesburg is 5,750 feet (1,753 meters) above sea level, which undoubtedly contributed to the fast time. Officials in the American AAU made light of the performance, claiming the course was downhill, although there is no mention of this in the South African newspapers of the time.

Holway and Donaldson met again at the Sydney Sports Ground on September 23, 1911, for a 130-yard race. The excitement was intense and an enormous crowd was on hand. Both men got off to perfect starts. At 80 yards Donaldson was two yards in front of the American, which he increased to five yards when he breasted the tape. The three timekeepers all caught Donaldson in 12 seconds flat—an astonishing 10 yards inside even time. The track was remeasured and found to be long by four inches. Of course no wind measurements were taken in 1911 and it was admitted there was a breeze. How much it contributed to the time we will never know. Journalists in Britain and America flatly refused to believe it.

Donaldson finally went to Britain, where sports journalists were convinced he would never be able to duplicate the "ludicrous" times he had run in Australia and South Africa. On October 10, 1912, at Taff Vale Park in Pontypridd, Wales, he raced South African Reginald Walker, the 1908 Olympic 100-meter champion, for the world professional 130-yard championship. Donaldson won by five yards in 12³⁄₁₆ seconds. With such a huge winning margin, he had time to turn and watch Walker finish. The time was eight yards inside evens, and showed the fans sprinting of a quality not seen since the glory days of Harry Hutchens in the old Sheffield Handicaps.

Donaldson's remarkable run convinced the British press. His greatest critic, W. L. Sinclair of the *Sporting Chronicle*, wrote, "Donaldson in his earlier career had put up some records which I would not accept. But after seeing the Australian defeat Walker on Saturday, I must admit today the greatest sprint runner in the world is with us. I refer to Jack Donaldson."

As a further test, the *Chronicle* offered £100 to anyone who could break Harry Hutchens's hallowed record of 300 yards in 30 seconds. Donaldson made the attempt on August 4, 1913, at a Sports Carnival in Weaste, Manchester. The "Blue Streak" started from scratch, giving Tom Brandon of Edinburgh a 28-yard start and allowing two other runners starts of 23 and 19 yards. Brandon won, beating Donaldson by a distance officially given as two yards, but some observers thought it was more like three to five.

Officials timed Donaldson with "Williams" dog-racing watches, which recorded to $\frac{1}{64}$ of a second. Two timers had him inside 30 seconds, but the third recorded $30\frac{2}{64}$. The average time was taken and Donaldson was credited with $29\frac{61}{64}$ seconds, breaking Hutchens's record by a minuscule $\frac{3}{64}$ of a second. There was much criticism of this, as many old-timers in the pedestrian fraternity thought the performance was inferior to Hutchens's feat of nearly 30 years earlier. Hutchens had a clear-cut win, and there was no difficulty in reckoning his time as there had been Donaldson's. The *Sporting Chronicle*, however, was satisfied with the official time and paid Donaldson the £100 prize money.

At five feet eight inches (1.7 m) tall and weighing 146 pounds (66.4 kg), Donaldson was deep-chested and long-legged, with a stride of almost nine feet. He raced Postle 21 times, and won on 15 occasions. Postle was very quick over the shorter distances but in the five matches the two ran over 100 yards, Donaldson won them all. Because he was a pro, the American press never gave Donaldson his due. In the 1920s, Charley Paddock made many attempts to break Donaldson's record of 130 yards in 12 seconds, but the best he could do was $12\frac{2}{5}$ at Pasadena on June 18, 1920. Paddock finally gave up in disgust and announced that 130 yards was an "unorthodox" distance.

Richard Perry Williams was an American sprinter who ran for the University of Pennsylvania in 1895 and as a professional from 1900 to 1908. He claimed to have set many amateur and professional sprint records, including 100 yards in 9.0 seconds on June 2, 1906, at Winthrop Massachusetts. Unfortunately, none of Williams's claimed records were reported in the newspapers and sporting journals of his day. Charley Paddock in his book *Track and Field* (1933) did not believe Williams's claims:

> R. P. Williams, of New London, Connecticut, claimed a number of astonishing sprint records, and his name still appears in the book as the "official" holder of many marks, but his competitive record does not compare well against the times with which he is credited. I mention this merely because many sports authorities of today, judging solely from Williams' marks, place him among the great sprinters of history. His professional contemporaries did not so rank him.

Professional running died out in England and America soon after World War I. The only places where it survived were in Scotland at Powderhall Stadium and the Highland and Border Games circuits and in South Australia in the Victorian Athletic League circuit.

### CHARLEY PADDOCK — "THE FASTEST HUMAN"

On March 26, 1921, at a USC–California dual meet, Jack James, a San Francisco sports columnist, coined the term "The Fastest Human." He had just seen Charles W. Paddock run 100 yards in $9\frac{3}{5}$ to tie the world record and 220 yards in $20\frac{1}{5}$, the latter a world record that finally surpassed Wefers's 1896 record of $21\frac{1}{5}$. James wrote: "Paddock had smashed the world's record. He had run faster than any human had ever been officially timed. He had earned for himself the title of 'The Fastest Human!'"

Paddock was born in 1900 in Gainesville, Texas, but his family moved to Southern California when he was seven months old. There, as a child, Paddock's favorite pastime was throwing rocks at the older boys and then running away, knowing they couldn't catch him. He was a rather plump

**R. P. Williams claimed many fast performances that were never verified (cigarette card, 1910, author's collection).**

youth who walked with a peculiar waddle. He grew into a powerful, barrel-chested young man and when he was 15 took up cross country running and the mile. His father, however, rightly steered Charley in the direction of becoming a sprinter. At 15, Paddock ran 220 yards in 21⅗ seconds and when he was 19 ran 100 yards in 9⅘ seconds. In 1919 Paddock, who had been an artillery officer in World War I, became world-famous for his sprinting and antics at the Inter-Allied Games at Paris, France. As 40,000 Allied soldiers watched, Paddock went through his pre-race ritual, which he described in his autobiography *The Fastest Human* (1932):

Just before he called us to our marks, I walked over to a wooden hurdle and rapped three times, crossing my hands as I did so. This had been a habit of mine from the time I had won my first race. I believe I had commenced "hitting on wood" with much the same idea in mind as the automobile driver has when he knocks on wood after saying, "I've never had an accident." I told myself: "I can win this race, but I am not taking any chances, and I am not going to be over-confident. Anything can happen." As the years passed I did not continue to engage in a monologue every time I stepped on a track, but just the same, I did not give up on hitting on wood. And its charm was potent before the Inter-Allied hundred. The moment I touched wood, the

**Charley Paddock, the first "Fastest Human," executing his famous "jump" finish (University of Southern California).**

gloom of the day, the cold air and the vast crowd were all forgotten. I was eager to be off.

Paddock won both the 100 and 200 meters at the Inter-Allied Games. When he returned home, he sought out and defeated the three American sprinters he felt he needed to beat to be considered the champion sprinter of the world. Fueled by a raw egg and a glass of sherry, Paddock won the 100 meters and finished a close second in the 200 meters in the 1920 Olympic Games.

By 1921, Paddock was at the top of the sprint world but as yet had set no world records. He had two weaknesses, a poor start and a short stride. Up to this point, he had been reluctant to work on his start. He loved the thrill of coming from behind and winning with his famous "jump" finish.

There were two styles of finishing a sprint race at the time. Arthur Duffey had used the "lunge" with success. Just as he came to the finish, he threw his chest out and his arms back, leaning into the tape, or "lunging" toward it. This finish gave the user about a one-foot advantage over someone who merely ran through the tape. Another finish, said to have been perfected by Bernie Wefers, was the "shrug." The runner using the "shrug" threw the side of the body into the tape with one arm held high overhead and the other pulled back. It kept the forward lean of the lunge but was said to give its user an additional six-inch advantage at the tape.

In 1916, while still in high school, Paddock began perfecting his own finish, the "jump," which only a few runners could use, as he explained in his autobiography:

A great many backhanded compliments have been tossed at the "jump finish." It has been referred to as a "grandstand" play and "the freak finish of a freak performer." The latter phrase has a certain amount of truth attached to it. Few can use the jump to advantage. It requires that the sprinter run high, "bounding" along. He must come down on the tape, gaining in speed and momentum as he makes his last leap, which after all is nothing more or less than an exaggerated final stride varying in length from ten to fourteen feet.... The jump has won so many more races than it has lost for me that I can do no less than recommend it to the sprinter who runs "high" and has the patience to learn it, and the courage to use it.

After much hard work in early 1921, Paddock found he had noticeably improved his start and increased his stride-length by six inches. It all paid off on March 26, 1921, when he chopped $\frac{2}{5}$ second off Wefers's 25-year-old 220 straight-course record by covering the distance in $20\frac{1}{5}$ seconds. A month later, at Redlands, California, on a bitter cold and rainy day, he broke the amateur world's marks in the 100, 200, 300 meters and 300 yards. In addition, he equaled the world's record of $9\frac{3}{5}$ seconds for 100 yards for the third time. Paddock set all of his records in just two races. In his first race, tapes and timers were stationed at 100 yards and 100 meters. In the second they were positioned at 200 meters, 220 yards, 300 yards and 300 meters. There were at least five watches at each tape and the wind as tested by handkerchiefs held at three points along the track was nil.

In the first race Paddock was off to a good start and led all the way. At 95 yards, he gave a mighty bound and flew over the 100-yard line in $9\frac{3}{5}$ seconds. He came down heavily, recovered, and took two quick strides before leaping for the tape at 100 meters. The second leap gave him $10\frac{2}{5}$ seconds for 100 meters, breaking Lippincott's old mark by a fifth of a second.

As Paddock rested for the next race, a small army of timers positioned themselves at the various distances and checked their watches. Paddock thundered down the track and with one jump passed the 200 meter and 220 yard marks. Speeding on around the sharp turn, he seemed to weaken and slow as he reached 300 yards and his sprint was nearly gone when he came to the last tape at 300 meters.

As he caught his breath, he learned that he had broken three more records. He had clipped $\frac{2}{5}$ second from Archie Hahn's 200-meter record of $21\frac{3}{5}$ seconds. At 300 yards, his time had been $30\frac{1}{5}$ seconds, beating Bernie Wefers's quarter-of-a-century-old amateur mark by $\frac{2}{5}$ second. At 300 meters, which he ran in $33\frac{4}{5}$ seconds, he had beaten the old record by 2⅗ seconds. Despite all these records, he had only tied Duffey's elusive 9⅗ second 100-yard record.

The five-foot, eight-inch (1.7 m) Paddock had a tremendous bouncing stride with knee-action so high that he sometimes kneed himself in the chin. His powerful leg-drive combined with a feather-footed stride made it appear that he hardly touched the track as he flew over it. In 1921 at Pasadena, in a 200-yard record attempt, he was timed in 10⅕ seconds for 110 yards. Although it was accepted as a record for 110 yards, it was not approved as a record for 100 meters even though the distance was 100.58 meters.

Five years later, he made an all-out assault on the 100-yard record, aided, he thought, by an improvement in timekeeping. Watches reading in ⅕ second, which had been in use for some 40 years, were being replaced by improved models that read in ⅒ second increments. This meant he had only to break the record by three feet instead of six. In May 1926, in a desperate struggle with Charlie Borah, a young sprinter from Southern California, Paddock used his jump finish to come from two feet behind at 98 yards to beat Borah by four inches in 9.5 seconds. Unfortunately, the International Records Committee didn't trust the newfangled ⅒ second reading watches and refused to ratify the record.

Paddock set records at all sorts of odd, seldom-competed, distances. At one of his record attempts, in the Penn Relays, the crush of fans craning their necks for a look at the "Fastest Human" caused a brick wall to crumble. Paddock sped through the falling bricks and vaulted over fans lying on the track to set a record of 17⅖ seconds for 175 yards. No one was seriously injured in the mishap.

In 1924, before the Paris Olympics, Bellin de Coteau, an eminent French doctor, examined Paddock and reported: "Paddock is fat, he has curvature of the spine, his shoulder blades stick out like those of the famous Spark-plug. His nasal respira-

tion needs attention and when he runs he looks exactly like a calf with two heads." Although favored to defend his 100-meter title, Paddock finished out of the medals.

British sprinter Harold Abrahams, who was featured in the movie *Chariots of Fire*, had gone out in the second round of heats in the 1920 Olympics and was determined to do better this time. In 1923, he enlisted the services of Sam Mussabini, a wily old coach who had known Harry Hutchens and used the methods of the professional sprinters. Mussabini put Abrahams on a rigorous training program. He helped him improve his start, and to ensure that he was not overstriding, put pieces of paper at various places on the track that Abrahams had to pick up with his spikes.

Mussabini gave Abrahams some last-minute advice before the 1924 100-meter final. "Only think of two things, the report of the pistol and the tape. When you hear one, run like hell till you break the other." Abrahams ran an Olympic record 10⅗ to win the gold medal with Paddock finishing fifth. Paddock redeemed himself somewhat in the 200 meters where he won the silver medal behind teammate Jackson Scholz.

Paddock was constantly on the carpet with the AAU, which suspended him many times. He always succeeded in getting himself reinstated at the last moment for the big meets. One reason he was able to avoid Duffey's fate was his tireless work to promote the sport he loved, which earned him many friends—some in high places. During the 1920s Paddock traveled endless miles throughout the United States giving lectures on track and field.

In 1928, when Jesse Owens was in junior high school in Cleveland, Ohio, Paddock visited his school and spoke to the students. "I met him later in the coach's office," said Owens, "and was so impressed that I decided right then that I would become the 'World's Fastest Human' by winning the 100-meter championship in the Olympic Games."

Paddock capitalized on his fame by starring in five "B" movies with such titles as *Nine and Three-Fifths Seconds*, (1925) and *Olympic Hero* (1928). Truly a giant in the history of sprinting, Paddock rejoined the Marines in World War II and perished in an airplane crash in Alaska in 1943.

## PERCY WILLIAMS—
### A RELUCTANT HERO

Near the end of the 1920s, the title of "World's Fastest Human" passed from Charley Paddock to a young Canadian named Percy Williams. Known as the "Human Flash," Williams was an unwilling candidate for the title of champion sprinter of the world, freely admitting that he never liked running. He was born on May 19, 1908, in Vancouver, British Columbia, and as a high school sprinter was puny and spindly—under five feet six and weighing only 110 pounds. He also had a bad heart, the result of rheumatic fever, and a bad knee, from playing football. Seemingly, his only assets were a magnificent pair of legs.

His coach, Bob Granger, played a vital role in Williams's success. Granger was such a track and field enthusiast that, on occasion, he went without eating to buy track shoes for his athletes. He recognized Williams's potential early and sheltered the shy young man and pushed him to develop his talent. Williams later admitted that, "Whatever I've done was through my coach, Bob Granger. Granger was everything."

In addition to a great pair of legs Williams had another talent, as Granger explained in a November, 1930 article in *American Magazine*:

> I was the only person who realized that while men like Borah and Paddock were masters of their own particular style of running, Percy Williams was master of two styles.... The "stretch" style—the effortless beautiful, flowing style that great runners use, never changing their

stride from the gun to the tape—Percy had that to perfection. But he also had the "drive," and had it under such remarkable control that he could "change gears" at will. This meant that he could start a 100-yard dash with the easy, flowing style, conserving his energy, and then, when his intuition directed, change suddenly into the drive and put on a burst that was, truly, like a flight.

In 1927 Williams had the first of many unhappy encounters with race officials. After winning the British Columbia sprint title and qualifying to run in the Canadian Championships, he prepared to make the long trip to Hamilton. The official responsible for Williams's travel thought the young sprinter was not good enough to compete in the championships and instead of sending Williams, used the ticket himself. A sympathetic sports fan bought Williams a ticket, but coach Granger had to work his way to the meet by washing dishes in the railway diner.

When Williams got to Hamilton the officials discovered that the track, which was supposed to have six lanes, had only five. This presented a dilemma when Williams, along with five others, qualified for the 100-meter final. Since there were two runners from Western Canada, the officials decided to toss a coin to see which one of the Westerners would drop out. Williams lost and was out of the final. He was allowed to run the 200-meter final, but faltered in the last 10 yards and failed to place.

The next year his luck improved. He qualified for the championships a second time and, along with coach Granger, who again washed dishes to pay his fare, went back to Hamilton for the championships. This time Williams performed brilliantly, winning the 100 meters (10⅗) and the 200 meters (22.0), and qualifying for the 1928 Amsterdam Olympics in both events. In July the Canadian team sailed for Europe on the liner *Albertic*. Williams's mother canvassed Vancouver to raise money to send coach Granger and he followed on a freighter.

In Amsterdam, Granger and Williams stayed in a cheap hotel near the red-light district. Granger diligently drilled Williams in starting, using a mattress placed against the wall to protect his protégé when he crashed into it. Williams, barely 20 years old and weighing 126 pounds, was a virtual unknown at the Games. The favorite in the 100 meters was 19-year-old American Frank Wykoff, the "Comet from the Coast," who had previously vanquished an aging Charley Paddock in the "sprint of the century."

The track, which had been finished only the day before the Games opened, was very soft. Sprint times were slow and got slower as the Games went on. Still, along with American Robert the "Flying Cop" McAllister and Jack London, Williams tied the Olympic 100-meter record of $10\frac{3}{5}$ in the heats, but few considered him a contender. He gave Granger a scare in the semifinals when he was left on his mark at the start, but recovered and finished second. The final included American stars McAllister and Wykoff, Wilfred Legg of South Africa, London of Great Britain and George Lammers of Germany.

Legg, then Wykoff, false started, but the third start was perfect. Quicker than a pickpocket can snag a wallet, Williams was out of his holes, with the others on his heels. At 70 meters the young Canadian was still in front. London made a valiant effort to catch him but Williams won by two meters in $10\frac{4}{5}$. Bob Granger watched the race from the tiny Canadian section of the stands. Tears streamed from his eyes and his hand bled from beating a barbed wire fence as he shouted "come on" to Williams.

The crowd was at first stunned, then went wild. Even the officials were surprised and had to delay the awards ceremony while they searched frantically for a Canadian flag and a phonograph record of the Canadian national anthem. Unlike Granger, Williams was not overjoyed at his victory. He wrote in his diary: "So I'm supposed to be the world's 100-meters champion. Crushed apples. No more fun in running now."

Despite his win in the 100 meters, Williams was given little chance in the 200. The Americans, Charley Paddock, Jackson Scholz and Charlie Borah, were the favorites, but Paddock and Borah failed to qualify for the final. Only two from each semifinal advanced and Williams considered his semifinal the most difficult race of his life: "I met Borah and Körnig and one of us had to go out," he later said. "I was third with a yard to go, but finally beat Borah." Granger felt that Helmut Körnig was the man to beat in the final and told Williams to stay with him and make his move near the end. Williams did just that, following a yard behind the German sprinter until they came out of the curve. With less than 50 meters to go he changed gears and flew by Körnig to win by a yard in $21\frac{4}{5}$.

Williams wrote in his diary: "August 1, 1928 — Well it's done. Won the 200m. Not so bad. Telegrams galore. The girl's team sent flowers to me. Hot Dog! McAllister, Paddock, Scholz, Borah and Wykoff all congratulated me."

In 1929 and 1930, Williams toured the United States, proving that he was the best sprinter of his day. He later said in an interview: "I think I came up with my best performances in the winter of 1929. I had never run indoors before, but I ran 22 races in 21 days and I came second in one and won all the others." His feats prompted humorist Will Rogers to tell his radio audience: "The United States must annex Canada to acquire Williams."

In August 1930, at the Canadian national championships in Toronto, the "Human Flash" set a world record of 10.3 for 100 meters. "It was the hardest race I have run this year," Williams said afterwards. His performance broke Paddock's 1921 record of $10\frac{2}{5}$ and was a full half-second faster than Williams had run in winning the Olympic title in 1928. The IAAF, which had finally agreed to accept records timed to the nearest .1 second, ratified the record.

Two weeks later, Williams ran in the British Empire Games in Hamilton. The weather was cold and wet and the 100-yard race started 40 minutes late. The finalists, after shedding their warm-ups, were kept waiting 10 minutes in the cold rain. Halfway through the race, Williams tore a muscle in his upper thigh. Remarkably, he staggered on and won the race in 9.9 seconds, but the damage was done. He maintained years later that had the muscle been surgically repaired promptly, his career might have been saved. But the injury never healed properly and at age 22 his reign as the best sprinter in the world was over.

In 1972, Williams was voted Canada's all-time greatest Olympic athlete. Always terribly shy and introverted, he felt very bitter about the treatment of athletes in his time, especially compared with the plush lifestyles of some race officials. His last days were not happy ones. He suffered from arthritis in his knees and ankles, a worsening heart condition and two strokes. Beset with so many problems, Percy Williams committed suicide in November 1982.

### Eddie Tolan and Ralph Metcalfe— First Great Black Sprinters

As the 1930s began, new sprint sensations appeared to replace the injured Percy Williams, many of them American and black. For reasons not completely understood and worthy of more research, American blacks were never prominent as sprinters before 1900. This is surprising in view of today's great black sprinters. Other 19th century professional sports such as boxing had black champions and Frank Hart was one of the best six-day pedestrians.

Track and field was one of the first collegiate sports to include blacks and a few black athletes had been selected for U.S. Olympic teams since the Games had begun.

**Percy Williams of Canada (left) leading in the men's 200 meter race during the eighth Summer Olympic Games, Amsterdam, Netherlands, 1928 (National Archives of Canada, PA-150993).**

Howard Drew was the first great American black sprinter. He tied Duffey's 100-yard record of 9⅗ and was also an outstanding 220 runner with a smooth running form much admired by track fans. In the 1912 Olympics, Drew was the favorite in the 100 meters, but pulled a muscle in winning his semifinal heat and had to withdraw.

Eddie Tolan and Ralph Metcalfe were the first black Americans who earned the title of "World's Fastest Humans." Thomas "Eddie" Tolan, Jr., and Ralph Metcalfe both came from the Midwest and were promising high-school athletes. Tolan was born in Denver, Colorado, in September 1908, and spent his early years in Salt Lake City where he reportedly put his outstanding speed to use by relieving farmers of their watermelons. He attended Detroit's Cass Technical High School and later ran for the University of Michigan.

Tolan, known as the "Midnight Express," was five feet six inches (1.7 m) tall and weighed 130 pounds (59 kg). He smiled often, raced while chewing gum, and could be easily identified by a bandage around his left knee to protect an old football injury.

In addition he wore horn-rimmed glasses held in place with adhesive tape. In 1929 he won the 100 yards at the Big-Ten Championship, at Evanston, Illinois, setting a world record of 9.5. Two weeks later, George Simpson from Ohio State University ran 9.4, but his mark was not allowed because he had used starting blocks. Later in 1929 Tolan won both sprints at the national AAU meet and on a tour of Europe he twice equaled the world 100-meter record of 10.4.

Ralph Metcalfe, the "Black Panther of Marquette," was tall and powerful. Like Charley Paddock, Metcalfe's starts were comparatively weak, but he had an extremely long stride and was noted for the strength of his finishes. Metcalfe was born in Atlanta, Georgia, on May 29, 1910, but grew up in Chicago and later attended Marquette University. The five-foot, 11-inch (1.8 m), 180-pound (82 kg) sprinter won the 1930 AAU Junior 100-yard title in 9.7 seconds. On June 11, 1932, he set a world record of 20.5 on a 220-yard straight course and tied Tolan's 100-yard mark with 9.5. Metcalfe dominated Tolan in the 1932 Olympic trials, winning both the 100 and 200 meters, with Tolan placing second and George Simpson third in both sprints. These victories made Metcalfe the favorite to beat the apparently fading Tolan in the Los Angeles Games.

Tolan had a weakness—he tightened-up when he was under pressure. To relieve tension, he chewed gum before a race. One day as he trained, he forgot to get rid of his gum before starting, and as he sped along he realized his chewing was at the same tempo as his striding. After confiding this to his coach, they decided that Tolan should keep chewing his gum while he ran and try to accelerate his leg movements by chewing faster. It worked. Tolan felt this new-found ability to change the tempo of his stride allowed him to race Metcalfe on even terms.

In the first semifinal of the Los Angeles Olympic 100 meters, Tolan was declared the winner. A finish-line photo, however, clearly showed him finishing third behind Daniel Joubert of South Africa and Takoyoshi Yoshioka of Japan. Yoshioka was one of the fastest starters in the history of sprinting, but tended to fade over the latter part of the race. In the second semifinal Metcalfe won easily with teammate George Simpson second and Arthur Jonath from Germany third. These six made up what turned out to be the most controversial Olympic sprint final ever.

Joubert false started, and on the restart Yoshioka was out of his holes the fastest and led for the first 20 meters. Tolan and Metcalfe, neither known for their fast starts, were also off well. By 50 meters, Tolan had caught the fading Japanese sprinter and moved slightly into the lead with Metcalfe a yard behind. As the rest of the field drew even with Yoshioka, Metcalfe began his famed finishing burst and from 80 meters on ran even with Tolan. The power of Metcalfe was pitted against the piston-like leg speed of Tolan and the two sprinters hit the tape together.

Hours later, the officials were still unable to pick the winner and decided to take a look at the film from the Kirby two-eyed camera which was being used for the first time in Olympic competition. One frame showed the runners hitting the finish line at the same instant, but the next showed that Tolan's entire torso had crossed the line but Metcalfe's had not. Based on this picture, Tolan was declared the winner by two inches and awarded the gold medal. The camera also recorded 10.38 for both men and the official (hand) timers gave Tolan and Metcalfe 10.3, which tied Percy Williams's world record.

To the end of his days, Metcalfe was convinced he had either tied or won the race. He later recalled: "I heard afterward that the officials believed that I was a certain winner in the 200 meters and that it would be nice to give the gold medal to Eddie Tolan since this was going to be his last Olympics." Because of the controversy, the AAU later changed the rules for picking the winner to read: "The competitors shall be placed in the order in which any part of their bodies reaches the nearer edge of the finish line." Under these rules, Tolan and Metcalfe would have finished in a dead heat. The AAU voted to recommend retroactively awarding the 100-meter title to both Tolan and Metcalfe, but Olympic officials never accepted their recommendation and the record books list Tolan as the winner.

Metcalfe was still the favorite to win the 200 meters and won his semifinal easily. Tolan also won his semifinal, although not as impressively. The other American, George Simpson, finished second and qualified also. In the final, as the runners came out of the turn onto the home straight, Simpson led by about a meter with Tolan closing fast. Metcalfe was strangely nowhere. Tolan passed Simpson with 50 meters to go and won by two meters in 21.2 — a world record. Simpson finished second and Metcalfe third.

Later, red-faced officials admitted that Metcalfe, who was never in contention, had started from a line three meters behind his proper mark. They offered him a rerun, but he graciously declined, saying he didn't want to jeopardize the American sweep. Metcalfe went on to win a gold medal in the 1936 Olympics and become president of his senior class at Marquette. In 1970 he was elected U.S. Congressman from Illinois.

Tolan was given a hero's welcome when he returned to Detroit but it was in the middle of the Depression and he soon found that two gold medals didn't add up to one good paying job. Within a year of his Olympic triumphs, he was broke and discouraged. "The honey of this life has turned to vinegar for me," he told a reporter. Finally he landed a steady but low-paying job as a clerk in the Detroit registry of deeds office.

Tolan went to Australia in 1934 to try to become the first man to win both the amateur and professional sprint champion-

Eddie Tolan, winner of the 100 and 200 meters in the 1932 Olympics (National Archives [306-NT-161.772 C]).

Ralph Metcalfe, a great sprinter who was overshadowed by Jesse Owens (Marquette).

ships of the world. With his good humor and wit, he proved to be an outstanding showman and a crowd favorite. At the World Professional Sprint Championships, held in March 1935 in Melbourne, he won the 75-yard race in 7.5 seconds and the 100 yards in 9.75 seconds. Austin Robertson from Australia won the 130 yards in 12.38 seconds, but Tolan came back to win the last event, the 220 yards, in 21.5 seconds. Tolan's three victories gave him the professional sprint championship of the world but not a lot of money.

## Jesse Owens—An American Hero

James Cleveland "Jesse" Owens was born on September 12, 1913, in Oakville, Alabama. The youngest of ten children, as a youth he suffered from bronchitis and growths on his legs and chest that mystified doctors. Young Owens picked cotton until his family moved to Cleveland, Ohio, in the early 1920s.

At Fairmont Junior High School, he met his longtime mentor and friend, Charles Riley, a wily old math teacher and part-time coach. Riley, as Bob Granger had done with Percy Williams, sensed Owens's future greatness and made the young man his life's work. Owens often ate at Riley's home, where Riley taught him track skills as well as good manners. Upon finishing high school in 1933, Owens had won 74 of his 79 sprint races.

He first gained national acclaim in 1933 at the National Interscholastic meet at Chicago's Stagg Field. In that meet he tied Frank Wykoff's 1930 world mark of 9.4 for 100 yards and ran the straightaway 220 in 20.7 seconds. In the fall of 1933 he accepted a partial scholarship to Ohio State University with the stipulation that his unemployed father be offered a job.

Owens was popular from the beginning at Ohio State and drew huge crowds to his performances. At the National Intercollegiate championships in Ann Arbor, Michigan, on May 25, 1935, he had perhaps the most remarkable hour in track and field history. Five days earlier, in a wrestling match with a fraternity brother, he fell down a flight of stairs and injured his back. He had to be helped into his running clothes and into a car for the ride to the track. When he tried to warm up, he was too stiff to run a warmup lap, stretch, or practice starts. At the start of the 100 the pain suddenly went away. "The pain was gone," he said later. "I don't know why. My back never hurt during that hour I competed, it didn't get better but it didn't worsen either."

He started his magic hour at 3:15 P.M. when he sprang smoothly from his holes and glided down the track in 9.4 seconds to equal Frank Wykoff's 100-yard world record. Ten minutes later he marked the existing world long-jump record with a piece of paper, then made his lone attempt in that event. He sailed six inches past the mark, covering 26 feet 8¼ inches (8.13m) for a record that would last for 25 years.

At 3:45 P.M., he ran the straightaway 220 and was well in front by the time he had gone 10 yards. He finished in a remarkable 20.3, .2 seconds better than Metcalfe's world record. This record was not beaten for 14 years. At 4 P.M. he ran the 220-yard low hurdles, and won by a full second in 22.6, breaking the world record by .4 seconds. Both his records at 220 yards were better than their 200-meter equivalents, so he was given credit for world marks at 200 meters also. He had broken five world records and tied a sixth in less than an hour—an unprecedented feat.

As astounding as Owens's achievements were, he was not head and shoulders above other American sprinters of the mid–1930s. In July 1935, at the AAU Championships, Eulace Peacock beat Owens twice, in the 100 meters in a wind-aided 10.2 and in the long jump. Owens and Peacock were considered by many to be another one-two sprint punch for the upcoming Olympics as Tolan-Metcalfe had been in 1932. Peacock was Owens's greatest rival and defeated him five straight times starting in July of 1935. In all, Peacock won seven of their 10 meetings. Owens himself admitted that Peacock was the only man he ever feared on the track.

Like Owens, Peacock was from Alabama. Born in Dothan, on August 27, 1914,

**Eulace Peacock, the only man Jesse Owens feared on the track (National Archives [306-NT-180292 C]).**

he moved to Union, New Jersey, about the same time Owens moved to Cleveland. Peacock enrolled at Temple University intending to play football but the coaches thought his talents could be put to better use on the track team. The burly Peacock competed with great success in European meets in 1934–1935, running two legitimate 10.3 times for 100 meters, and losing only two races. Sadly, Peacock never made an Olympic team. In the 1936 Penn Relays in Philadelphia, he tore his right hamstring, and the injury didn't heal in time for the Olympic trials that year. With the next two Olympics canceled, Peacock, the man who had Jesse Owens's number, never had a chance at Olympic glory.

Adolf Hitler had hoped to turn the 1936 Olympic Games in Berlin into a showcase for proving the superiority of the Aryan race. Owens would play a key role in refuting this myth. He tuned up for the Games by setting a world record in the 100 meters. On June 20 at the NCAA Championships in Chicago, under ideal conditions (aiding wind, 1.2 m/s), he won the final of the 100 meters in 10.2. This record-breaking performance would not be surpassed until 1956.

In his semifinal heat on the first day of the Olympics, Owens again ran the 100 meters in 10.2, but it was wind-aided. He drew the inside lane for the 100-meter final which could have been a disaster since the lane had been chewed up in previous races. Fortunately there was an extra lane and the officials wisely moved everyone out one lane. Owens got a good start and built a two-meter lead by 50 meters. Metcalfe, with his customary poor start, got away last but came within a meter of Owens at the tape and finished second. Owens was timed in 10.3.

On Tuesday morning, August 4, Owens easily qualified for the 200-meter final. Later that day, in a memorable duel with German Luz Long, who later became his close friend, Owens won his second gold medal by long jumping 26 feet 5⁵⁄₁₆ inches (8.06m).

On Wednesday afternoon Owens became the first man to break 21 seconds for 200 meters around a curve. He cruised around the soggy, red clay track in the final of the 200 meters smoothly, almost effortlessly, to win his third gold medal. His time was a world record of 20.7, surpassing Tolan's record of 21.2 by half a second.

Neither Owens nor Metcalfe had been slated to run the 4 × 100-meter relay and neither had practiced exchanging the baton. The powerful American team was almost in a class by itself and many believed they could win by 15 meters with any combination of sprinters they chose to put on the track. On the morning of the final trial heat, the American coaches, Lawson Robertson and Dean Cromwell, replaced the two Jewish runners, Marty Glickman and Sam Stoller, with Owens and Metcalfe. According to Glickman, Owens protested, saying: "Coach, let Marty and Sam run, they deserve it. I've already won my three gold medals." Cromwell answered, "You'll do as you're told." With Owens leading off and handing off to Metcalfe, the U.S. team won easily in 39.8 seconds, a world record.

In 1998, the U.S. Olympic Committee (USOC) presented Glickman, then 80, a plaque to partly atone for the gold medal he was not allowed to compete for 62 years earlier. The USOC conceded that Glickman and Stoller were kept off the 4 × 100-meter relay team because they were Jewish.

Although Metcalfe's star never shone as brightly as Owens's, some track rating systems rank him ahead of Owens. Metcalfe's career lasted longer than Owens's and he won many more championships. In Chicago, on June, 11, 1932, Metcalfe ran 100 meters in 10.2. The NCAA ratified the time as a record, but for some unexplained reason neither the AAU nor IAAF approved it.

Shortly after the Games the AAU began a tour of Europe to raise money to pay for their trip to Berlin. Owens was the man everyone wanted to see, but he yearned to go home. Not only did he have a stack of offers from American promoters wanting to capitalize on his fame, but his many Olympic races and his competing every day on the tour had left him exhausted. He performed to a packed White City Stadium in London, then announced that he was going home. "I'm burned out and tired of being treated like a head of cattle," he told the press. The AAU suspended him for life for refusing to finish the tour and Owens never ran another race as an amateur. He had a year of eligibility left at Ohio State but didn't return to school. Except for exhibition races as a professional his running career was over.

Owens performed many exhibitions throughout his career. In the spring of 1935 at Ohio State he ran 100 yards with a 20-yard running or "flying" start. Paddock had done the "flying 100" in 8.9 seconds and

Wykoff, 8.6. Owens's time of 8.4 was written up in *Ripley's Believe It or Not*.

He missed running and was constantly in need of money, but with professional track dead in America, Owens had few opportunities to earn money with his athletic talents. He did manage to run exhibition handicap races against horses, dogs, cars and the 1936 Women's Olympic 100-meter champion Helen Stephens. Owens sometimes raced against the fastest local runners, often spotting them 10 yards and beating them by the same amount.

After a series of economic and occupational mishaps, Owens settled down as a representative for the Atlantic Richfield Company and at the request of the president, made several world tours to promote sports and international understanding. In later life, Owens was able to use his popularity and speaking ability to earn a good living on the banquet circuit. In 1971, he developed pneumonia and was forced to give up his heavy cigarette smoking. He was saddened in 1978, when his old friend and rival Metcalfe died of a heart attack, and less than a year later Owens himself became ill filming a TV commercial. Doctors found lung cancer. He returned to his home in Phoenix, Arizona, where he died in March 1980.

Owens was more than an outstanding athlete. The author can remember hearing him speak at a sports banquet at the Florida Relays in the early 1970s. The graying Owens, dressed in a neat business suit, was no longer physically imposing, but he still held the audience spellbound with his eloquent, smoothly-delivered speech. Twenty-five years later, the author is sorry to say he can't remember a word Owens said. But he will never forget the feeling of awe from being in the presence of a man who, with his running and his class, had shattered Hitler's illusion of a master race.

On May 15, 1948, American Mel Patton, in a duel with Lloyd LaBeach from Panama, lowered the 100-yard record to 9.3.

Jesse Owens, probably the best known track and field athlete of the 20th century (United States Olympic Committee).

Mel Patton ran the first official 9.3 100 yards in 1948 (National Archives [306-NT-778B-3]).

After several false starts Patton was off flying, while LaBeach was left at the post. At 20 yards Patton had a three-foot lead. LaBeach managed to close in the final 20 yards, but couldn't catch Patton, who hit the tape a foot in front. The official watches read 9.3, 9.3 and 9.4, and the rules said if two of the three watches agreed that was the official time. Patton went on to win the 200 meters in the 1948 Olympics and set a world straightaway 220-yard record of 20.2 at the 1949 USC–University of California meet.

## BETTY ROBINSON—FIRST WOMAN OLYMPIC SPRINT CHAMPION

Organized track and field for women dates back to the 1895 "field day" competition at Vassar College in New York. Women's track meets were also held in Australia, New Zealand, and South Africa early

in the 20th century. The first women's dual track meet in the United States took place in 1903 between Montclair High School in New Jersey and the Pamlico Athletic Association. Of the six events contested three were running events—50 and 75 yard sprints and a 300-yard relay. The first listing of women's athletic records appeared in the 1904 Spalding Almanac.

In Paris, France, in October 1903, 3,000 young women competed in a road race. Starting from the Place de la Concorde, the women ran a 7.5-mile (12 km) course to Nanterre. A crowd of 20,000, mostly men, turned out to watch. The winner, Jeanne Cheminel, finished in an hour and 10 minutes.

Alice Milliat, head of the Fédération Féminine Sportive de France, requested in 1919 that the International Olympic Committee (IOC) add women's track events to the Olympic Games, but her request was denied. In March 1921 the Fédération Sportive Féminine Internationale (FSFI), also headed by Milliat, held the first international women's track meet in Monte Carlo. Five countries participated in 11 events and the Games were repeated the following year with an increase in the number of athletes, teams and events. In 1926, the IOC reconsidered the proposal to add women's events to the Olympics and five events (100, 800, 4 × 100-meter relay, high jump and discus throw) were added for the 1928 Games in Amsterdam.

The winner of the women's 100 meters at Amsterdam was as much of a surprise as Percy Williams's victory had been. Elizabeth "Betty" Robinson was born in Riverdale, Illinois, in 1911. When she was 12, her teacher was so impressed when he saw her running to catch the train that took her home from school that he encouraged her to start running. She trained with the boys' track team at her high school since there was none for girls. In Chicago, on June 2, 1928, in her first outdoor meet, the slim, smiling, young woman equaled the 100-meter world record of 12.0.

Robinson edged Canada's Myrtle Cook for first place in her semifinal heat of the 100 meters at the Amsterdam Olympics. In the final — the highlight of the day's program — six nervous, jumpy young women made their way to the starting line. None had ever experienced anything like the pressure of an Olympic 100-meter final and their inexperience showed. Myrtle Cook of Canada, the favorite, made two false starts and was disqualified. When the starter waved her off the track, she seemed not to understand for a moment, then burst into tears. She soon had company in her misery when Leni Schmidt from Germany made her second false start. But instead of tears, Schmidt shook her fist at the starter. The surprised starter waved the irate sprinter off the track and at the same time tried to comfort Cook, who sat near the starting line sobbing. When the officials finally got the two disqualified sprinters off the track, Cook continued crying, but Schmidt left vowing vengeance upon the starter should they meet again.

Robinson was not nervous and jittery, but was worried about the other Canadian, Fanny Rosenfeld, who had beaten her by a whisker in the first round of heats. When the gun sounded, Rosenfeld was out fast, but near the halfway mark, Robinson pulled even. From that point on they ran stride-for-stride with the 16-year-old Robinson winning by an eyelash in 12⅕. The finish was so close that the judges picking first and second disagreed. Robinson completed her first Olympics by winning a silver medal as a member of the 4 × 100-meter relay team.

After the 1928 Olympics she continued her running, and in July of 1929 ran the 100 yards in 11⅕ seconds for a world record. Two years later, she barely survived a plane crash that left her in a coma for two months with a cracked hip and a broken leg. Doctors told her she would never compete again. But three years later, she went for a run just for the exercise, and found she could still run, although not as fast as before.

**Betty Robinson, winner of the first Olympic 100 meters for women in 1928 (United States Olympic Committee).**

Unable to bend her bad knee enough for the crouch start, she qualified for the 1936 Olympics as a member of the U.S. 4 × 100-meter relay team. The favored German team had set a world record of 46.4 in their qualifying heat and in the final ran their fastest runner first to try to build an insurmountable lead over American anchor, the great Helen Stephens. Although the German team was leading by eight meters at the last exchange, they dropped their baton, and the Americans won with 46.9, giving Robinson her second gold medal.

Mildred (Babe) Didrikson, one of the 20th century's most gifted athletes, specialized in hurdles and field events and dominated the 1932 Olympics, but set no running records.

Stella Walsh lived in the United States but competed for Poland. In her 20-year career she set nearly 100 world records at distances up to 200 meters. Competing under her given name, Stanislawa Walasiewicz, she won the women's 100 meters in the 1932 Olympics with a time of 11.9 seconds. She also held the women's 200-meter record from 1926 to 1942. Walsh was married and lived for years in Cleveland, Ohio. She was killed in 1980, caught in the cross fire during a robbery at a store where she was shopping. An autopsy revealed that she was biologically a man, making it difficult to assess her(?) athletic career.

### Helen Stephens— World's Fastest Woman

Walsh's greatest rival was Helen Stephens, a tall, slender farm-girl from Callaway County, Missouri. Stephens loved to run and as a child was able to beat all the boys she knew. She delighted in hunting rabbits by running them down. As a young girl she raced her cousin, who rode a horse, the one-mile trip to school each morning. "I could always hold my own with that horse" she explained, but added modestly, "he was wind broke and wasn't very fast."

**Helen Stephens (second from right) winning the 100-meter final at the 1936 Olympics. Stella Walsh is on the far left (United States Olympic Committee).**

When she was 15, her high school physical education teacher timed her in 5.8 seconds for 50 yards. The time tied Elizabeth Robinson's world record and prompted the instructor to have his watch checked before realizing he had a possible future Olympic champion on his hands.

Stephens, known as the "Fulton Flash," achieved additional fame in 1935 at the national AAU track meet in St. Louis. Most of the 4,000 spectators had come to see the 1932 Olympic sprint champion Stella Walsh. Stephens easily defeated Walsh in the 50 meters, winning in 6.6 seconds, then remarked "Who is Stella Walsh?" On June 1, 1935, at the Missouri Outdoor Interscholastic Championships, the 17-year-old Missourian equaled Walsh's world record of 11.8 seconds for 100 meters. Later in 1935, she won national AAU titles in the 100 and 200 meters and the discus throw.

The 1936 Olympic crowd eagerly awaited the duel between Stephens and Walsh. They roared with approval when Stephens finished 10 meters ahead of the field in her 100-meter qualifying heat in a wind-aided 11.4 seconds. In the final, before 90,000 spectators, she got away to a slow start but again destroyed the field with a time of 11.5. Walsh finished two meters back in 11.7. Both times were wind-aided. In the 4 × 100 relay Betty Robinson handed off to Stephens, who anchored the American team. On the same exchange, the German team, leading by eight meters, dropped its baton. Stephens, who died in 1994, always insisted, "I would have won that race even if they hadn't dropped the baton."

Adolf Hitler took a liking to the almost six-foot-tall (1.8 m) American sprinter and invited her to his private quarters in the stadium. Stephens later said that when she arrived, Hitler "hugged and pinched her, and then invited her to spend the weekend with him." She declined and instead gave him "a good old Missouri handshake" and asked for his autograph. Stephens passed one of the earliest sex tests at the 1936 Olympics after a Polish reporter had accused her of being a man. Ironically, the reporter's own countryman, Walsh, would not have passed the test.

On August 10, 1936, in Dresden, Stephens ran 100 meters in 11.5, and, earlier in 1935, had run 100 yards in 10.8 seconds.

Helen Stephens being congratulated by Hitler (National Archives [42-HD-0148]).

Both these marks were apparently valid, but never approved by the IAAF. Stephens was voted 1936 Associated Press Sportswoman of the Year, and retired from amateur athletics in 1937. In her brief three-year amateur career she ran over 100 races and was never beaten.

The last great female sprinter of the first half of the 20th century was Francina Elsje "Fanny" Blankers-Koen from the Netherlands. Blankers-Koen competed in the 1936 Olympics as a high-jumper and in the 4 × 100-meter relay but finished out of the medals. The next two Olympics were canceled and by 1948, Blankers-Koen was 30 years old with two children and starting her 12th season under the coaching of her husband, Jan Blankers. That year, in preparation for the London Olympics, she ran 100 yards in 10.8 seconds and equaled Helen Stephens's 100-meter record of 11.5. Still, because of her age she was written off by many for the 1948 Games. The "Flying Dutch-Woman" performed brilliantly, however, and duplicated her idol Jesse Owens's feat of winning four gold medals.

In the 1948 Games, Blankers-Koen easily won the 100 meters in 11.9. In the 80-meter hurdles she used her superior speed to come from behind and edge out Maureen Gardener of Great Britain with a world-record 11.2. She later admitted that she might have returned home after winning those first two events but was persuaded to continue by her husband. "I had had enough. I was exhausted, I was in tears and I was missing my two children," she said. "But my husband told me that if I went home then, I would regret it if I didn't run."

She won the newly added 200 meters by six meters in 24.4, and was in fourth place when she received the baton for the anchor leg of the 4 × 100-meter relay. She won for the Netherlands in almost the last stride. As phenomenal as her showing was, it would have been even better if she had been permitted to enter the long and high jumps. She held the world records in both, and the winning jumps at London were well short of her marks.

Blankers-Koen's Olympic performances were so electrifying that she silenced forever any legitimate argument that women didn't belong in Olympic track and field. Many physical education authorities of her time frowned on track and field for women. It was "injurious to the future mothers of the land," they proclaimed. In an interview after the 1948 Olympics Blankers-Koen replied: "My best answer to them is that all four members of the Netherlands relay team at London are mothers of the healthiest children you can find anywhere in Holland." Blankers-Koen closed

Fanny Bankers-Koen, female track and field athlete of the century (United States Olympic Committee).

out her career by setting a 220-yard record of 24.2 in 1950. In 1999, the IAAF voted her female athlete of the century.

## Quarter-Mile

*God made me devout — and he also made me fast.* — Eric Liddell

### THE SADDEST OF ALL OLYMPIC FINALS

The 1908 Olympics were loaded with controversy, mostly between the British host and the Americans. Possibly the most bitter dispute in Olympic history resulted from the 400-meter final. Only the semifinal heat winners made the final. Three Americans won their heats — John Taylor, with 49⅘, John Carpenter with 49⅖ and William Robbins with 49. The other runner to make the final was Lt. Wyndham Halswelle, a long-striding Scot who had set an Olympic record of 48⅖ in winning his heat. Halswelle was a near legend in Scotland, having accomplished the Lon Myers–like feat of winning the 100, 220, 440 and 880 in the Scottish Championships of 1906.

Of the Americans, John B. Taylor from

the University of Pennsylvania, who had set an intercollegiate record of 48⅕ for the quarter in 1907, was the most highly regarded. The 400-meter final was not in lanes and the start was not staggered. Because the length of the track was a third of a mile, the race was run along two straights and only one turn. Carpenter had the inside, next came Halswelle, then Robbins with Taylor on the outside. At the sound of the pistol Carpenter took the lead, followed by Robbins and Halswelle.

The three leaders were bunched as they approached the turn and it looked like anybody's race. In the turn, Carpenter forced Halswelle to the extreme outside of the track. Suddenly a number of officials rushed onto the track, tore down the tape across the finish, and declared the race void. Carpenter crossed the line first in the already canceled race in approximately 48⅖. The official judging the curve declared a foul, ruling that Carpenter had cut in front of Halswelle.

Carpenter was disqualified and a rerun scheduled for Halswelle, Robbins and Taylor. The American officials, headed by commissioner James E. Sullivan, felt Carpenter had won the race fairly and refused to allow Robbins and Taylor to participate in the rerun. Two days later Halswelle ran the distance unopposed in 50 seconds to win what British running historian Peter Lovesey has deemed "The saddest of all Olympic finals."

Halswelle described the race in a letter published in *The Sporting Life*:

> I did not attempt to pass the Americans until the last corner, reserving my effort for the finishing straight. Here I attempted to pass Carpenter on the outside, since he was not far enough from the curb to do so on the inside, and I was too close up to have crossed behind him. Carpenter's elbow undoubtedly touched my chest, for as I moved outward to pass him he did likewise, keeping his right arm in front of me.
>
> In this manner he bored me across

quite two-thirds of the track, and entirely stopped my running. As I was well up to his shoulder and endeavoring to pass him, it is absurd to say that I could have come up on the inside. I was too close after half way round the bend to have done so. Indeed, to have done so would have necessitated chopping my stride, and thereby losing anything from two to four yards.

Carpenter, in his description of the race, didn't believe his disqualification was warranted:

> As we approached the last bend Robbins had the pole and was leading by a yard. I made my effort there, and I certainly ran wide, as I have done every time I have been on the track. Halswelle had lots of room to pass me on either side.
>
> It is ridiculous to talk of a team "boring" or picketing as good a man as Halswelle in a quarter-mile race. No team could do it. We had nothing of the kind in view; we just raced him off his feet and he couldn't stand the pace.

The British and American rules for running the 400 differed. American rules allowed Carpenter to cross in front of Halswelle if he were two yards in the lead. Both the British and Olympic rules prohibited such crossing under any conditions and the Americans had been informed of these rules. American Caspar Whitney, in a 1908 editorial in *Outing Magazine*, had the last word on the unhappy incident:

> Sportsmen will always regret that the Americans refused to run the race over as ordered by the referee. No matter how incensed they may have been; no matter how sure they may have felt of the injustice of the decision, when they entered the Games they subscribed to its rules and agreed to abide by the decisions of the judges; the decision of the judges in this case was final, and the Americans should have kept their mouths shut and abided by that decision.

Finish of 1908 400-meter final. John Carpenter of the United States is looking back at Wynd-ham Halswelle, whom he has forced to the extreme outside. Carpenter was disqualified and Halswelle won the gold medal in a walk over (*Outing*, September 1908).

John Taylor, one of the two Americans who were not allowed to participate in the rerun, did run the 400-meter leg of the 1,600-meter medley relay. The American team won, making Taylor the first black American to win an Olympic gold medal. Taylor returned to Philadelphia a hero, but died suddenly from typhoid on December 2, 1908. Neither Halswelle nor Carpenter had much enthusiasm for running after the Olympics, and Halswelle was killed at the battle of Neuve Chapelle in 1915. The "bor-ing" incident lead to some needed changes in the administration of the Games. In fu-ture Olympics the 400 meters would be run in lanes and the officials would not be from the host nation but from international gov-erning bodies.

ERIC LIDDELL—
AN INSPIRED RUNNER

The next great quarter-miler was Eric H. Liddell, Scotland's most famous athlete. No watch could measure the spirit of Eric Liddell and perhaps no runner ever came closer to running on pure inspiration. The story of Eric Liddell, along with teammate Harold Abrahams, is told in the 1981 movie *Chariots of Fire*. Although the movie takes some liberties with historical facts, it is the most successful film yet made with a run-ning theme.

Liddell was an outstanding 100-yard sprinter, having covered the distance in 9.7 seconds. Yet he refused to run the 1924 Olympic 100 meters at Paris when he found that the heats were to be held on Sunday. In-stead, he concentrated on training for the 400 meters which he considered his next best event.

After finishing third in the 200-meter final, behind American stars Scholz and Paddock, Liddell was given little chance to reach the final of the 400 meters. Experts agreed that the race was beyond his best distance and his running form was terrible. He ran with an ungainly energy-wasting style, his head far back, arms flailing and knees pumping.

Liddell ran his first 400-meter heat in 50⅕, finishing second, and later that day won his quarter-final in a personal best 49.0. The next day he won his semifinal in 48⅕— another personal best and only ⅖ seconds slower than the Olympic record. He was clearly peaking at the right time, but winning the final seemed an insurmountable task. Swiss runner Joseph Imbach had run 48.0 in one of his heats and the American star, Horatio Fitch, had run a seemingly effortless 47⅘ in his semifinal heat.

For the final, Liddell drew the dreaded outside lane, where, for most of the race, he would not be able to see his rivals. Liddell shook hands with all the finalists before they took their positions and when the pistol sounded, he was off like a shot. He flashed past 200 meters in 22⅕ seconds— only .3 seconds slower than he had run in finishing third in the 200-meter final. Guy M. Butler of Britain followed in second place three meters back.

As the runners came off the bend into the straight, Fitch began closing fast. The favored American caught Butler and pulled within two meters of Liddell. Though apparently completely exhausted by the fast early pace, somehow Liddell summoned a hidden reserve. With his head back, mouth open, and arms waving, he increased his lead over Fitch to five meters, winning in a world record 47⅗.

When Liddell graduated from the University of Edinburgh in July 1924, the vice-chancellor quipped: "Mr. Liddell, you have shown that none can pass you but the examiner." After he received his degree and was crowned with a wreath, his fellow stu-

dents carried their hero the quarter mile to St. Giles Cathedral. Forced to make a speech, Liddell centered it on the words inscribed over the entrance gate of the University of Pennsylvania: "In the dust of defeat as well as in the laurel of victory there is glory to be found if one has done his best." Those who had done their best and failed to win were owed as many honors as those who received them, he added.

Later, in an interview, Liddell was asked how he managed to run at such a fantastic pace with his curious style. "The secret of my success over the 400 meters is that I run the first 200 meters as hard as I can. Then, for the second 200 meters, with God's help, I run harder."

Shortly after the 1924 Olympics, Liddell went to China to begin work for the

Eric Liddell, the "Flying Scotsman" (National Archives [306-NT-6528 B]).

London Missionary Society. Five years later, some way down a world 400-meter ranking list, an entry showed that Liddell had run 49.0 "somewhere in China." At the beginning of World War II he was captured by the Japanese forces occupying China. Eric Liddell died in 1945 of a brain tumor in a prison camp in North China.

## BEN EASTMAN AND WILLIAM CARR— CLASSIC DUELS AT 400 METERS

The track world would never have known "Blazing" Ben Eastman if physical education had not been a requirement for graduation at Burlingame High School in San Mateo County, California. Ben and his brother Sam had managed to dodge all the physical education classes until their senior year. Their hobby of camping in the High Sierras and taking long hikes gave them all the exercise they thought they needed. But they wanted their diplomas, and in the last half of their senior year they found they could substitute track for physical education. Almost overnight Ben became a running sensation.

Early in 1932, during his sophomore season at Stanford University, Eastman tied Ted Meredith's world record of 47.4 for the quarter mile. On March 26, 1932, in a special record attempt at Palo Alto, California, the six-foot, one-inch (1.8 m) 155-pound (70 kg) Eastman destroyed Meredith's record. Stanford coach Dink Templeton was suffering from arthritis and had been unable to leave his hospital bed for months. Just before the race, he phoned Eastman: "Don't tie up. Go right out from the gun and run just as fast as you can. Run easily, without effort, but run like hell." Eastman sprinted the first 220 in 21.3 and although he faded badly in the last 20 yards, he broke the old 440 record by a full second. His remarkable time of 46.4 seconds remains the largest improvement in either the 400-meter or 440-yard records ever made by an amateur or professional. Two weeks later,

"Blazing Ben" Eastman held world records at 440 and 880 yards (Stanford University Athletics Department).

Bill Carr, the "Arkansas Flyer," defeated Ben Eastman and set a world record in the 1932 Olympic 400-meter final (University of Pennsylvania).

on April 9, Eastman set a world record of 1.51.3 for the half mile, knocking .3 seconds off Dr. Otto Peltzer's 1926 record.

Eastman appeared to be the world's best quarter-miler by far, but there was a surprise waiting in the East. William Arthur Carr, known as the "Arkansas Flyer," was an outstanding relay runner for the University of Pennsylvania. Before 1932, the compact, dark-haired Carr seldom competed in the open 440 and had recorded a best time of 48.4 seconds. Carr faced Eastman in the quarter mile at the 1932 IC4A championships and, to almost everyone's surprise, came from behind to win in 47.0. The story was repeated at the 1932 Olympic trials. Carr again passed Eastman near the finish to win in 46.9 to Eastman's 47.1.

The rivalry was renewed at the 1932 Olympics in Los Angeles. Eastman held the word record for the 880 as well as the 440 going into the Games, and may have actually been better at the longer distance. He didn't run the 800 meters in the Olympics, partially because his coach, "Dink" Templeton, felt Eastman should have been selected to run the Olympic 800 based on his world record.

The Olympic 400 meters would decide, once and for all, whether Carr, the fast finisher from the East, or Eastman, the front-runner from the West, was the world's best. There was a thunderous outburst from the Los Angeles crowd as the two Americans came to the line. Eastman, the favorite, started from lane two and Carr from lane four. They got away smoothly, with the long-striding Eastman bolting into the lead and sprinting the first 100 meters in 10.8 to Carr's 10.9. Still going flat out, Eastman passed the halfway point in 21.9, having built a .2 second lead over Carr.

The pace was too "hot," however, and in the third 100 meters Eastman slowed to 11.8 and the relentless Carr cut the lead to .1 second. Both men slowed even more over the last 100, but Carr was the stronger and passed his teammate with 80 meters to go and snapped the tape two meters ahead with a world record of 46.2. Like Eric Liddell, Carr and Eastman did not back off or "float" the mid part of their 400-meter race. Neither ever let up.

The two men never raced each other again. After the Olympics, Eastman moved up to the half mile and on June 16, 1934, set a world record of 1:49.8. Following a 20-month layoff he ran in the 1936 Olympic trials, but failed to make the team as a half-miler. Carr was involved in an automobile accident in 1933, breaking his hip and ending his running career. During his brief career, Carr was never beaten at 400 meters or 440 yards.

Following the trail blazed by Tolan and Metcalfe in the shorter distances, Archibald Franklin Williams was the first great black quarter-miler. At Berkeley he ran for the famous coach Brutas Hamilton, whom he respected greatly. Williams once commented, "I think he had more to do with whatever success I had, not only on the track but in life, than anyone else. He was always gentle, always positive, and he got results out of us that no other coach could have."

Williams improved rapidly under Hamilton, knocking two full seconds off his 440 time in one year. On June 19, 1936, at the NCAA meet in Chicago, he passed the 220 in 21.6 on his way to 440 yards in 46.5 (around one turn). His time at 400 meters was a world record of 46.1. A week later, Jimmy Lu Valle ran the 400 meters around two turns in 46.3. The pair went to Berlin hoping to duplicate the Carr-Eastman double of 1932.

Williams won his semifinal in 47.2 and Brown qualified right behind Lu Valle (47.1) in the second semifinal with 47.3. Lu Valle and Williams went out hard in the final and Godfrey Brown from Britain in lane six appeared to be out of the race. Brown eased up coming off the second turn, then as if he suddenly realized he could beat the two Americans, he unleashed a tremendous finishing burst that carried him past Lu Valle and nearly past Williams as well. The unofficial Zielbildkamera photo-finish system gave Williams 46.66, Brown 46.68, and LuValle 46.84.

The next great quarter miler was Rudolf Harbig of Germany. Harbig was born on November 8, 1913, at Dresden and started his career in 1932 at age 19 as a cross country runner. In 1934 he discovered he had more speed than endurance and switched to shorter distances and ran the 100 meters in 10.6 and the 200 in 21.5. His foundation of cross country for endurance and several years of sprinting to develop speed enabled him to attack the middle-distance records with great success.

### DR. GERSHLER AND THE ORIGIN OF INTERVAL TRAINING

Harbig was coached by Dr. Woldemar Gerschler, a professor of physical education at Turenne College in Germany. Gerschler was one of the originators of "interval training," which stressed running repeated short distances at relatively high intensity with "intervals" of rest that gave incomplete recovery. During 1935–1940, working with 3,000 "average" patients, Gerschler and a cardiologist, Dr. Herbert Reindel, developed the basic principles of interval training.

The distance run was chosen to cause the heart rate to peak at around 180 beats per minute. Then the runner rested for up to 90 seconds. When the heart rate returned to 120–125 beats per minute, he began the next run. If the heart rate failed to return to 120–125 beats per minute within 90 seconds the workout was terminated. The goal of interval training was to increase general endurance by enlarging the heart. Gerschler and Reindel found that after 21 days of interval training, heart volume could be increased by 20 percent.

The development of a scientifically-based, easily applied training method was of enormous importance in the history of running. Although others had developed similar training methods, they were based on trial and error or intuition and were usually kept secret. Gerschler and Reindel gave interval training to the world and soon it was adapted to all distances from 400 meters to the marathon. Harbig proved the merits of interval training at Frankfurt on August 12, 1939, when he ran 46.0 to shave .1 second off Archie Williams's three-year-old 400-meter record.

### HERB MCKENLEY— THE MOST FRUSTRATED OLYMPIAN

Harbig's record stood until 1948 when it was broken by Herbert McKenley of Jamaica. McKenley attended Boston College and the University of Illinois after an impressive career at Calabar High School in Jamaica. On June 5, 1948, tuning up for the 1948 Olympic Games, McKenley ran 440 yards in 46.0 seconds at Berkeley. A month later, in a heat of the AAU Championship at Milwaukee, he ran the 400 meters in 45.9, becoming the first man to dip under 46 seconds.

Liddell, in the 1924 Olympics, and Eastman, with less success in 1932, had tried

Herb McKenley from Jamaica was a great 400-meter runner who had bad luck at the Olympics (National Archives [306-NT-642-7]).

to turn the 400 meters into a sprint from the gun. McKenley, with his "maximum speed, minimum deceleration" efforts carried these tactics to the extreme.

At the London Olympics in 1948, he was considered the most likely gold-medal winner of the Games. In the 400-meter final, he hit the 200-meter mark in 21.1, the same as the winning time in the 200-meter final, and led for the first 395 meters. But in the last five meters, his teammate Arthur Wint caught a tired McKenley and won by a foot. McKenley would never admit that he had run the first 200 meters too fast. He insisted that he had gone even faster for the first 200 in setting his world records. It was the third 100 meters, he believed, that cost him the race, as he related in *Herb McKenley Olympic Star* (1974): "I felt so relaxed at 200 I just kept on running at that pace. My 300 was 33 seconds; halfway down the home-stretch it seemed the entire stadium had fallen on me."

In 1952 at the Helsinki Games, McKenley showed his versatility by finishing second to American Lindy Remigino in a photo-finish 100-meter final. Two days later, McKenley ran his favorite event, the 400 meters. In the final he and his teammate George "Hurricane Herbert" Rhoden both crossed the finish line in 45.9 but the photo finish camera gave Rhoden the gold medal. McKenley closed out his Olympic career by running a magnificent third leg of the 4 × 400 relay to bring his team from 15 meters behind. Then Rhoden held off Mal Whitfield of the United States, to give Jamaica the victory and McKenley his only Olympic gold medal.

## *Half Mile—800 Meters*

### "Peerless" Mel Sheppard

Melvin B. Sheppard, who ran for the Irish-American Athletic Club, was born in 1883 at Almonesson Lake, N.J. He won AAU half-mile titles in 1906, 1908, 1911 and 1912, but his lasting fame came from his performances in the 1908 Olympics. Shortly before the London Olympics, Sheppard was rejected as a candidate for the New York police force because examining doctors diagnosed an enlarged heart.

At the Games in London, Sheppard showed few signs of dropping dead from heart disease. In the heats of the 1,500 meters, where only the winner advanced, Sheppard drew the same heat as teammate J. P. Halstead, of Cornell, considered the best miler in America. Sheppard defeated Halstead by a yard in 4:05, after a terrific struggle.

In the 1,500-meter final, the favorite was British world record holder H. A. Wilson—the first man to run the 1,500 meters in under four minutes (3:59$\frac{4}{5}$). Wilson had qualified easily in 4:11$\frac{2}{5}$. Coach "Mike" Murphy, who knew that Sheppard ran best when he was angry, talked to him just before the final. "Mel you might as well stay in the stands," Murphy is reported to have said. "You don't have a chance." Sheppard marched off steaming. In the race, Wilson took the lead on the third lap, but turning into the stretch, Sheppard shot past with 15 yards to go. He held on to win by a yard in 4:03$\frac{2}{5}$.

The next day in the final of the 800 meters, Britain's I. F. Fairbairn-Crawford set a very fast pace in an effort to draw Sheppard out, with teammate T. H. Just ready to take over on the second lap. The plan backfired when Just, who expected to pass Sheppard in the stretch, had nothing left, and was not only beaten by the American, but also by Emilio Lunghi of Italy and Hanns Braun of Germany. Sheppard had covered the first lap in 53 seconds and won easily in 1:52$\frac{4}{5}$, a world record. The American star ran another fast 800 meters when he anchored the winning 1,600-meter medley relay for his third Olympic victory.

In July 1910, Sheppard ran 1,000 yards in 2:12$\frac{2}{5}$ seconds, clipping $\frac{3}{5}$ of a second from Lon Myers's mark of 29 years' standing—a record that nearly every middle-distance champion in that period had tried to beat. Sheppard died in 1942 at age 58 from "acute indigestion."

## TED MEREDITH—A CLASSIC OLYMPIC 800-METER FINAL

In the 1912 Olympics at Stockholm, eight men qualified for the 800-meter final. Six were Americans, including Mel Sheppard, the defending champion, and James Edwin "Ted" Meredith, a 19-year-old Pennsylvania schoolboy. Hanns Braun of Germany, who had finished second in the London Olympic Games of 1908, was also in the final. Braun, a fast finisher, was expected to be the main threat to Sheppard in his bid to win his second Olympic 800 meters. The American plan was similar to the one the British had tried in the previous Olympics. They would try to take away Braun's closing sprint by setting a blistering pace right from the start.

Coach Mike Murphy, after consulting the other coaches, decided that the young and inexperienced Meredith would be the "sacrificial lamb" and set the pace to kill off Braun. Meredith agreed to this strategy but when the race started Sheppard had a plan of his own. Sticking with the tactics that had won him the 800 meters in the previous Olympics, he went all out from the start. He flew over the first 400 meters in 52.4 seconds—even faster than he had gone four years earlier. Meredith followed, along with Braun, then the other Americans. Both Meredith and Braun closed on Sheppard as they rounded the last turn. Sheppard fought desperately and managed to hold off Braun but Meredith, running on the outside, kept coming and slipped by Sheppard for the victory. His time of 1:51.9 was a world record. Sheppard and Ira Davenport took the silver and bronze medals. Both were timed in 1:52.0, also breaking the record. Braun finished fourth in 1:52⅕. Only .8 seconds separated the first six finishers in one of the greatest 800-meter races in history.

Ted Meredith was an intense runner who won a gold medal in the 800 meters in 1912 and held both the 440- and 880-yard world records (*New York Times*, March 26, 1916).

Meredith kept going to complete 880 yards in 1:52½ which was also a world mark. On his return to America he entered the University of Pennsylvania and became an intercollegiate track star. In a dual meet between Cornell and Pennsylvania on May 13, 1916, he improved his 880-yard record to 1:52⅕, running the first 440 in 54⅘. Two weeks later at Cambridge, Massachusetts, in the IC4A championships, Meredith showed his ability as a quarter-miler. Although he was forced to pass the field on a turn, he still set a world record of 47⅖ seconds. At the Penn Relays in 1916 he ran a fabulous last leg in the mile relay, being timed in 46 seconds and gaining 20 yards on Willcox, of Harvard, a 48-second quarter-miler.

Meredith had exceptional speed, the "strength of an ox" and great fighting spirit, but swung his arms like the blades of a windmill when he ran. He also found it difficult to stay in top form. After a layoff he needed almost twice as much training as

Otto Peltzer, a German doctor, set world records in the 800 and 1,500 meters (National Archives [306-NT-56474]).

the ordinary runner to recover his fitness. He was equally talented at 400 and 800 meters but preferred the shorter distance believing it required less training.

### OTTO PELTZER—THE MAN WHOSE SHORTS WERE TOO SHORT

At the British Championships of 1926, 26-year-old Otto Peltzer, the German champion at 400 meters, 1,500 meters and 400 meter hurdles was on hand to race Douglas Lowe of Britain at 800 meters. Peltzer had missed the 1924 Olympics because the Germans were not invited. The race at Stamford Bridge was a classic, featuring 27,000 roaring spectators, a scorching pace and a world record.

When Peltzer removed his warm-ups, the starter looked him over and informed him that his shorts were too short. After all, the Queen was in the audience. An embarrassed Peltzer raced back to the dressing room to look for a longer pair. None were to be found, so he desperately pulled his shorts off and turned them around backwards. After putting them on again and pulling them as low as possible, he sprinted back to the starting line. The starter allowed him to join the race and after a false start the German champion let Lowe set the pace, as he hung back in fourth place.

Near the 400-meter mark, which Lowe passed in 54.6, Peltzer smoothly moved into second place. About 300 meters from the tape Peltzer challenged for the lead. Lowe answered and the two ran stride for stride for a hundred meters before the German eased, seemingly beaten, then somehow summoned the energy to come back with a final burst to win. Peltzer's time of 1:51.6 decisively beat Ted Meredith's 10-year-old world record of 1:52.2, and Lowe, three yards back, was inside the old record as well. Lowe, after analyzing his defeat, concentrated on quarter-miling during the 1927 season to improve his speed.

## Douglas Lowe—Double Olympic 800-Meter Champion

Douglas Lowe was the first man to win the Olympic 800 meters twice. In the 1924 Paris Olympic final he had been sixth at the end of the first lap, but with 200 meters to go made his move and won in 1:52.4. Lowe's chances for defending his 800-meter title in the 1928 Games looked dim. In the U.S. trials, Lloyd Hahn ran 800 meters in 1:51.4 and a week later, Sera Martin of France set a world record of 1:50.6 seconds.

In the 1928 Games at Amsterdam, Lowe drew an easy qualifying heat and won in 1:55.8, but Hahn (1:52.6) and Martin (1:53) had to fight hard to win theirs. An injured Peltzer finished fifth in the semifinal and didn't advance. In the final, Hahn tried to run away from the field with a 53-second first 400 meters. Lowe, however, stayed at his shoulder, keeping the pressure on. With 100 meters to go, Lowe took off and destroyed the field with a finish that won him the race by eight meters. His year of training for greater speed had paid off. Lowe was a tactical runner, with a fine finishing kick. He was more interested in winning than in fast times.

Women ran the Olympic 800 meters for the first time in 1928. Inga Gentzel of Sweden, who had recently set a world record of 2:20, was the favorite. Kinue Hitomi from Japan set the early pace, followed by Lina Radke of Germany. With 300 meters to go, Radke made her move with Gentzel and Hitomi going with her. Radke won in 2:16.8, with both Hitomi and Gentzel also under the old record. Six of the nine runners sprawled on the ground from exhaustion after the race and two were carried away on stretchers. The Olympic governing body overreacted and banned the women's 800 meters. The event was not restored to the Games until 1960.

Lowe was followed on the world 800-meter scene by countryman Tommy Hampson, who also had a plan for winning the Olympic 800 meters. He reasoned that a time of 1:50 would be needed to win in Los Angeles in 1932. This would mean running a world record in an Olympic final—no easy feat. Instead of relying on a finishing kick, Hampson planned to achieve his victory with even pacing.

In 1925 British scientist A. V. Hill, who had won the Nobel prize for medicine in 1922, published a paper, "The Physiological Basis of Athletic Records." Hill concluded that for races that took longer than about 50 seconds, even pacing used the least energy and was the optimum pacing strategy for setting records. Later researchers found that Hill's conclusion was based on bad data, but the paper was widely read and contributed greatly to the trend toward more even-paced running.

Hampson wrote, "I was convinced, having studied some of Professor Hill's researches and knowing the work of the 'oxygen-debt' theory, that the Finnish runners were correct when they maintained that the most economical method of running was to keep as near as possible to an even pace throughout." He planned two evenly paced laps of 55 seconds each and worked on even pacing for all of 1931 and 1932. He ran several races during those years, including the British AAA Championships, with lap times that were consistently within ⅖ second of each other.

In the Los Angeles Olympic final, Phil Edwards from Canada led off at a near-sprint to cover the first 200 meters in 24.4 seconds and the first lap in 52.8. Hampson ran his own race 20 meters back, passing the 400 meters fifth in 55 seconds—right on schedule. Then as the leaders slowed, Hampson's steady pace began to reclaim the lost ground. By the back straight he had overtaken them all without increasing his speed. Another Canadian, Alex Wilson, had stayed on Hampson's shoulder from the start and had the benefit of even pacing without the work of setting it.

Wilson took the lead on the final

Tom Hampson set a world 800-meter record in the 1932 Olympics by running a perfectly paced race (National Archives [306-NT-172. 801 C]).

curve, but Hampson stayed with his plan, knowing that he was on a world-record pace. Hampson drew even with Wilson, and out of the corner of his eye saw the white form of the Canadian fade from view just as he felt the tape break across his chest. The time was 1:49.8 seconds. By running laps of 55.0 and 54.8, Hampson had an Olympic victory, a world record, and had become the first man to run the 800 meters under 1:50.

In 1936 Ben Eastman ran 880 yards in 1:49.8 and was given credit for tying Hampson's record. Two other American milers, Glenn Cunningham (1:49.7 in 1936) and Elroy Robinson (880 yards in 1:49.6 in 1937) improved the 800-meter record marginally.

## "LONG" JOHN WOODRUFF—
### FIRST GREAT BLACK
### MIDDLE-DISTANCE RUNNER

John Woodruff, a near giant for a runner at six feet four inches (1.9 meters) and 183 pounds (83 kg), was an outstanding 800-meter runner from the University of Pittsburgh. As a freshman in 1936 he ran 1:49.9 in his semifinal of the 1936 American Olympic trials. In the Berlin 800 meter final, his inexperience almost cost him the gold medal.

The American coach, Lawson Robertson, warned Woodruff before the race to stay clear of entanglements. Unfortunately, on the first lap he became badly boxed in and was unable to free himself. The long-striding Woodruff took the only option open to him: He came to an almost complete stop. The other runners went on, leaving him in last place. With a furious rush,

John Woodruff won the 800 meters in the 1936 Olympics (National Archives [306-NT-112, 166]).

he ran out into the third lane and caught and passed the whole field. When he eased up on the final turn, Phil Edwards from Canada passed him. But Woodruff sprinted again and went on to win the gold medal by two meters. After the 1936 Olympics, Woodruff was never beaten in a half-mile race.

In 1938, Englishman Sydney Wooderson, who already held the mile record, turned his attention to half-miling. Running in a specially designed handicap race at Motspur Park, Surry, the diminutive, almost frail looking Wooderson smashed the record. Wooderson started from 10 inches behind the starting line in case the course turned out to be short. Following his "rabbits" he passed the quarter mile in 52.7 and caught all of them by the home straight. With a superlative effort, he broke the 800-meter tape in 1:48.4 and continued for 5.1 yards to the 880-yard mark in 1:49.2 — both world records.

### RUDOLF HARBIG— AN ASTONISHING 800-METER RECORD

On July 15, 1939, on a 500-meter track at Milan, Italy, Rudolf Harbig ran the greatest 800 meters of the first half of the 20th century. Mario Lanzi of Italy, the favorite, had set a new Italian record of 1:49.5 for 800 meters a month earlier. The Italian raced the first 400 meters in 52.0, with Harbig several yards back. Having reached the 600 meters mark in a killing 1:20, Lanzi was dismayed to find Harbig still on his shoulder. Harbig sprinted the last 200 meters to win in an astonishing 1:46.6 — a record that would last for 16 years. Harbig, who also held the 400-meter record of 46.0, broke the world record for 1,000 meters in 1941 with 2:21.5. He might have gone on to greater achievements had he not been killed fighting in East Prussia in 1944.

Rudolf Harbig, in all white, racing Mario Lanzi of Italy. Harbig's 800-meter record of 1:46.6 lasted 16 years (National Archives [131-GR-218 15]).

## *Mile—1,500 Meters*

*The art of running the mile consists, in essence, of reaching the threshold of unconsciousness at the instant of breasting the tape.*— Paul O'Neil

By 1915, Walter George's 1886 mile record of 4:12¾ had been on the books for 29 years. Only amateur Tommy Conneff (4:15⅗ in 1895) and professional George B. Tincler (4:15⅕ in 1897) had even come close. In 1913, American amateur John Paul Jones from Cornell sprinted his final lap in an amazing 58 seconds to clock 4:14⅖ and come a bit closer. Jones's last lap time would not be surpassed for many years in a major race.

At Cambridge, Massachusetts, on July 16, 1915, Norman S. Taber, a Brown University runner and later a Rhodes Scholar, made an assault on George's record. Taber, who had won a bronze medal in the 1912 Olympics, had spent six months preparing for the attempt. He chose the Harvard stadium track, which judges and timers agreed was the fastest they had ever seen. The effort was billed as a handicap race but instead of giving reasonable handicaps, the handicaps were adjusted to allow the other runners to act as pacers.

J. W. Ryan, with a 10-yard start, led Taber through the first quarter in 58 seconds. Then Taber caught D. J. Mahoney, who had started with a 120-yard handicap. Mahoney led him through the second and third quarters in 67 and 68 seconds, then J. M. Burke, who had been loitering ahead of them with a huge 355-yard handicap, took the pacing duties. Taber passed Burke coming into the straight and covered the final quarter in 59⅗ and the mile in 4:12⅗.

He had broken George's 4:12¾ record by .15 seconds. This lowering of the record

Norman Taber ran 4:12⅗ to break Walter George's 1886 mile record in 1915 (from George Orton, *Spalding's Distance and Cross-Country Running*, 1916).

by the difference between 4:12¾ and 4:12⅗ may have been entirely because the newer watches timed in ⅕ second increments rather than ¼ seconds. In addition, there were objections raised because the record was not set under true racing conditions. Nevertheless, the performance was accepted as a world record and set a precedent for orchestrated record attempts that has continued to this day. Taber's performance also marked the end of an era. George's mile record was the last for a commonly contested track distance to be held by a professional.

### Paavo Nurmi— "I Never Really Concentrated on the Mile"

The first runner to lower George's mile record decisively was Paavo Nurmi, the "Phantom Finn." In 1923, 27-year-old Edvin Wide of Sweden, who had run 1,500 meters in 3:56.7, was at his peak and challenged Nurmi to a race. Nurmi, on finding that Wide's best distance was the mile, agreed to a race at that distance. During the spring, Nurmi concentrated on speed, and brought his 800-meter time down to 1:56.3. What Nurmi had in mind is uncertain, but some sources reported that he planned an evenly paced race of four 62-second laps to give him a 4:08 mile.

The race took place on August 23, before a crowd of 18,000 in the Stockholm Olympic Stadium. If Nurmi had planned an evenly paced race, Wide never allowed him to use the plan. Wide jumped into the lead and pushed the pace for the first quarter which he covered in 58⅗. Nurmi, drawn into the fast pace, followed a short distance behind. The Phantom Finn, stopwatch in hand, challenged Wide for the lead on the second lap and the two men ran past the half-mile nearly even in 2:03⅕.

The pace was too fast for Wide, who began to fade on the third lap. Nurmi reached the ¾-mile mark in 3:06⅗ as Wide struggled to stay with him. On the last lap

Nurmi glanced back at Wide, then slowly left him. He passed 1,500 meters in a record 3:53 and went on to win by 18 yards in 4:10$\frac{2}{5}$, beating Taber's eight-year-old record by 2$\frac{1}{5}$ seconds.

With the mile record in hand, Nurmi moved up to longer races and except for his 1,500-meter/5,000-meter double in the 1924 Olympics, never concentrated on the mile again. In 1940, he predicted that the four-minute mile would be broken within 10 years, adding: "I never specialized in the mile, but I honestly believe that if I had concentrated on the mile, I could have driven the time down between 4:06 and 4:07 fifteen years ago.... It will be run at an even speed—four 60-second quarters. That is less exertion and that is the way it will be done."

On September 11, 1926, in Berlin, Otto Peltzer ended Nurmi's reign as 1,500-meter record holder. Peltzer's opponents were Nurmi and Wide. Nurmi didn't relinquish his record without a struggle as he took the lead and held it for the first three laps. When he looked around and saw Peltzer and Wide still with him, in typical Nurmi fashion, he increased his speed. But Wide charged past as they went down the backstretch, and Nurmi was unable to respond.

With 60 meters left, Peltzer caught Wide and for 20 meters they ran shoulder to shoulder. Then Peltzer summoned a reserve and pulled away to win by about three meters. Almost unnoticed, Nurmi crossed the line third. For the first time the 1,500-meter record was better than the mile mark—Peltzer's winning time of 3:51 was equal to a mile in 4:09.5. Although injuries and misfortune kept Peltzer from winning any Olympic medals, he was one of the best middle distance runners of his day. Later in World War II he managed to survive a Nazi concentration camp only because of his superior fitness and knowledge of physiology.

Up until the late 1920s the world had seen two superb milers—Walter George, running his splendid duels with Cummings in the 1880s, and Nurmi in the 1920s. The 1930s brought a new crop of milers and a golden age of miling. Peltzer, who had run a 46.5-second 400 meters on a relay, had shown what a miler with speed could do. Many of this new breed of milers could run the quarter mile under 50 seconds and the last lap of an all-out mile race in under 60. The world followed these matches with great interest and the winners' names became household words. In the United States, running the mile indoors became the rage with the most famous venue being Madison Square Garden. The smoky air and enthusiastic, noisy crowds close enough to touch the runners had an almost magical effect, inspiring many magnificent performances.

### Jules Ladoumègue—First Under 4:10

Frenchman Jules Ladoumègue, born at Bordeaux on December 10, 1906, got things rolling in 1930. Ladoumègue, a temperamental but talented runner, had won the silver medal in the 1,500 meters at the 1928 Amsterdam Olympics with 3:53$\frac{4}{5}$. He was at the top of his form in October 1930 when he lowered the 1,500 meter record to 3:49$\frac{1}{5}$.

He next broke Tommy Conneff's ancient three-quarter-mile record of 3:02$\frac{4}{5}$ on Sept 13, 1931, when he ran 3:00$\frac{3}{5}$. On October 4, 1931, in Jean Bouin Stadium in Paris, Ladoumègue went after Nurmi's mile record in a specially staged race. The weather was perfect, with no wind. Rene Morel, a 1:54 800-meter runner, set the early pace, passing 440 yards in 60$\frac{4}{5}$ and 880 in 2:04$\frac{1}{5}$. On the third lap Morel slowed and by three quarters of a mile, passed in 3:08, Ladoumègue was all by himself but 1.3 seconds behind Nurmi's record pace. He pushed the entire last quarter and passed 1,500 meters in 3:52.4—0.6 ahead of Nurmi's pace. Finishing with a 16.8-second last 120 yards, he covered the mile in 4:09$\frac{1}{5}$ to become the first man to come within ten seconds of the "magic" four-minute mile.

**Jules Ladoumègue of France. In 1931, he became the first man to run the mile under 4:10 (National Archives [306-NT-778C-3]).**

Now a national hero, Ladoumègue was favored to win the Olympic 1,500 meters in the Los Angeles Games of 1932. But the French Athletic Federation, much to the disappointment of Ladoumègue and the disgust of the French public, banned him for life for receiving under-the-table payments from meet promoters.

## JACK LOVELOCK—THE LEGEND

John Edward "Jack" Lovelock was born on January 5, 1910, at Cushington, New Zealand. He was an introspective, analytical, runner who kept careful records of both his triumphs and his failures. Throughout much of his career he suffered from insomnia and chronic knee problems. During his early years in New Zealand he practiced running on one side of a stone wall with a friend running on the other side. His friend's job was to watch for Lovelock's head to make sure it didn't rise above the

wall. By doing this he eliminated much of his bobbing up and down, making his running smoother and more efficient. After years of practice, Lovelock, who was noted for his slight build, curly blond hair and broad smile, developed an almost perfectly smooth running form with magnificent acceleration when he needed it.

In the fall of 1931 at age 22 he went to Oxford as a Rhodes Scholar to study medicine. One of his first visits was to the famous Iffley Road three-laps-to-a-mile track, where races were still being run clockwise. Twenty-three years later Roger Bannister would run the first sub-four-minute mile here, but on a new counterclockwise 440-yard track.

In May 1932, in a match at Iffley Road, Lovelock was anxious to impress the New Zealand Olympic Selection Committee. Aided by pace makers, he pushed the pace from the beginning and surprised everyone with a new British mile record of 4:12. He had never broken 4:20 before this race. The committee selected Lovelock for the New Zealand team, but he was not yet ready for top-flight international competition. He finished a disappointing seventh in the 1932 Olympic 1,500 meter final in Los Angeles, which was won by Italian Luigi Beccali in 3:51.2.

## CUNNINGHAM AND BONTHRON— AMERICA'S BEST

Lovelock's greatest rival was Glenn Cunningham, the "Kansas Iron Man" who finished fourth at Los Angeles. Cunningham, born on August 4, 1909, in Atlanta, Kansas, was the greatest American miler in the first half of the 20th century. When he was seven, young Glenn and his older brother, Floyd, were badly burned when they accidentally poured gasoline on hot coals attempting to start a fire in a pot-bellied stove in their one-room schoolhouse. Despite their burns, both boys ran the two miles back to their home. Floyd died nine days later and doctors initially feared that Glenn's legs would have to be amputated.

After a long, painful recovery, Cunningham gradually learned to walk again. When he discovered that it hurt less to run than to walk, he started down the road to becoming a strong, superbly fit runner. Cunningham could run the quarter-mile in 47.2, but with part of one arch and several toes destroyed by the fire it was difficult for him to sprint at the end of a race. To compensate, he developed a strategy of running a devastating third lap to take the sprint out of his rivals, then finishing them off with an even faster last lap. The scars on his legs hindered him throughout his career, requiring long warm-ups and causing him to adopt a light training program emphasizing speed.

The other outstanding American miler of the 1930s was William Robert "Bonny" Bonthron, born November 1, 1912, in Detroit, Michigan. As a youngster he fell from an apple tree and landed on an electric wire, burning his left leg so badly that it required a series of skin grafts. Bonthron was as talented as Cunningham, but didn't have Cunningham's love of running and admitted he didn't care to set records, but wanted only to win. He also admitted that he enjoyed playing baseball or golf more than running track. Bonthron entered Princeton in 1930 and soon became an outstanding collegiate middle-distance runner. He often doubled and even tripled in the 880, mile, and two miles in dual meets and usually won all three.

His first international race was in his junior year when he met Lovelock in the mile at Princeton in the July 15, 1933, meet pitting Oxford-Cambridge with Princeton-Cornell. The threat of rain during the day kept the crowd down to 5,000, but the rain never came and the hot weather and hard, fast track were ideal for a record.

Lovelock always planned his racing strategy carefully and sometimes practiced for months for a single race. Teammate

Forbes Horan was to act as pacemaker and hit the quarters in 61, 2:03 and 3:06. But when the gun sounded it was Bonthron who shot into the lead and the slender New Zealander followed him instead. Bonthron led through the first lap in 61 seconds and the half in 2:03 — just the pace Lovelock had hoped for. When Bonthron began to slow, Horan took the lead but was unable to keep up the planned pace and Bonthron was soon back in the lead.

They passed the three-quarter-mile mark in 3:08, two seconds slower than Lovelock had planned. With 300 yards to go, Bonthron surged and moved three yards ahead of Lovelock. He soon eased slightly and Lovelock was back on his shoulder. Coming off the last curve Lovelock made his own move and Bonthron couldn't respond. Lovelock continued his sprint to the tape, finishing with a world record 4:07.6. Bonthron finished six yards back in 4:08.7, also under the old record. Lovelock had run the last lap in 58.9 seconds to Bonthron's 60. When it was announced that Bonthron had also broken the old record he just said: "Aw nuts, he beat me."

Luigi Beccali was the first outstanding Italian miler. He had won the 1932 Olympic 1,500 in a dramatic and unexpected fashion by overtaking the field in the final meters. On September 17, 1933, he took aim at the world record for the "metric mile" in an Italy vs. Great Britain dual meet in Milan. Beccali's main opposition was Reginald Thomas, a 4:13 miler and three-time AAA Champion. The powerful Beccali followed his pacers to a 60-second 400 and 2:04 800, with Thomas trying to stay with him. His pacers ran out of steam at 1,000 meters and Beccali was forced to take the lead. Thomas dropped back, and with no one to push Beccali, the pace lagged. After passing 1,200 meters in 3:07, Beccali unleashed a tremendous finish, covering the last 300 meters in 42 seconds and the 1,500 meters in a record 3:49.0.

In 1934 the rivalry between college

seniors Cunningham and Bonthron led to two more records. On June 16, at Princeton, a crowd of 25,000 watched in amazement as Cunningham followed Gene Venske for the first lap in 61.8, then took the lead. He passed the half in 2:05.8 then stepped on the accelerator and ran his rival Bonthron into the ground with a withering 61.8 third quarter. To this he added a 59.1 last lap, leaving Bonthron plodding and exhausted 40 yards back. Cunningham's time was 4.06.8, a world record. Bonthron's only comment after the race was: "There will be other races and other days."

Bonthron evened the series by defeating Cunningham in the mile a week later at the NCAA Championships in Los Angeles. The following week in the AAU Championships in Milwaukee, he made it two out of three by sprinting past his rival at the

Bill Bonthron (left) from Princeton defeating Glenn Cunningham and setting a 1,500-meter world record (3:48.8) in Milwaukee on November 7, 1934 (National Archives [306-NT-94507]).

tape to win the 1,500 meters in 3.48.8, clipping .2 seconds off Becalli's world record. Bonthron's performances in 1934 earned him the Sullivan award as the top American amateur athlete for that year.

Lovelock and Cunningham continued their running careers seriously after college, but Bonthron reduced his training to lunchtime runs on a department-store roof and made only token appearances in Princeton meets. After a long layoff, he tried to recover his form and make the Olympic team in 1936, but his fitness had declined so much that he finished a disappointing fourth in the trials. He joined Eulace Peacock and Ben Eastman as American runners with great potential who stayed home for the 1936 Olympics.

During 1936 Lovelock trained for the 5,000 meters as well as the 1,500 and was undecided up to the last minute whether to run one or both races at Berlin. Lovelock planned his strategy for the Berlin 1,500 meters carefully. He realized that based on 800 meter times, he would most likely be the slowest of the favorites. To compensate, his old friend and Oxford teammate Jerry Cornes agreed to set a fast early pace to keep the kickers at bay. Lovelock, who had recently run some fast times at distances longer than the mile, including two miles in 9:04, planned to use his new-found endurance to start his sprint 300 meters from the tape rather than his customary 100. He felt Cunningham, who held the mile world record (4:06.8) was the man to beat.

The vast Berlin Olympic stadium was packed on August 6, 1936, as the 12 finalists came to the starting line for the 1,500 meters. The field was the finest yet assembled for a middle distance race. Six of the veteran group had competed in the Olympic final at Los Angeles four years earlier. Analysts expected a tactical race between Beccali (the 1932 Olympic champion), Cunningham and Lovelock.

Jerry Cornes, the silver medalist in Los Angeles, took the early lead as promised until one of the two Germans in the race took over and led briefly. Cunningham was well back, followed by Lovelock, running with his silky smooth style and in his black New Zealand uniform looking like the American's shadow. Shortly after the first lap, passed in 61 seconds, Cunningham took the lead and Lovelock went with him into second place. Cunningham controlled the pace for the second lap and slowed to 2:05 at 800 meters. At the beginning of the third lap the Swede Eric Ny, with a long raking stride, moved into second, separating Cunningham and Lovelock.

Near the end of the third lap, Ny passed Cunningham and cut in, grazing the American and knocking him off balance onto the grass infield. Miraculously, Cunningham, after running two paces on the grass, recovered and got back on the track without any noticeable loss of speed. In a few strides he had overtaken Ny on the inside, but Ny spurted back into the lead. Despite the collision, Cunningham had run the third lap in 61 seconds. All the while Lovelock clung to the "Kansas Iron Man."

With 320 meters to go, Lovelock came up on Cunningham's outside, accelerated past and drew even with Ny. Cunningham moved up, ready to counter Lovelock's sprint, but Lovelock eased off slightly causing Cunningham to relax for an instant as they came within 300 meters of the finish. Then, with catlike quickness, Lovelock sprang into the lead. "I made a quick, sudden move which never was anticipated," Lovelock wrote in his diary. "I knew I'd won or lost the race when I whisked by Cunningham. My cards were on the table. He had to top me or I'd haul in the pot."

Cunningham desperately gave chase, as did Beccali. But Lovelock had gained a vital three yards and no one could catch him. Twenty yards from the tape the soft-striding New Zealander glanced down for footsteps behind his right shoulder. Seeing none, he eased slightly, and glided through the tape five yards ahead of Cunningham.

Lovelock's time was announced as a world record of 3:47.9. He had run the last 400 meters in 56.8 seconds. Cunningham, finishing second, also broke the old world record with 3:48.4. Beccali finished third in 3:49.2. An elated Lovelock considered the race an artistic creation and wrote in his diary that night: "It was the most perfectly executed race of my career."

Interviewed shortly after the race, Cunningham couldn't hold back the tears. "These legs—they weren't right, they're no good," he said. The cold, damp weather in Berlin had caused his legs to become stiff and sore. Cunningham went on to run many fine races after the Berlin Olympics. In March 1938, on Dartmouth College's springy, 6⅔ laps-to-the-mile board track, he ran 4:04.4. His quarter-mile splits were 58.5, 64, 61.7 and 60.2. The performance was never recognized as a record because it was in a handicap race and was made indoors. After his running days Cunningham

Jack Lovelock set a world record in winning the 1,500 meters at the 1936 Berlin Olympics (**National Archives [306-NT-91884]**).

and his wife operated a ranch for troubled children for over 30 years.

Lovelock retired from running shortly after the Berlin Olympics, became an orthopedic surgeon, and in 1947 moved to New York. Suffering double vision from two riding accidents, he joked: "One of these days I shan't be able to see where I'm running." On the morning of December 29, 1949, he stumbled and fell beneath a subway train at Church Street Station in Brooklyn. The man was gone, but his magnificent Olympic victory, which was filmed for Leni Riefenstahl's classic movie, *Olympia,* will be remembered as long as anyone cares about the history of the mile foot race.

### Sydney Wooderson— An Unlikely World Champion

Sydney Charles Wooderson was a most unlikely-looking man to hold the title of world champion miler. Many mile record holders look as though they would have made good models for the ancient Greek sculptors when they carved statues of their gods. Wooderson was a pale, five-foot, six-inch (1.7 m) 126-pound (57 kg) solicitor's clerk who wore thick-rimmed glasses and could have passed for a man 20 years his senior. Although he was shy, uncommunicative and diffident, he had gritty determination and was highly competitive and self-confident. His many gutsy performances and especially his "blistering" kick made him one of Britain's most admired athletic heroes.

Wooderson had won four of six matches with Lovelock prior to the Berlin Olympics and would have been a contender in the 1,500 final had he not suffered an ankle injury requiring surgery. Like many milers of the time, his training program was light by today's standards. He did two to four miles of easy striding five times a week in the winter. In the summer he typically ran two miles of sprints on Monday, 2 × 660 fast on Tuesday, 1½ miles fast on Wednes-

day, a three-quarter-mile time-trial on Thursday, rest on Friday and race on Saturday.

At Motspur Park, London, on August 28, 1937, Wooderson attacked Cunningham's 4:06.8 mile record. His club, the Blackheath Harriers, had arranged a special handicap to aid him. Reggie Thomas led Wooderson through the first quarter in 58.6, and the half in 2:02.6 seconds. At the bell, the pace had slowed to 3:07.2, but Wooderson ran the last lap in 59.2 to set a world record of 4:06.4. Walter George, then 79 years old, was at the finish to congratulate Wooderson, the first Englishman to hold the mile record since George himself in 1886.

World War II interrupted Wooderson's career, and in 1944 he suffered a severe bout of rheumatic trouble. He made a remarkable recovery, however, and went to Sweden in 1945 and ran his best ever mile of 4:04.2, losing a close race to Arne Andersson.

Sydney Wooderson leading Arne Andersson in the mile at Wimberly Stadium, August 6, 1945 (National Archives [306-NT 231-C-1]).

## HÄGG AND ANDERSSON— ON THE BRINK OF THE FOUR-MINUTE MILE

World War II brought an end to the record ambitions of most runners, but not in neutral Sweden. There, Gunder Hägg and his friend and rival Arne Andersson waged a more humane war on the track and brought the mile record tantalizingly close to four minutes. As it was for George and his countryman Cummings, the success of Hägg and Anderson was largely the result of two extremely talented runners pushing each other to new heights. The war and the lack of an Olympic arena to showcase their magnificent duels conspired to deny them much of the recognition they deserved.

Gunder Hägg was born on December 31, 1918, at Albacken, Sweden. He was five feet, 10 inches (1.8 m) tall, weighed 150 pounds (68 kg) and started racing in 1936 at age 17. Hägg did much of his training on springy surfaces of leaves, moss and pine needles on forest paths in summer and through deep snow in winter. He used a form of training called *Fartlek* or "speed play." The method was named and publicized in the mid–1930s by the Swede Gosta Holmer. *Fartlek* consisted of running through the forests for one to two hours, accelerating, decelerating, running uphill and down. It was exhilarating, demanding and effective when used by a runner who could judge the correct combination of hard and easy running he needed. It did away with monotonous intervals on a track, but it was unscientific and depended heavily on the runner's good judgment.

Andersson, a year older than Hägg, was born at Trollhättan on October 27, 1917. Where the taller, thinner Hägg flew over the track with an easy, feathery stride, Andersson steamed and puffed, driving himself forward with powerful strokes like a steam engine. He became the Swedish 1,500-meter champion at the age of 18 and early in his career sometimes trained as much as four

hours a day running through the forest. By hard work he would eventually progress to become Hägg's equal in the mile, but he would never match his rival at the longer distances.

Hägg first attracted attention in August 1941, by breaking Lovelock's 1,500-meter record by running 3:47.5. A year later, he ran 4:06.2 to break Wooderson's mile record, with Andersson only a yard behind. Andersson equaled this time a week later, but Hägg, within two months, lowered it again to 4:04.6.

Hägg had a sensational year in 1942, setting 10 world records at distances from 1,500 to 5,000 meters while winning all 32 of his races. Andersson was able to push Hägg but didn't have the speed at the end of a race to beat his smooth striding rival.

America wanted to see "Gunder the Wonder" and despite it being the middle of World War II, the AAU sent cable after cable to Sweden inviting Hägg to America. Hägg was anxious to go and prepared for a flight to the United States in May 1943. When these plans fell through, he was forced to make a long, perilous journey on the *Saturnus*, a safe-conduct ship. The trip took 26 days and the tanker had to pass through minefields where two previous Swedish safe-conduct vessels had been sunk.

Hägg ran eight races in the four months he stayed in the United States and won them all. He set no world records in America, partially because the best American milers, Bill Hulse and Gil Dodds the "Flying Parson," couldn't push him. He also may have been tired from his previous year's record-setting spree.

Meanwhile, back in Sweden, Andersson had become a teacher posted to a school outside Stockholm. Here he discovered the benefits of shorter but tougher training sessions and developed a more economical running style. Like Hägg, he trained on a forest path, pushing the uphills. Unlike Hägg, Andersson did a lot of jogging, limbering-up exercises and often about ten

**HAGG**

**Gunder Hägg ran the mile in 4:01.4 in 1945 (U.S. Army Air Force Relief Society Poster).**

40 yard sprints. Even this minuscule amount of speed work would prove of great help in his finishing duels with Hägg.

On July 2, 1943, Hägg, along with the rest of the world, was shocked to hear that Andersson had run the mile in 4:02.6, in Göteborg, cutting two full seconds off Hägg's mile record. Not only did Andersson break the mile record, but the second place finisher, Rune Gustafsson, had equaled Hägg's best time of 4:04.6. Three days later Andersson cut 2.1 seconds from the best recorded time for the three-quarter mile when he ran the distance in 2:56.6. On August 15, Hägg, who was still in America, grimaced when he read that Andersson had also annexed his 1,500 record. In a race in Göteborg, Andersson had run the "metric mile" in 3:45.

The 1944 season found Hägg back in Sweden and the two great rivals were soon dueling each other again. It was the newfound finishing burst of Andersson pitted against the long sustained drives of the front-running Hägg. On July 7, 1944, in Göteborg, Hägg got his 1,500 meter record

back by defeating Andersson by seven yards in 3:43.0, the equivalent of a mile in 4:00.8. Eleven days later, Andersson came from behind with a devastating kick to beat Hägg by three yards and lower the mile record to 4:01.6. In all, Andersson defeated Hägg six out of seven times in 1944.

Finally, in July 1945, in Malmo, Sweden, Hägg and Andersson made their closest approach to the four-minute mile. Andersson, the mile record holder, was the favorite over Hägg, the 1,500 meter record holder. Pettersson, the pacemaker, led them through the 440 in a blazing 56.5, then slowed to 1:59.2 for the 880 before stepping off the track. Hägg took the lead and passed the three-quarter-mile mark in 3:01 with Andersson close behind.

Unfortunately, Andersson had stepped on an empty cartridge shell which a careless starter had dropped on the track. Unable to kick it off, he had to run the entire race with the shell impaled on one of his spikes. It's hard to say how much the uneven stride caused by the stuck shell cost Andersson, but he didn't have his usual kick at the end. If he had, one or both runners would probably have broken four minutes. Hägg finished with a 60.0 last lap, beating Andersson by six yards and setting a world record of 4:01.4. Hägg commented after the race: "I was full of running tonight. I could have made four minutes if I'd had the competition to press me harder."

Eight months later, both men were declared professionals for accepting excessive expense money. Hägg, satisfied with his many achievements, accepted his plight, but later said, "It would be better if there was no hocus pocus about this professionalism. It is not easy for a poor boy who is a good athlete to refuse to accept large sums of money when they are offered him for just a few minutes of running." Andersson remained inconsolable for years and turned to cycling to vent his frustrations. The four-minute mile would have to wait for a new generation of milers.

## Two to Ten Miles

*Water which doesn't run goes sour.—*
Paavo Johannes Nurmi

### ALFRED SHRUBB—
### A "MODERN" DISTANCE RUNNER

Early in the 20th century, Alfred Shrubb, a slim, almost flimsy-looking little runner, carried on W. G. George's British legacy of versatility and record breaking. Born at Slinfold, in Sussex, England, in 1878, Shrubb discovered his running talent when, as a youth, he heard a fire bell clanging. Rushing outside he chanced to meet F. J. Spencer, champion of the Horshan Blue Star Harriers, who suggested they run to see the fire which was three or four miles away. Shrubb, running through the night, beat both Spencer and the horse-drawn fire engine and was invited to join the Blue Star Harriers.

Unlike George, Shrubb loved cross country and once said: "Of all branches of athletics there can be nothing superior to cross country running for either pleasure or health." He was almost unbeatable at the sport and delighted at skimming across rough terrain and plowed fields while his rivals plodded. Shrubb won the British national championships four years in a row, beginning in 1901, and became the first international cross country champion in 1903 and retained the title in 1904.

By 1903, Shrubb was at the height of his powers and started his record-breaking spree. His first record was three miles in 14:17⅗ at Stamford Bridge in London on May 21, 1903. On May 31, at Ilford, Shrubb surpassed Bill Lang's ancient 9:11½ two-mile record when he ran 9:11.0 for the distance. A year later he improved his two-mile record to 9:09⅗ and set a new three-mile record of 14:17⅕. On November 5, 1904, in Glasgow, inspired by the skirling of bagpipes and the roar of the crowd, he broke William Cummings's ten-mile record

with 50:40⅗. He kept going to set a new one-hour record of 11 miles, 1,137 yards (18.74 km).

His record breaking came to a halt in 1905 when the AAA suspended him for life, charging him with receiving excessive travel expenses on a tour of Australia. After that, Shrubb ran successfully as a professional. One of his most memorable races as a pro was a victory at 10 miles against a relay of five runners. Shrubb ran several professional marathons but never mastered the race. After he retired from running he coached at Harvard in 1907 and later in 1920 became the first professional coach of the Oxford University Athletic Club.

For training he refined and extended

Alfred Shrubb was the world's best runner from two to 15 miles in the early 1900s (from Alfred Shrubb, *Long Distance Running and Training*, 1909).

George's methods. Shrubb ran twice a day except on Sunday. His weekly mileage was 35–40 miles, mostly steady runs at a medium-to-fast pace with little speed work. Shrubb retained George's custom of long walks interspersed with his running. If he were not racing, he would usually run a time-trial once a week.

Shrubb proved that a short (just under five feet), economical stride could be effective in setting records. Despite being modest and unassuming, he sometimes played with his opposition. He would deliberately slow for while, allowing the other runners to catch up, then sprint away with ease. He frequently requested the timers not give him lap-times, considering them an unnecessary and artificial aid. Shrubb's career was remarkable in that he achieved his records without the aid of either pacemakers or other runners of comparable ability to push him. His suspension and never competing in the Olympics kept him from receiving some of the recognition he deserved.

### Hannes Kolehmainen— First of the Flying Finns

After Shrubb came the light-hearted, uninhibited Hannes Kolehmainen, first of the outstanding Finnish distance runners. Finland has an illustrious history in 20th century distance running. From 1912 through 1952, runners from Finland won ten of the sixteen 5,000-meter and 10,000-meter races in the Olympics.

Hannes Kolehmainen had three brothers and a sister. All were outstanding athletes, but Hannes was clearly the best. Cross country skiing and sibling rivalry played an important role in the early training of the Kolehmainens. Almost every night the brothers would go for ten- to 15-mile jaunts on skis at as hard a pace as they could set. On Sundays and holidays they would treat themselves to 50 or 60, sometimes as high as 80, miles, always finishing with a burst of speed.

In 1906 the Kolehmainen brothers took up road running to keep in shape during the summer. Unable to reach the top level in skiing, in 1909 they made running their primary sport. The brothers preferred the marathon, but Hannes, after being informed by a doctor that he had a weak heart, turned to shorter distances.

In 1910, at age 20, Hannes began training in earnest for the 1912 Olympics. His training system, developed from the experience of his older brother Willi, emphasized long, easy runs and walks. As he approached a race, he would shorten the distance and quicken the pace. Hannes was a strict vegetarian and in addition to running, his training included gymnastic exercise, deep massage and sauna baths.

At the 1912 Games he won gold medals and set records in the first Olympic 5,000-meter and 10,000-meter races. He got his third gold medal by winning the rugged five-mile (8 km) cross country race by 60 meters.

Although Kolehmainen won most of these races easily, Jean Bouin from France gave him all he could handle in the 5,000 meters. Bouin was a handsome 23-year-old from Marseilles who always ran with a toothpick in his mouth. The previous winter he had set a world record (30:58⅕) for 10,000 meters and also won the international cross country title.

Bouin set another world record (15:05) in his heat of the 5,000 meters. In the final, Kolehmainen took an early lead, then he and Bouin sped away from the rest of the field to battle for the gold. On the last lap Bouin unleashed a furious finish but Kolehmainen stayed with him. The lead changed hands eight times over the last 400 meters but Kolehmainen hung on and in the last 20 meters drew ahead and won by a step. Kolehmainen's winning time of 14:36⅗ was almost 30 seconds better than Bouin's world record. Significantly, Kolehmainen had run almost even splits of 7:17 and 7:19⅗ for each half of the race, predating the even pacing of Nurmi.

**Hannes Kolehmainen (809) and Jean Bouin battling for the gold medal in the 5,000 meters at the 1912 Olympics (author's collection).**

The Olympic Games of 1916 were canceled and Bouin, after improving Shrubb's one-hour record to 11 miles, 1,442 yards (19.015 km) in 1913 was killed at Flanders in 1914. Kolehmainen was not actively involved in World War I but was deprived of the competition that would have pushed him to greater heights. His fluent style, with a smooth stride, holding his arms high, was a highlight of the Stockholm Games and became the trademark of Finnish runners for the next 40 years. Although Kolehmainen represented Finland in the Olympics, he lived in Brooklyn, New York, from 1912 to 1921 earning a living as a mason. When the news of Kolehmainen's three victories at the 1912 Stockholm Games reached Finland, a whole generation of young Finns took up

distance running in hopes of winning Olympic honors. Among them was 15-year-old Paavo Nurmi.

### Paavo Nurmi—The Strange, Silent Man of Åbo

Paavo Johannes Nurmi was born on June 13, 1897, on the outskirts of Turku (also: Åbo), in Southern Finland. His father was a frail man with a weak heart. The elder Nurmi died of a heart attack when Paavo was 13, and the young Finn was forced to leave school and help support his mother and the five children. As a delivery boy, young Nurmi struggled up the steep slope to the Turku railway station many hundreds of times, pushing a heavily laden cart. Later, he would attribute his unusually powerful back and leg muscles to these exhausting climbs.

Although he was inspired by the feats of Hannes Kolehmainen, Nurmi's early development as a runner was slow and gave no inkling of his future greatness. Up until 1917, he trained only in the summer and did no speed work. He developed his high leg-lift and a good sense of pace by following the local train for runs of two to three miles, kicking high to avoid stubbing his toes in the roadbed.

The quiet, meditating Nurmi joined the army in 1918. The combination of maturity and more time to train led to rapid improvement in his running. He entered the annual Finnish Army March in which he was required to travel 9.3-miles (15 km) in full uniform, carrying a rifle and 55-pound pack. Nurmi astounded his superiors by running the entire distance in 59 minutes. That summer he improved his 5,000 time to 15:31 and his 10,000 time to 32:56. These times put him in the top three in his country in both events.

In 1919, Hannes Kolehmainen encouraged Nurmi to vary the speed of his training runs and to include speed work. The speed training paid off and in 1920 Nurmi set a Finnish record for 3,000 meters. He was selected for the 1920 Antwerp Olympic Games, with the 10,000 meters expected to be his best event.

The first Olympic final Nurmi ran was the 5,000 meters, in which his racing inexperience was evident. On the third lap he bolted into the lead and overextended himself. Starting the last lap, the fading Finn still clung to the lead, but the five-foot, three-inch (1.6 m) Frenchman, Josef Guillemot, was on his heels. Guillemot sprinted past Nurmi on the final straight and won by five seconds in 14:55³⁄₅. Three days later in the 10,000-meter final, Nurmi showed he was a quick learner. He let Guillemot set the pace and when the Frenchman started his finishing sprint too soon, Nurmi passed

him near the end to win the gold in 31:45⅘. Nurmi later won the cross country race, giving him two gold medals and one silver.

Returning to Finland a national hero, Nurmi shunned publicity and instead carefully weighed his achievements and made plans for the future. His defeat in the 5,000 meters troubled him. In order to prevent a similar occurrence in the future, he devised a strategy that he would use the rest of his career. Instead of racing the other runners he would race the clock. He would train himself to run a race in a time no one else could equal. Even pacing was best, he decided, and he would use his stopwatch to make sure he stayed on pace. This way, he could avoid sprinting the last lap with a runner who had more speed than he. Nurmi decided to do whatever it took to make him fit enough to run the times he had set for himself.

After leaving the army, Nurmi entered the Industrial School at Helsinki. He excelled in mathematics, which he used to good purpose in his running. His analytical mind led him to adopt a disciplined, regimented training program. He was at his best during the years of 1921–1925, when he was unbeatable from 1,500 to 20,000 meters. No runner since Walter George had dominated over such a wide range of distances. The "Phantom Finn" suffered a serious setback in the third week of April of 1924. He fell on an icy road, injuring his knee, and for a week could do no training. In May he resumed training too soon and injured the other leg. Finally, in June, with the help of traditional Finnish massage and sauna baths, he was able to resume normal training.

His training for the 1924 Olympics was quite rigorous, although no one knows exactly how he went about it. He preferred to train alone and was secretive about what he did. If another runner wanted to join him, he set a pace that soon left the intruder far behind and gasping for breath. This created a belief, probably true, that he trained very hard.

While Nurmi was preparing for the 1924 Olympics, Finnish distance runner Ville Ritola, who lived in New York but competed for Finland, broke Nurmi's 10,000 meter record by 4⅘ seconds. Finnish Olympic officials suggested that Nurmi leave the 10,000 meters to Ritola at the 1924 Games and concentrate on the 1,500 and 5,000 meters. Unfortunately, the final of the latter two events were to be held only an hour apart. On June 19, Nurmi tried an experiment to see if he could contend for both medals. He ran the 1,500 meters in 3:52⅗, covering the first lap in 57.3 seconds and less than an hour later ran the 5,000 meters in 14:28⅕. Both these times were world records. Still, Nurmi was disappointed at not being able to defend his 10,000-meter title. He wanted a chance to sweep all the Olympic running events from 1,500 to 10,000 meters, which would have been a superhuman achievement.

At first it looked like Nurmi might be upstaged at the 1924 Games in Paris. On the second day Ritola won the 10,000-meter final easily in 30:23⅕. A Finnish newspaper story suggested that Nurmi had skipped the 10,000 because he was no match for Ritola. The report incensed Nurmi. He was said to have gone to a secluded track while Ritola was winning the Olympic 10,000 meters. There with a stopwatch in hand, he reportedly ran the 10,000 meters alone in 29:58 — 25 seconds faster than Ritola's gold-medal-winning time. Although this story is part of the Nurmi legend, it is probably untrue. Ritola also won the 3,000-meter steeplechase in world record time and was the favorite for the 5,000.

The 1,500-meter final was set for July 10 at 3:45 P.M. Nurmi's greatest threat was expected to come from Hyla Stallard from England. Nurmi made sure the race would not go to the "kickers" by taking an early lead and pushing the pace. He reached 400 meters in 58 seconds and finished the first lap on the 500-meter track in 1:13, with Stallard 25 meters back. Nurmi looked at his stopwatch and smiled. He was exactly on pace. He reached 1,000 meters in 2:32, having slowed in the second lap by six seconds. At the bell signaling the last lap, Nurmi calmly looked at his watch, carefully tossed it onto the grass, and rapidly moved 40 meters into the lead.

Only Stallard, running with a throat infection and a painful stress fracture in his foot, gave chase. The Englishman spurted from seventh to second and made up many yards on the leader. Nurmi, sensing someone was within striking distance, easily shifted into a faster gear and won his first gold medal of the Games by 25 meters in 3:53⅗, only a second off his world record. Despite the challenge from Stallard, Nurmi had coasted the last 500-meter lap in 1:21⅗.

At 4:45 P.M., 56 minutes after the finish of the 1,500 meters, the 5,000 meters began. Nurmi's task was much more difficult this time. His main opposition would come from Ritola, who had just set a world record in the 10,000 meters, and Edvin Wide of Sweden. At the start, Wide rushed into the lead with Ritola close behind. The two men realized Nurmi must be tired from the 1,500 meters and were determined not to let him coast in this race. They passed 1,000 meters in 2:46⅖—an exceedingly fast pace for a 1924 5,000 meters. A serene Nurmi checked his watch occasionally, but paid little attention to the two men in front of him.

During the third lap Nurmi began to move up, leaving the slower runners and approaching the two leaders. At 2,000 meters, covered in 5:43⅗, Wide still led the three front-runners. Shortly after the halfway mark, Nurmi again looked at his watch, and, deciding it was Ritola and Wide he had to beat, not the watch, he tossed it onto the grass and moved into the lead. Ritola passed Wide, gaining second place and led briefly at 3,000 meters. But by 4,000 meters Nurmi was back in front and on the last lap increased the pace relentlessly. Ritola, who later said he was "full of running" that day, hung with him and at one point drew even.

For a few tense moments the two titans battled on even terms, but in a few strides Nurmi was two meters ahead. He finished composed and confident, with Ritola beaten but only a meter behind. Nurmi's winning time was 14:31⅕, only three seconds off his world record. There was no victory lap for Nurmi. Unperturbed by one of the greatest doubles in track history, he calmly recovered his watch and warm-ups and walked out of the stadium.

Two days later, along with Ritola and Wide, Nurmi ran the 10,000 meter cross country race. It was unbelievably hot — 97 degrees Fahrenheit (36 degrees C) according to some accounts — when the race began at 3:30 P.M. In addition, the course was unusually difficult, including stone paths that were covered in knee-high thistles and weeds. Ritola and Wide were still with Nurmi at 3,000 meters, but by 7,000 meters

Paavo Nurmi dominated running from 1,500 to 10,000 meters in the 1920s (National Archives [306-NT-329Y-1]).

Ritola was 100 meters behind with Wide 50 meters farther back. Many of the rest of the field had dropped like flies from the intense heat. Nurmi finished, then removed his shoes and reportedly showed a faint smile when Ritola struggled across the finish line in second place.

Only 15 of the 39 starters completed the race. The sad state of the majority of the runners prompted Olympic officials to ban cross country running from future Olympic Games. The following day, most of the other cross country runners were recuperating in bed or in the hospital. But not Nurmi; he was winning the final of the 3,000-meter team race with ease in 8:32, defeating Ritola by 80 meters. The win completed the greatest running exhibition the modern Olympics had yet seen.

After the Olympics, as if to show the Finnish selection committee he could have won the event in Paris, Nurmi broke Ritola's 10,000 meter record by 17 seconds, running 30:06.1. He then left for America to participate in the winter indoor season. During this tour he became the first runner to break nine minutes for two miles when he ran the distance indoors in 8:58⅕. Americans by the tens of thousands came to see the emotionless, unsmiling, balding legend, who ran with a bounding stride, rolling his body and carrying his arms high. Nurmi ran almost daily, completing 48 "amateur" races in America in 1925. His tour earned promoters nearly a million dollars. Neither did Nurmi go home empty handed. With the "lowest pulse rate and the highest asking price" of any runner of his time, he was said to have returned to Finland a rich man.

Some felt that Nurmi over raced on his American tour, but he answered, "Well I used to practice in mornings and afternoons." He developed inflamed Achilles tendons and never again was quite up to the form he displayed in Paris. During his slow decline in the years 1926–1933, he was still quite formidable, using tactics and cunning to replace his lost form. In the 1928 Olympic

Games, at age 31, he gained his ninth gold medal by winning the 10,000 meters but lost the 5,000 to Ritola and finished second in the steeplechase. In October of that year Nurmi set a ten-mile record of 50:15 on his way to a record 11 miles, 1,648 yards (19.21 km) in one hour.

Nurmi trained hard for the 1932 Olympics and planned to end his Olympic career like his hero Kolehmainen — with a victory in the Olympic marathon. He was favored to win, but the condition of his Achilles tendons caused some to doubt he could do it. On the eve of the race, the IAAF declared him a professional, making the question academic.

In the 1952 Olympics at Helsinki, Nurmi received one last Olympic honor. He carried the torch into the stadium and the cheers of the Olympic athletes and the crowd left no doubt of their admiration and respect for the great runner. When he had lit the flame in the bowl at one end of the arena, he passed the torch to a slight, elderly man, unrecognized by most of the crowd, who lit the beacon at the top of the Helsinki tower. This was Hannes Kolehmainen, the first of the Flying Finns.

After Nurmi's running career was over, he became a successful businessman, living a Spartan existence. Late in his life it was discovered that he was renting one of his expensive apartments at half price. The tenant was his old rival, an aging, sickly Ville Ritola, who had returned to his homeland to spend his declining years. Paavo Nurmi died of heart problems in 1973 at age 76. At his funeral, Finnish President Urho Kekkonen praised the great runner this way: "People explore the horizons for a successor. But none comes and none will, for his class is extinguished with him."

The Flying Finn's presence was still felt for many years. As he had idolized Kolehmainen, a new generation of Finns, copying Nurmi's training and running style, continued his legacy. The most notable was probably Taisto Maki, who, in 1939, became

the first man to break 30 minutes for 10,000 meters when he ran 29:54.6. Gunder Hägg, who didn't really like to run races longer than the mile, made a rare assault on the 5,000-meter record in his spectacular record-breaking year of 1942 and came away with 13:58.2, the first sub–14-minute 5,000 meters.

## EMIL ZATOPEK—THE MOST HUMAN OF ALL RUNNERS

Czech Emil Zatopek, the runner who would replace Nurmi as the dominant force in distance running, was born in Moravia, on September 19, 1922. Nurmi had been known for his stoic personality and his even-paced, watch-in-hand, running. Zatopek was characterized by a massively intense training program, an awkward running style, and a pained facial expression when he ran. Off the track he was perhaps the warmest and most outgoing of all the great distance runners to date.

After grammar school, Zatopek got a job in a shoe factory in Ziln, where he was born, and in the evenings attended school. In 1941, the factory sponsored a road race to advertise its brand of shoes. The students ran through the streets wearing tee-shirts painted with the factory's initials. Nineteen-year-old Zatopek, who had no intention of becoming a runner, tried to avoid the race, protesting that he had a cold and a sore knee. His supervisor insisted that everyone run and Zatopek had no way out after he was examined by a doctor and declared fit. He finished second, and was surprised to find himself disappointed in not winning. Based on his performance, the local athletic club invited him to join and he soon began to take a serious interest in running.

His first efforts were at 1,500 meters, and in 1943 he set a new Czech record of 4:01. The performance was enthusiastically received by his countrymen although it was 15 seconds slower than Hägg's world record.

It showed that Zatopek had potential and caused him to concentrate both his mental and physical energies on running. At the end of World War II, he was drafted into the army, where he was given time for training and leave for competition. He was commissioned a second lieutenant in 1947 and decided to make the army his career.

Zatopek had no coach, but was intelligent and inquisitive enough to devise his own training methods. In 1945, Arne Andersson visited Czechoslovakia and Zatopek was very impressed with the Swede's level of fitness. He concluded that his own training was not rigorous enough and borrowed Nurmi's idea that to become faster at a longer distance he should run shorter distances many times at faster speeds. Although Zatopek didn't invent interval training, he did extend it to distance running and willingly shared his training methods with other runners. He evolved a rigorous interval-training program featuring massive numbers of 200- and 400-meter repetitions.

Zatopek did no gymnastics or weight training, but ran alone, every day, in wind, rain, blizzard or heat-wave. In bad weather he ran in military boots and sweat clothes. Usually he ran on a track, but if his military duties took him where there was no track, he ran through the forest. By 1948 his training consisted of five 200-meter sprints, 20 400-meter runs, then five more 200-meter sprints. He ran the 200s in about 34 seconds and started the 400s as fast as possible, but ended them in 70–75 seconds. He varied the ratio of 200s to 400s, doing more 200s to improve his speed and more 400s to improve endurance. His rest interval was a 200-meter jog that took about a minute. Whereas Nurmi relied greatly on his stopwatch, Zatopek almost never used one when he trained. "You must listen to your body," he insisted. "You must feel hard and feel easy." At one stage in his training, he ran 400 meters 60 times a day for 10 straight days. Zatopek reasoned that if he ran as

hard as possible in training the races would be easy. Few could argue that anyone, before or since, trained harder than Zatopek.

When the Olympics resumed in London in 1948, Zatopek was 25 years old. Viljo Heino of Finland, who loved to destroy his opponents by sudden bursts of speed, was the favorite to win the 10,000 meters. Zatopek planned to run an even pace of 71-second laps which would give him a world record of 29:35. Feeling he might not be able to hear the lap timers, he told his coach to raise a white pair of shorts if his laps were faster than 71, a red shirt if he were slower. While Heino pulled the field through a series of surges, Zatopek, with his even pace, gradually moved up from 17th place and eventually took the lead. His form was awful — worse than Deerfoot's, worse than Eric Liddell's. With every step his body rolled and heaved, his head lurched back and forth with his tongue lolling from his mouth. He ran with such agony etched on his face that one reporter wrote: "Zatopek ran like a man who had been stabbed through the heart."

The crowds loved him, not only for his running talent and his perhaps exaggerated anguish, but also because, off the track, he was humble, friendly and accessible. The words "Zat-o-pek, Zat-o-pek," resounded through the stadium as the "Beast from Prague" won the 1948 Olympic 10,000 meters in 29:59.6, a new Olympic record, 47.8 seconds ahead of Alain Mimoun of France in second place. Zatopek was well aware of his less-than-perfect style, saying, "I shall learn to have a better style once they start judging races according to their beauty. So long as it's a question of speed then my attention will be directed to seeing how fast I can cover ground." Zatopek's upper body motions no doubt wasted precious energy, but his legs moved effortlessly in smooth short strides. His knee lift was minimal and he ran with almost no bounce.

In qualifying for the 5,000-meter final, Zatopek, either through inexperience, pride, or sheer competitiveness, waged a meaningless but exhausting struggle trying to win his heat. In the final, run in a torrential rain, he suffered a mental lapse and with a lap to go, found himself in third place, 40 meters behind the leader. Regaining his concentration, he noticed that the two men in front of him were slowing. He launched himself into a furious sprint that took him past Slikhuis of Holland and brought him to within a meter of Belgium's Gaston Reiff at the finish. Zatopek was disappointed with his performance, realizing he could have won had he stayed nearer the front or started his sprint sooner.

From 1948 to 1952, Zatopek solidified his claim to being the world's best distance runner. During this period he won all his 38 races at 10,000 meters as well as all his 5,000 meter races. In the spring of 1951, he skied into a fir tree and tore a ligament which delayed the start of his training until April. By September he was again running well but had done little speed work. Having promised a world record for 1951, he finally decided to follow the footsteps of Deerfoot, Shrubb, Bouin and Nurmi by trying for a record in the classic one-hour run.

Zatopek ran 12 miles, 269 yards (19.6 km) on September 15, 1951—a world record. But he was not satisfied and, realizing 20 km was within his grasp, he tried again two weeks later. This time his effort proved to be one of his most memorable performances. All went well until 10 miles (16 km), when he got a stitch, but he pressed on. The side-stitch eased, to be replaced by bone-deep fatigue. At 59 minutes, an official fired a gun warning that there was one more minute left. Zatopek, doubting he could cover 20 km within the hour, was amazed when he went by the 20-km mark without hearing the gun. He pressed on and 52 meters later the gun sounded ending the race. His 5,000 meter splits were as follows:

1. 14:57
2. 14:56
3. 15:01
4. 14:57

He passed 10 miles in 48:12, 20 km in 59:51.8 and finished the hour with 12 miles, 808 yards (20,052 meters). All these were world records. Three years earlier Zatopek had won the Olympic 10,000 meters in 29:59. In setting his new one-hour record he had run twice that distance at a faster pace.

Zatopek was at his peak at the 1952 Helsinki Olympics. The night before the 10,000-meter final, an Australian reporter burst into Zatopek's room at midnight. Most runners would have been irate at having their sleep disturbed before a big race, but not Zatopek. Instead of angrily throwing the man out, he graciously gave him a 20-minute interview. Then when he discovered the reporter had no place to spend the night he offered to share his room.

In the final, the red-shirted Zatopek started from the second row in a field of 33. He surged hard at 8,000 meters, dropping Frenchman Alain Mimoun, his only real opposition. Zatopek's winning time of 29:17 was an Olympic record and made him the first man ever to win back-to-back Olympic golds in the 10,000.

Two days later in his 5,000-meter heat, Zatopek "conducted" the race, chatting with his opponents and offering advice. Slowing almost to a walk, he dropped back to eighth place to encourage American Curtis Stone. Zatopek then sprinted back to the lead group and pointed out those who would qualify for the final. On the last lap, the Russian Anufriev started a sprint to win the heat. Zatopek, smiling to show that he had learned his lesson, let him go. There may have been method to his clowning—he finished third, qualifying for the final in 14:26, the slowest qualifying time of any of the favorites. He knew he would need every bit of energy he could summon to win the 5,000-meter final.

The field was unusually strong in the 5,000 meter final. The German Herbert

Schade had won his heat in Olympic record time and Reiff would be looking for his second gold at this distance. Zatopek was also concerned with the up-and-coming young British runners Chris Chataway and Gordon Pirie. By the beginning of the bell lap, Reiff had faded out of contention and Zatopek was positioned perfectly, on the shoulder of Schade who had led most of the way. As "Za-to-Pek! Za-to-pek!" rang through the stadium, he launched himself into his powerful finish. To his surprise, at the start of the back straight three men — Chataway, Schade and Mimoun — swarmed past his right shoulder like angry bees. With 300 meters to go Zatopek had been moving away from the field; with 250 to go, he was fourth and out of the medals.

Chataway, in the lead, began to struggle as Mimoun and Schade gained on him. Zatopek unleashed a furious second charge — the most dramatic moment of the 1948 Olympics. Running wide around the curve, he flew by them all. Chataway, exhausted, tripped on the concrete edge of the track and fell. Mimoun and Schade fought on, but only Zatopek had anything left. With agony, power and pride etched on his face, he sprinted to the tape, winning the greatest victory of his career. His time was an Olympic record 14:06.6 — his last 400 meters had taken only 57.9 seconds, the last 200 meters 28.5.

The following morning, newspapers carried the news that Zatopek would run the marathon. Although he had done marathon-type training, he had never raced the distance and many experts gave him little chance of winning over an experienced, deep field. Zatopek considered Jim Peters of Britain to be his most dangerous opponent. Peters indirectly owed his marathon career to Zatopek. In the 1948 10,000-meter final, Zatopek had lapped the Englishman causing him to at first retire from running then move up to the marathon distance.

On June 14, 1952, only six weeks earlier, Peters had run a marathon in 2:20:42 —

almost five minutes under the old world's best. Zatopek found in the local newspaper that Peters's number was 187. He then sought out Peters to confirm that the number was truly his. "Hello, I'm Zatopek," he said, then explained that because he knew nothing of marathon pacing, he might follow him for a while to get used to the pace.

Peters went out hard and led early, covering five km in 15:43 and 10 km in 31:55. Zatopek struggled to keep him in sight. At about 15 km Zatopek and Gustaf Jansson of Sweden caught Peters and the three ran together for the next four kilometers. Shortly before the halfway turn-around, Zatopek, who spoke six languages, noticed that Peters seemed to be slowing and spoke to him in English: "Jim, the pace? Is it good enough?"

Peters, who was just about done in by the pace and heat, but didn't want to admit it, answered. "Pace too slow."

Zatopek looked at Peters calmly for a few moments then said. "You say too slow. Are you sure the pace is too slow?"

"Yes," Peters answered.

Zatopek shrugged his shoulders and a moment later, took Peters at his word, opening a gap of about ten meters. He glanced back to see if Peters was going to make a response — seeing none, he gradually accelerated away.

Peters continued to fade, finally collapsing at 20 miles (32 km), suffering from cramps. By 22 miles (35.4 km) Zatopek led a fading Jansson by 65 seconds. Reports from the press car following the leader noted that he seemed to be running easily. Zatopek suffered blisters, a headache and was exhausted at the end "But it was the most pleasant exhaustion I have ever known," he admitted. He ran alone into the almost hysterically cheering stadium two-and-a-half minutes ahead of second place Reynaldo Gorno of Argentina. People of all countries, creeds and colors rose to honor him with "Zat-o-pek, Zat-o-pek." He even managed a smile as he won his third gold medal in Olympic record time of 2:23.03. Zatopek's marathon victory is unique in Olympic history. No other runner has been able to win the marathon and any track race in the same Olympics.

After his running days Zatopek remained in the army and became a sought-after athletic advisor. In 1968 Soviet tanks rolled through Prague to suppress a Czech bid for independence. To show their support for the new government, Zatopek and his wife Dana, also a gold medal winner in the javelin in 1952, signed *The Manifesto of 2,000 Words*, a statement of defiance against the old Soviet-backed government. For this he was stripped of his colonel's rank and purged from the Communist Party.

For the next 22 years, Emil and Dana lived in a sort of political limbo. Unable to find work in Prague, he finally was hired by a geological survey team, where he dug ditches and did other construction work.

**Emil Zatopek won the 5,000 and 10,000 meters and the marathon in the 1952 Olympics (National Archives [306-NT-778C-2]).**

He later became a "sports spy," reading foreign sports journals to find out what coaches in other countries were doing. During this period Zatopek was visited by Ron Clarke of Australia, who had set 18 world records but never won an Olympic gold medal. When Clarke got ready to leave, Zatopek gave him a small box and told him not to open it until he was on the plane. When Clarke opened the box, he was astounded to find one of Zatopek's Olympic gold medals with a note that read: "Dear Ron, I have won four gold medals. It is only right that you should have one of them. Your friend Emil."

With the end of the Cold War in 1990, the Czech defense minister issued a public apology to Zatopek.

## Cross Country

There is no rigid definition of a cross country course, but the emphasis is running in a natural setting. IAAF guidelines for a course are as follows:

> The race shall be run over a course confined, as far as possible, to open country, fields, heath land, commons and grasslands. A limited amount of plowed land may be included. If the course passes through woodland without any clearly defined path or track, it must be clearly marked for the runners. The traversing of roads of any description should be limited to the minimum.

The first International Cross Country Championship was held at Hamilton Park, Glasgow, in 1903, with England, France, Belgium and Finland taking part. Alfred Shrubb won individual titles the first two years and his teammates took the team titles. England dominated the early championship races, winning the first 14. Only France and Belgium were able to beat the British harriers during the first half of the 20th century.

Although the United States did not send a team to the international meet in the early years, cross country was popular with American coaches and runners. It provided a natural form of running not possible on the track, as well as valuable conditioning for other sports. Cross country was introduced in the Olympics at the Stockholm Games in 1912. Teams were made up of three runners and the distance was five miles (8 km). The race started in the stadium and returned to the stadium track after 4,000 meters, then repeated the course to finish in the stadium. A large number of runners dropped out after only one lap. The 1920 race was held at Antwerp over a one-lap course that started and finished in the stadium. Forty-eight ran with Finland winning, beating Great Britain and Sweden.

The race at Paris in 1924 proved to be the undoing of cross country as an Olympic sport. It was run over 6.6 miles (10.6 km), starting and finishing at the stadium on a very hot day. Forty runners started, but only 15 finished. After this race, cross country was cut from the Olympic Program.

The dropping of cross country was unfortunate since the sport had a long tradition and was contested in many countries. In addition, it seems absurd to have argued that a six-mile (10 km) cross country race was more dangerous or life-threatening than a marathon run under similar weather conditions. The international cross country championship race continued. Outstanding individuals were England's Jack Holden, who won four times from 1933 to 1939, and Alain Mimoun, an Algerian competing for France, who also won four times beginning in 1949.

Women's cross country began in the 1920s, and France held a Women's National Championship in 1923. The first English Women's National Championship was held at Luton in 1927. The first international women's match was in 1931 at Douai, in France, but international women's championships were not held regularly until 1967.

## The Marathon and Beyond

*I'll keep on running as long as my legs will carry me.* — Clarence DeMar

After the wildly popular victory of Spiron Louis in the 1896 Athens Olympics, marathoning spread to other countries in Europe and to America. Although the New York City Knickerbocker Athletic Club held America's first marathon at the Columbia Oval in September of 1896, the Boston Marathon, first held on Patriot's Day April 19, 1897, would become the most famous. The IAAF, official keeper of world running records since 1914, has never approved of a world record for the marathon. It maintains that courses vary so much that it is impossible to compare performances on different courses. It is still interesting and instructive to keep track of the improvement in marathon times. Instead of world record we will use the term "world best."

The marathon, if run hard, takes a significant toll on even a well-trained runner. Many marathon runners of the early 20th century trained lightly and had little regard for even pacing. As a result, several of these early races were filled with drama and uncertainty as runners collapsed or were forced to withdraw at various stages of the race.

The 1908 Olympic Games in London added immeasurably to the popularity of the marathon, so much so that the length of the event became forever fixed at the rather odd distance of 26 miles, 385 yards used that year. The marathon distance had been approximately 25 miles for previous Olympic marathons. It was intended that the London race should be 25 miles with the last ⅓ mile inside the stadium.

In order for the grandchildren of King Edward and Queen Alexandra to easily view the start, officials selected the grounds of Windsor Castle to begin the race. Starting at the castle meant the course would be well over 25 miles. Selecting a starting point under the nursery windows, 700 yards from Queen Victoria's statue, they arranged the course so that it would measure exactly 26 miles to the entrance of the stadium. Instead of ending with a full lap of the track, it was decided that the proper place for the finish was in front of the Royal Box, making the course 26 miles, 385 yards.

There is a legend that Queen Alexandra, who had agreed to present the prizes, arrived at the stadium at the last moment and, "stamping her dainty foot," insisted the finish-line be moved to the front of the Royal Box. But this is a myth. A program published before the day of the race clearly listed the length of the race as 26 miles, 385 yards. By 1924, 26 miles, 385 yards (42.195 km) would become the standard distance for the marathon. In 1908 the increased distance brought defeat, but also lasting fame, to a gritty little Italian candy maker named Dorando Pietri.

Tom Longboat, a Canadian Onondaga Indian who had won the 1907 Boston Marathon in record time, was the favorite. Pietri, the Italian champion, and Charles Hefferon from South Africa were also expected to do well. British runners Fred Lord and Jack Price went out very fast — 5:02, 10:11 and 15:42 for the first three miles. Despite the hot, muggy weather, they covered five miles in 27:01 where Lord dropped back. Price continued this "suicidal pacing," passing the ten-mile mark in 56:53. By 14 miles the heat had taken its toll on Price and Hefferon swept into the lead with Pietri and Longboat in third and fourth. The well-drilled team of 12 Americans was back in the pack. Coached by Mike Murphy, they had covered up to 30 miles in practice and were running a conservative, even paced race. The leading American was Johnny Hayes, a 22-year-old shipping clerk from New York City whose best showing

had been a second place at Boston earlier that year.

The field dwindled from 75 to 27 as the race wore on. Just before 20 miles, Longboat, who was in second place, suddenly fell to the ground, bleeding from his nose and mouth. He got up and tried to continue, but medical officials refused to allow him to go on. Hefferon ran on in the steamy heat, passing 20 miles in 2:02:26, with Pietri almost four minutes behind. Pietri slowly began to reel in the fading South African and cut his lead to 3:18 at 21 miles, 2:47 at 22 miles, and 2:00 at 24 miles. With a mile to go, Pietri passed Hefferon. Hayes, by this time the strongest of the medal contenders, also went by Hefferon a short time later.

Approaching the stadium, Pietri began to slow and his handlers gave him a minute dose of strychnine.* Nearly spent, he entered the stadium in a delirium and to the horror of the crowd of 70,000, wobbled in the wrong direction and collapsed. Doctors and officials rushed to the little Italian, dragged him to his feet, and started him off around the track in the proper direction. He staggered and would have fallen a dozen times but for the assistance he received. Hayes arrived in much better shape and finished in 2:55:18, 30 seconds after Pietri had been dragged across the finish line. The Italian flag was quickly raised in victory, prompting the outraged Americans to lodge a protest, since 70,000 spectators had seen the officials break the rules in helping the Italian. Pietri was carried away on a stretcher and rumors spread that he had died. An hour later, to the dismay of the emotional thousands, Pietri was disqualified and the gold medal awarded to Hayes. Pietri recovered quickly. The drama and controversy surrounding his collapse made headlines the world over and led to "marathon fever."

Hayes returned to New York a hero.

*The rules for 1908 stated that "No competitor either at the start or during the progress of the race may take or receive any drug." American Thomas Hicks, winner of the 1904 St. Louis marathon, was the first known drug user in the Olympic marathon. His handlers gave him concoctions of brandy, raw eggs and strychnine several times in the last ten miles.

Dorando Pietri of Italy finishing the 1908 Olympic marathon. His disqualification led to a boom in interest in the marathon (*Outing*, September 1908).

The bizarre Olympic marathon had generated so much publicity that American sports promoters scrambled to organize a profusion of amateur and professional marathons to take advantage of it all. On November 29, 1908, in New York's Madison Square Garden, Hayes and Pietri, now professionals, faced each other in a race reminiscent of the nearly forgotten go-as-you-please races of the 1880s. Hayes, dogging Pietri the whole way, was never more than a few paces behind. But the Italian won the 262-lap race around the tenth-of-a-mile indoor track by 60 yards, covering the 26.2 miles in 2:44.

Tom Longboat was Pietri's next opponent. Longboat's collapse at the London Olympics had probably been caused by the heat, although there were persistent rumors that he had been drugged. Longboat was a talented, versatile runner, whose personality was as colorful as his name. He was born on the Six Nations Reserve near Ontario, Canada, and as a youth worked as a farm laborer. He discovered his gift for distance running while chasing runaway horses. It was reported that he could capture the strongest strayers inside of 15 miles.

Twenty-five thousand persons tried to get into Madison Square Garden on Tuesday evening, December 15, 1908, to watch the two men run. Ten thousand more were turned away, some holding tickets. Thousands of Italians waved their hero's national flag, and an equal number of Canadians cheered continuously for Longboat. Pietri led until the 25th mile, where he began to show signs of severe distress and soon collapsed. Longboat took it easy on the last mile and won in 2:45. He received $3,000 from the gate money and Pietri got $2,000. On January 2, 1909, in Buffalo, New York, Pietri and Longboat raced again with similar results. This time Pietri dropped out at 18 miles.

Alfred Shrubb, owner of all distance records from two to 15 miles, but a novice at marathon running, took on Longboat at Madison Square Garden on February 6, 1909. Shrubb, never one to put much stock

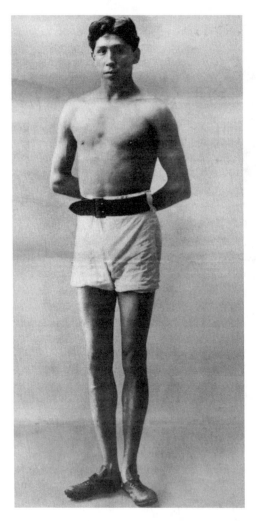

Tom Longboat, a great marathon runner from Canada (*National Police Gazette*, April 11, 1908).

in even pacing, started off much too fast, with the awkward but more experienced Longboat content to run his own race. Shrubb opened a lead of nearly a mile, but by just over 25 miles he was overextended and near collapse. He slowed to a walk and sipped some beef tea, but couldn't get going again. Longboat passed him easily and completed the distance in 2:53, well off his best time.

Thirty thousand New Yorkers jammed the Polo Grounds on April 3, 1909, to see the six best professional long-distance run-

ners in the world try for a piece of a $10,000 purse. Ten thousand more watched from Coogan's Bluff. Longboat, Pietri, Shrubb and Hayes were all entered, as was Matthew Maloney of Brooklyn, who had recently set the American amateur record for the marathon with a 2:36 in a race from Rye, New York to downtown Manhattan. Making his debut in this country was France's Henri St. Yves, a barely-five-foot (1.5 m) tall waiter who was virtually unknown in America.

The young Frenchman led early, going out with a 5:14 first mile. At ten miles, Shrubb caught St. Yves and the two ran to-

Henri St. Yves, the world professional marathon champion in 1909 (from Alfred Shrubb, *Long Distance Running and Training*, 1909).

gether for the next eight miles. Pietri continued in third, but Longboat, in fourth, began to falter. Hayes and Maloney were far back. St. Yves passed 20 miles in a fast 1:57. Overextended, Longboat quit shortly after 20 miles and Shrubb retired at 25. Hayes and Maloney gained on Pietri, but the stubborn Italian clung to second place. St. Yves pushed the last half-mile amid deafening roars from the crowd and finished in 2:40.

After this race, interest in professional marathoning in the United States declined. The runners were exhausted and the public lost interest when the rivalries played out and the newness wore off.

The Finnish Olympic Committee in 1920 considered Hannes Kolehmainen, now age 30, too old for Olympic competition. They gave his 5,000 and 10,000 meter spots on their team to talented younger men. Kolehmainen took the only spot open to him, the marathon, and his performance marked a turning point in Olympic marathons. The superbly trained Finnish legend proved that the Olympic marathon was a race rather than a survival test.

Christian Gitsham of South Africa and a Belgian, August Broos, were the early leaders, but the 31-year-old "Flying Finn" reached the halfway point in the lead in 1:13:10, followed closely by Gitsham. At 24 miles Gitsham dropped out and Juri Lossman of Estonia began to challenge for the lead. Kolehmainen managed to hold off Lossman and win by 100 meters. Although he was obviously tired at the end of his record-breaking race, he still had the energy to smile. His winning time of 2:32:35⅘ for the 26.55-mile (42.75 km) course would have been approximately 2:30 on a now standard 26.2 mile course.

## CLARENCE DEMAR—KING OF THE BOSTON MARATHON

In America, the Boston Marathon continued to grow in popularity, eventually becoming an international race. One of the reasons for its popularity was the legendary Clarence "De Marathon" DeMar. Born on June 7, 1888, in a suburb of Cincinnati, DeMar ran the marathon in the 1912, 1924 and 1928 Olympics, with his best finish being third in 1924. He ran no world-best times and except for his running in the Boston Marathon he would not be rated a great marathoner. But at Boston he reigned supreme, winning a record seven times starting in 1911. He also placed second three times and third twice, and had three other top ten finishes. DeMar's string of Boston victories is all the more remarkable because he ran the race only once (1917) during what were potentially his best years (from age 22 to 33).

On October 12, 1925, DeMar fought a neck-and-neck battle at the inaugural Port Chester, New York, marathon with Albert "Whitey" Michelsen, who won by 2½ minutes in 2:29:01.8. Michelsen's time stood until 1935 as the only sub 2:30:00 marathon run on a 26-mile, 385-yard (42.195 km) course. DeMar's second-place time was 2:31:07⅘, his fastest on a full-length course. His best performance was probably at Boston in 1922 when he finished the 24.7 mile course in 2:18:10. This is equivalent to about 2:27 on a standard 26.2-mile course. DeMar's last Boston victory was in 1930 when he was 41. In all, he ran Boston 33 times, the last at age 65.

DeMar prepared carefully for his marathons. His training started about six months before the race. For his first Boston Marathon in 1910, he trained by running seven miles to or from work each day with occasional long runs of 15–20 miles added. His only speed work was 10-mile races. By trial and error he discovered how to increase his mileage without becoming injured. Before the 1911 Boston race, his first win, he was up to 100 miles a week for the two months before the race, including several 20 mile-runs.

DeMar ran over 1,000 road races in his 49-year career, his last at age 69, only a year

Clarence DeMar, "Mr. Boston Marathon" (**National Archives [306-NT-160690C]**).

before he died in 1958. Doctors examined his heart after his death and found that his coronary arteries were unusually large — two to three times normal size — with only mild atherosclerosis. The autopsy proved that DeMar had not been foolish in resuming his running in 1917 after being warned that he had a weak heart. Nothing was found to suggest that 49 years of strenuous running had damaged his heart.

### Kee Chung Sohn— A Delayed Victory Celebration

Except for the sleeping giants in North and East Africa, the 1930s saw quality marathons by runners from almost everywhere on earth. The Koreans and Japanese were especially prominent during this period, and between them produced all the world best times from 1930 to 1950. On March 31, 1935, in Tokyo, 22-year-old Fusashige Suzuki from Japan came into his own and lowered the best on record marathon time to 2:27:49.

On November 3, 1935, in Tokyo, 23-year-old Korean-born Kee Chung Sohn fought off a side-stitch early in the race, and after the turnaround, ran away from his opposition and finished with 2:26:42, a world best. Sohn claimed to have trained by carrying sand in his baggy pants and rocks strapped to his back. Korea had been conquered and occupied by Japan since 1910. The only way for Sohn to compete internationally was on the Japanese team. When running for Japan, he was called Kitei Son.

The temperature at the 1936 Berlin marathon soared to a 10-year high of 94 degrees Fahrenheit. Defending champion Juan Zabala from Argentina was the favorite. In 1932 at age 20 he had run 2:31:36 to become the youngest Olympic marathon champion. Zabala went out fast and was among the leaders in the early going. Sohn, fearful of the heat, started slowly but worked his way up to fifth by five kilometers. By 15 km Zabala led by over a minute-and-a-half. But by the half-way turnaround, reached in a fast 1:11:29, he had begun to slow and his lead had shrunk to less than a minute.

On the way back Sohn stepped up the pace and at the 28th kilometer, he and lanky Englishman Ernie Harper caught the fading Zabala. The former champion knew he was finished after running with the leaders for just 100 meters. A short time later Sohn broke away from Harper and stretched his lead to two minutes as he finished in 2:29:19.2 and became the first to better 2:30 in an Olympic marathon.

Instead of a moment of great joy, the victory ceremony was an ordeal for Sohn. "It was unendurable humiliating torture," he said later. "I hadn't run for Japan. I ran for myself and for my oppressed Korean people. I could not prevent myself from crying. I wished that I had never come to Berlin." Fifty-two years later in 1988, Sohn, age 74, experienced some of the joy he had missed so long ago. He was given the honor of carrying the Olympic flame into the sta-

Kee Chung Sohn from Korea (left) running with Ernest Harper of Britain in the 1936 Olympic marathon. Chung won, but had to wait until 1988 to celebrate (National Archives [242-HD-313]).

dium in the Seoul Olympics, this time wearing the colors of Korea.

On April 19, 1947, a brilliant international field of 156 runners assembled in Hopkinton, Massachusetts, for the 51st running of the Boston Marathon. Soldiers from the U.S. Army occupational forces had helped raise money to send a three-man team from Korea. This first group of Oriental runners to enter Boston included 1936 Olympic champion Kee Chung Sohn, 12th

place Olympic finisher Seung Yong Nam, and five-foot, one-inch (1.5 m) Yun Bok Suh. Sohn withdrew because of a foot injury, but told the race officials, "You won't miss me, Suh is by far our best runner."

The pace was fast, with Hietanen from Finland and Suh running shoulder to shoulder until about 16 miles. As they ran up the first of the series of Newton hills that collectively make up "Heartbreak Hill," a fox terrier that had been dogging Suh tripped the Korean and he fell, bruising a knee. Suh jumped to his feet and soon caught the Finnish champion and went into the lead. With five miles to go, Suh had the race in hand and extended his lead to four minutes at the finish. His time was a sparkling world best of 2:25:39.

## Arthur Newton and the Bunion Derby

Six-day go-as-you-please races died out in the late 1880s as public interest turned to other sports and fads. Over the years, several unsuccessful attempts were made to revive multi-day racing. Promoters tried two-man team races with international teams and races shortened to 10 and 12 hours per day. But none caught on and ultra running was at a low ebb until 1922. That year Arthur Newton, a 39-year-old South African farmer, began to astound the world with ultra-running feats of a quality not seen since the days of Littlewood, Albert and Rowell.

Newton, who was born in Weston-Super-Mare, England, in 1883 emigrated to South Africa in 1901. Ten years later he applied for and was granted 1,350 acres of land to begin a new occupation as a cotton and tobacco farmer. His running career came about because of a dispute he had with the South African government involving the resettlement of native South Africans on land they had given him. He applied for an exchange of farms, but was refused. He wrote in *Races and Training* (1948): "Winning a widely-advertised annual race, I thought, would enable me to turn a spotlight on this cause which would in turn bring about legislation to rectify matters." At age 39, when many men began to settle into their easy chairs, he embarked on a career as an ultra-long-distance runner.

After an unsuccessful 26-mile "trial" race with a train, Newton discovered the fallacies of the long-distance training methods of his day. "I decided to ignore practically everything I had read and start all over again with sound common sense methods," he wrote. Entirely self-coached, he developed an uncanny ability to identify and correct the errors he made in his training and racing. On May 24, 1922, only five months after starting his training program, he ran the South African 54.6-mile Comrades ultra marathon and won by 30 minutes in eight hours 40 minutes. The following year a much fitter Newton returned to make shambles of the race, winning by two hours.

Newton, who lacked the speed to race successfully at marathon distances and below, concentrated on 50-mile and longer races and developed an extremely efficient running style. By 1924 he had shortened his stride to three feet seven inches (1.1 m), and did not lift his feet more than a couple of inches from the ground as he ran. In developing his running form, Newton had advice from Walter George, who had trained with the master of efficient running, Charles Rowell, in the 1880s. Like Rowell, Newton kept his arm action to a minimum, letting his hands flap like a seal's fins to aid relaxation.

After his decisive victory in the 1923 Comrades ultra marathon, Newton made his first attempt at setting a world record, choosing a 50-mile out-and-back course on the Comrades route beginning in Maritzburg. Despite the uneven, dusty and unpaved roads, Newton ran the distance in 5:53:05, lowering the amateur record by 20 minutes and astounding road running officials.

In 1928 at age 45, Newton traveled to England where he overcame snow and floods to break the amateur record for 100 miles by 22 minutes, running the distance in 14 hours 22 minutes. In March 1928 he came to America to enter Charles C. Pyles's "Bunion Derby," a professional transcontinental foot race from Los Angeles to New York. Billed as "the greatest test of human endurance in history," this epic 3,422-mile race consisted of 84 daily stages of between

30 and 75 miles. The runner with the lowest total time was to receive a prize of $25,000.

An unprecedented 15 million Americans saw the race and it may have attracted greater newspaper coverage than any other sports event in history. Although Pyle rivaled P. T. Barnum in the ability to separate the public from its money, he lost $100,000 on the venture. Pyle discovered that it was extremely difficult to make money from a public who could view the runners for free in his "hop step and limp" race across America.

The race had 199 starters from 15 countries. Among the amateurs, professionals, crackpots and eccentrics from age 16 to 63, were some of the best distance runners in the world. Willie Kolehmainen, older brother of Olympic hero Hannes Kolehmainen, and Arthur Newton were probably the most famous. Pyle led the procession in a custom-made bus and hired football legend Red Grange and former sprint world-record holder Arthur Duffey as officials.

Running at a punishing 5:48 minutes-per-mile pace, the favorite, Willie Kolehmainen, led the race the first day, but he paid the price two days later when he was forced to quit with a torn muscle. Newton fared better and won stage after stage through the brutal Mojave Desert and mountains of Arizona. Near Flagstaff, with over a nine-hour lead, a bad ankle forced him to quit. Pyle wisely made Newton, who was headline material, a "technical advisor" to counsel, encourage and mother the remaining runners— a task the stoic Newton performed admirably.

Arne Souminen of Finland then led for several hundred miles, before he, too, was forced out. Peter Gavuzzi, an Englishman of Italian parentage, hailing from Liverpool, led next. But Gavuzzi suffered from dental trouble which prevented him from taking proper nourishment. He grew weaker by the mile and leading by six hours, he was forced to quit after 2,800 miles.

Andy Payne, a shy 20-year-old part-Cherokee from Claremore, Oklahoma, took the lead over the latter stages. Like most of the others, he suffered many hardships. Payne contacted tonsillitis and had to run for days with a fever and sore, swollen throat. From Ohio to New York, 55 steadfast runners continued without losing a single man. In order to speed up the race, which was losing more money each day, Pyle lengthened each day's run to 75 miles. Most of the runners stayed in the race solely for the satisfaction of completing it since they had no chance at finishing in the top 10 and receiving any of the prize money.

Only a few hundred spectators saw the runners arrive in New York. Off the Weehawken Ferry hobbled 55 gaunt runners burned black by the sun. Some were in rags, some were barefoot, others wore bandages instead of shoes. One contestant, Eugene German, seemed able to move only crab-wise. They ran, walked and limped to Madison Square Garden, the official finish of the race. Payne, who won by 15.5 hours, used his $25,000 winnings to pay off the mortgage

**Andy Payne, winner of the first Bunion Derby (author's collection).**

OFFICIAL PROGRAM

PRICE
25¢
Pay no more

C.C.Pyle's
Second Annual
INTERNATIONAL-TRANS-CONTINENTAL
FOOT RACE
NEW YORK
TO
LOS ANGELES
1929

Program for the second Bunion Derby Transcontinental Race (author's collection).

on his father's farm in Claremore. Having been told by a doctor that the race had shortened his life by 10 years, he permanently retired from running. One sad aspect of the race was that there were no women involved.

Pyle excluded women, which prompted Will Rogers, who knew Payne's family and had become captivated by the race, to quip "they wouldn't let his [Payne's] 16-year-old sister enter. She's better than Andy."

Despite injuries and advancing age, Newton refused to abandon long distance running. He entered the second Bunion Derby in 1929, this time from New York to Los Angeles. He was forced out of the race when he was hit by a car, breaking his shoulder blade. The majority of the 91 starters in the second race were veterans, hardened by the first race. This race was much closer than the previous year's, with a dramatic struggle between New Jersey policeman John Salo and Englishman Peter Gavuzzi. On the last stage of the event, Salo passed Gavuzzi and won the 3,685-mile, 78-day race by a mere three minutes. Despite the excitement and quality of the race, Pyle went bankrupt and none of the 19 finishers were paid.

By 1931 Newton owned all the long-distance records from 27 to 100 miles. Yet there was one more record he wanted badly — the 24-hour record of 150 miles, 395 yards (242 km) set by Charles Rowell during the first 24 hours of a six-day race in 1882. Newton wrote in *Races and Training*:

> I had long since made up my mind to have a shot at it before I faded out and as I was now nearly fifty it was evident I couldn't put it off much longer…. After talking things over with one of the actual competitors in those long-ago races— they had taken place almost half a century earlier — I got a fair idea of what was required.

Newton made the attempt at the Hamilton Arena in Ontario on April 4, 1931. Because he had often become giddy from circling small indoor tracks, he had a square 12-laps-to-a-mile track with banked corners constructed. Instead of constant turning, he preferred short straight-aways and sharp turns. Among the other starters were Australian Mike McNamara, the 100-mile indoor record holder; Canadian Philip Granville and Lin Dilks, the American record holder for 100 miles.

Before the start, the two favorites,

Arthur Newton, a great ultra runner in the 1920s and 1930s (National Archives [306-NT-79743]).

Newton and McNamara, made plans for a stop at 100 miles for a quick hot bath. They agreed to leave the track separately, but to take the same time for their stops. That way neither would gain an advantage. The plan was thwarted when photographers insisted the leaders stop at 100 miles for photographs. After a stop that stretched to nine minutes McNamara went off for his bath, but developed a cramp which required massage and extended his bath stop to 19 minutes. Newton, a gentleman and believer in fair play, spent a full 19 minutes soaking in his tub also.

McNamara was unable to resume and Newton pushed on far in the lead, trying to divert his mind from the fatigue and bone-aching discomfort. At long last he was informed that he was within a mile of 150. Perked up by the news, he increased the pace to 10 miles an hour. When the 24 hours were up, he had covered 152 miles, 540 yards (245.3 km) and had beaten Rowell's record by just over two miles.

In 1934 at age 51 Newton closed out his career by running his fastest ever 100 miles in 14 hours, six minutes.

# VII

## The Modern Superstars
## (1950–2000)

*The record breakers drive themselves to a common but unachievable goal ... the ultimate in excellence, which can never be reached and all this is done in the certain knowledge that the record will be only borrowed, it is not theirs to keep.*
— Sebastian Coe (1986)

### Technical Advances

#### AUTOMATIC TIMING

In the late 1930s, Lorenzo del Ricco of Los Angeles invented a new type of camera that would eventually revolutionize race timing. This camera, which was initially used for judging the finish of horse races, took a continuous picture of the finish through a vertical slit. The image was focused onto a strip of film that moved at a uniform speed proportional to that of the horses crossing the finish line. A normal camera's shutter freezes time, stopping movement. With a slit camera, however, the absence of a shutter causes fixed objects to become blurred and only objects moving at a speed proportional to the film speed are recorded clearly.

Unlike a high-speed movie camera, the slit camera had no gaps between frames and the runners crossing the finish line (along with a time base) were recorded on a single strip of film. This made a quick and accurate determination of all the runners' times and places possible. An early version of the slit camera, the "Racend-Omega Timer," was used for the Olympic Games in London in 1948.

Early slit-camera photo finish systems cost a quarter of a million dollars and required six operators, but cheaper and

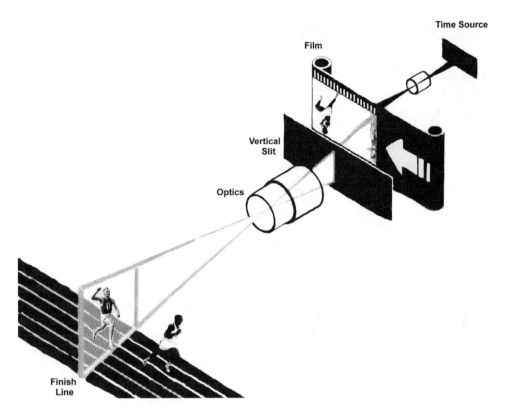

**Operation of slit camera photo finish system (drawing by author).**

improved versions soon followed. Improvements included quartz-controlled clocks, miniaturized components and digital electronics that allowed near real time computer displays of the finish. A slit-camera photo-timing system built by Bulova was used from 1948 onward in the United States at AAU and NCAA championships. Omega photo-finish systems were used for the 1952, 1956 and 1960 Olympic Games, as well as for other major meets such as European and Pan-American championships. These systems were used to help decide the order of finish, but not for the official times. The 1972 Olympics were the first to have official times taken directly from the photo-finish equipment.

In January 1977, more than 100 years after its first use, automatic timing became mandatory for setting world records at 400 meter and shorter distances. Since January 1981 photo-finish systems have been used at major meets to time all races up to 10,000 meters to .01 seconds. One reason for the slow acceptance of automatic timing was that it gave times that were up to .24 second slower than hand timing for 100–200 meter races and up to .14 second slower for 400 meters. These greater-than-expected differences are caused by human reaction time for manually starting and stopping a watch being different. Most human timers anticipate when a runner crosses the finish line, making the reaction time for stopping their watches less than for starting them. With proper training, a manual timer can be taught to reduce this bias considerably.

Since starting is such an important part of a sprint race, several efforts have been made to make starting fairer. The farther a runner is from the gun, the longer it takes for him to hear it. To insure that all the runners heard the gun at the same time, race officials introduced loudspeakers for each sprinter in the 1968 Olympics.

**Slit camera photo finish (Omega Sports Timing).**

### Smart Starting Blocks

Technicians from the German firm, Junghans, installed pressure-sensitive switches in the starting blocks at the 1972 Olympics in Munich to aid the starter in judging false starts. When a runner exerted a preset force (88 pounds) on the block's footpads, a switch closed signaling that the runner had moved. If this signal occurred less than .12 seconds after the gun was fired an alarm sounded. The starter then had the option of declaring a false start and recalling the runners or letting the race continue. It was thought that no runner could react to the gun in less than .12 seconds. Tests had shown that an elite sprinter's first muscular response to the gun usually took from .12 to .20 seconds.

When it was discovered in the mid–1980s that some very fast starters could react to the gun in the .11–.12 second range, the reaction-time limit was reduced to .10 sec-

onds. Another problem was that some large male sprinters sometimes tripped the pressure switches with just their body weight resting on the footpads. The pressure sensor system is not perfect and further refinements will undoubtedly be made to it.

In the 1950s all-weather "rubber-asphalt" composition tracks began to come into use. The Mexico Olympics in 1968 were the first to be held on this new surface, which proved to be more uniform, easier to maintain and faster than cinders. A composition track can be made faster for sprinting by making it harder, which increases energy return to a runner's legs. In 1987 the IAAF passed a rule limiting the hardness of composition tracks.

Even with all these technical advances, there are still two uncontrolled variables affecting races—winds and the altitude of the track. The rules currently disallow sprint performances with trailing winds of more than two meters per second. Even legal winds of 2 m/s can cause sprinters to run as much .1 second faster or slower than they would have run with no wind.

For races up to 400 meters, runners can be assured of a faster than normal time if they run at altitude. Conversely, the thinner air at high altitudes causes times for distances greater than 1,500 meters to suffer. Some of the sprint records set at the 1968 high-altitude Olympic Games in Mexico City were on the books for nearly 30 years before they could be broken at sea level. The trend in recent years has been to include wind information with 100 and 200 meter record lists. Records for distances shorter than 800 meters made at high altitudes are usually denoted with an "A"—sometimes called the "Scarlet A" because it stigmatizes a record.

## Drugs—The End of the Age of Innocence

One of the things that makes a runner great is the burning desire to be the best.

Like Achilles, who was willing to trade a long life without honor for a few years of glory, some if not many runners are determined to reach the top no matter what the risk.

In the second half of the 20th century, biochemists, endocrinologists and other medical scientists have had more and more influence on running at the highest levels. Drugs, mostly stimulants, have been used by runners since the time of the Ancient Greeks. But all the stimulants in the world won't make a mediocre runner a champion. Only in the last 50 years have truly effective performance-enhancing drugs become available. In the 1950s anabolic steroids became widely available and began to have a profound impact on running, particularly sprinting. The IAAF finally started "day of the event" drug testing in 1974. This method of testing proved largely ineffective and was replaced by random testing in 1989. Still, the testing never seemed to quite catch up with the cheating technology.

Canadian sprint coach Charlie Francis, at the 1989 Dubin Inquiry into drug use in Canada, explained why he approved of Ben Johnson's steroid use: "It's pretty clear steroids are worth approximately a meter. He [Johnson] could decide to set up his starting blocks at the same level as the other international competitors—or he could set up his starting blocks a meter behind."

If one believes everyone else is doing it, the morality of using performance enhancing drugs becomes hazy, allowing cheaters to rationalize their behavior. Currently the track world is struggling with the drug problem but, as yet, has no solution in sight.

In writing about runners of the recent past, there is a tendency to want to omit known drug users and de-emphasize the achievements of runners from countries known to have had systematic drug-use programs. The author has tried to avoid this. Like it or not, drug users are a part of running history. If a runner described in this section failed a drug test, it is noted. All others are assumed to have set their records and won their gold medals without the aid of drugs. In writing history, it seems unfair to pretend that a record-breaking performance never happened, as Sullivan did with Duffey's records. Proof of drug use lessens or possibly nullifies an athlete's achievements, but it can never erase them from the news reports of the time when they were made.

## Sprinters—Men

*I find it very difficult to look on modern sprinters with the same sort of admiration as those from the earlier age of innocence, I don't know why some of the contemporary great sprinters are great, you can never be sure if they have done it legitimately and to my mind that's destroyed the whole ethics of the sport.*—Peter Radford (1988)

The Olympic year of 1956 was one of the most productive in the history of sprinting. That year Jesse Owens's 20-year-old record of 10.2 seconds for 100 meters was beaten five times by three different sprinters, all from America. Three of the 10.1s were run at an international military meet in Berlin's Olympic Stadium. Willie Williams, a hard-luck sprinter from the University of Illinois who never made the Olympic team, ran smoothly from start to finish on August 3 recording the world's first legal 10.1. The wind at his back was only .7 m/s.

On the following day, Williams won the first semifinal in 10.3. In the second, Ira Murchison from Chicago, the fastest legal starter since Japan's Takayoshi Yoshioka in the 1932 Olympics, got away fast and was never threatened. Three official timers again registered 10.1. The trailing wind was 1.0 m/s.

In the final on August 5, the two new record holders lined up in adjacent lanes to settle who was really the "world's fastest human." Murchison got off to his usual great start but Williams managed to close the gap and the two were about even after 40 meters. Williams inched ahead, but at 30 meters from home, Murchison started to pull even. Williams fought off the challenge and won by a foot in another 10.1.

Leamon King of the University of California equaled the 100-yard record of 9.3 and ran 10.1 for 100 meters on October 20, and again ran 10.1 for 100 meters on October 27.

### BOBBY MORROW—WHITE HEAT

Despite all these great performances, the dominant sprinter of the 1950s was smooth-striding Bobby Joe Morrow, a rangy, dark-headed sprinter from Abilene Christian College in Texas. Morrow proved that a sprinter's greatness can't be measured by a watch alone. Born on October 15, 1936, in Harlingen, Texas, he was considered by many to be the most relaxed sprinter of all time, even more so than his hero Jesse Owens. At Harlingen High School, Morrow was an outstanding football tailback and sprinter. During his senior year, he won 17 straight 100- and 220-yard races and was the state champion in both events.

"We always concentrated on relaxation," said Morrow, in describing his training at Abilene Christian.

> We trained so your cheeks would bounce up and down when you ran, making sure your arms were relaxed and we worked on that every day of the week. I worked on starting a lot because I never tried to roll with the gun like a lot of other sprinters, so consequently I was usually behind at the start and had to make up a lot of ground. I was never a great starter.

As a freshman at Abilene Christian in 1955, Morrow was undefeated at both sprints until the AAU championships, where he

Willie Williams, from the University of Illinois, never made the Olympic team but ran the world's first legal 10.1 for 100 meters on August 3, 1956 (National Archives [III SCA-4749 SC 485568]).

finished fourth in the 220. His 30-race winning streak for 100 yards ended in April 1956 at the Drake Relays in Iowa. During a torrential downpour, big David Sime from Duke University leaped out of the blocks to beat Morrow by a yard.

Sime, the "Blur in Blue," was one of Morrow's greatest rivals, especially at 200 meters. Shortly after his victory over Morrow, however, he was thrown by a horse and injured a groin muscle. On June 9, Sime tied the world record for 100 yards with 9.3 seconds. Minutes later he ran the straight-course 220 in 20.0 for a world record but aggravated his injury, which kept him off the Olympic team.

Morrow, with his emphasis on relaxation, was able to avoid serious injury until 1959. He was undefeated during 1956 in 200-meter and 220-yard races, winning the major collegiate and national titles. The Olympic trials were held in late June with

Morrow winning both the 100 and 200. Murchison and Thane Baker from Kansas State were also selected for the 100 meters. Andy Stanfield, a Seton Hall graduate, and Baker qualified in addition to Morrow for the 200 meters. Leamon King earned a spot as the fourth sprinter for the 4 × 100 relay team.

The 1956 Olympic 100-meter final in Melbourne was loaded with fast sprinters. Besides the Americans there were fast starting Hector Hogan from Australia, who had equaled Mel Patton's 9.3 seconds for 100 yards; Manfred Germar from Germany; and Michael Agostini from Trinidad, who had run the straight 220 in 20.1. By the time the 100-meter final was held, the cinder track was chewed up and the runners had to face a cold 5 m/s headwind. It looked like an almost certain sweep for the Americans. All three had qualified without going all out, while of the others only Agostini qualified easily. Morrow had regained the 10 pounds (4.5 kg) he lost during a virus attack and looked confident.

When the gun sounded, Hogan jumped into the lead while the others seemed left at the post. Morrow, with his great acceleration, soon ran down the Australian and passed him at 50 meters. The Texan pulled away to win easily by two meters in 10.5. Baker lunged past Hogan at the finish to win the silver medal, and Murchison took fourth.

For the 200-meter final, Morrow was worried that Andy Stanfield, the defending Olympic 200-meter champion from 1952, might beat him. Luckily, Morrow drew lane three, where he could watch his major rivals— teammates Stanfield in lane four and Baker in the outside lane. At the gun, all were off well and coming into the straight the three Americans were out in front. Powering past everyone, jaw muscles waggling in his familiar style, Morrow sprinted down the straight to win by 1.5 meters over Stanfield, with Baker third.

Morrow's winning time of 20.6 was a

world record that finally erased the 20.7 mark first made by Jesse Owens in the 1936 Olympics. "Ever since I started sprinting, I wanted to emulate the great Owens," said

**Bobby Morrow, from Abilene Christian College, won both the 100 and 200 meters at the 1956 Olympics (Abilene Christian University).**

Morrow after the race. The American 4 × 100 relay team had little trouble in winning the gold medal, with a great start from Murchison and smooth handovers to King, Baker and finally Morrow. The Texan broke the tape in 39.5, to erase the world record set by the Owens-led team in 1936 by .3 seconds.

Between 1956 and 1958 Morrow ranked as the top sprinter in the world, equaling world records at 100 and 220 yards and winning all the major championships he entered. In 1959, injuries began to hinder his career and he was unable to make the 1960 Olympic team. After his career in track and field, Morrow became a rancher. He was the last great American sprinter of the 20th century who happened to be white.

## Armin Hary — Thief of Starts

By the end of the 1950s, America had dominated the sprints for almost 30 years, but this was about to change. In 1958 a young, blond German named Armin Hary began to make a name for himself by winning the European Championships 100 meters in 10.3. At first, the rise of the fast starting Hary caused only mild interest in the world track scene and few thought he would challenge the powerful Americans in the 1960 Olympic Games. After all, when the Olympic year began, the world 100-meter record of 10.1 was held by four sprinters: Willie Williams, Ira Murchison, Leamon King and Ray Norton — all Americans.

Ray Norton from San Jose State earned his share of the world record at a meet in San Jose in 1959. Norton, widely regarded as the world's best sprinter, won both sprints at the U.S.–U.S.S.R. meet and the Pan American Games. In addition to Norton, America also had the improving Frank Budd and a healthy Dave Sime. Of the nine sprinters who jointly held the 9.3-second world record for 100 yards, only Hogan of Australia was not an American. At 200 meters, only Britain's Peter Radford could

claim a share of the world record of 20.5 with Americans "Stone" Johnson and Norton.

For years Germany had turned out such world-class sprinters as Huber Houben, Helmut Körnig, Arthur Jonath, Heinz Fütterer and Manfred Germar, only to see them beaten in the international championships, usually by the Americans. Hary changed that trend. Starting as a decathlete in 1956, he soon found that by far his best event was the 100 meters. He had marvelous reactions and acceleration and was willing to work hard in training. During the winter of 1957-58, he worked tirelessly with his coach Bertl Sumser and became one of the fastest starters ever.

Hary improved his already great start by perfecting what the German press called the "Blitz Start." He found a way to steal two or three strides on the rest of the field in the first five meters — if he were not called back for jumping the gun. His trick was to wait until all the other runners had gone into the "set" position. He would then come to the set position himself, pause for an instant, then take off. Since the starter had to wait for the last sprinter to become "set," often as not Hary's start would coincide with the gun.

Hary freely admitted he was taking advantage of a loophole in the rules, saying: "Rudolph Valentino was called the Thief of Hearts. As far as I know, he was never in prison. So what I do is not a crime. I am the thief of starts. It goes back to the rules of the game, and I'm a born player." The rules were eventually changed to require all sprinters to come to the "set" position at the same time, but throughout his short career, Hary used the "Blitz Start" with great success.

On a warm, sunny evening in Zurich, Switzerland, on June 21, 1960, Hary rocketed off his customized starting blocks — before the gun — and won easily from an international field, recording 10 flat. The starter had tried to recall the men, but his second shot failed to fire. The officials declared a false start and Hary protested, claiming that it was not his fault that the starter had been unable to recall the runners. Fifty minutes later he was allowed a rerun, but only two of his original six rivals agreed to race again. This time with a fair start, Hary won easily by three meters. Of the three timers, one timed him in 10.1, the other two in 10.0. With a tail wind of only 0.6 m/s, it was legal. Hary had made sprinting history by becoming the world's first 10-flat 100-meter runner.

Three weeks later, on July 15, 1960, Canadian Harry Jerome, at the national trials in Saskatoon, became the second man to run 10 flat. The following wind of 1.8 m/s was just under the limit. Despite these two world records, neither Hary nor Jerome was expected to beat the Americans Norton and Sime when the Olympics began in Rome.

In the second qualifying round in Rome, Hary used his famous "Blitz Start" to set a new Olympic record of 10.2, beating Dave Sime in the process. The next day in the first semifinal, Jerome pulled a muscle at 50 meters and crashed to the track. In the second semifinal, Hary led all the way. With the exception of Jerome, all the favorites qualified for the final.

For the final, Sime drew lane one and Hary the outside lane. On the first start, both Hary and Sime left before the starter fired the gun, but neither was penalized. When the starter tried a second time, Hary jumped, and he was warned that one more false start and he would be out. Finally, on the third try, the field got away with Hary a meter in the lead at the five-meter mark. Big Dave Sime, who had gotten a terrible start, accelerated fast, but Hary managed to hang on. As he hit the tape, Sime lunged desperately before crashing to the track. The crowd couldn't tell who won, but the photo finish showed Hary winning by a foot over Sime with Radford third. Hand timing gave Hary 10.2 and the unofficial automatic timer read Hary 10.32, Sime 10.35 and Radford 10.42.

Hary won his second gold medal as a member of the German 4 × 100 relay team. His team finished second to the United States team of Budd, Norton, Johnson and Sime, but the Americans were disqualified after Budd and Norton exchanged the baton out of the passing zone. The 200 meters, which Hary did not enter, was won by a lanky Italian chemistry student, Livio Berruti, in a world record-equaling 20.5. Lester Carney from the United States was second and Frenchman Abdoulaye Seye third. A short time after the Games, Hary injured his knee in an auto accident, ending his running career.

## BOB HAYES—THE BULLET

Stinging from defeat in both sprint races at the 1960 Olympics, American track fans longed for a world's fastest human. Frank Budd from Villanova looked like he might be the man on June 25, 1961, when he ran the first "accepted" 9.2 in winning the AAU 100-yard title. Budd's record illustrated the vagaries of hand-timed sprint records. Paul Drayton and Dave James finished only a yard back. Neither had run as fast as 9.4 that year, and the unofficial Bulova automatic timing gave Budd 9.36.

Robert Lee "Bob" Hayes was born on December 20, 1942, in Jacksonville, Florida, where he grew up in the "Hell's Hole" slums. In 1960 he won a scholarship to Florida A&M University in Tallahassee to play football. Most of Hayes's sprinting was done while he was at Florida A&M and was in addition to his primary sport of college football.

Hayes was a powerful man—almost six feet (1.8 m) tall and weighing more than 190 pounds (86 kg). He wrote in his autobiography *Run Bullet Run* (1990):

> I was a football player who just happened to have world class speed, and I looked like a football player. Coaches, reporters, and all kinds of track experts commented

throughout my track career that I looked out of place on the track because of my muscular build and my big butt, which I carried high coming out of the starting blocks, instead of low, the way sprinters are supposed to. Bud Winter, the famous track coach at San Jose State, who developed sprinters like John Carlos and Tommie Smith, once observed that I ran like I "was pounding grapes into wine," and John Underwood, who covered track for *Sports Illustrated,* wrote that "Hayes does not run a race so much as he appears to beat it to death." My "style," if you want to call it that, was to run knock-kneed and pigeon-toed.

Hayes burst onto the sprint scene with 9.3 for 100 yards in a heat of the National Association of Intercollegiate Athletics (NAIA) Championships in Sioux Falls, South Dakota, on June 2, 1961. This equaled the world record, but Frank Budd's 9.2 three weeks later made it academic. On a "slow" track in Miami in February 1962 Hayes equaled Budd's mark with a 9.2 of his own. Although Hayes got off to a bad start into a 2 m/s headwind, two of the five timers gave him 9.1, while three read 9.2. Unfortunately the mark was not ratified because the starter, to save a few cents on ammunition, had used a .22-caliber pistol instead of the required .32-caliber model.

At the Coliseum Relays in Los Angeles on May 19, 1962, Hayes met Frank Budd, his rival for the title of world's fastest man. After two false starts the race finally got off, and Hayes finished the 100 meters in 10.2, beating Budd by about two yards. Nobody called Frank Budd the world's fastest human after that.

The 1963 AAU championships were held at the Old Public Schools Stadium in St. Louis on a new "rubberized" track, a mixture of rubber, crushed rock, and asphalt. Hayes, after coasting to 9.3 for 100 yards in the opening round, found the new surface to be the fastest he had ever run on and decided to go all out in the semifinals. After two false starts he stumbled a bit, but

by the midway point was five yards ahead and finished in 9.1, a world record. Hayes's time was the first world record to be set on a composition track. At first the IAAF refused to ratify it, but when it became evident that composition tracks would be commonplace, it was finally approved.

Hayes ended his brief running career with a dazzling display of speed at the 1964 Tokyo Olympic Games. Ironically, he was lucky to even be on the team. He had been forced to miss the preliminary Olympic trials with a pulled muscle, but was given special permission to advance to the final in Los Angles. There he qualified for the 100 meters easily with a 10.1. He also qualified for the 200 meters by finishing third, but the USOC gave his spot to Henry Carr, who finished fourth.

Hayes breezed through his first heat of the Tokyo Olympic 100 meters in 10.4 and his second in 10.3. In the semifinal he decided to open up and give the competition something to think about. He got out of the starting blocks in a flash and blasted down the track to win by three meters. A few minutes later, the announcement came over the loudspeakers: "Nine point nine seconds for Robert Hayes of the United States." Automatic timing gave him 9.91, the world's first sub 10.0 with auto timing. The capacity crowd of more than 75,000 went wild, but then groaned when the announcer added that Hayes's time didn't count as a record because the tail wind was 5.3 m/s, more than double the legal limit.

In the final, Hayes drew lane one, which had been chewed up by the 20-km walkers. He asked for another lane, but his request was turned down. When the gun sounded, he got another good start, although Cuba's Enrique Figuerola was about a half a step ahead of him. After 10 meters, it was Hayes, Figuerola and Jerome neck and neck, but by 25 meters, Hayes had moved a little ahead of Figuerola, with Jerome third. By the second 25 meters, when Hayes had gotten into full stride, he

**Bob Hayes after winning the 100-meter gold medal in Tokyo in 1964 (United States Olympic Committee).**

blasted past Figuerola, increasing his lead with every step. Hayes hit the tape two to three meters in the lead. The unofficial automatic timing gave him 10.06 and a winning margin of 0.19 seconds over Figuerola. The following wind was 1.1 m/s. His victory margin was the largest in an Olympic 100-meter final up to that time. Harry Jerome, the joint world record holder, finished third. The winning time was ratified as a world record–equaling 10.0. Afterwards Hayes commented, "My lane felt a little soft. I would have run faster in one of the other lanes."

He was even more impressive when he anchored the 4 × 100 relay. "Just get me close to the leaders," he told his teammates before the race. But he hadn't counted on being so far behind — he took the baton in fifth place. The other anchor men, led by Jocelyn Delecour from France, were as much as three meters ahead kicking up a cloud of cinders with their spikes.

Hayes took the baton and exploded down the track, trying to avoid the cinders which were stinging his eyes. He began to pick off the leaders one by one, first the Jamaicans, then the Russians, the French and finally the Poles. Making up six meters on some of the best sprinters in the world, he won by three meters in a world record 39.0. It is difficult to time individual runners in a relay accurately but the slowest estimate of Hayes's leg was 8.9 with most being 8.6-8.7.

Hayes lost only two of 62 races at 100 yards/meters during his career. Both losses came after he had been ill. After the Tokyo Olympics, at age 22, he gave up track to play professional football for the Dallas Cowboys. He was so successful at getting open for long passes that pro teams were forced to adopt the new "zone defense" to counter his amazing speed.

Injuries ended his football career in 1975 and soon after Hayes went through the lowest point of his life. After returning to Dallas in 1977 he worked as a telemarketing executive. He was befriended by an undercover police officer who arrested him in 1978 for selling cocaine and Quaaludes. Beginning in 1979, he spent 10 months in prison for the offense. After rehabilitation for drug and alcohol abuse, he returned to Florida A&M and completed his bachelor's degree in elementary education in 1994. He has spent much of his time in later years speaking out against drug abuse and urging athletes to get their college degrees.

The decision to give Hayes's 200 meter slot to Henry Carr at the Tokyo Olympics proved to be a wise one. Hayes had run the 220 in 20.1 on a straightaway, but because of his awkward style, his best time running the curve was only 20.5. Carr, who was born in Montgomery, Alabama, and attended college at Arizona State, had run 220 yards around a turn in a world record 20.3 in 1963, and improved this to 20.2 in April 1964. His greatest competition at Tokyo was expected to come from Paul Drayton from Villanova, who had run 20.4 for 220 yards around a turn. Running in lane eight in the Olympic final, Carr won easily in 20.3 (auto time, 20.36) over Drayton who finished second with 20.5. Carr, a versatile performer who had run 100 yards in 9.3 and 100 meters in 10.2, also anchored the U.S. 4 × 400 relay team at Tokyo to a world record with a blazing 44.5 split. Carr became a defensive back for the New York Giants football team in 1965.

## JIM HINES AND CHARLIE GREENE

The only 100-meter sprinter to get close to Bob Hayes in 1964 was Charlie Greene from the University of Nebraska. But Greene could only manage sixth place at the Olympic trials that year. Greene, from Pine Bluff, Arkansas, raced in dark sunglasses, and he delighted in explaining, "Hey, these aren't sunglasses, they're re-entry shields." He was challenged for the title of world's fastest human by Jim Hines from Texas Southern University. On May 13, 1967, at Houston, Texas, Hines ran 9.1 to tie Hayes's 100-yard mark.

At the AAU championships on June 20, 1968 in Sacramento, seven Americans, plus Jamaica's Lennox Miller and France's Roger Banuuck, tied or broke the existing world record of 10.0 for 100 meters. Hines ran 9.8 in his first heat, but the tail-wind of 2.8 m/s was over the limit. In his semifinal he recorded the world's first legal 9.9 for 100 meters. He won by inches over Ronnie Ray Smith from San Jose State, who was given 9.9 also. Five minutes later, Greene joined the hand-timed 9.9 club in winning his semifinal. The Bulova photo timer showed 10.02 for Hines and 10.09 for Greene. The following wind for both semifinal races was .8 m/s. In the final Greene edged Hines with both men being hand timed in 10 flat.

The other great sprinter of this era was Tommie Smith, who was born in Atworth, Texas, in 1944 and ran for San Jose State. On May 7, 1966, at San Jose the six-foot, four-inch (1.9 m), 188-pound (85.4 kg) Smith ran an incredible 19.5 seconds for the straight-away 220. Although the wind was 1.9 m/s at his back, he still took .5 seconds off the record set by Dave Sime in 1956. On June 11, 1966, Smith ran the 220 around-a-turn in 20.0. Since both the straightaway and around-a-turn 220-yard races were re-placed by the 200 meters around-a-turn in the late 1960s, Smith's times remain the best-on-record performances for 220 yards.

In a July 24, 1966, 4 × 400m relay, fol-lowing legs by Robert Frey (46.3) and Lee Evans (44.5), Smith ran a 43.8 leg (the first ever under 44). He handed off to Theron Lewis, who ran 45.0 to bring the team home in 2:59.6, the first 4 × 400 run in under three minutes.

The 1968 U.S. Olympic trials were held at Echo Summit, California (2,250 meters above sea level), on September 12, where conditions were expected to be similar to those in Mexico City. Jim Hines strength-ened his claim as America's best sprinter by winning the 100 meters in a hand timed 10 flat with Greene second and Mel Pender third. Ronnie Ray Smith finished fourth and was selected for the 4 × 100 relay.

In the 200, Tommie Smith was beaten by a goateed, jive-talking 23-year-old John Carlos from Harlem, New York, who fin-ished in 19.7, to Smith's second-place 19.9. Carlos's record-beating time was never ap-proved. The tail wind of 1.9 m/s was just inside the limit but Carlos's new track shoes had 68 brush-like spikes instead of the legal limit of six (now 11). The brush-spike shoe was designed by Puma for composition tracks and offered improved stability and traction but was never approved of by the IAAF.

In the 1968 100-meter Olympic final in Mexico City, Hines got off to a great start. He took the lead with 30 meters to go and won in an auto-timed 9.95. This was the first auto-timed 100 meters in less than 10 seconds with a legal wind reading. It was aided, however, by Mexico City's 2,250-meter altitude. Jamaican Lennox Miller was second in 10.04 and Greene, who had strained a muscle in winning his semifinal, finished third in 10.07.

The American 4 × 100 meter relay team made up of Greene, Pender, Ronnie Ray Smith and Hines set a world record of 38.24. Poor baton passing caused Hines to be two meters behind in third place when he got the baton for his anchor leg. Storming past the field, he finished a meter clear of the Cuban Figuerola then gleefully threw the baton into the crowd.

Fast times were also expected in the 200 meters and the fans weren't disap-pointed. Tommie Smith breezed to an Olympic record-tying 20.3 in his heat and Australian Peter Norman brought the Olympic record down to 20.2 in winning his qualifying heat. Carlos had an anxious moment in the second round — he almost lost his footing when he hit a wet spot as he rounded the curve.

In his semifinal, Carlos, running in lane one, ran the turn hard and led all the way, lowering the Olympic record again, this time to 20.1. Smith caught Greg Lewis from Australia with 80 meters to go and won his heat in 20.1 also, but in doing so pulled a muscle in his right groin. The pain was so sharp and so intense that he thought for a moment he had been shot by a sniper. The final was only about two hours away and his chances looked dim. "I didn't think I was going to make it," he said later. A team doctor applied ice, gave him three aspirins and wrapped him from the waist to the lower edge of his running shorts.

Carlos, in black socks and wearing an "Olympic Project for Human Rights" but-ton, was out fast in the final. He attacked the turn, and led by a meter and a half going into the straight. Showing no sign of his in-jury, Smith was also off quickly and entered

Jim Hines winning the 1968 Olympic 100 meters. On the far left is Jamaican Lennox Miller, who finished second. On the far right is Charlie Greene, who finished third (National Archives [306-NT-778C-2]).

the straight in second. He poured on the speed and passed Carlos at 140 meters. Five meters from the finish, Smith threw his long arms in the air and broke into a wide smile. Norman, coming from far behind, passed Carlos to take the silver medal. Smith was auto-timed in a world record 19.83, with Norman at 20.06 and Carlos 20.10.

At the awards ceremony, Smith and Carlos appeared shoeless in black socks and scarves. They stood with bowed heads and clenched black-gloved fists held high for the playing of the national anthem. Smith later explained the symbolism of their dress and actions. Their clenched fists, Smith's right and Carlos's left, stood for black power and unity. The scarves symbolized their blackness. The shoeless, black-stockinged feet were symbols of black poverty.

The incident produced mixed reactions. Some hailed it as a gesture of independence and for a worthy cause. Others were offended and embarrassed. The International Olympic Committee (IOC), fearing that the Games might degenerate into socio-political symposiums, threatened to expel the whole U.S. team if Smith and Carlos were not severely disciplined. After issuing an apology, the USOC removed the two sprinters from the team.

## VALERY BORZOV—
## THE UKRAINE EXPRESS

Valery Borzov proved that no country or region of the world has a monopoly on great sprinters. Born on October 20, 1949, in Sambor, Ukraine, he was the first male

John Carlos and Tommie Smith giving the Black Power salute at the 1968 Olympics (United States Olympic Committee).

athlete from the Soviet Union to win Olympic gold medals at any distance less than 5,000 meters.

By the time he was 12 years old, the efficient talent selection methods of the Soviet Union had spotted his sprinting potential and started him on his way to becoming a champion sprinter. He was first taught to love sports. After that he learned relaxation by running 100 meters holding a paper tube in his mouth. The only way to keep from crushing the tube was to relax his jaw muscles. Borzov studied films of great sprinters to determine optimal sprinting techniques such as the best push-off angle and the most effective body incline coming out of the blocks.

In 1969 Borzov won the European Championships in Athens on a new Tartan track. Next, he defeated the best American sprinters in a U.S.–U.S.S.R. meet in Leningrad in 1970 and again at Berkeley in 1971. Borzov also won the 1971 European Championships in Helsinki, running 10.27 for the 100 and 20.30 for the 200. In June 1972, Borzov raced Pietro Mennea of Italy in Milan and won by a scant margin as both equaled

the European record with a hand-timed 10.0.

Despite his success, it looked like Borzov would have his hands full in the 1972 Olympics in Munich. At the U.S. Olympic Trials in Eugene, Oregon, Eddie Hart from the University of California ran a hand-timed 9.9 seconds to equal the 100-meter world record. Florida A&M's Reynaud Robinson, a close second, also had 9.9. The third finisher, Robert Taylor, finished in 10.0. Opposition was also expected from Jamaica's 1968 Olympic silver medalist Lennox Miller and Hasely Crawford from Trinidad.

The first round of heats for the 1972 Olympic 100 meters began at 11:00 A.M. on August 31. Borzov, Hart and Robinson all qualified easily for the quarter-finals, which were to start later that day at 4:15 P.M., with the semis and the final to be run the following day. Unfortunately, Hart and Robinson never made it to their quarter-final races. Their coach, using a schedule that was a year-and-a-half old, thought they were to run at 7:00 P.M. When the Americans saw on a TV that their races were about to begin, they rushed to the stadium, but Hart and Robinson's races had already been run. Taylor made it just in time to run his semifinal heat and advance to the final. Hart later described losing the most important race of his life — the race to the stadium.

> I remember us driving to the stadium, speeding the wrong way down one-way streets, swerving around police cordons. I had got half way down the tunnel which connected the practice track and the stadium when my race went off. I was just seconds from making it.

The 100-meter final was run with almost no wind, in slightly chilly weather and under overcast skies that seemed to reflect the somber mood of the American fans who were minus their two fastest sprinters. The remaining American, Taylor, was still a threat, along with Miller and Crawford. At the gun, the field got away together, but by 30 meters Borzov began to pull away and was not challenged. He finished in 10.14, throwing his arms high above his head in an uncharacteristic display of emotion, with Taylor a meter behind and Miller third. Borzov said after the race that he didn't have to go all-out to win. "I made the greatest effort in the finals and I gave 90 percent of what I had to give." Although some felt the race would have turned out differently had Hart and Robinson ran, Borzov had beaten the best American sprinters six times in six matches before the Games.

In the final of the 200 meters Borzov cemented his claim as the world's fastest human. Running in lane five, he got off to a great start. Coming off the turn into the stretch, American Larry Black in lane one and Pietro Mennea of Italy in lane two closed for a moment, but then Borzov began to increase his lead with every stride. With 10 meters to go he was two meters in the clear. Five meters out he looked back then threw his hands in the air, finishing in 20.00 with Black second in 20.19. Borzov anchored the Soviet 4 × 100 meter relay, taking the baton in fifth place, with Hart far ahead in the lead. With another strong run, Borzov caught everyone but Hart to give his team a silver medal.

In the Montreal Olympics four years later Borzov was past his prime but still gave a good account of himself. Hasely Crawford took the gold, with Jamaica's Don Quarrie second. Borzov just edged out American Harvey Glance for the bronze. This was the first time a male 100-meter Olympic champion had returned and won a medal in the same event. Borzov also ran the 4 × 100 meter relay in Montreal, anchoring the Soviet team to another silver medal.

On May 11, 1974, Ivory Crockett, a five-foot, six-inch, (1.7 m) 141-pound (64 kg) sprinter from Southern Illinois University set the last world record at the classic 100-yard distance. Running on a Chevron track in the University of Tennessee's Tom

Valery Borzov, the only great sprinter from the Soviety Union, won the 100- and 200-meter races in the 1972 Olympics (photograph by Mstislav Botashev, courtesy of Nikolai Botashev).

Black Classic, Crockett exploded from his blocks with the best start of his life and was never challenged. Nearing the tape, he threw his arms up in triumph and looked over his left shoulder at Reggie Jones two yards back. Four watches caught Crockett in 8.9, 9.0, 9.0 and 9.1, with the official time being 9.0.

Crockett's record was equaled by Houston McTear from Baker, Florida, in the 1975 Florida high-school state-championship meet. McTear, extremely gifted and one of the fastest starters ever, qualified for the Olympic team in 1976 but could not compete because of injuries. After that he faded into obscurity, never fulfilling his early promise.

In 1976 all English distances except the mile were removed from the record books. The era of the 100 yards, which had begun with Englishman Jem Wantling's perhaps mythical nine second 100 yards on a turnpike road in about 1822, strangely ended with the same 9.0 as the best time on record.

## CARL LEWIS—
## ATHLETE OF THE CENTURY

Frederick Carlton Lewis had a long and stellar career as a sprinter and long jumper. In four Olympic Games he won nine gold medals and one silver. He also won eight gold medals at the World Championships and six times anchored U.S. 4 × 100-meter relay teams to world records. In addition, he had 15 auto-timed sub–10 second races for 100 meters—more than any other sprinter of his day. He also set two world records in the event.

Lewis was born in Birmingham, Alabama, but grew up near Philadelphia. His parents were both track coaches and his sis-

Ben Johnson defeating Carl Lewis in the 100-meter final in Seoul in 1988. Lenford Christie of Great Britain is third (Ted Grant, National Archives of Canada, PA-175370).

ter Carol was a world-class long jumper. As a young boy, Carl was small, shy and overshadowed by Carol, who called him "Shorty." In 1971, his father introduced him to Jesse Owens, then 57 years old. Lewis was greatly impressed by the legendary sprinter whose initial advice was "to have fun."

When he was 15 and in his second year of high school, Lewis finally started growing and sprouted so suddenly (two inches in a month) that he had to walk with crutches for three weeks while his body adjusted. As a high school junior, his time for 100 yards plummeted from 10.6 to 9.3 and as a senior he improved his long jump to 26 feet eight inches (8.13 m), a national high-school record.

In 1979 Lewis entered the University of Houston. There he was coached by Tom Tellez, who honed young Lewis's sprinting form. Lewis finished fourth in the 100 meters at the 1980 Olympic trials. This qualified him for the team as a member of the 4 × 100 relay, but that was the year of the Carter Administration–mandated boycott of the Games.

During the winter of 1980-81, Lewis went through a weight-training program to develop his strength. On May 16, 1981, he ran the 100 meters in 10.00 in Dallas with no wind. This was the first legitimate auto-timed, non-windy, non-altitude "even time" mark ever recorded for 100 meters. On May 14, 1983, at Modesto, California, in the S & W Invitational, he ran 9.97 seconds, becoming the first auto-timed sprinter to break evens for 100 meters with no qualifications. Others had previously run under 10, but there had always been something such as altitude or winds that cast doubt on the performance.

In 1984, at the Los Angeles Olympics, Lewis duplicated Jesse Owens's feat of winning four gold medals. In the 100 meters he ran 9.99 to win by 2.5 meters, beating fellow American Sam Graddy (10.19) and Canadian Ben Johnson (10.22). He added the gold medal for the long jump with his first leap — 28 feet (8.53 m) into the wind. He won the 200 in an Olympic record 19.80 seconds and topped it all off by running an 8.94 anchor leg on the victorious 4 × 100 relay team. Because Lewis had appeared to be somewhat cold and aloof during the Games, the expected commercial endorsements never happened.

Because of his height (6 feet, 2 inches/ 1.9 m) Lewis nearly always played catch up, reaching his top speed behind the shorter, faster starters. His greatest strength was over the last 30 meters. While other sprinters often strained and tightened near the finish, Lewis was able to stay relaxed and maintain near-perfect form all the way. In 1999 the IAAF voted him the top male athlete of the century.

### BEN JOHNSON — TIME IN A BOTTLE

Finishing third to Lewis in the 100 meters at the 1984 Los Angeles Olympics was Benjamin Sinclair Johnson, a Canadian who had emigrated from Jamaica in 1976. Johnson joined the Optimist Track Club in Toronto in 1977, where he was coached by former Canadian sprint champion Charlie Francis. At first Johnson was skinny (93 pounds/42 kg) and awkward, but under Francis's coaching he steadily became stronger and faster. He was noted early for his explosive, leaping start. In August 1981 at the World Cup trials in Venezuela, the 19-year-old Johnson finished second in the 100 meters in 10.25 — his best performance up to that time.

According to Francis in *Speed Trap* (1990), he met with Johnson in September of 1981 and discussed using anabolic steroids. Both men said they believed that most of the world's top sprinters were taking steroids and that if Johnson was to be competitive at the highest level it was necessary for him to take them also. Johnson began taking the steroid dianabol in late 1981 and eventually proved, without doubt, that the combination of talent, hard training and steroids produced results.

By 1984 he had established himself as one of the best sprinters in the world. At the World Track and Field Championships 100-meter race in Rome in August 1987, he shattered Calvin Smith's altitude-aided world record of 9.93, by a full .1 second. In running his 9.83 he beat a field of elite sprinters, including his chief rival Carl Lewis, who finished in 9.93. In 1988 at the Seoul Olympics Johnson won the gold medal in the 100-meters, running an amazing 9.79 with Lewis second in 9.92 and Linford Christie from England third in 9.97. Two days later, the biggest news story of the Games broke. Johnson had been disqualified based on an "endocrine profile" that showed he had used the steroid stanazolol. He lost his gold medal, his world record and was suspended for two years.

Steroids had been used by track & field athletes since the 1950s and were legal until 1974 when the IAAF banned them. "Day of the event" drug testing proved inadequate for catching steroid users. A runner on steroids could grow larger muscles and train harder, yet still easily pass the drug test. It was only necessary to let the drugs clear the system before being tested. This usually took from two to three weeks with an extra week often added for insurance. A few steroid users miscalculated the clearance time or were otherwise careless and got caught.

As a result of Johnson's failed drug test, the Dubin Commission was formed in 1989 to investigate drug use by Canadian athletes. The IAAF tacitly admitted their testing didn't work when they took away Johnson's 1987 record of 9.83 for the 100 meters. Up to that time, Johnson had passed over 20 drug tests including one when he set the record. Johnson's admission at the Dubin Inquiry that he had taken steroids since 1981 was what cost him the record.

Johnson returned to competition in January 1991 and ran in the 1992 Olympics in Barcelona but failed to make the final. His best 100-meter time in 1992 was 10.16, which placed him 22nd on the world list. On the indoor circuit that winter his times began to improve and he ran 50 meters in 5.65, only .04 seconds off his own world best. On January 17, 1993, after an indoor meet in Montreal, he tested positive for testosterone and he was banned again, this time for life.

Interviewed in 1996, Johnson insisted he was not the only sprinter on steroids who ran in the Seoul Olympics in 1988. "There was no cheating," he said. "We ran on equal terms and the best man won. They know it. I know it. That's all that counts. Yes, I was taking steroids, but so was everyone else on the starting line that day."

In 1989 the IAAF began random drug testing which made it more difficult for steroid users to pass the drug tests. Some turned to masking agents, switching samples and various other tricks to beat the tests. Others switched to new drugs not currently being tested for, such as Human Growth Hormone. None of the women's sprint records set in the 1980s (when women's sprinting was dominated by the Soviet Bloc and steroid use among runners of those countries was common) were broken in the 1990s after random drug testing became more widely practiced.

With Johnson's feats nullified, Carl Lewis received the 1988 Olympic gold medal and became the first sprinter to win two golds in the 100 meters. He also became the world record holder with his 9.92 at Seoul. Lewis's mark was beaten by his Santa Monica Track Club teammate Leroy Burrell, who ran 9.90 on June 14, 1991, in New York.

Lewis regained the record on August 25, 1991, in Tokyo, running on a specially designed extra-hard track nicknamed "the magic carpet." He came from behind in the last 10 meters to defeat Burrell and lower the record to 9.86. In 1994 in Switzerland, Burrell took .01 seconds off Lewis's record by running 9.85. With Burrell injured and age creeping up on Lewis, neither made the 1996 U.S. Olympic team at 100 meters, although Lewis won his fourth gold in the long jump. Nambia's Frank Fredericks and Trinidad's Ato Boldon, who won their semifinals in 9.94 and 9.93 were the favorites for the gold at Atlanta. In the final there were three false starts and defending champion Linford Christie was disqualified for starting .082 seconds after the gun fired. When they were finally away, the quickest legal starter was Fredericks with a .143 second reaction time. Fredericks and Boldon were in the lead at 60 meters, but Donovan Baily of Canada powered past them both to win in 9.84, and become the new world's fastest man. Baily, who was born in Jamaica and moved to Canada at age 13, later won a 150-meter race against Michael Johnson when the American pulled up lame.

Maurice Greene, from Kansas City, Kansas, made his first national impact in 1995 when he beat Carl Lewis in a wind-aided 9.88 at the Texas Relays. He failed to qualify for the Atlanta Olympics, finishing seventh in his quarterfinal heat at the U.S. trials. He then went to Los Angeles and trained under 1972 Olympian John Smith, who helped him improve his sprint mechanics.

On June 16, 1999, Greene became the 20th century's last fastest human. The venue was the Olympic Stadium in Athens, Greece, and Greene's opposition consisted of training partner Alto Boldon from Trinidad, Frank Fredericks from Namibia and Bruny Surin of Canada. The start was even, but Greene and Boldon soon moved ahead of the others. At 70 meters they were still together, but then Greene took off and left Boldon behind to win in a world record 9.79. Boldon was second in 9.86 and Surin third in 9.97. Greene's world record 9.79 had at last equaled Ben Johnson's drug-aided time of 1988.

Later in 1999, at the World Championships in Seville, Greene defended his title in the 100 meters with a 9.80, then won the 200 meters in 19.90, becoming the first man to win both events at the worlds.

## MICHAEL JOHNSON—
## SHIFTING INTO HYPER-DRIVE

Michael Johnson was the star of the 1996 Olympics. Johnson was born on September 13, 1967, in Dallas, Texas, and attended Baylor University, where he quickly became a world class sprinter. He was noted for his rigid, upright running style with minimal knee lift. His best race was the 200 but he gradually learned the intricacies of the 400 and began to excel at that distance also. Before the Olympic Trials in 1988, he developed a stress fracture in his left fibula and didn't make the team.

In 1992 Johnson decided to concentrate on the 200 and skip the 400, but bad luck struck again. He was the favorite to win the 200 meters in Barcelona, but two weeks before the Olympics opened he dined on a mixture of grilled and smoked meats and came down with food poisoning. The resulting 10-pound (4.5 kg) weight loss sapped his strength and he was eliminated in the semifinals of the 200 meters when the best he could manage was sixth in 20.78. He did get a gold medal for running on the winning 4 × 400 relay team.

In 1996 Johnson persuaded the IOC to change the schedule at the Atlanta Olympic Games so he could attempt an unprecedented 200–400 double. At the 1996 U.S. Olympic trials he qualified for the 400 meters in 43.44, the third fastest time ever. In the 200-meter final he finished in 19.66, breaking the altitude-aided 19.72 world record that Pietro Mennea had set in 1979 at Mexico City.

On July 29 at the Olympic Games in Atlanta, Johnson set an Olympic record of 43.49 in winning the 400. Three days later in the 200 final his main rival was Frankie Fredericks, who four weeks earlier had ended Johnson's two-year 200-meter winning streak.

At the gun, Fredericks shot into the lead. Johnson reacted quickly, but after four steps he stumbled slightly. He recovered, caught Fredericks at 80 meters, and then seemed to shift into another gear. "I did know, off the turn, I was running faster than I ever have," he said later. He crossed the finish line four meters ahead of Fredericks in an amazing 19.32 seconds—a time many experts thought no sprinter would run until a couple of decades into the 21st century. In his amazing race Johnson ran 10.1 for the first 100 meters and 9.2 for the second.

**Michael Johnson won gold medals for the 200 and 400 meters in the 1996 Atlanta Olympics. He also set world records at both distances (Baylor University).**

## Sprinters—Women

*Most people don't realize that you work a lifetime to run 9, 10, 11 seconds, and you can't plan for it.... It takes a very special person to be mentally tough for 9 seconds.*— Wilma Rudolph (1960)

The 1950s were the "golden age" of women's sprinting in Australia. In 1949 the Dutch superstar Fanny Blankers-Koen toured Australia and shockingly was beaten both at 100 yards and 100 meters by a young sprinter named Marjorie Jackson, the "Lithgow Flash." Jackson became the first woman to run 100 yards in 10.7 seconds in March 1950 and won both the 100 and 200 meter races at the 1952 Olympics in Helsinki. In the 200 meters she lowered the world record to 23.4 in one of the early rounds. She lost a chance for a third gold medal due to a bad baton exchange between her and teammate Winsome Cripps in the 4 × 100 relay. After the Olympics, on October 4, 1952, in Gifu, Japan, Jackson broke the 100-meter record with 11.4. This record was beaten by another Australian, Shirley Strickland, when she ran 11.3 on August 4, 1955, in Warsaw, Poland.

Betty Cuthbert was known as Australia's "Golden Girl," but she was never quite sure whether it was for the color of her hair or the four Olympic gold medals she won. Cuthbert was born in Sydney in 1938, along with twin sister Marie. She won her first race at age eight and went on to win many schoolgirl titles, but never considered herself Olympic material. In 1956 she made remarkable progress and set a 200-meter world record by running 23.2 in Sydney on September 16.

Cuthbert, in her book *Golden Girl* (1966), explained how she won the gold medal in the 100 meters at the Melbourne Olympic Games in 1956:

> I never relaxed for a fraction of a second and kept driving as hard as I could till I felt the little white tape break in two. Toward the end my mouth was open so wide it began hurting but I thought, "You can't stop to shut it now." So it stayed open till I thought my jaws were going to split. I'd done it. I'd won the highest prize in amateur sport — an Olympic Gold Medal.

In the 200-meter final, Cuthbert drew lane five, and her most dangerous oppo-

nent, East German Christa Stubnick, lane six. Cuthbert knew she would have to catch the East German by the time they came off the curve in order to win. She got a terrific start, caught Stubnick by 80 meters, and was clear of the field. She finished in 23.4, to win her second gold medal. In the 4 × 100 relay Cuthbert anchored the Australian team to yet another gold. The team's time of 44.5 took .7 seconds off the old world record.

Cuthbert had a difficult time with her new-found fame. She was shy and only 18 when she won her three gold medals. After she pulled a hamstring at the Olympics in 1960 her coach, June Ferguson, suggested she move up to the new Olympic race for women — the 400 meters — at the Tokyo Olympics in 1964. Cuthbert wrote in her autobiography of the fire that drives a world champion athlete.

> It was a gold medal or bust. I didn't care what happened to me physically — I

Betty Cuthbert setting a world record for the 60 meters (Australian Archives, Series A1200, caption number L35230. Commonwealth of Australia copyright, used by permission).

could tear both hamstrings, put that bone in my foot out of joint for good, rip all the tendons in my ankles but I had to get over that line first. I was going to punish myself as I'd never done before, for that 400-meter final was going to be my personal D-Day.

True to her word, in the 400-meter final in Tokyo, Cuthbert got off quickly and held off Anne Packer of Great Britain to finish in 52.0 and win her fourth gold medal. Cuthbert is the only runner, male or female, to win Olympic gold medals in the 100, 200 and 400 meters.

## WILMA RUDOLPH—THE EBONY GAZELLE

Wilma Rudolph was born June 23, 1940, in Clarksville, Tennessee. Double pneumonia and scarlet fever left her unable to walk until age 10. While attending Burt High School in Clarksville, where she was a star basketball player, she was "discovered" by Ed Temple, the celebrated coach at Tennessee State. Rudolph participated in Temple's summer track program and made rapid progress. In 1956 at the Melbourne Olympics, 16-year-old Rudolph did not make the final of the 200 meters, but she and her three "Tigerbelle" teammates won a bronze medal in the 4 × 100 meter relay.

Her running dreams were almost dashed in 1958 when she became pregnant. "I was mortified," she wrote later. But her family agreed to take care of her child and coach Temple waived his rule against mothers on his team. After graduation and the birth of her daughter Yolanda, the tall (5-foot, 11-inch/1.8 m), graceful Rudolph enrolled at Tennessee State University. "By the time my sophomore year began things started falling in place nicely," she wrote in her book *Wilma* (1977). "Yolanda was doing fine with my family back in Clarksville, my grades were holding, and I was running well. In fact I was running better than ever. My speed was tremendous after I had the baby; I was much faster than before."

On July 9, 1960, in Corpus Christi, Texas, Rudolph smashed Betty Cuthbert's 200-meter record by .3 seconds when she ran 22.9 to become the first woman to break 23 seconds for the distance. At the 1960 Olympics in Rome, she won the 100-meter gold medal after tying the world record of 11.3 in the semifinals. She wrote in her book, *Wilma*,

My start was relatively good. I came out second or third in the field, and my speed started increasing the further I went. When I reached 50 meters, I saw that I had them all, and I was just beginning to turn it on. By 70 meters, I knew the race was mine, nobody was going to catch me.

She won the 200-meter final in 24.0. Earlier in her opening heat she had set an

**Wilma Rudolph won three gold medals at the 1960 Rome Olympics (United States Olympic Committee).**

Olympic record of 23.2. Then she combined with her three Tigerbelle teammates to win the 4 × 100 relay in 44.5, following a world record of 44.4 in the semifinals. When Rudolph returned home from Rome, Clarksville held a parade and an integrated banquet, one of the first of its kind in the history of the city. On July 19, 1961, in Stuttgart, Germany, she lowered the 100-meter record to 11.2. The following year, at age 22, she retired from the track, leaving the sport at an even earlier age than Jesse Owens to whom she was often compared. "I don't know why I run so fast," she was quoted as saying. "I just run." Wilma Rudolph, whose ability, grace and charisma endeared her to millions, died of cancer in 1994.

### Wyomia Tyus—Double Olympic 100-Meter Champion

Wyomia Tyus, another member of Ed Temple's Tigerbelles, was the first Olympic sprinter to win two gold medals in the 100 meters. Tyus, born on August 29, 1945, in Griffin, Georgia, began her track career as a high school high jumper. When she struggled to clear four feet (1.2 m), she decided to switch to sprinting. Tennessee State coach Ed Temple recognized her potential when he saw her compete in the Georgia high school championships. He later nicknamed her the "Machine," because "You could just wind her up like a machine, and she'd do everything so well."

In 1964 at Tokyo she was just a freshman but equaled the world record of 11.2 in her quarterfinal and went on to win the 100-meter gold medal. Another Tigerbelle, Edith McGuire, finished second and won the gold in the 200 meters with an Olympic record 23.05. Both won silver medals as part of the 4 × 100 meter relay team.

Four years later in Mexico City, after being told she was "washed-up," Tyus did a little dance called the "tighten-up" to loosen up before the 100-meter final. She beat teammate Barbara Ferrell and Polish superstar Irena Szewinska by a meter to win another gold medal and set a world record of 11.0 seconds (auto time 11.08). Running anchor on the 4 × 100 relay, she got her third gold medal by leading the U.S. team to a world record 42.88. After the 1968 Olympics, Tyus retired from running. In 1973, she returned to competition with the professional International Track Association (ITA) and in 1974 was the top women's money-winner.

Ed Temple was one of America's greatest track coaches. He coached the Tigerbelles at Tennessee State for 43 years until he retired in 1993. Although he wasn't even allowed to offer scholarships until 1967, he trained 40 Olympians who won 17 gold medals. All but one of the 40 graduated.

### Irena Szewinska—First Great Sprinter from Eastern Europe

Irena Szewinska of Poland was the "Queen of the Track" in the 1960s and 1970s. She was the first of a long list of outstanding sprinters from Eastern Europe. Her career, beginning in 1964 and ending in 1980, spanned five Olympics. She won seven Olympic medals with golds in the 200 (1968) and the 400 (1976), and she was the only runner to hold world records at 100, 200 and 400 meters.

One of Szewinska's greatest triumphs was her 1974 victory over East German Renate Stecher at an international meet in Potsdam, East Germany. Stecher had been undefeated at 200 meters for four years going into the race. Szewinska's winning time of 22.21 was the first official automatically-timed women's record. Her lifetime bests were 11.1 for 100 meters in 1965 and 1968, 22.21 for 200 meters in 1974, and 49.25 for 400 meters in 1976.

### Chi Cheng—First Woman to Run "Even" Time

Chi Cheng from Taiwan developed into a marvelous athlete but it took a long

Wyomia Tyus (white shirt) was the first sprinter to win 100-meter gold medals in two Olympic Games (United States Olympic Committee).

time. She competed in the 80-meter hurdles at the 1960 Rome Olympics as a 16-year-old, but went out in the first round. Vince Reel, a coach from the United States, noticed her performance and when he met her again in 1962 in Taiwan, they agreed that she would come to California to train. She competed at Tokyo in 1964, but did little better than at Rome. Finally, in Mexico City in 1968 she managed a bronze medal in the 80-meter hurdles. After that her career took off.

In 1969 she won 66 out of 67 competitions and in 1970 she was undefeated in 83 running, jumping and hurdling events. She was the first woman to run 100 yards in even time (10.0) and set records at 100 meters (11.0) and 200 meters (22.4). Cheng retired in 1973 and returned to Taiwan in 1980 where she was immensely popular and was elected to the national senate in 1981.

## RENATE STECHER—A GREAT SPRINTER FROM EAST GERMANY

Renate Stecher was the first of many East German women who dominated the sprints and middle distances in the 1970s and 80s. In the Munich Olympics of 1972 Stecher won the 100-meter gold medal with a world record 11.07 and came back to win the 200-meters in another world record (22.40). She anchored the 4 × 100 meter relay team for East Germany and just missed winning her third gold medal when she took over the baton a stride behind West Germany's Heidi Rosendahl. Everybody expected Stecher to make up the one-meter deficit. However, Rosendahl ran the race of her life, losing only a half meter, and held on for the gold medal. Four years later in Montreal, Stecher got her gold medal in the 4 × 100 relay plus a silver in the 100 and bronze in the 200.

Another East German, Marlies Göhr, was one of the most durable sprinters ever. She made her Olympic debut at Montreal as a member of the gold-medal-winning 4 × 100 meter relay team. At Dresden on July 1, 1977, she ran 10.88 to became the first woman to break 11 seconds for 100 meters with automatic timing. The aiding wind was 2.0 m/s.

Although sprinting of the 1970s and early 1980s was dominated by women from Eastern Europe, Evelyn Ashford, born in

Evelyn Ashford won the 100-meter gold medal in the 1984 Los Angeles Olympics (AAF/LPI 1984, 60987 J2).

Louisiana in 1957, was an exception — an American who competed on even terms with the Eastern Europeans. Ashford grew up in California and received one of the first women's athletic scholarships to UCLA. She was fifth in the 100 meters at the 1976 Olympics but by 1979 was the best sprinter in the world. At the 1979 World Cup in Montreal she defeated Marlies Göhr to win the 100 and Marita Koch to win the 200. Ashford was bitterly disappointed by the U.S. boycott of the 1980 Olympics. In 1983 she lowered the 100-meter record to 10.79 in a high-altitude (7,200 feet/2,195 meter) race in Colorado Springs.

At the 1984 Olympics, she won gold medals in the 100 (10.97) and 4 × 100 relay. The 100-meter triumph was lessened somewhat by the absence of Göhr whose East German team boycotted the Games that year. Three weeks later in Zurich, Ashford met Göhr and defeated her with a world record of 10.76. She made the U.S. Olympic team again in 1988, and won a silver medal in the 100 and another gold running on 4 × 100-relay team. In 1992, at age 35, she won her fourth Olympic gold medal, again on the 4 × 100 relay team.

### FLORENCE GRIFFITH JOYNER— GODDESS OF THE WIND

Florence Griffith Joyner, "Flo-Jo," who was born in 1959 in California, surpassed the achievements of all other sprinters of her era. While attending UCLA she had bests in the 100 meters of 11.23, 11.12 and 11.06 as a sophomore, junior and senior and 22.81, 22.39 and 22.23 in the 200 meters. After graduating in 1983 with a degree in psychology, she improved her 100-meter time to 10.99 in 1984 and won a silver medal at the Los Angeles Olympics in the 200 (22.04).

She went into semi-retirement from track in 1986, working full-time at a bank. For a second job she styled hair and fingernails. In April 1987 she returned to track, and at the World Championships in Rome ran the first two rounds of the 200 meters in a colorful skin-tight suit similar to a speed skater's. She finished second and ran the third leg on the gold medal–winning U.S. 4 × 100 meter relay team.

In June 1988 she ran 10.89 for 100 meters and 22.15 for the 200. A month later she went to the U.S. Olympic Trials in Indianapolis sporting a remarkable set of newly developed muscles and was a favorite to make the team in both sprints. In the first heat of the second round of the 100 meters she ran a jaw-dropping 10.49. The performance broke Evelyn Ashford's 1984 world record of 10.76 by .27 seconds. Diane Williams was second in 10.88, with Gail Devers third in 10.98. The legitimacy of this amazing performance is still being argued. Winds were kicking the nearby triple jump wind gauge to nearly 5 m/s, but the gauge used for the 100 meters registered an improbable 0.0 for her race. The IAAF approved the record but the Association of Track & Field Statisticians annotated it as "probably strongly wind-assisted." Griffith Joyner ran 10.61 to win the Olympic trials final with a legal 1.2 m/s aiding wind. Many consider this her best performance.

At the Seoul Olympics she won both sprints by huge margins. She won the 100-meter gold medal with a wind-aided 10.54 ahead of Ashford (10.83) and East Germany's Heike Drechsler (10.85). In the final of the 200 she broke the world record with 21.34. Grace Jackson of Jamaica was second (21.72) with Drechsler again third (21.95). Griffith Joyner ran the third leg of the U.S. 4 × 100 relay team, handing off to Ashford. The U.S. team won in 41.98 with East Germany second. American coach Terry Crawford had Griffith Joyner anchor the 4 × 400 relay to give her a chance to tie Fanny Blankers-Koen's feat of winning four gold medals in a single Olympics. Despite Griffith Joyner's 48.08 split, the Soviet team beat the Americans by three meters with a world record 3:15.18.

After retiring from track in February 1989 Griffith Joyner designed and modeled clothes. She also worked with children, both through sports programs and by writing a series of children's books. On September 21, 1998, she died unexpectedly in her sleep. Her premature death brought intense media speculation that it was caused by the effects of taking performance-enhancing drugs. An autopsy, however, showed she suffocated as the result of an epileptic seizure. Primo Nebiolo, president of the IAAF gave perhaps the most moving of many tributes to Flo-Jo: "I will never forget this extraordinary athlete who stunned the world in Seoul 10 years ago with her amazing sprints and spectacular outfits. Sadly, her life has passed as rapidly as her races."

Florence Griffith Joyner running in the 1984 Olympics. Her world records at 100 and 200 meters set in 1988 stayed unbroken for the remainder of the twentieth century (AAF/LPI 1984, 56570 RL).

Griffith Joyner overshadowed all other female sprinters for the rest of the 20th century, but mention should be made of Jamaican Marlene Ottey and American Gail Devers. Over a long career Ottey consistently rated near the top. In 1991 she had the eight fastest 100-meter times of the year and in Milan in 1996 became the world's second fastest woman with 10.74 for 100 meters. Ottey's career came to an abrupt end when she failed a drug test in 1999.

Gail Devers was treated for Graves' disease before the 1992 Barcelona Olympics. Her body reacted so violently to the radiation used to treat the disease that doctors considered amputating her feet, but she opted for diet and medication instead. She returned to the track in time to win the 100 meters at the 1992 Barcelona Games in a photo-finish 10.82 against a 1 m/s breeze. She almost won another gold in the 100-meter hurdles but, with a commanding lead, she tripped and fell. In the 1996 Atlanta Olympics Devers duplicated Wyomia Tyus's feat of winning two gold medals in the 100 meters. This time the finish was so close that second place Ottey protested, thinking she had won. After studying the photo finish the judges declared Devers the winner, although she and Ottey were both timed in 10.94

If anyone can break Flo-Jo's 100-meter record, it may be Marion Jones from Southern California. Jones was born in 1975 in Los Angeles to a mother who emigrated from Belize and a father from Louisiana. She was an active child who participated in ballet, soccer, basketball and gymnastics. By the age of 10, she was an age-group national champion in track, by 12 she was competing internationally, and by 15 she was running 22.76 for the 200 and 11.17 for the 100.

In high school in Thousand Oaks, California, Jones set the national prep record for 200 meters five times and long-jumped 22 feet, ½ inch (6.72 m). At the University of North Carolina she was an outstanding basketball player, making third team all-

American. She broke a bone in her foot in April 1995 playing basketball and reinjured it in December, ending her 1996 Olympic hopes. In May 1998 she replaced Ottey as the "world's second fastest woman" when she ran the 100 meters in 10.71 and later said:

> As a child, I saw Flo-Jo on television running her 10.49 without realizing what it meant. Now, after my 10.71, I know what it means. What I don't understand is the attitude of other sprinters. They look at Flo-Jo's record and say, "We can never do that." In my opinion, that's the main reason that women's sprints have made no progress in the last 10 years.

## Men's 400 Meters

By the early 1950s the great trio of Jamaican sprinters McKenley, Wint and Rohden had brought the 400-meter record down to just under 46 seconds (45.8 by Rohden). With a few exceptions, Americans dominated the event for the rest of the century. At the Pan Am Games in Mexico City in March 1955, Louis Jones, a graduate of Manhattan College in New York, blazed the first 200 meters in 21.1 seconds. He held off rival Jim Lea of the U.S. Air Force to win in 45.4 before falling to the track unconscious. Lea, who finished second in 45.6, was also inside the old world record. Track observers found the new record hard to believe until they took into account the 7,400 foot (2,256 m) altitude of Mexico City.

Lea, who held the 440-yard record of 45.8, and Jones met again in California at the U.S. Olympic trials for 1956. Running in lane eight, Jones again went out very fast for the first 200 (21.3). He beat Lea by half a second, running 45.2 to break his own world record. Despite these record-breaking performances, both Jones and Lea ran poorly at the Melbourne Olympics and finished out of the medals. The gold medal went to Charles Jenkins, the third American on the team, who won with 46.7.

Otis Davis was the first man to break 45 seconds in the 400 meters (University of Oregon).

Otis Davis was a student at the University of Oregon where he played basketball. He started running the 400 at age 26 and made remarkable progress, making the 1960 Olympic team by finishing third at the trials. In the Olympic final in Rome the South African Mal Spence led for the first 200 meters, with Davis and the German Karl Kaufmann about six meters back. Davis then sprinted the next 100 meters in 10.8 seconds to move seven meters into the lead with Kaufmann second. Kaufmann came back and dueled Davis to the finish. They crossed the line together with the photo finish giving the race to Davis. Hand timers gave both men 44.9, and the photo timer gave Davis 45.07 and Kaufmann 45.08.

## LEE EVANS—A 400-METER RECORD THAT LASTED 20 YEARS

Lee Edward Evans, born in 1947 in Madera, California, burst into prominence in 1966, his first year out of high school. He attended San Jose State and was undefeated at 400 meters in 1966 with a number one world ranking and an AAU championship. The following year he again ranked first and won the AAU and Pan American titles. On May 20, 1967, in a classic race with his teammate and friend Tommie Smith, Evans suffered his first defeat. Evans set the pace for the first half of the race (21.5–21.7), but Smith was able to use his superior speed over the last 50 meters to win in 44.5, taking .4 seconds off the world record. Evans finished in 45.3.

At the 400-meter final in Mexico City, Evans was under enormous pressure from the events surrounding the black power demonstration of two days earlier. Starting

Lee Evans set a 400-meter world record in the 1968 Olympics that lasted for 20 years (San Jose State University sports information office).

in lane six, he ran 100-meter splits of 10.4, 10.7, 11.1 and 11.8 to win the gold medal in 43.86 to teammate Larry James's second place 43.97. The combination of altitude and a superb performance made for a record that lasted until 1988. Although a Black Power advocate, Evans did not disrupt his victory ceremony.

The best 400-meter runner of the 1970s was six-foot, two-inch (1.9 m), 195-pound (88.6 kg) Cuban Alberto Juantorena, known as "El Caballo" (the horse) for his powerful nine-foot (2.7 m) stride. He ran his first 400-meter race in 1971 and a year later competed in the Olympics in Munich, where he was eliminated in the semifinals. He won all of his 400-meter races in both 1973 and 1974 before having two operations on his foot in 1975. In 1976, at the Montreal

Alberto Juantorena from Cuba won both the 400 and 800 meters at the 1976 Olympics (photograph by Mstislav Botashev, courtesy of Nikolai Botashev).

Olympics, he accomplished the unprecedented feat of winning gold medals in both the 400 and 800 meters. His 44.26 in winning the 400 at Montreal was the fastest non-altitude time until 1987. Alonzo Babers from the U.S. Air Force Academy ran almost as fast (44.27) in winning the gold medal in the 1984 Los Angeles Olympics.

### BUTCH REYNOLDS—BREAKING 44 SECONDS AT SEA LEVEL

Harry Lee "Butch" Reynolds was born on June 8, 1964, in Akron, Ohio. In high school his best 400 meters was 48.1, but the six-foot, three-inch (1.9 m) Reynolds improved dramatically the following year when he ran 45.47. During his track career at Ohio State University he was hampered by injuries much of time. He ran in the 1984 U.S. Olympic trials but was eliminated in the semifinals. In 1987 Reynolds approached the season cautiously, doing a lot of background miles and weight training and clocked 44.09, the fastest non-altitude 400 meters up to that time.

Reynolds took aim at Evans's venerable record on August 17, 1988, in Zurich. He started from lane four with Nigerian Innocent Egbunike in five and Danny Everett in six. Only Steve Lewis in lane three was expected to pose problems for Reynolds during the early stages. Egbunike roared through the first 200 in 20.9 (Evans ran 21.1, Reynolds 21.4). With 150 meters to go, Lewis made a spurt, but it lasted only about 30 meters. Reynolds reached 300 meters in 32.1, which was 0.1 faster than Evans' pace. Rounding the last curve, Reynolds pulled away from everyone, head up and arms pumping powerfully. He finished in 43.29, having covered the last 100 meters in 11.2, 0.4 better than Evans.

"Finally, it's over," he said. "The thing everyone said I had to do has been achieved. And it's a clean record — no altitude, no wind, nothing to tarnish it."

Six weeks later at the Seoul Olympics,

Steve Lewis sprinted to a big lead and despite a furious finish, Reynolds could not make up the distance. Lewis came in first (43.87), and Reynolds second (43.93). Reynolds's running career was changed forever in August 1990 in Monaco, when he tested positive for the anabolic steroid nandrolone. He began a long series of appeals all the way to the U.S. Supreme Court to have the verdict overturned. The resulting two-year ban caused him to miss the 1992 Olympics. He sued the IAAF and an Ohio judge found in his favor, awarding him $27.3 million in damages. The IAAF refused to accept the judgment and added four months to his suspension. In the 1996 Olympics Reynolds was unable to finish his 400-meter semifinal because of leg cramps.

After suffering a variety of leg and hip injuries in 1997-98, Michael Johnson, then 31 years old, arrived in Seville for the 1999 World Championships fitter than ever. He ran 43.95 in his semifinal, easing up well ahead of the finish line. On August 26, starting in lane five in the final, Johnson finished with a blazing last 150 meters to record 43.18 and break Reynolds's 11-year-old record by .11 seconds. Johnson set the record wearing specially designed shoes that had glass-filled sole plates with flexibility and stiffness tuned to his running style. Johnson joined Tommie Smith as the only men to hold both the 200 and 400 meter world records.

## Women's 400 Meters

The IAAF first began recognizing world records for the women's 400 meters in 1957, and the event was added to the Olympic program in 1964. Russian Maria Itkina, whose career lasted from 1952 to 1966, was the first to run the distance in less than 54 seconds when she ran 53.4 in 1962.

Shin Geum Dan, the only runner from North Korea to set a world record, lowered the record to 51.9 in Pyongyang in October 1962. Her career was hampered by the isolationism of her native country, and many of her records were not recognized by the IAAF. She was banned from the 1964 Olympics for competing in the 1963 "Games of the Emerging Forces" meet in Indonesia that was not sanctioned by the IAAF. In 1963 she ran the 400 meters in 51.4 and lowered that time to 51.2 in 1964. She was ranked first in the world at 400 meters from 1960 to 1964.

Irena Szewinska started as a sprinter and late in her career moved up to the 400 meters and quickly showed her excellence. One hundred and twenty-five years after Henry Allen Reed ran sub–50 on a turnpike road, she became the first woman to run under 50 seconds for 400 meters. At the Kusocinski Memorial Meet on June 22, 1974, she went out very fast and passed 200 meters in 22.9. The tall veteran runner reached 300 meters in 36.0 and covered the final 100 in 13.9 to record 49.9 and take 1.1 seconds off the world record. Actually, 49.9 for 400 meters is equivalent to 50.2 for 440 yards. Szewinska did run a sub–50 second quarter equivalent at the Olympic Games in Montreal in 1976 when she won the gold medal in 49.29 and set another world record.

### MARITA KOCH—GREATEST WOMEN'S 400-METER RUNNER

Marita Koch, from East Germany, had a personal best of 10.81 for the 100 meters and was the first woman to run under 22 seconds in the 200 meters (21.71). But her best distance was 400 meters, where she lost only two races in eight years and lowered the world record an amazing seven times. Koch did not have the muscular build of many of the East European middle distance runners. Instead she was tall, thin and long-legged (five feet, seven inches/1.7 m, 140 pounds/64 kg) and ran with a light, flowing stride.

Koch was born February 18, 1957, in

Wismar, East Germany. Her first sport was team handball, but she was considered too short and too slow. At a school sports day, Koch competed in some sprint races. "I knew right away that I had speed. I was the fastest girl and I beat all the boys, too," she said later. She began competing seriously in 1972 at age 15 (60.3 for 400 meters) and was coached by Wolfgang Meier, a former sprinter.

Koch attended the University of Rostock where she completed an 11-year program to become a doctor of pediatrics. "The sprints are all connected for me," she once said. "In order to run fast in the 400, I have to have good performances in the 100 and 200." In 1975 she had bests of 11.7, 23.92 and 51.60, but an injury forced her to withdraw from the 1976 Olympics in Montreal, where she had been expected to do well. In Leipzig, East Germany, in 1978 she ran 49.19 for her first 400-meter record. Before the end of the year she had improved this to 48.94, becoming the first woman to run under 49 seconds.

She easily won the gold medal for the 400 meters at the 1980 Moscow Olympics in 48.88 seconds, with the Czech Jarmila Kratochvilova second in 49.46. Kratochvilova proved to be Koch's greatest rival. She broke Koch's record on August 10, 1983, at the World Championships, running 47.99 to become the first woman under 48 seconds. Kratochvilova, who had an incredibly muscular physique, once commented: "It's obvious that running 400 meters in less than 49 seconds is a thing which takes away from your beauty." Koch regained the record at the 1985 World Cup by running 47.60. Two years later she retired. In the 15 years since Koch ran 47.60 for 400 meters, no woman came close to her mark.

## Men's 800 Meters

*It's an interesting aspect of half-miling that the fast times have always been gained* *when the first lap has been fast. The records have been set by runners who have belted through the first quarter and then concentrated on hanging on for the second. Nine times out of ten the runner will fold on the second lap but the tenth always manages to hang on—and up goes another record.*—Peter Snell (1965)

### Mal Whitfield—Double Olympic 800-Meter Champion

Malvin G. "Marvelous Mal" Whitfield, born in Bay City, Texas, in 1924, dominated the 800 meters during the early to mid–1950s. He set world records for both 880

Mal Whitfield won Olympic gold medals in the 800 meters in the 1948 and 1952 Olympics (National Archives [306-NT-642-F-2]).

yards (1:48.6) and 1,000 meters (2:20.8), but was more concerned about winning. His range was similar to that of Lon Myers, extending from 100 meters in 10.7, and 400 meters in 45.9, to a mile in 4:12.6.

In the 1948 London Olympic 800-meter final, Whitfield's main competitor was Arthur Wint, a six-foot, five-inch (1.96 m) Jamaican with an 11-foot (3.4 m) stride. Taking the lead at the end of the first lap, Whitfield held off Wint to win by .3 seconds in 1:49.2. Whitfield was the world's number one ranked 800 meter runner in three of the four years leading up to the 1952 Olympics. In 1951, the year he was not rated, he flew 27 missions as a tail-gunner in a B-26 bomber in Korea.

Wint was again Whitfield's main competition for the 800-meters gold medal in the 1952 Helsinki Olympics. This time Wint seized the lead from the start. But with 170 meters to go, Whitfield easily went past him and won by two yards. Whitfield's winning time was the same as four years before. Known for his smooth stride, Whitfield appeared to "coast downhill" as he ran. He spent many years practicing before a mirror and lifting weights to improve his form. Whitfield ran to win, not to set records. Despite his talent, he never approached Rudolf Harbig's 1:46.6 800-meter record set in 1939.

Roger Moens, a police inspector from Belgium, broke Harbig's record in August 1955 at the Bislett Games in Oslo. A pacesetter led the first lap in 52.0 seconds, with Moens and Norwegian Audun Boysen a step behind. On hearing the time, Moens decided to go for the record. Although Boysen challenged him, Moens held on to win by 0.2 seconds in 1:45.7, beating Harbig's record by .9 seconds. Two months before the 1956 Games, as he was training on a tennis court on a dark day, Moens's glasses fogged up and he ran into a support post. The resulting injury ended his Olympic hopes for 1956.

With Moens out, the favorite for the 1956 Olympic 800 meters was Tom Courtney from Newark, New Jersey. Courtney described how he felt before the race.

As I stepped onto the track, I felt my legs go rubbery. I saw over 100,000 people in the stands, and before I knew it, I had collapsed onto the infield grass. "Can it be," I remembered thinking, as I lay there gazing up at the sky, "that I'm so nervous I'm not going to be able to run?" Then I realized how ridiculous I'd look, flat on my back on the grass as they started the race. I guess the humor of that image made me lose my nervousness. I was able to recover, get up and jog to the starting line.

On the final turn Courtney moved up to teammate Arnie Sowell's shoulder. "With 140 meters to go, Sowell started to sprint," Courtney remembered:

I thought to myself, he's crazy, he's going to tie up and I'm not going with him. But at 120 meters to go I started my sprint. Sure enough I took the lead and edged past Sowell just as he was starting to tie up. At that point Derek Johnson came through on the inside. I was tying up — basically finished — but I can remember from other races that there was more there if I really forced myself to do it.

Courtney gathered himself and spurted again. With a desperate drive he threw himself at the tape to win by inches. Never before in an Olympic 800-meter final had a leader been passed in the last 50 meters and come back to win. Courtney had extended himself so much that he was unable to walk or talk for an hour after the race.

## PETER SNELL—THE MAN IN BLACK

One of the greatest upsets in Olympic 800-meter history occurred in Rome in 1960. An extra qualifying heat was added and for the first time the runners had to run four races in three days. Roger Moens, the

**Tom Courtney winning the gold medal in the 1956 Olympic 800 meters (Fordham University).**

world record holder at 1:45.7, after four frustrating years of waiting, was the clear favorite. George Kerr of the West Indies and Paul Schmidt of Germany were expected to be his main opposition.

Peter Snell, a 21-year-old New Zealander was unknown, with a best time of 1:49.2. He was running for the experience and to get ready for the 1,500 meters at Tokyo in 1964. Snell had trained under Arthur Lydiard, first building endurance, then strength, then speed. His endurance training was unprecedented for a half-miler — 100-mile weeks, including exhausting 22-mile circuits in the hilly and densely bushed Waitakere Ranges in New Zealand.

In the final, Christian Wägli from Switzerland led through the first 400 meters in 51.9 and was still leading at 600 meters in 1:19. With 200 yards to go, the field in front of Snell was three wide. He had the choice of staying on the inside or trying to run around the field. Staying inside, he hoped the front runners would split and allow him through. Moens was in front, followed closely by Kerr as they swung onto the straight and the runners spread out to make their drives to the tape. Snell found a gap in the front, and edged past the fading pacemaker Wägli, to draw even with the leaders. With a clear path to the tape and only 20 yards to go, he put every ounce of effort into his finish and flung himself across the tape the winner.

In four races in three days Snell had run heats of 1:48.1, 1:48.6, and 1:47.2. His gold medal winning 1:46.3 was 2.9 seconds under Whitfield's Olympic record.

On February 3, 1962, a week after setting a mile world record of 3:54.4, Snell went after the 800-meter record on a grass track at Christchurch, New Zealand. Trying to catch his pacemaker, Snell ran the first 200 meters in 24.6. He eased slightly to 26.0 for the second 200 then took the lead and sprinted the third 200 in 25.7. He began to slow and his legs wobbled as he struggled around the last curve. But he still held on, running 28.0 for the last 200 and 1:44.3 for 800 meters and 1:45.1 for the half-mile. He had broken Moens's 800-meter world record by 1.4 seconds and Courtney's half-mile record by 1.7 seconds.

In the 1964 Tokyo Olympics, Snell's goal was to win both the 800 and 1,500 meters—a feat not accomplished since A. F. Hill from Britain did it in 1920. In the 800-meter final he again found himself boxed in on the second lap, but this time he was

more confident. He dropped back and went around the field to finish in 1:45.1—an Olympic record. Snell also won the 1,500 meters. He retired in 1965 and later earned a Ph.D. in exercise physiology.

In 1966 in Terre Haute, Indiana, 19-year-old Jim Ryun shocked the world as well as himself when he broke Snell's half-mile record. Ryun was not trying for a record, only to win and help his team. Since he had to race a mile the following day, he didn't want to push too much. He had planned to run the first 440 yards in 52 seconds, but the leader ran only 52.9 and Ryun followed in 53.3. As he came out of the curve onto the backstretch, Ryun exploded, passing 660 yards in 1:19.4 and finishing the

Dave Wottle came from the back of the pack to win the 1972 Olympic gold medal in the 800 meters (United States Olympic Committee).

last 220 in 25.5 for a new half-mile record of 1:44.9.

Since no record had been expected, his 800-meter time was not taken. Ryun's performance was stunning in that his second 440 yards were run an unprecedented 1.7 seconds faster than his first. In the 1972 U.S. Olympic trials 800-meter final in Eugene, Oregon, Ryun committed a tactical blunder by sprinting too soon. He took the lead on the back straightaway with 300 meters to go and flew down the backstretch, covering 200 meters in 24 seconds. But with 50 meters to go, his legs turned to putty, then to lead. Dave Wottle, Rick Wohlhuter and Ken Swanson all swept past him for the three Olympic team spots. The winner, Wottle, described himself as "wholly a kicker," and insisted he was "not a half-miler." Yet he had tied the world 800-meter world record with his 1:44.3.

Yevgeniy Arzhanov of the Soviet Union, unbeaten in the previous three years, was the heavy favorite to win the 800-meter Olympic final in Munich. Kenya's Mike Boit and Robert Ouko led the first 200 meters in 24.5, then settled back to 27.8 for the second. Wottle trailed in last place. Irritated by the slowing pace, which threatened to play into the kickers' hands, Arzhanov began his sprint with 300 meters to go. He took the lead and reached 600 meters in 1:19. Wottle, still in last place, finally made his move. Running mostly on the outside, he went around the entire field in the last 200 meters. Arzhanov was still leading with three meters to go but Wottle edged past to win by .03 seconds—1:45.86 to Arzhanov's 1:45.89. Wottle's 200-meter splits show that his furious sprint to overtake the leaders was an illusion. The other runners came back to him. He ran a remarkably even paced race with 200-meter splits of 26.4, 26.9, 26.4 and 26.2.

Marcello Fiasconaro, a South African whose father was an Italian airman, competed for Italy during the early 1970s. In a 1973 meet between Italy and Czechoslova-

kia in Milan, Fiasconaro broke Snell's 11-year-old 800-meter record. In the same stadium where Harbig had set his famous 800-meter record 34 years earlier, Fiasconaro ran the first lap in 51.2 and came back with 52.5 for 1:43.7, taking .6 seconds off Snell's record. Unfortunately, injuries kept Fiasconaro out of both the 1972 and 1976 Olympic Games and after retiring he returned to South Africa.

Rick Wohlhuter, a Notre Dame alumni, "tripped on a sunbeam" and fell in his heat, failing to qualify for the Munich 800-meter final. He came back in 1973 to lower the world record for the half mile to 1:44.6 in Los Angeles. Using Mark Winzenried as a pacer, Wohlhuter ran a perfectly paced race with 440-yard splits of 52.3 and 52.3. Wohlhuter added the world record for 1,000 meters on July 30, 1974 when he ran 2:13.9, taking 2.1 seconds off the record held by Daniel Malan of South Africa. Going into the Montreal Olympic Games in 1976, Wohlhuter was a favorite to win the 800 meters, along with Mike Boit of Kenya. But with the African boycott, Boit was unable to compete and a newcomer from Cuba, Alberto Juantorena, was expected to challenge Wohlhuter.

In the final, Wohlhuter led the field through the first 200 meters in 25.5. Juantorena had caught up by 400 meters, which they both passed in 50.9. By 600 meters (1:17.4) the Cuban had taken the lead, with Wohlhuter struggling to stay with him. Juantorena powered to the finish, winning in 1:43.86, a world record. Ivo Van Damme of Belgium passed a spent Wohlhuter in the last 30 meters for second. Two days later Juantorena completed his historic double by winning the gold medal in the 400 meters.

SEBASTIAN COE—
SPEED OVER DISTANCE

Sebastian Newbold Coe, born September 29, 1956, at Chiswick, England, had a silky smooth stride and could maintain a sustained sprint farther than any other runner of his time. Coe began running at age 13 and tried sprinting and long jumping before switching to middle distance and cross country. Early in his running career, his father Peter became his coach and stressed low mileage, high-quality speed work, strength training and diverse gym sessions.

Coe set the first of his 11 world records on July 5, 1979, at Oslo's Bislett Stadium. Jamaican Lennie Smith set a fast early pace, just under 25 seconds for the first 200, and led the first lap in 50.6. Running alone, Coe maintained his rhythm all the way to the tape, covering the third 200 in 24.3 and the fourth in 27.4. His time of 1:42.33 was 1.1 seconds faster than Juantorena's old record. "It was a strange feeling," Coe later wrote "like being on autopilot; I was mentally outside what my body was achieving, and it just felt beautiful."

Coe put the 800-meter record out of reach for runners of his generation on June 10, 1981, in Florence. Eleven runners toed the line at 11:00 P.M. on that calm, balmy evening. Kenyan Billy Konchellah led the first 400 in 49.7, with Coe striding smoothly just behind. Coe then took the lead and passed the 600-meter mark in 1:15.0, needing only a 27.2 last 200 to break his record, but it didn't come easy. "It seemed like the track was turning uphill," he said later. "It was as hard a race as I have run for a long time. In the last 30 meters I was beginning to tie up, but apart from that there was no problem." He covered the last 200 meters in 26.8 for 1:41.73.

Six days later Coe blazed the first 800 meters in 1:44.6 en route to a record 2:12.18 for 1,000 meters. He took 1.22 seconds from his own record of 2:13.40 made at the same meet a year before. Despite being the world record holder and heavy favorite, Coe finished second in both the 1980 and 1984 Olympic 800-meter races.

Joaquim Carvalho Cruz from Brazil won the 1984 Olympic 800 meters in 1:43.00

Joaquim Cruz (left) from Brazil wins a heat of the 1984 Olympic 800 meters. (AAF/LPI 1984, 44935 GL).

to Coe's 1:43.64. Cruz then went after Coe's 800 record and came within .04 seconds, running 1:41.77 in Cologne on August 26, 1984. Despite many injuries Cruz managed to win the 800-meter silver medal at the 1988 Olympic Games, finishing second to Kenyan Paul Ereng.

### WILSON KIPKETER— FASTEST 800 METERS OF THE 20TH CENTURY

Kenyans dominated the 800 meters in the 1990s with the greatest being Wilson Kipketer. He came from the Nandi Hills region of the Great Rift Valley, where he attended school with future stars Peter Rono and Joseph Tengetei. At age 16 Kipketer ran the 800 meters in 1:46. Instead of following in the footsteps of many other Kenyan runners to U.S. universities, in 1990 Kipketer moved to Denmark to run and study electrical engineering.

He won the 800 at the 1995 World Championships running for Denmark. Because he had not met the seven-year citizenship criterion, he was unable to represent Denmark in the 1996 Olympics at Atlanta and did not compete. Instead, he set his sights on Coe's 800-meter record. In July 1997, after he had broken 1:43 nine times, he ran a 48.1 first 400 meters then finished with 1:41.73 to equal Coe's 16-year-old 800-meter record.

Five weeks later on August 13 at the Weltklasse meet in Zurich, he broke Coe's 800-meter record — at the time the oldest track world record on the books. The field included seven of the year's fastest 800-meter runners, but Kipketer paid attention only to the pacemaker who covered the first 200 in 22.9 and the 400 in 48.1. Kipketer followed in 23.0 and 48.3. He reached 600 meters in 1:14.5 and as the crowd of 25,000 chanted his name he finished with a 26.7 last 200 to set a world record of 1:41.24. But his season wasn't over.

Eleven days later on a hot, still, afternoon at Cologne, France, Kipketer followed "rabbit" David Kiptoo to 200 meter splits of 23.7 and 25.4, taking the lead at 570 meters. He ran alone to 1:14.4 at 600 meters and running smoothly, seemingly without effort, finished in 1:41.11 to break his own world record.

## Women's 800 Meters

After the disastrous women's 1928 Olympic 800-meter final, when several of the runners collapsed at the finish, the women's 800 meters was dropped from the Olympic program until 1960. Other than the Australians in the 1960s, women from Europe, especially the Soviet Union, dominated the race.

In 1954, Nina Otkalenko of the Soviet Union won the first 800-meter European championships in 2:08, and in 1955 lowered the world record to 2:05. Another Soviet, Lyudmila Shevtsova, became the first Olympic gold-medal winner when the event was reintroduced in Rome in 1960. Australia's Dixie Willis led the race to the 700-meter mark, but stepped off the track, exhausted. Shevtsova out-sprinted Willis' steammate, Brenda Jones, to win by a meter in 2:04.3, a world record.

In 1962 Willis, the Australian 400- and 800-meter champion, took a huge chunk off the world record. Running in her hometown of Perth on March 3, 1962, she defeated New Zealand's Marise Chamberlain by .2 seconds while lowering the record to 2:01.2.

Breaking two minutes proved difficult and there is some controversy over who should get credit for it. Shin Guem Dan from North Korea ran 1:59.1 at the "Games of the New Emerging Forces" meet in Djakarta in 1963. Her performance was not recognized by the IAAF, who did not sanction the meet and declared the participants ineligible to compete in the Tokyo Olympics. In 1964 Dan ran 1:58.0 at Pyongyang, but that mark was not recognized by the IAAF either. Despite the nonacceptance of her marks, she was rated first in the world in the 800 meters in 1961, 1963, and 1964.

West German Hildegard Falck, originally a swimmer, switched to track at age 17 and won the West German Junior 800-meter title in 1967. She was West Germany's 800-meter champion in 1970, 1971 and 1973. At the West German championships in July 1971, Falck ran the 800 meters in 1:58.5 to become the first woman to break two minutes with IAAF approval. A year later at the Olympics in Munich, Svetla Zlateva of Bulgaria led the field in the 800-meter final to 600 meters, where Falck took the lead and won the gold medal in 1:58.6. Nile Sabaite from the Soviet Union was second a meter behind.

In the 1972 Olympics, Svetla Zlateva ran an Olympic record 1:58.9 to win her heat, but could manage only 1:59.7 for fourth place in the final. At the Balkan Games in 1973 she blazed her first lap in 56.5 then slowed to 61.0 for the second. Her time of 1:57.5 knocked 1.1 seconds off Flack's record.

Three months before the Montreal Olympics Velentina Gerasimova of the Soviet Union ran a stunning 1:56.0 in the Soviet Championships. She was expected to be a favorite at Montreal but finished sixth in her semifinal in 2:01.0 and was eliminated.

Tatyana Kazankina of the Soviet Union dominated women's middle distance running of the mid–1970s. Kazankina, who was five feet, three inches (1.6 m) tall and weighed only 106 pounds (48 kg), made amazing progress in 1976 and was a last-minute addition to the Soviet team at 800-meters. She won the gold medal in Montreal by sprinting the last 150 meters to set a world record of 1:54.9. Kazankina also won the 1,500 meters at Montreal, again by using a very fast finishing sprint.

Another Russian, Nadezhda Olizarenko, finished second in the 800 meters at the 1978 European Championships in Prague. A month before the 1980 Moscow Olympics at the Pravda Prize athletic meet, she led from the start with 57.1 for the first 400 and 57.8 for the second, equaling Kazankina's record of 1:54.9.

In the Moscow Olympics she ran two fast qualifying heats of 1:59.3 and in the semifinals ran 1:57.7. Olizarenko again led from the start, finishing the first lap in 56.4 seconds, and held on for a 57.0 second lap to win by 15 meters in a world record 1:53.43. She missed the 1984 Los Angeles Olympics because of the Soviet boycott but came back to finish her career with a win in the 800 meters at the 1986 European Championships.

## JARMILA KRATOCHVILOVA— TOTAL MUSCLE DEVELOPMENT

Czech Jarmila Kratochvilova's unusually strong body was said to have been developed by years of hard work on a farm. A member of her family recalled how, at age 12, she could toss a pitchfork of hay up into the loft as well as any grown man. At age 20 in 1971, her best 400 meters was only 60.2, but she improved steadily until 1980 when she ran 49.46 to finish second to Mirita Koch in the Moscow Olympics. She moved up to 800 meters in 1982 and ran 1:56.69. Her previous best had been 2:11.4 in 1975.

In July 1983, just before a meet in Munich, she suffered a cramp in her upper thigh and decided to switch from the 400 to the 800 meters. Running laps of 56.1 and 57.2, she set the current 800-meter world record of 1:53.28. "I have, never run the second lap so loose or with such intense joy of ease," she said afterward, "I didn't know the splits; I took the lead at the 400 and didn't realize the pace until the start of the home-stretch when I saw 1:40 ... I ran a little harder and so it happened."

Two weeks later, she was sensational at the World Championships in Helsinki, and accomplished a difficult 400/800 double. She won the 800 meters in 1:54.68 only 33 minutes after winning her 400-meter semifinal. The next day she ran the 400 meters in 47.99 to become the first woman to break 48 seconds.

## Men's 1,500 Meters—Mile

*The mile — the Anglo Saxon standard of distance — has captured the imagination of athletes and spectators alike in a way that its nearest metric equivalent, 1,500 meters, has never done. It was a popular event long before any one dreamt of the magic four minutes. It is a distance that seems to present a perfect test of judgement, speed and stamina.* — Roger Bannister (1955)

## Roger Bannister and the Race to Break Four Minutes

Four-minute-mile madness began in 1933 and 1934 when Jack Lovelock, Glenn Cunningham and Bill Bonthron began running the mile in about 4:08. There are apocryphal stories that both Lovelock and Cunningham actually ran under four minutes in practice. Cunningham seemed to have actually believed he had beaten four minutes, but his coach admitted years later that the whole thing had been a psychological ploy designed to give his runner confidence in his first national competition. Cunningham ran 4:28.9, but his coach subtracted 30 seconds from his time leaving the young Cunningham thinking he had run 3:58.9.

Lovelock's alleged performance is not so easily explained. Writing in the *British Medical Journal* of June 27, 1987, Dr. John Etheridge told a fantastic story of how in 1935 Lovelock ran a solo mile on the Paddington track in 3:56. Later that year, according to Dr. Etheridge, Lovelock ran another practice mile at Motspur Park in 3:52.2, "neither breathless nor distressed at the finish." While Lovelock was truly a great miler, he never came close to these performances in public. Although Dr. Etheridge may have been quite sincere, his recollections of events 52 years earlier are difficult to take seriously.

In all probability World War II delayed the first sub–four-minute mile by nearly 10 years. Men like Gunder Hägg, Arne Andersson and Sydney Wooderson seemed capable of it. Had they been able to train normally and run against other world class milers during the war years, either they or one of their contemporaries would probably have dipped under four minutes.

Roger Gilbert Bannister enrolled in Exter College, Oxford, in 1946. Although his idol was Wooderson, he seemed to have more in common with Lovelock. Like Lovelock, Bannister was self-coached at Oxford and had to do his running when his medical studies would permit it. Because of their limited time and light training, both preferred to get in top shape for only a few important races each year.

Despite his lack of training, Bannister was the number one-ranked miler in the world in 1951, running a best time of 4:07.8. Ten days before the 1952 Helsinki Olympic 1,500-meter final, he ran a three-quarter-mile time trial at Motspur Park in 2:52.9. Each lap was faster than the previous— 58.5, 57.5 and 56.9. Although world records were no longer kept for the three-quarter-mile distance, Bannister's time was four seconds under the unofficial record and equivalent to a mile in approximately 4:00. The performance convinced him that he was capable of winning the Olympic 1,500 meters, even if he had to break the world record to do so.

The next day the bottom fell out of his hopes when he read that an extra round of heats had been added to the Olympic 1,500 meters. He feared that with his light training he couldn't possibly run three hard races on consecutive days. Sure enough, Josy Barthel from Luxembourg just nipped American Bob McMillen for the gold medal. Both were timed in 3:45.2. Werner Lueg from Germany was third (3:45.4) and Bannister fourth (3:46).

With his Olympic hopes dashed, Bannister decided in 1953 to make an assault on the four-minute mile. He knew he would have to hurry. Others were approaching four minutes, especially John Landy of Australia and Wes Santee of the United States. In February 1953, Bannister started running what has come to be called the "Bannister workout." It consisted of 10 × 440 with rest intervals of two minutes. He initially averaged about 63 seconds per lap, which was more strenuous training than he had ever done and left him exhausted for several days. But the workout fit into the half-hour period that he was able to spare for training. Near the end of 1953, he consulted with Austrian coach Franz Stampfl, who recommended a six-month winter training program of intervals and weight lifting.

Wes Santee, the "Kansas Cowboy," was from Ashland, Kansas, just 100 miles east of Glenn Cunningham's home of Elkhart. Like Cunningham before him, and Jim Ryun after, Santee attended Kansas University. Santee's training consisted of a mixture of cross country and interval work totaling 30–35 miles a week. His interval training for the mile often consisted of five 440s, starting at 60 seconds and ending with about 52.

On June 5, 1953, in Compton, California, he began to show his potential. Following a slow first half in 2:05, Santee came back with 1:57 to dazzle the crowd and record a mile time of 4:02.4. Meanwhile, in England, Bannister was running personal bests of 4:03.6 and an unofficial 4:02.0.

The other contender in the race to break four minutes, Australian John Landy,

John Landy from Australia (right) became the second man to break the 4-minute mile (Australian Archives, Series A7135, Caption Number 041/1. Commonwealth of Australia copyright, used by permission).

Wes Santee from the University of Kansas came close to being the first to break the 4-minute mile (University of Kansas sports information office).

had begun a training program in 1953 that was more severe than that of either Bannister or Santee. It involved weight lifting and running a total of about 200 miles (322 km) a month. By April 1954, he had won six mile races all in times of less than 4:03.

In the same month, Bannister managed to average 61 seconds for his 10 440s, but couldn't reach his target of 60 seconds. Realizing he was stuck, he and training partner Chris Brasher took a break and drove to Scotland for a few days of rock climbing. After four days, they returned and to his surprise, Bannister found his times for the 440s had dropped to 59 seconds. Now he was ready.

He decided to make the effort on May 6, at Oxford. His training partners, Chris Brasher and Chris Chataway, were to play key roles in the effort. Santee and Landy were mostly on their own in their efforts to dip under four minutes, but Bannister opted for the team approach. Brasher, who was capable of a half mile in 1:55, would lead Bannister and Chataway through that distance in 1:58. Chataway, who eventually dipped under four minutes himself, would take over for the third lap and lead for as far as he could manage. Bannister's preparations were meticulous, and included filing his spikes to needle-like sharpness and putting graphite on the soles of his shoes to prevent cinders from sticking to them.

Roger Bannister, the world's first sub–four-minute miler (National Archives [286NP-UK-1873]).

Rain and high winds caused him to almost postpone the effort. But near race time the winds dropped and the rain stopped and he decided to go ahead. This was Bannister's first race for eight months. All that time he had been storing nervous energy for one supreme effort. When the gun sounded, he found himself "full of running." Pacemaker Brasher led the first lap in 57.5. Bannister, thinking the pace was too slow, shouted "faster." Running in a tight group with Brasher shielding the other two from the wind, they passed the half-mile in 1:58.

Midway through the third lap Chataway took over as planned and led through three quarters of a mile in 3:00.5. Bannister now knew that all he had to do was run a 59-second last lap. With 300 yards to go, a spent Chataway dropped back and Bannister found himself, as he later put it, "where no man had yet ventured." Cheered on by an enthusiastic Oxford crowd of 1,200, he unleashed his kick with 230 yards to go and finished in 3:59.4. Breaking the four-minute mile was considered by many to be the "sublime achievement" in the long history of British running, the "Everest of athletics."

After Bannister showed it could be done, runners poured through the four-minute-mile "barrier" like wild horses through an open gate. On June 4, 1954, Santee, despite the cold, windy, weather at Compton, California, ran 3:42.8 for 1,500 meters—a world record. He continued to the mile mark but "tied up" in the last 100 yards because of the cold. He struggled on to finish in 4:00.6. Had the conditions been better, he would almost certainly have broken four minutes. Less than a year after this meet Santee ran afoul of the AAU for expense money violations and at age 23 was declared a professional, ending his running career.

On June 21, 1954, in Turku, Finland, Landy ran 3:57.9 to surpass Bannister's record. Pushed to an all-out effort by Chataway, he clocked 3:41.8 at 1,500 meters to smash Santee's record as well. Landy's performance set up "the mile of the century," an August 1954, meeting of the world's two sub–four-minute milers at the British Empire Games in Vancouver.

In Vancouver, with the world anxiously awaiting the outcome, Bannister struggled to stay in contact with Landy, but fell seven yards behind on the first lap. He almost lost contact when Landy stretched his lead to nearly 12 yards at the half mile. But Bannister ran a strong (59.6) third lap and cut Landy's lead to two yards at the three-quarter-mile mark. Coming out of the last curve, Landy glanced to his inside to see where his rival was. At the same instant, Bannister sprinted by on the outside to win by five yards in 3:58.8 to Landy's 3:59.6.

The first American to run the mile under four minutes was 20-year-old Don Bowden from the University of California, Berkeley. After his final exams on June 1, 1957, Bowden traveled to Stockton, California, for the Pacific Association AAU Championships. His previous best performances that year had been 1:47.8 for the half mile on a muddy track and a 4:01.6 mile leg of a distance medley relay. His strategy was simple — run a four-minute pace for as long as he could. He had no rabbits or anyone to push him but still managed splits of 59.7, 2:00.8 and 3:00.6. After three laps he still felt great and gave it everything he had to finish in 3:58.7, to the delight of the 2,500 spectators. Bowden, who was six feet, three inches (1.9 m) tall and weighed 160 pounds (72.7 kg), ruptured his Achilles tendon in 1960, ending his career without running under four minutes again.

Derek Ibbotson was an uninhibited, easy-going runner from Huttersfield, England. Occasionally he trained hard and there was no denying his natural ability. He regained the world record for Britain on July 19, 1957, at London's White City Stadium. Ibbotson ran a sparkling 56.9 last lap to record 3:57.2. The first four men finished under four minutes.

## HERB ELLIOTT—A GOLDEN MILER

*Thrust against pain. Pain is the purifier. Walk towards suffering. Love suffering, embrace it.*— Percy Cerutty (1956)

In October 1956, 18-year-old Australian Herbert James Elliott was a spectator at the Olympic Games at Perth. When he saw Russian Vladimir Kuts, in his titanic struggle with tenacious Englishman Gorden Pirie, young Elliott became hooked on running and decided to commit himself seriously to the sport. He left home in late 1956 to train with Percy Cerutty, possibly the most unorthodox running coach the world has ever known.

The legendary Cerutty thought of running as a way of life and expected his athletes to give their body and soul to the sport. He elevated a foot race to a test of character. Central to his teaching was embracing adversity and growing from it. In his book *The Golden Mile* (1961) Elliott wrote, "Percy helped me to world records not so much by improving my technique, but by releasing in my mind and soul a power that I only vaguely thought existed."

Cerutty believed that if anybody presumed to tell others what to do he must be prepared to do it himself. Elliott wrote:

> The day before any important race he would run four laps of the nearest oval, usually the equivalent of a mile, with all the speed he could muster, and then stagger over to me, eyes bulging and tongue lolling. "Well, you may be able to run faster," he'd gasp, "but tomorrow you can't run any harder than that."

After only two months of training at Cerutty's running camp at Portsea, Elliott ran a mile on January 12, 1957, in 4:06.0, breaking Ron Clarke's Australian junior record by .8 seconds. In May 1957, Elliott began a rigorous training program that emphasized, in addition to running, lifting heavy weights, swimming in the surf, eating uncooked vegetables and running up steep sand dunes to exhaustion. He seldom ran more than 60 miles (97 km) a week, but the mileage he did run was extremely intense. He thrived on this program and in January 1958 ran his first sub–four-minute mile (3:59.9).

On August 6, 1958, at Santry Track in Dublin, Elliott became the mile world record holder. Fellow Australian Alby Thomas ran a blistering first lap of 56 seconds followed by another Australian, Merv Lincoln, then Elliott in 56.4. On the final curve of the second lap Elliott moved to within a yard of the leader Thomas as the timer announced 1:58. Elliott later described how he felt at that point: "That's a fair sort of half-mile. And I didn't even feel I've been running. Maybe there's a chance for a record. Look out Alby. I'm coming." He tore past Thomas on the third lap but could sense someone on his heels. On the curve, to Elliott's amazement, Lincoln shot past. Lincoln held the lead for only 50 yards, but his challenge was enough to get Elliott to the bell lap as the timer called out 2:59. Passing Lincoln, Elliott drove on. Sprinting the last 120 yards in 14.9, he finished in 3:54.5, 20 yards ahead of Lincoln who also broke the old world record with his 3:55.9. Elliott had bettered the record by 2.7 seconds, the largest margin in the 20th century. Only Walter George in 1886, when he broke William Cummings's record by 3⅘ second, had lowered the record by a greater amount.

Three weeks later in Göteborg Sweden, Elliott was even more impressive, this time at 1,500 meters. After getting boxed in at the start, he was in seventh place at the end of the first lap. He caught the leader, Thomas, at 800 meters (1:57.5) and suddenly felt strong and confident. Scorching the third lap in 58.0, he reached 1,200 meters in 2:55.5. He covered the last 300 meters in 40.5 seconds and finished in 3:36 — equivalent to a mile in 3:53.3.

After a year of inactivity, Elliott closed out his international career at the 1960

Rome Olympics with probably his greatest race. Because of the qualifying heats and the extreme pressure, most Olympic 1,500 meter finals are slow tactical races. Not since Jack Lovelock in 1936 had a runner set a world record in one. Elliott felt tired after two laps of the final and he couldn't understand the lap times, which were called out in Italian. But, as planned, he accelerated gradually and took the lead with 600 meters to go. When he started the last lap, he saw Cerutty waving a towel over his head, signaling that a world record was possible.

He wrote in his autobiography,

Half a lap from the tape I made up my mind to sprint, but I was so swept with fatigue it's doubtful whether the pace increased. All I knew then was that I was trying to sprint and therefore the effort mounted accordingly. The finish straight appeared to stretch into eternity. And trying to reach the tape was like one of those nightmares in which you run frantically from a terror behind you, never making headway. The medal burned in my consciousness and dragged me on until I was through the tape and it was over.

He had won by 20 meters in a world record 3:35.6.

During his short (1957–1961) career, which ended when he was 22, Elliott ran 36 mile and nine 1,500 meter races. He won them all, running 17 sub–four-minute miles. In looking back over his career he reflected: "I had trained so hard, and was so mentally tough because of it, that the only person who could have beaten me was a mentally tougher person, and there weren't any around."

Arthur Lydiard from New Zealand and German Waldemar Gershler, the inventor of interval training who was described in the previous section, were probably the two most influential running coaches of the 20th century. Lydiard believed in using

**Herb Elliott was undefeated in the mile and 1,500 meters during his entire career (Australian Archives, Series A1200, Caption Number L35388. Commonwealth of Australia copyright, used by permission).**

"periodization," or breaking down the training year into various "phases" in order to peak a runner one or more times a year. He found that a peak racing performance was usually possible when a long buildup period consisting of low-intensity, high-volume training, was followed by a period of high-intensity, low volume training. Lydiard's periods were base training, hill training, and speed training. He advocated running up to 100 miles (160 km) a week in the base period at just slower than the runner's maximum steady-state speed.

Peter Snell was Lydiard's most famous pupil. Besides having good basic speed (47.9 for the 440) Snell was a powerful man who

was able to use his strength to accelerate past other runners at the end of a race. On January 27, 1962, on a 385-yard grass track at Wanganui, New Zealand, he broke Elliott's mile record by .1 second when he ran 3:54.4. The world longed for a race between the two great runners from down under, but with no prospects of a money payoff, Elliott could not be coaxed out of retirement.

Already the owner of an 800-meter gold medal from the Rome Olympics of 1960, Snell set his sights on an "impossible" double — winning both the 800 and 1,500 meter gold medals at Tokyo in 1964. Not since Britain's Albert Hill in 1920 had a runner won both events. The double was thought impossible because it demanded six high-pressure races in eight days. During the six months previous to the Games, Snell trained harder than ever before, covering 1,000 miles (1,610 km) in a ten-week period.

He won the 800-meter gold easily in 1:45.1. Because of his fatigue from the 800 final, he considered his first 1,500 heat on the following day his most critical race. Luckily, he drew a slow heat and qualified for the next round without trouble. After being boxed in early in the final, he freed himself and began his sprint half a lap from the finish. With his powerful legs tearing huge chunks of cinders from the track, he covered the last 200 meters in 25.4 to win the gold medal. A month later, in Auckland, he set a world record of 2:16.6 for 1,000 meters and five days after that broke his own mile record with 3:54.1. Despite all of his success, Snell lived in Elliott's shadow and like Elliott, had no rivals who could push him to his limit.

Michel Jazy of France finished second to Elliott in the 1960 1,500 meter Olympic final and was one of the favorites for the 1,500 gold at the 1964 Games. But he elected to run the 5,000 meters instead and unfortunately for him, started his sprint too soon and faded to fourth in the race, won by Bob Schul of the United States. Highly disappointed, Jazy bounced back in a mile race on June 9, 1965, run on a rutted track at Rennes, France. He was fourth at the end of the first lap in 57.3. By the half, passed in 1:56.5, he had moved up to third. He took the lead at the bell (2:57.4) and pulled away from the field to finish in 3:53.6 to knock half a second off Snell's record. Jazy, who also held the world record for two miles in 8:22.6, was better at setting records than winning championships or Olympic medals.

### JIM RYUN—DRIVEN BY A DREAM

On June 5, 1964, the track world was astounded to hear that Jim Ryun, a 17-year-

old high-school student from Wichita, Kansas, had run a mile in 3:59. Ryun began his running career as a 15-year-old high school sophomore in the fall of 1962 when he went out for cross country. That fall he ran a mile trial in 5:38. He improved rapidly with a training program of 10–15 mile runs and intervals. By June 6, 1963, his mile time had plummeted to 4:07.8.

He was aided greatly in his quest to become the first high-school sub–four-minute miler by his coach, Bob Timmons. Previously, Timmons had coached Archie San Romani, Jr., to a high school mile record of 4:08.9 and realized that Ryun was ahead of San Romani at the same age. "Timmie first made public the 4-minute goal," Ryun wrote in his autobiography *In Quest of Gold* (1984). "And I began to desire it with a far greater intensity than before—the hunger to accomplish what no one else had ever done."

Ryun qualified for the 1964 U.S. Olympic team in the 1,500 meters, edging Jim Grelle for third in a photo-finish 3:41.9. At the 1964 Tokyo Games he was weakened by a virus and finished a disappointing last in his semifinal heat. His Olympic bad luck had begun.

As a freshman at the University of Kansas, Ryun set the world record for the half mile with 1:44.9 and just missed the mile record by a tenth of a second with 3:53.7. On July 17, 1966, at the University of California's Edwards Field, Berkeley, he made another assault on the mile record. Tom Von Ruden agreed to pace the first lap, Rich Romo the second and Wade Bell the third. Ryun had hoped to reach the half in 1:56.

When the race began, Ryun stayed close to the front, covering the first lap in 58 seconds and the half in 1:55.6. On the third lap the pace slowed and Ryun surged past Bell to complete three laps in 2:55.3. Only Snell and Jurgan May of Germany had covered the first three laps of a mile race that fast, but both had died in the final 440.

With a half lap to go Ryun began to tie up, but knowing a record was possible, drove on, forcing his weary legs to keep moving. The 15,000 spectators roared with approval as he crossed the finish in 3:51.3, breaking Michel Jazy's world record by 2.3 seconds.

A year later on June 23, 1967, at Bakersfield, Ryun improved his record slightly. Leading all the way, he ran 59, 1:59, and 2:57.4 for the first three laps then floored the accelerator on the last lap, running it in 52.5 to finish in 3:51.1. "When I crossed the finish line, I was hardly fatigued," Ryun wrote. "There was none of the usual post-race nausea. (My first order of business after most races was to find a bathroom or other solitary spot where, in peace and quiet, I could proceed to lose my lunch.)"

Ryun ran his greatest race in the United States vs. British Commonwealth meet on July 8, 1967. The temperature was 95 degrees and Ryun's main opponent was the remarkable Kip Keino from Kenya. Keino, the first great African middle distance runner, loved to fling his orange cap onto the infield when he made his move at the end of a race. No one wanted to lead and the first lap went in a slow 61 seconds. Then Keino, who did not have a superior finishing kick and disdained a slow pace, swept into the lead and covered the second lap in 56 seconds with Ryun on his heels. Keino continued his torrid pace and reached the end of the third lap in 2:55. Then Ryun accelerated slightly and eased up alongside the Kenyan. Side by side they ran, then Ryun sprinted hard, looked back a couple of times, and moved away from his rival to finish 15 meters ahead with a world record 3:33.1. His time was equivalent to a 3:48.6 mile. His last half mile had been run in 1:51.3, his last three-quarters in 2:48.7.

After 1967, Ryun's running fortunes began to decline. He wrote in his autobiography, "Running was the only life I had known for five years now, but a drudgery was gradually setting in. After some 15,000 to 20,000 miles and between 2,500 and 3,000 hours of running, it was no longer fresh and invigorating." In May of 1968 Ryun became ill with mononucleosis which set back his training for the Mexico Olympics. He planned to run both the 800 and 1,500 meters at the Mexico Games, but in the 800-meter final at the trials, he found that his awesome kick had deserted him. He still managed to qualify in the 1,500 meters, and despite the altitude of Mexico City, he was the favorite.

In the 1,500 meter final at Mexico City, Ben Jipcho, Keino's teammate, took the field through the first lap in 56 seconds. Keino followed in third place about six meters back and Ryun, who refused to be drawn into what seemed a suicidal pace, ran last in 60. By the 800-meter mark, passed in 1:55, Keino had moved to the front and opened a commanding lead. On the third lap he accelerated, leaving Jipcho far behind, and reached the end of three laps in 2:53 — a searing, unbelievable pace for a race run at the altitude of Mexico City.

Ryun made his move on the final lap, but it was too late. Keino went through the

Ben Jipcho (564) congratulates Kip Keino (566), who has just won the 1968 Olympic 1,500 meters (National Archives [306-OG-228]).

tape 20 meters ahead in 3:34.9 to win the gold medal with Ryun second in 3:37.8. Ryun, Keino and Jipcho were all criticized by the press— Ryun for holding back and the Kenyans for using team tactics. In truth, on that day and at the altitude of Mexico City, it seems unlikely that anyone could have beaten Keino in anything except a slow paced, kicker's race.

Four years later in the 1972 Munich Olympics Ryun had his third shot at Olympic gold. In the second round of 1,500 meter qualifying heats, he was running easily with about 500 meters to go. He tripped and fell heavily on the inside rail. Scrambling to his feet, he tore off after the pack 100 meters ahead, but he had no chance to qualify. American officials tried to get him reinstated, citing a spike hole in his shoe as evidence that he had been tripped. Their pe-

Jim Ryun, America' best miler (University of Kansas sports information office).

tition was denied. The judges ruled that the fall was Ryun's fault.

In the 1,500-meter final, Keino found the pace at 800 meters too slow (2:01.4) and ran the third 400 meters in 55.1. But Finland's Pekka Vasala not only matched Keino's third lap, but ran an even faster last lap in 53.5 to win the gold medal with 3:36.33. Keino won the silver medal with 3:36.81.

His Olympic career over, Ryun joined the professional ITA circuit and ran with mixed success until 1976. In 1996 he was elected to the U.S. House of Representatives for Kansas.

The next great miler was Filbert Bayi, born in 1953 at Karatu, Tanzania, 90 miles from Mt. Kilimanjaro. Best known for his courageous "catch-me-if-you-can" front-running tactics, he gave the first indication of his future greatness when he defeated Kip Keino at the African Games in January 1973. After his defeat Keino told the young Tanzanian, "If you train harder, one day you'll be the greatest."

In the 1,500 meters at the 1974 British Commonwealth Games at Christchurch, New Zealand, Bayi faced John Walker and Rod Dixon of New Zealand, Mike Boit and Ben Jipcho of Kenya and Brendon Foster of England — four of the best milers of the era. Bayi led the first lap in 54.4 with Boit on his heels. He continued to pull away and by 800 meters (1:51.8) led by 12 meters. He slowed on the third lap, but still reached the bell lap in 2:36.75. The crowd roared as Walker powered to within two meters of Bayi on the last turn. Bayi managed to hang on to win in a world record 3:32.16, beating Walker by .36 seconds.

On May 17, 1975, at the Freedom Games in Kingston, Jamaica, Bayi ran the fastest mile to date where the winner led from start to finish. This time his opponents were Americans Marty Liquori, Rick Wohlhuter and Tony Waldrop and Irishman Eamonn Coghlan. Bayi started fast as usual and passed the 400 meters in 56.9. On the second lap he slowed, reaching 800 meters in 1:56.6. Coghlan followed in 1:58 and Liquori in 1:58.4. On the third lap, Coghlan and Liquori caught up, but Bayi effortlessly glided away to pass three quarters in 2:55.3 with his pursuers falling farther behind. Bayi became the first African mile record holder when he finished in 3:51.0, to clip .1 second off Ryun's record. Liquori was second in 3:52.2, Coghlan third in 3:53.3 and Wohlhuter fourth in 3:53.8. Bouts of malaria and the African boycott of the 1976 Olympics hampered Bayi's subsequent running career, but he did win a silver medal in the steeplechase at the 1980 Moscow Games.

After improving his personal best by over four seconds in his effort to catch world-record setting Bayi in the 1974 Commonwealth Games, John Walker joined Jack Lovelock and Peter Snell as legendary milers from New Zealand. Like Snell, he was a powerful runner with a great finish. Like Lovelock he had blond hair, but Walker's was long and flowed in the breeze as he sped along.

Walker was the first to run 100 sub–four-minute miles, although American Steve Scott amassed 137 in his career to Walker's total of 127. On August 12, 1975, at Göteborg, Sweden, where Hägg and Anderson had run many great miles in the 1940s, Walker became the first man to dip under 3:50 for the mile. A pacesetter led him through the first lap on the new Tartan track in 56.3 and the half mile in 1:56.2. Walker took the lead and reached the bell lap in 2:53.5. He completed the last lap in 55.9 to finish in 3:49.4 and lower Bayi's record by 1.6 seconds.

At the 1976 Montreal Olympic Games, Walker hoped to win the 800–1,500 double but didn't make it past the first round of 800 trials. With Bayi out of the 1,500 final no one wanted to take the lead. Walker ran the last 400 in 52.7 to win the wild sprint to the finish in 3:39.17 and add an Olympic gold medal to his list of achievements.

## COE, OVETT AND CRAM— THE RETURN OF THE BRITISH

Sebastian Coe, at five feet, nine inches (1.7 m) and weighing 121 pounds (55 kg), possessed a smooth bounding stride with 46 second 400-meter speed and sustained acceleration second to none. Countryman Steve Ovett at six feet, one inch (1.8 m), 154 pounds (70 kg) was a strength runner, outstanding from 400 meters to the half marathon. Both men had excellent coaching, Coe by his father Peter, Ovett by Harry Wilson who modeled his training methods on Percy Cerutty's. Ovett, a year older than Coe, arrived on the world scene a couple of years before his rival. At age 18, he ran his first sub–four-minute mile in 3:59.4 on July 17, 1974. Coe ran his first sub-four on August 30, 1976 (3:58.3) when he was a month shy of his 19th birthday.

Coe got in the record books first when, in a 41-day span in the summer of 1979, he set world records for 800 meters (1:42.4), 1,500 meters (3:32.1) and the mile (3:48.95). Up to that time Ovett had not pursued records, but in July of 1980 he took Coe's mile record with 3:48.8 and equaled his 1,500 meter record. Coe responded on July 1, by running a first lap of 51, the 800 meters in 1:45.2, then continued to 1,000 meters in 2:13.4 to break the world record at that distance.

In the 1980 Olympics in Moscow, Coe was a heavy favorite at 800 meters and Ovett, who had won 45 straight mile and 1,500 meter races, looked unbeatable at 1,500 meters. Coe, who later felt he "choked," finished second to Ovett in the 800 meters. In the 1,500 final, the first 800 meters went in a snail-like 2:04.9 before Jurgen Straub from East Germany made his move, running the third lap in 54.6 with Coe on his heels. Coe, confident he could maintain his speed longer than anyone else, won the relentless drive to the tape, covering the last 800 meters in 1:48.5. Straub finished second and Ovett third.

After the Moscow Olympics, Coe and Ovett continued to break each other's world records. On August 19, 1981, Coe lowered Ovett's mile record to 3:48.53. Seven days later Ovett reclaimed the record with 3:48.4 at Koblenz Germany, but on the same day Coe got it back with 3:47.33 at Brussels.

Apart from the Olympic Games, Coe and Ovett raced each other only twice in their careers. In the 1972 English Schools cross country meet, Ovett finished second and Coe 11th. They both ran in the 1978 European 800-meter final in Prague, but were so intent on watching each other that East German Olaf Beyer slipped past them both to win. The Coe-Ovett rivalry was based on chasing records and media hype. Ovett wrote in his book *Ovett — An Autobiography* (1984):

I was aware, as was Seb I am sure, that if we did race then a lot of money would be generated — one figure quoted was a quarter of a million pounds. At the time, none of it would have gone into the Coe and Ovett bank accounts.... I knew the sport was changing fast, that commercial avenues were opening up for competitors and that rule changes would not be long in coming — so I preferred to wait.

In 1982 promoters planned three Coe-Ovett races, in Nice, London, and Eugene at 800 meters, 1,000 meters and the mile. But before any of them took place Coe suffered a stress fracture and Ovett injured himself by running into a stone church railing.

In 1983, a third English miler, Steve Cram from Gateshead, joined Coe and Ovett in the quest for middle-distance records and Olympic medals. Cram, blond, superbly talented but often injured, had run a mile in 3:57.04 on July 2, 1977, when he was only 17. In 1983 he beat Ovett for the first time in winning the World Championships 1,500 meters and repeated the victory a month later in London.

Ovett lost his 1,500 meter record

**Steve Ovett, left, finishing a heat of the 800 meters at the 1984 Olympics (AAF/LPI 1984).**

briefly to Sydney Maree, who was born in South Africa but emigrated to the United States in 1979. Maree ran 3:31.24 in a handicap race at Köln, Germany, on August 28, 1983. A week later on September 6, Ovett ran a magnificent 1,500 meter race at Rieti, Italy, to regain the record. With a fierce wind blowing, he was led through the 400 in 54 and the 800 in 1:52. He reached 1,200 meters in 2:49 and pushed on to lower the world record to 3:30.77.

Going into the 1984 Olympics in Los Angeles, the three British runners seemed, on paper, to be set to sweep the 1,500 meter medals. In reality, Cram had lost valuable training because of ankle and calf injuries. Coe was hampered by toxoplasmosis, a blood infection, and the smog in Los Angeles would cause Ovett to suffer severe breathing difficulties.

In the 800-meter final Coe finished second to Cruz of Brazil. Ovett, barely able to breathe, was last. In the 1,500 final, Steve Scott, who had finished second to Cram in

Seb Coe (359) and Steve Cram (362) finished first and second in the 1,500 meters at the 1984 Los Angeles Olympics. The runner leading here is Abascal of Spain, who finished third (AAF/LPI 1984, 65784 GL).

the 1983 World Championships, led through 800 meters in 1:56.8. Heading into the bell lap, J. M. Abascal of Spain was in the lead, followed in a row by Coe, Cram and Ovett. But Ovett stepped off the track on the turn, leaving a three-man race. With 300 meters to go, Cram inched ahead of Coe, who was in second. But Coe accelerated and squeezed between Abascal and Cram into the lead,

and using his superior speed, easily sprinted home to win his second 1,500-meter gold medal.

Cram had his best year in 1985. On July 15, at Nice, France, he ran an epic 1,500-meter duel with Moroccan Said Aouita. Sprinting the last 350 meters, he became the first man under 3:30 when he finished in 3:29.67 to Aouita's 3:29.71. On July 27 at the Bislett

Games in Oslo, Cram ran the last lap in 54.2 to defeat Coe and lower the mile record to 3:46.32.

Of the three great British milers, Coe would have to be regarded the most successful since he won the most Olympic medals and set the most world records. The only blemish on his marvelous career was his inability to win the Olympic 800 meters in 1980 and 1984. He was not a strength runner and his low-mileage, high intensity training may not have been suited to running a fast 800 meters after many heats. Ovett and Cram were nearly his equals and had fortune smiled on them, perhaps either could have matched Coe's medal and record totals.

Said Aouita was born the first son of a paper-mill worker in Kenitra, Morocco, 80 miles (129 km) north of Casablanca. In 1979, at age 17, he gave up soccer to take up running. He finished third in the 1,500 meters at the World Championships in 1983. Although he was favored to win the Los Angeles Olympic 1,500 meters, he skipped the event because he was injured and felt he didn't have the speed and power to run all the heats required. Instead he concentrated on the 5,000 and won the gold medal in 13:05.5, at the time the third-fastest 5,000 meters ever run.

After his defeat at 1,500 meters by Cram in July 1985, Aouita bounced back five weeks later to take the record himself. In the race held on August 23 in Berlin's Olympic Stadium, Volker Blumenthal of West Germany led for the first 800 in 1:53.5, with Aouita a step back. Then Ireland's Frank O'Mara took over and led to 1,100 meters in 2:35.25. Aouita took the lead and covered the last 300 meters in 41.0 to break Cram's record with 3:29.46.

Aouita kept his training methods secret, traveling between training camps in Switzerland, Mexico City, Rome and Boulder, Colorado. He was a great front-runner who often pushed himself to his limit. This may have led to some of his frequent in-

**Said Aouita from Morocco running the 5,000 meters in the 1984 Los Angeles Olympics (AAF/LIP 1984, 65417 RL).**

juries. He was one of the most versatile runners ever with personal bests of 46.9 for 400, 1:43.86 for 800, 3:29.46 for 1,500, 3:46.76 for the mile, 7:32.94 for 3,000, 8:13.45 for two miles, 12:58.39 for 5,000 and 27:26.11 for 10,000 meters. No middle-distance runner before Aouita had shown such excellence over this wide a range.

## NOUREDDINE MORCELI—
### GIFTED OF GOD

Noureddine Morceli (NOR-eh-deen MORE-seh-lee) of Algeria dominated the 1,500 meters and the mile from 1990 to 1996. Born in 1970 the sixth of 10 children, he grew up in the town of Sidi Akacha, on Algeria's Mediterranean coast. "I am gifted by God," he was quoted as saying, "and I prove it by working very hard. From age 11, I wanted to be a world champion."

By the time he was 16, Morceli had run the 1,500 meters in 3:50 and in 1988 finished second in the World Junior Championships 1,500. That fall he enrolled at Riverside Junior College in California where he was coached by Ted Banks. In 1989 Morceli ran a mile under four minutes for the first time and broke 14 minutes for 5,000 meters as well. During his stay at Riverside he made no secret that he wanted to set world records. He continued to improve and by the summer of 1990 had run the fastest 1,500 (3:32.60) of the year.

Heading into the 1992 Olympics at Barcelona, Morceli was the favorite in the 1,500 meters. In the final, the first 800 was run in 2:06, which was slower than in the women's 1,500 final. Morceli became boxed in on the last lap. He freed himself by going four lanes wide, but it was too late. Fermin Cacho from Spain won the gold with 3:40.62, with Morceli seventh in 3:41.7. Morceli was crushed after his defeat. "I run to be known as the greatest runner, the greatest of all time," he said. "I could not eat or sleep for a week after I lost in the Olympics. I have to win or die."

Less than a month later, on the fast track in Rieti, Italy, Morceli atoned for his poor Olympic showing. Taking aim at Aouita's seven-year-old 1,500-meter record, he followed his pacesetters through a blazing 53.8 first lap and 1:51.6 for 800 meters. He took the lead with just over a lap to go and passed 1,200 meters in 2:47.3. He ran the last 300 in 41.5 to finish with a record of 3:28.86.

A year later on September 5, 1993, Morceli returned to Rieti in even better shape to try for the mile record. Two of his countrymen led him through 400 in 54.4 and 800 in 1:51.8. Morceli took over at 1,200 meters, which he passed in 2:48.75. He reached 1,500 meters in 3:29.57 and covered the last 109.3 meters in 14.8 seconds to record 3:44.39 to beat Cram's mile record by 1.93 seconds. This was the biggest improvement in the 1,500 record since Ryun had lowered it by 2.3 seconds 27 years earlier.

In 1995 Morceli took 1.49 seconds off his own 1,500 meter record. His younger brother Ali led him through 600 meters. With 600 meters to go the elder Morceli took the lead and ran a 54 last lap to record 3:27.37.

By 1996 a rising star from Morocco named Hicham El-Guerrouj (ee-SHAM El gah-ROHSH), known as the "Prince of the Desert," began to challenge Morceli for supremacy of the mile and 1,500. El-Guerrouj had produced the year's fastest 1,500 and was co-favorite along with Morceli to win the 1,500-meter Olympic gold medal in Atlanta. Just before the bell in the final, El-Guerrouj drew even with Morceli, who was leading and trying to stay out of trouble. El-Guerrouj fell after tripping over Morceli's foot. Morceli continued on to win, but El-Guerrouj finished last.

El-Guerrouj was bitterly disappointed, but after the race, King Hassan, the Moroccan monarch, called to tell him not to worry. He was young and there would other Olympic Games. After being ranked as world's number one miler for a record seven years in a row, Morceli's reign at the top finally ended. On July 14, 1998, at Rome, El-Guerrouj ran a perfect race to erase Morceli's 1,500 meter record. His pacer led him through 400 in 55, 800 in 1:50.7, and 1,200 in 2:46.3. Breaking away from his pacemakers, he finished in 3:26.00 to take 1.37 seconds off Morceli's 1,500 record.

On July 7, 1999, in Rome, one year

after setting the world record for 1,500 meters, El-Guerrouj ran a remarkably even-paced race to break the mile record. The pacemakers took him through 440 yards in 55.1; 880 yards in 1:51.6, and the three-quarter mile mark in 2:47.9. It was an unusual record attempt in that El-Guerrouj was pushed on the final lap by Kenya's Noah Ngeny. El-Guerrouj ran the final lap in 55.2 to set a world record of 3:43.13. Ngeny, who had previously never run under 3:50, also broke the old record with 3:43.40. This was the first time that two men had broken the world record in the same race since 1958, when Australians Herb Elliott (3:54.5) and Merv Lincoln (3:55.9) both ducked under Derek Ibbotson's 3:57.2 mark for the mile.

On July 7, 1997, Kenyan Daniel Komen became the first man to run two sub–four-minute miles back to back. The table below shows how runners have been able to extend the distance they are able to run at a four-minute mile pace.

If this trend continues, 20–25 years from now someone should be able to break 16 minutes for four miles.

## Women's 1,500 Meters—Mile

The IAAF didn't recognize records for the women's 1,500 meters until 1967, although 1,500 meter races had been included in some meets as far back as 1922. Progress was rapid once the 1,500 became an official event and by 1972 when the race was introduced in the Olympics, times had improved dramatically.

The mile for women has even less of a history, since most of the great middle-distance runners from Eastern Europe have concentrated on the 1,500 meters. On May 29, 1954, only three weeks after Bannister's first sub–four-minute mile, Diane Leather, also of Great Britain, ran a mile in 4:59.6 to become the first woman under five minutes. Leather ran the mile under five minutes 15 times, getting down to 4:45.0 in 1955.

Anne Smith of Great Britain became the first official record holder at 1,500 meters when she ran the distance in 4:17.3 on June 3, 1967. She continued running to finish the mile in 4:37.0. Three months later Maria Gommers from the Netherlands lowered the 1,500 record to 4:15.6.

On July 2, 1969, Paola Pigni from Italy improved the 1,500 record to 4:12.4. Born in Milan, Pigni was the international cross country champion in 1973 and 1974. Pigni became the first woman to run the mile under 4:30 when she covered the distance in 4:29.5 in 1973.

Pigni's 1,500 record had lasted only 10 weeks when on Sept 20, 1969, at the European Championships, Czech Jaroslava Jehličková sprinted from eighth place to win in 4:10.7. Karin Burneleit from East Germany took the record under 4:10 on August 15, 1971, when she ran 4:09.6 at the European Championships in Helsinki. Burneleit finished fourth in the 1972 Olympic Games in Munich.

On July 18, 1972, during a heat of the Soviet championships, Lyudmila Bragina began a new era in the women's 1,500. Running laps of 66.5, 65.5 and 67.0, she reached the tape in 4:06.9 to take three seconds off the 1,500 record. At the Munich Olympics

| Miles | Date | Time | Runner | Years to double distance run at 4 min/mile pace |
|-------|------|------|--------|--------------------------------------------------|
| ½ | 1854 | 1:58 | Henry Allen Reed | — |
| 1 | 1954 | 3:59.6 | Roger Bannister | 100 |
| 2 | 1997 | 7:58.6 | Daniel Komen | 43 |

she lowered the record three more times. In her qualifying heat on September 4, she ran 4:06.5, and in the semifinal on September 7, 4:05.1. Despite her records the final was no sure thing as all 10 finalists had run 4:09 or better in the semifinals. In the final on September 9, Ilja Keizer from Holland led the first 400 meters in 62.5. At 700 meters Bragina moved into the lead and passed 800 meters in 2:10. She reached the bell lap in 2:58.6 and kept her 12-meter lead the rest of the way, crossing the finish in 4:01.4. Bragina, who had run her last 800 meters in 2:06.1, took 3.7 seconds off her own world record.

### TATYANA KAZANKINA

The first woman to go below four minutes for the 1,500 meters was Russian Tatyana Kazankina. She was born in 1951 in Petrovsk and ran 4:19 for the 1,500 at age 19. In June 1976, she improved dramatically,

Tatyana Kazankina from the Soviet Union set world records and won Olympic gold medals at both 800 and 1,500 meters (photograph by Mstislav Botashev, courtesy of Nikolai Botashev).

running 4:05.2. Ten days later she ran 4:02.8 and six days after that she covered the first 800 meters in 2:05.5 and went on to record an amazing 3:56.0. This broke Bragina's record by more than five seconds.

At the Montreal Olympics in 1976, she won the 800 in 1:54.9 and came back four days later with a 56.9 last lap to win the 1,500 meters in 4:05.5. Kazankina trained twice a day, running from 12 to 18 miles. After giving birth to a daughter in 1978 she was again in top form in 1980 and lowered her 1,500 record to 3:55.0 in Moscow on July 6. She won her second 1,500 meter gold medal at the Moscow Olympics with 3:56.6 and two weeks later in Zurich went after her own 1,500 meter record. Teammate Tatyana Providokhina led her through the first 400 in 58.5, and the 800 in 2:04.5 before dropping out at 900 meters. Running the final 600 meters alone, Kazankina covered the last lap in 60.5 to finish in 3:52.47 and set a record that would last for 13 years.

In 1984 at a Paris international meet, Kazankina was selected to take a drug test but refused. According to IAAF rules, an athlete who refuses to be tested is presumed guilty. The IAAF suspended her for 18 months, ending a brilliant career.

America's greatest female middle-distance runner of the 20th century was Mary Decker Slaney, who was born in 1958 in New Jersey. Slaney moved to California at age 11 and started running a year later. She was only 14 when she was selected to run in the U.S. vs. U.S.S.R. meet in Richmond, Virginia. At 15 she astounded the track world by running the mile in 4:37.4 and the 800 meters in 2:02.4. Between ages 15 and 16, she grew six inches (15 cm) and gained 25 pounds (11.4 kg), which may have contributed to severe leg pains that required a series of operations.

By 1980 she had dropped her mile time to 4:21.68 — the best by a woman up to that time. She set a 5,000 meter world record of 15:08.26 early in June of 1982 and lowered her world's best mile to 4:21.46 later that month. In July she set a world record at 10,000 meters when she ran 31:35.3. Slaney became the first woman to run under 4:20 for the mile with a 4:18.08 in Paris in July 1982. After colliding with South African Zola Budd in the 1984 Olympic 3,000 meter final, Slaney fell and injured her hip. She came back strong in 1985 to run 800 meters in 1:56.90, 1,000 meters in 2:34.8 and again lowered her mile world record, this time to 4:16.71.

Throughout her long career, Slaney was bothered by various leg problems requiring approximately 20 surgeries. In 1983 she proved that at her uninjured best, she was equal to any of the East Europeans. She out-kicked the field in the first World Championship 3,000-meters in Helsinki, and then outran a trio of aggressive Soviets to win the 1,500 also.

In June 1996, in the twilight of her career, Slaney failed a routine drug test at the U.S. Olympic trials. The test showed an

**Mary Slaney leads the 1984 Olympic 3,000 meters. Barefoot Zola Budd is running on her shoulder (AAF/LPI 1984, D62199).**

unusually high ratio of testosterone to epitestosterone. The USA Track and Field (USATF) governing body took no action, but the IAAF suspended her in May 1997 and the USATF was forced to follow suit. Slaney and her attorneys argued that her drug test was flawed. In September 1997 the USATF lifted its suspension, but in April 1999 an IAAF arbitration panel ruled that Slaney had taken testosterone and gave her a two-year retroactive suspension.

### Qu Junxia

In 1993 the world looked on in disbelief as Chinese women made shambles of the world middle-distance records. They destroyed the 1,500, 3,000 and 10,000 meter records in their national games in Beijing, then won all the middle distance races at the Stuttgart World Championships in August. Known as "Ma's Army" for their coach Ma Junren, the performances of these women were so extraordinary that many observers insisted, without any proof, that they must be on drugs. Junren attributed the Chinese success to his selection of runners from rural areas. These women were used to hardships, he insisted, and readily tolerated his combination of high mileage, intense speed work and altitude training.

Junren recruited Qu Junxia from the Dalaian school in Liaoning. Initially, she was said to lack talent but was "able to handle more hardships then the others." In 1990, at age 19, she won the World 1,500-meter Junior Championships and finished fifth in the World Cross Country Championships. At the Barcelona Olympics in 1992, she won a bronze medal in the 1,500.

On September 11, 1993, in Beijing, the Chinese women made a planned assault on Tatyana Kazankina's 13-year-old 1,500-meter world record. Qu Junxia's teammate Liu Dong led through the 400 in 57.1, the 800 in 2:00.7, then stepped off the track. Then Qu Junxia took over and ran the next lap in 64.5. With 200 to go, Wang Junxia,

the 3,000 and 10,000-meter world record holder, tried to take the lead, but Qu Junxia held her off and broke Kazankina's world record by 2.01 seconds with 3:50.46. Wang Junxia also broke the old record with 3:51.92. In all, seven of the Chinese women finished under 4:00. Qu Junxia's time of 3:50.46 is equivalent to a mile in 4:08.9.

Russian Svetlana Masterkova won gold medals in both the 800 and 1,500 meters in the 1996 Olympics in Atlanta. On August 14, 1996, at Zurich, she set a mile world record of 4:12.56. Her performance is equal to 3:53.8 for 1,500 meters, so the mile record still lags the 1,500 record. How soon will women run the mile in less than four minutes? Many attempts have been made to project the progression of world records into the future with notable lack of success. In addition, some if not many of the current records may be contaminated by drug use. Interestingly, Masterkova's time is close to the record set by Walter George in 1886. It took men nearly 68 years to go from George's 4:12¾ to Bannister's 3:59.4. The only safe prediction is that it won't take women anywhere near that long.

## Men's 5,000–10,000 Meters

### Vladimir Kuts—
### The Indefatigable Russian

Vladimir Kuts, born in 1927 in the Ukraine, took up where Zatopek left off. Kuts, short, stocky and tough, started running at the late age of 22 after serving in the Soviet navy as a gunner. Like many of his contemporaries, he admired Zatopek and emulated his idol's training methods. Instead of confining himself to repeat 200 and 400 meters, he added longer distances of up to 2,000 meters. He didn't make the workouts any easier. His training was so rigorous that he needed massage and two days of rest per week to get through it. Kuts probably never heard of Deerfoot, but lacking a finishing kick, he developed surging, front-running tactics similar to those the great Indian runner had used nearly 100 years earlier.

He lost his first race with an aging Zatopek in 1953, but came back in the European championships on August 24, 1954, to run away from both Zatopek and Chataway and set a world record of 13:56.6 for 5,000 meters. In a classic, televised race in London's White Stadium on October 13, 1954, Kuts led for nearly the entire race, but Chataway hung with him and won by two feet in a record 13:51.6. Ten days later in Prague, Kuts got the record back by running 13:51.2.

He lost the record again to Sándor Iharos of Hungary who ran 13:50.8 on September 10, 1955. Coached by the famous Mihaly Igloi, Iharos set world records at 1,500, 5,000 and 10,000 in 1955–1956. The Hungarian uprising in 1956 prevented Iharos and the other Hungarians from reaching their potential at the Melbourne Olympics.

Kuts regained the record with a 13:46.8 at Belgrade on September 19, 1955, but Iharos reclaimed it on October 23, 1955, when he ran 13:40.6. On June 19, 1956, at Bergen, Norway, Gordon Pirie defeated Kuts and lowered the record again to 13:36.8. A gracious loser, Kuts gave Pirie his Soviet warm-up sweater with CCCP on the front as a memento.

By mid–1956, Kuts was able to do 25 × 440 repeats in 63–67 seconds with only 30-second rest periods. On September 11, in Moscow, he received a great boost to his confidence when he lowered the 10,000-meter record to 28:30.4. A month earlier a dejected Kuts had said, "I am not fast enough to win anything at the Olympics."

At Melbourne, Kuts and Pirie engaged in one of the most memorable Olympic 10,000 finals ever. Kuts seized the lead and ran the first lap in 61 seconds with Pirie, "as if attached by an invisible string," staying right with him. After settling to a 68–69 second pace, Kuts made his first sustained surge on the fifth lap, but Pirie hung on. After 3,000 meters, Kuts surged again, sprinting the straight and slowing to almost a jog on the curve. He repeated the tactic on the 10th, 11th and 12th laps. Everyone but Pirie had fallen back as Kuts passed 5,000 meters in 14:07, just .4 seconds off Zatopek's 5,000-meter Olympic record. Kuts sprinted again on the 15th and 17th laps, but Pirie still hung on grimly.

For 20 laps the determined Englishman clung desperately to Kuts's shoulder. Then Kuts moved out to the third lane and slowed so abruptly that Pirie's momentum carried him into the lead. Kuts rested for a half lap, following and watching his rival. Suddenly Kuts surged again. This time Pirie did not follow. Kuts later said that if he had seen any sign of strength in Pirie's face he would have cracked himself, but the look on Pirie's face was unmistakable — he was finished. In the remaining laps a deathly pale Pirie drifted back through the pack, like a leaf on the wind, as Kuts won the Soviet Union's first ever Olympic gold medal in 28:45.6.

Five days later Pirie, the 5,000-meter world record holder, was expected to give Kuts stiff competition in the 5,000 meter final. This time Pirie decided not to follow Kuts but hoped to run a more even pace and catch him between bursts. The strategy failed when Kuts opened a 10-meter lead and went on to win his second gold medal easily in 13:39.6 with a broken Pirie second in 13:50.6.

Kuts set his final world mark in the 5,000 on October 13, 1957, when he ran 13:35 in Rome. During his career, the great Ukrainian runner lowered the world record in the 5,000 four times (22.1 seconds total). No other runner had improved the record by so large a margin. Although Kuts was sometimes described in the Western press as a "Soviet Automaton," in reality, he was friendly and very human. After he retired from the track to become a coach, he

**Vladimir Kuts (photograph by Mstislav Bota-shev, courtesy of Nikolai Botashev).**

suffered a series of four heart attacks. Sadly, in 1975, after battling alcoholism and obesity, he died at age 48 a forgotten hero.

New Zealander Murray Halberg, who was coached by Arthur Lydiard, ran world-class times from 800 to 10,000 meters in the 1960s. When he was 17 years old, Halberg suffered a shoulder injury playing rugby football that left him with nerve damage and a withered left arm. He wrote in *A Clean Pair of Heels* (1963):

> Before the accident I used to run slightly off balance. After it, I adjusted myself to running with the arm tucked up, pumping myself along with my right arm. And my balance seemed better. It supports the theory that there is something good in everything if you care to look for it.

Halberg won the 1960 Olympic 5,000 meter gold medal in one of the most exciting and tactically brilliant races ever. Al-

though he had run 800 meters in 1:51 and could run a 54-second lap at the end of a hard 5,000, he was unsure that he was fast enough to out-sprint a field that included some outstanding finishers. He and Lydiard devised a bold plan for the race that Halberg executed perfectly.

When the race started, Halberg ran in last place until the seventh lap, then gradually moved up with the leaders. With three laps to go he sprinted a full half lap, gaining a 10-meter edge on the surprised front runners. He went on to complete the lap in 61 seconds and widen his lead to 20 meters with the German Hans Grodotski in second place. On the next lap he slowed only slightly (64 seconds) as he struggled to hold on to his lead. When he came to the bell lap, he was obviously in distress, rolling his head and baring his teeth. Grodotski slowly began to narrow the gap as the crowd of 60,000 asked each other if the gritty New Zealander could hang on. Looking back again and again, Halberg began to falter as his lead shrank to 12 meters. With 100 meters to go he was still 10 meters in the lead and from somewhere he summoned the energy for a final drive. He reached the finish 1.2 seconds ahead of Grodotski, clutched the tape in his hands, and fell exhausted on the infield.

## RON CLARKE

During the mid–1960s Ron Clarke made vast improvements in the world records from two miles to 20 km, but never won a major title. Clarke set a world junior record of 4:06.8 for the mile in 1956 and was rewarded by being chosen to carry the Olympic torch into the stadium at Melbourne. He began serious training in 1961 at the age of 24 and on December 18, 1963, broke the world record for 10,000 meters with 28:15.6.

Clarke ran three times a day and covered about 100 miles a week. He trained nearly every day even if injured or ill and gradually increased the quality of his training as his career progressed. He ran mostly on grass and roads, and much of his training was done over extremely hilly courses. Usually he went to the track once a week, for some quick 200s, or some 100/100s (sprint the straights/jog the curves).

In 1964 at the Tokyo Olympics, Clarke was a heavy favorite to win the 10,000 meter final. Other outstanding runners in the huge field of 38 were Pyotr Bolotnikov of Russia, Murray Halberg of New Zealand, Ron Hill of England, Mohamed Gammoudi of Tunisia, Mamo Wolde of Ethiopia and an unheralded American part-Sioux Indian from Kansas, Billy Mills.

Pyotr led the field through a 64-second first lap, then Clarke moved to the front to push the pace. At 5,000 meters Mills was on the ropes. He was within seven seconds of his best time for the distance and considered dropping back or even quitting but somehow managed to stick with the leaders. At the bell, only Gamoudi and Mills remained with Clarke. As they approached a lapped runner, Mills moved up on Clarke's shoulder. Mills described the wild last lap in *Tales of Gold* by Lewis H. Carlson (1986):

We were coming off the first curve with another curve to go, about 375 yards from the finish, when Clarke saw that I had boxed him in, he gave me a little nudge. I nudged him back, and then he leaned into me a little, and I leaned into him. Then he lifted me up and pushed me into the third lane. I thought I was going to fall, and my legs started to buckle. But I recovered and started to close back on Clarke's shoulder. Just then Gammoudi broke between Clarke and me, knocking Clarke to the inside and me to the outside, but neither of us really stumbled. Gammoudi pulled probably 12 to 15 yards ahead, and I'm three or four yards behind Clarke.

With 60 yards to go, Clarke caught Gammoudi and struggled to a six-inch lead. Then suddenly it was all over as Mills came sprinting down the outside, his finishing burst so furious and so unexpected that neither Gammoudi nor Clarke could respond. Mills went through the tape, his hands held high in triumph, followed by Gammoudi and then Clarke. The time was 28:24.4. Mills's previous best for 10,000 meters had been 29:10.4. His victory made him the only American to win an Olympic gold medal at 10,000 meters.

In the 5,000-meter final, which was run on a muddy track in a driving rainstorm, Clarke tried a series of surges but faded badly near the end. The Americans struck gold twice as Bob Schul, who had trained under Igloi, sprinted the last 300 meters in 38.7 seconds to win America's first gold medal in the 5,000. Clarke finished a disappointing ninth.

After Tokyo, Clarke continued his record setting spree, setting 15 more world records at distances from two miles to

Ron Clarke (204) and Derek Clayton share the lead in a 10,000 meter race in Melbourne, March 30, 1969 (Australian Archives, Series A1200, Caption Number L80677. Commonwealth of Australia copyright, used by permission).

20,000 meters. He was in excellent condition for the 1968 Mexico City Olympics. But, like most distance runners who had lived and trained at sea level, he could not cope with the altitude. He finished fifth in the 5,000 and sixth in the 10,000. During his career Clarke broke the 5,000 meter world record four times and reduced the record by a total of 18.4 seconds. His best performance was 13:16.6 on July 5, 1966. In the 10,000 he was the first runner to break 28 minutes and he lowered the record by a total of 38.8 seconds. His best performance was 27:39.4 on July 14, 1965.

## Lasse Viren—Carrying on the Norwegian Tradition

The Finns were so dominant at distance running during the first third of the 20th century that some thought their genes must make them especially suited for running long distances. After a gap of 36 years, Lasse Viren brought his country back to the forefront of distance running. Viren, unlike Nurmi, Zatopek and Kuts, concentrated almost exclusively on the Olympics. Although he set world records at two miles, 5,000 and 10,000 meters, his place in running history comes from winning the 5,000 and 10,000 meters in both the 1972 and 1976 Olympics.

In 1971, Viren went to Kenya, where he trained rigorously at high altitudes, logging many miles. On August 14, 1972, he tuned up for the Munich Olympics by setting a new two-mile record of 8:14. At Munich, Viren was fourth and last to qualify in his heat of the 10,000. In their heats, favorites Dave Bedford of England and Emiel Puttemans from Belgium thrilled the crowd with fast times of 27:53.4 and 27:53.6 — extravagant displays that Viren considered "sheer madness."

In the final, Bedford led off with a first lap of 60.6 then tried a series of surges which failed to drop the lead pack. On the fourth kilometer, Viren tripped and fell, but calmly got to his feet again, losing only

three seconds. In only 230 meters he had caught everyone but the leader Bedford. With 1,000 meters to go, Viren began a relentless drive to the finish, running each 100 meters faster than the last. Only Puttemans could stay with him and in the end, he too had to give way as Viren ran the last 100 meters in 13.8 to set a world record of 27:38.4.

In the 5,000 Viren faced a strong field that included Puttemans, Ian Stewart, Mohamed Gammoudi and American Steve Prefontaine. The young, charismatic, front-running Prefontaine had run 13:22.8 in the American trials and stated bluntly that he would run the last mile in four minutes. The race started lazily with no one wanting to take the lead. With a mile to go, Prefontaine accelerated as promised and covered the next lap in 62.5. Only Stewart, Puttemans, Gammoudi and Viren managed to stay with him. Prefontaine ran the next lap in 61.2, but Viren hung on and even took the lead. The next-to-last lap went in 60.3 as Viren, Gammoudi and Prefontaine struggled for the lead. On the homestretch, Prefontaine tied up badly as Viren swept to victory followed by Gammoudi and Stewart. Viren had run the last mile in 4:01.2.

In 1974 Viren suffered a leg injury which made running nearly impossible. Finally, in early 1975, he underwent a successful operation to remove extra ligaments that had become attached to his injured muscle. In May 1975, Steve Prefontaine, who was expected to battle Viren in the Montreal Olympics, tragically died when his MG sports car flipped as he was returning home from a party. Saddened by his friend and rival's death Viren commented: "When Pre was in the race the sun always shone."

At the Montreal Olympics, Viren set his sights on duplicating Zatopek's feat of winning the 5,000, 10,000 and marathon. Including qualifying heats, Viren would have to race a prodigious 72,000 meters in eight days with the marathon starting only 24 hours after the 5,000 final. Zatopek had not been required to run a qualifying heat for the 10,000 and had three days' rest between the 5,000 final and the marathon.

Viren got off to a good start as he won the 10,000 with relative ease, running the second half in 13:31.3 to finish in 27:40.38 with Carlos Lopes second and Brenden Foster third. In the 5,000 final, Viren faced stiff challengers in New Zealand's Rod Dixon and Dick Quax as well as Foster, Stewart and Hildenbrand. The race started slowly and looked like a repeat of Munich. With 2,000 meters to go, Viren glided to the front and the race was on. He covered the next two laps in 60 seconds each, but failed to drop the lead pack. "I was the fugitive now, and I had to flee as if my life depended on it," he was quoted as saying.

Going into the last lap Viren held a small lead. First Dixon challenged and was repelled, then Viren noticed another runner in black forcing his way past. Somehow Viren found one last gear and it was just enough. He crossed the finish in 13:24.76, followed in less than a second by Quax, Hildenbrand and Dixon.

After a fitful night trying to rest, a depleted Viren made a gallant effort at winning a third gold in the marathon. But he could not overcome the combination of a lack of recovery time and a strong marathon field. He shadowed Frank Shorter, the favorite, but at 16 miles (26 km), Shorter surged and Viren was forced to drop back. Viren struggled on and finished a credible fifth in 2:13:10.8.

Rolf Haikkola, Viren's coach, borrowed marathon-type training from Lydiard, short intervals from Igloi, hill running from Cerutty and long steady runs from Nurmi. Viren also trained at altitude in Brazil and Kenya. His favorite tactic was to steadily increase the pace beginning about four laps from the finish. At the Olympic Games in Moscow, youth and perhaps luck had run out for Viren as he finished fifth in the 10,000 final. The race was won by Miruts Yifter, a diminutive Ethiopian air force captain known as "Yifter the Shifter" for his fierce finishing kick. Yifter, who also won the 5,000, had been one of the favorites at Montreal before the African boycott. He raced opponents rather than the clock and never set a world record.

Henry Rono was a Nandi tribesman from Kenya who attended Washington State University in the late 1970s. In the summer of 1978 he amazed the track and field world by setting world records in the 5,000 (13:08.4), the 10,000 meters (27:22.4), as well as the 3,000 meters and the steeplechase. He added a second world record for 5,000 meters in 1981 (13:06.2). While at Washington State, Rono won two NCAA track championships and three NCAA cross country titles. He missed both the 1976 and 1980 Olympics because of boycotts and remained in the United States when his running days were over. Rono's career was hampered by weight and alcohol problems. He graduated from Washington State with a degree in psychology but had difficulty adapting to life in the United States. After spending time in homeless shelters in New York and Washington D.C., by late 1999 he was working in Albuquerque, New Mexico, as a skycap.

### HAILE GEBRSELASSIE— VERY BIG IN THE HEART

As the 20th century drew to a close, Ethiopian Haile Gebrselassie (HIGH-leh geh-bruh-suh-LAH-see) continued the legacy of Abebe Bikila, Mamo Wolde and Miruts Yifter. Gebrselassie led a group of East Africans who shattered the 5,000 and 10,000 meter records with unprecedented regularity.

Born in 1973, young Gebrselassie often chased down any of the family horses that broke loose. The barrel chested five-foot, three-inch (1.6 m), 117-pound (53 kg) Ethiopian first achieved international fame by winning the 5,000 and 10,000 World Junior Championships in 1992. The following year at the Stuttgart World Championships, he won the 10,000 and finished second in the 5,000. Then in 1994, he broke Said Aoutia's 1987 world Record in the 5,000 by 1.4 seconds when he ran 12:56.96 in Hengelo, Holland.

In 1995 Gebrselassie astounded the world with his record-breaking performances. In May, he ran 8:07.46 for two miles, breaking Kenyan Moses Kiptanui's world record. The following week in Hengelo, he broke the 10,000-meter record by nine seconds when he ran 26:43.53. Later in the year, he won the World Championship 10,000 again and on August 16, he regained the 5,000 meter record that had been broken by Kiptanui (12:55.30) on June 8. Gebrselassie took nearly 11 seconds off Kiptanui's record, running 12:44.39.

The 1996 Olympic 10,000 final, run in searing Atlanta heat, was a classic. Paul Tergat (TER-got) from Kenya took the lead at the halfway point and tried to pull away from the field. Despite covering the second 5,000 meters in 13:11, he could not separate himself from Gebrselassie, who sprinted past to win in 27:07.34, a new Olympic record. The hard track surface caused so much damage to Gebrselassie's feet that after the 10,000 he was unable to run the 5,000.

On August 23, 1996, Moroccan Olympic bronze medalist Salah Hissou took five seconds off Gebrselassie's 10,000 record. But on July 4, 1997, in Oslo, Gebrselassie was ready to reclaim the record. He lapped a world class field, breaking Hissou's record by seven seconds with his 26:31.32. The following month Gebrselassie won the 10,000 meters for the third time at the World Championships.

In Zurich, on August 13, 1997, Gebrselassie and Daniel Komen battled for the 5,000-meter world record. With about 150 meters to go, Gebrselassie sprinted past Komen, who had led up to that point. Gebrselassie won with a world record of 12:41.86, three seconds better than his pre-

vious mark. Komen was upset because he felt he had done all the work, yet Gebrselassie got the record. Using his own pacers in Brussels on August 22, Komen ran 12:39.74 to take the record. Later that evening, Tergat broke Gebrselassie's 10,000 record by running 26:27.85.

In June 1998, in Helsinki's Olympic Stadium, Gebrselassie ran the last mile of the 5,000 in 3:58 to finish in 12:39.36 and reclaim, by a mere 0.38 seconds, the record he lost to Komen the previous summer.

Gebrselassie's training is based on how he feels. He runs an hour in the morning and an hour in the evening for a total of about 18 miles (29 km). To improve his speed, he does 800-, 400- and 200-meter repetitions in the weeks leading up to major races.

During his career (through 1999), Gebrselassie has lowered the 5,000-meter record by a total of 19.03 seconds. Only Vladimir Kuts, with a lifetime total of 22.2 seconds, has done better. In the 10,000 Gebrselassie has improved the record by 20.91 seconds compared to Zatopek's 40.8 and Ron Clarke's 38.8. In 1998, Walt Disney Inc. produced a biographical motion picture, *Endurance*, that chronicled Gebrselassie's rise to fame and Olympic glory.

## Women's 3,000, 5,000 and 10,000 Meters

*I do feel more relaxed without them. It's just a question of plucking up courage to go out in an Olympic stadium for the first time as the only runner in the Games with bare feet.* — Zola Budd (1984)

Records for the women's 3,000 meters were first recognized by the IAAF in 1974, and the event was introduced in the Olympics in 1984. Lyudmila Bragina, who set three world records at 1,500 meters in the 1972 Olympics, moved up to the 3,000 late in her career. In 1974 at the U.S. vs. U.S.S.R. meet in Durham, North Carolina, she set her first record at the distance with 8:52.8. Grete Waitz from Norway lowered the record to 8:46.6 in 1975 at Oslo and again to 8:45.4 in 1976 in the same city. Bragina regained the record in 1976 when she ran 8:27.2 at another U.S. vs. U.S.S.R. meet at College Park, Maryland.

The Chinese, in their Beijing record assault in 1993, lowered the record three times, with Wang Junxia setting the current record of 8:06.11 in the final. In 1996, in order to bring the women's events more in line with the men's, the 3,000-meter race was replaced on the Olympic program by the 5,000 meters and the top women began to concentrate on the new distance.

The 5,000-meter race for women has only been in existence on a world level since the early 1980s. The first woman to break 15 minutes was Ingrid Kristiansen of Norway when she ran 14:58.89 in Oslo in 1984. Zola Budd, from South Africa, was an extremely talented runner whose career was hampered greatly by her home country being banned from international competition. Budd, running barefoot, broke the 5,000-meter record in 1985 with 14:48.07. In 1986 Kristiansen regained the record from Budd by running 14:37.33. Fernando Ribeiro of Portugal improved the record slightly to 14:36.45 in 1995.

The 10,000-meter race was given world record status for women in 1981. First under 32 minutes was Mary Decker Slaney in 1981 when she ran 31:35. By 1985 Ingrid Kristiansen had broken 31 minutes with 30:59.42 at Oslo. A year later she returned to lower the record to 30:13.74. In 1988 Soviet Olga Bondarenko won the first Women's Olympic 10,000 at Seoul with 31:05.21.

## Ingrid Kristiansen

The dominant female runner at 5,000 and 10,000 meters in the 1980s was Ingrid Kristiansen of Norway. Born in 1956, she tried cross country skiing before turning to running. She is the only runner, man or woman, to simultaneously hold world records for 5,000 (14:37.33) and 10,000 meters (30:13.74) and the marathon (2:21:06). Her accomplishments include gold medals for 10,000 meters at the World Championships (1987) and the World Cross Country title in 1988. Kristiansen also won the Stockholm, Houston, Boston, Chicago, London and New York City marathons.

## Wang Junxia

Wang Junxia, the most famous runner from coach Ma Junren's "Family Army," came from a poor peasant family in Northeast China. In 1992, her best 10,000 meters was 32:29. But at the 1993 World Championships in Stuttgart, the 20-year-old five-foot, three-inch (1.6 m) 99-pound (45 kg) Junxia won easily over a class field, running 30:49.30, and finishing with a devastating kick. Two weeks later at China's National Games, she became the first woman to break 30 minutes for 10,000 meters running 29:31.78, demolishing Ingrid Kristiansen's World Record by 43 seconds. Junxia ran the second half of the race in 14:26, the fastest 5,000 meters yet run by a woman. Three days later, she ran 3:51.92 to surpass the world record for 1,500, but finished second to teammate Qu Junxia. The next day in a qualifying heat of the 3,000 meters Junxia broke Tatyana Kazankina's nine-year-old world record by 10 seconds, running 8:12.19. The following day she ran an almost unbelievable 8:06.11.

These performances rocked an incredulous track and field world. Track experts could not explain how the Chinese women, with almost no tradition at running, could suddenly make shambles of the world distance records. Vague reports came from China of marathon-a-day training, strict military discipline, secret turtle-blood potions and beatings. In addition there was a strange revelation that 11 of Junren's runners had undergone appendectomies in the summer of 1994.

Junxia finished 1993 by winning the World Cup Marathon after earlier running 2:24 in her first 26.2 mile effort. In 1994 her only international race was a win in the Asian Games 10,000 with 30:50.34. In early 1995 she broke with coach Junren and formed a rival training group in Shenyang. At the 1996 Olympics in Atlanta, Junxia attempted the 5,000–10,000 double, which required 30,000 meters of racing. She won the 5,000 in 14:59.88 while trying to conserve her energy, but in the 10,000-meter final homestretch, Fernando Ribeiro saw a gap open up on the inside and shot by Junxia to win the gold by a second. In 1998 Junxia retired from running, moved to the United States, and enrolled at Colorado State University.

## Cross Country

Worldwide interest in cross country grew steadily in the second half of the 20th century. In the 1950s and '60s the North African countries Tunisia, Morocco and Algeria began sending teams to the international championship race. This race came under the IAAF's jurisdiction in 1973 and was renamed the World Cross Country Championships. In pre–IAAF days, 15 was the largest number of teams competing, but by 1997, 72 countries sent 731 runners to the race.

Beginning in 1981, Ethiopia won the men's team title for five straight years, but from 1986 to 1999, Kenya won 14 in a row, with usually Ethiopia or Morocco finishing second. John Ngugi of Kenya won the race five times between 1986 and 1992 and countryman Paul Tergat did likewise beginning in 1995. Near the end of the 20th century the IAAF tried to make the championships more open by reducing the size of teams from seven to six and introducing shorter races to attract more middle-distance runners. The changes made little difference, as the Africans still dominated.

The English Cross Country Union began a women's 2.5-mile international championship in 1967 at Barry, South Wales, with the men's event. England won the team championship and Doris Brown of the United States the individual title, which she retained over the next four years. Up to 1975 the United States and England fielded the strongest teams, then the Soviet Union dominated until 1990. Norwegian Grete Waitz won five titles in six years between 1978 and 1983 and Lynn Jennings of the United States won three times starting in 1990. With the demise of the Soviet Union, the North Africans began to dominate. From 1990 to 1999, Kenya won six times with Ethiopia winning twice and Portugal once.

## The Men's Marathon

*The marathon is my only girlfriend. I give her everything I have.* — Toshihiko Seko (1985)

### JIM PETERS — A MOST GALLANT MARATHON RUNNER

James Henry Peters, born in Homertown, London, on October 24, 1918, applied the massive training methods pioneered by Zatopek to the marathon and changed the race forever. He began his series of amazing performances in 1952. When he retired in 1954, he had run four of the six fastest marathons up to that time. Peters knew only one way to run a marathon — all out from the front, regardless of the competition or race conditions. Unfortunately this trait led to a premature end to his career.

Peters was a competent track performer, winning the AAA six-mile and 10-mile titles. But after being lapped by Zatopek in the 1948 Olympic 10,000-meter final, he felt humiliated and decided to retire from running. His coach Albert "Johnny" Johnston convinced him that he had promise as a marathon runner and urged him to give the longer race a try. In November 1949, at age 31, Peters began training for the marathon.

At the time, most marathoners trained by running long distances at a slow pace three or four days a week using long walks to supplement their running. Peters ran every day, keeping the pace fast, and omitted the walking. He wrote in his autobiography *In the Long Run* (1955): "The body has got to be conditioned to stand up to the stresses and strains which it is going to meet in an actual race and therefore it is useless running at a 6-min/mile pace if you hope to race at 5½ min/mile."

By late 1951 Peters had increased his training runs from seven to 10 a week. He found that all this short but fast training gave him more speed and stamina than he ever had before.

In the 1952 AAA marathon, Peters took the lead from the beginning and covered the first 15 miles (24 km) in 1:17:23. He increased his lead to nearly three minutes at 20 miles (32 km), but his legs began to ache and he slowed slightly. Feeling tired over the last three miles, he thought he was going to have a slow time. When he ran into the stadium, excited timekeepers were looking incredulously at their watches. His time was 2:20:42. He had beaten Yun Bok Suh's world best by almost five minutes.

Peters continued with his rigorous training. "I rarely ran more than 16 miles (26 km) a day in training," he wrote. "But I did good, fast quality miles. You see, speed and stamina are yoked together. And if you do a lot of speed work, the more you do, you build up the stamina to do a marathon."

His dropping out at 30 km in the 1952 Olympic Marathon won by Zatopek was a major disappointment. Peters may have not been fully recovered from his 2:20.42 performance six weeks earlier, and he had arrived at the Games after a harrowing nine-hour flight on a York transport plane. The plane was struck by lightning and Peters, exposed to a cold draft from an open door, became violently ill. He arrived in Helsinki sick, stiff and with a headache. In 1953 he resumed his marathon running, lowering the world best twice more, running 2:18.40 and 2:18.34, becoming the first marathoner to run the distance under 2:20.

His last great race was on June 26, 1954, when he defended his British national title at the Polytechnic Marathon. In the 10 months previous to this race he had covered 4,474 miles (7,204 km) in practice. He did not go all out at the "Poly" because he wanted to save something for upcoming races in Vancouver and Berne. Still, he managed to run 2:17:39.4, another world best.

In August 1954, Peters flew to Vancouver for the Empire Games where he, along with Bannister and Landy's "mile of the century," were the star attractions. Vancouver proved to be his last marathon. Several things conspired to make this race a disaster for the gritty world champion. The course was unusually hilly and on driving over it several times, the odometer in the car Peters was riding in consistently read 27 miles (43.5 km). He protested to the officials who claimed it was only 250 feet over distance.

The race was held at noon on a very hot day. Many runners of Peters's day drank very little during a marathon, considering it a sign of weakness. Peters expected teammate Stan Cox, who was in superb condition, to give him a tough race. Worst of all, Peters had no one on the course to give him his position during the race, which led to his running needlessly fast over the latter part of the course.

The runners began with three tough miles winding up a long hill. Peters started slowly, but soon went surging through the field with Cox following. At eight miles (12.9 km) he sprinted up another hill, breaking away from Cox and taking the lead. From then on Peters continued to build on his lead. He wrote in his autobiography:

By the time I came to the last feeding station, which was only half a mile from the stadium, I still thought that Stan was close behind. I was completely unaware that at somewhere about 24 miles, poor Stan had collapsed from sunstroke and had run into a telegraph pole — so that with less than ¾ mile to go, I actually had a lead of nearly 3.5 miles from the next competitor.

If only I had known that, I could have *stopped* at the last feeding station, had a good sponge down and trotted in slowly.

In a horrifying scene reminiscent of Dorando Pietri in the 1908 London Olympics, Peters entered the stadium like a puppet with some of its strings broken. He collapsed on the track then managed to get up, then collapsed several more times before Mick Mayes, the masseur for the British team, caught him and helped carry him to his dressing room. The race was won by Joe McGhee of Scotland, who had himself collapsed five times during the race and was waiting for an ambulance when he heard Peters was out. He got up and stumbled to the finish to win in 2:39:36.

After a week's stay in the Shaughnessy Hospital, Peters decided to retire. His ordeal had been so terrifying that he was not sure he would survive another collapse in the heat. He also believed it likely that the 1956 Olympic marathon in Melbourne, the race he most wanted to win, would be run in hot weather.

In 1976, Peters was invited back to Vancouver to symbolically rerun the last lap of the race. In characteristic fashion, he shed forty pounds (18 kg) before going back. Twenty-four thousand fans were on hand to see the great marathon runner triumphantly finish the lap that had given him so much trouble 22 years earlier.

## ABEBE BIKILA— TRIUMPH AND MISFORTUNE

Although Algerians Boughera El Ouafi in 1928 and Alain Mimoun in 1956 both won Olympic marathons, they ran under the flag of France. Abebe Bikila, a thin, high cheek-boned Ethiopian, was the first black African to win an Olympic gold medal while competing for his native country. His colorful personality, and one of the most fluid and efficient running styles ever seen, made him perhaps the most admired and respected marathoner ever.

Bikila was born in Debre Birhan, Ethiopia, on July 7, 1932, the same day of the Olympic Marathon in Los Angeles. He grew up herding cows and drinking huge amounts of milk. In 1951 he enlisted in the 5th Infantry Regiment of the Imperial Bodyguard. His regiment stressed physical fitness and at first Bikila preferred playing soccer. One day while working out on the track, he happened to see a group training for the Melbourne Olympics. Their smart track uniforms and the admiration everyone seemed to have for them prompted Bikila to announce to his surprised friends, "One day I too will go to foreign lands as a track athlete."

In 1955 at age 22 Bikila began his running career. At first he was self-coached, but in 1959 he went to a training camp sponsored by the Ethiopian government. The camp was at 6,000 feet (1,829 m) above sea level. Onni Niskanen, a Swede who had been hired in 1946 to coach Ethiopia's military athletics, became Bikila's coach. At the camp, Bikila ran once a day doing a mixture of cross country and road runs at distances up to 20 miles, with occasional repeat 1,500 meter runs on the track.

It did not take Niskanen long to recognize Bikila's gift for running. In August 1960, in a competition to select the Ethiopian Olympic team, Bikila ran the marathon in 2:21:23. Although the race was at an altitude of 6,000 feet, Bikila's time was still two minutes under Zatopek's Olympic record. Niskanen decided to keep the performance quiet, not wanting to put undue pressure on Bikila, who had never run outside Ethiopia.

At Rome in 1960, the Olympic marathon was held at night for the first time because of the heat and was run entirely outside the Olympic stadium. The favorites were world record holder (2:15:17) Sergey Popov of Russia, Rhadi Abdesselem of Morocco and Barry Magee from New Zealand. A problem arose for Bikila when he discovered that his running shoes were worn out. After buying a new pair and finding they gave him blisters, he quietly informed his coach he intended to run barefoot. He was used to running without shoes, although in most of his recent training he had worn them.

The strategy that Bikila used in most of his marathons was to start slowly and accelerate gradually to the constant-pace speed he wanted to run. Once he caught the leader he would follow until the leader began to tire. If the leader never slowed, Bikila would attempt to break away at a predetermined point in the race. Shortly after the start, a group of four moved to the front — Keily of Great Britain, Vandendriessche of Belgium, Rhadi of Morocco and Bikila. At about 11 miles (18 km) Rhadi put on a burst and gained a 200-meter lead on everyone but Bikila, who was left 60 meters back. By 12.4 miles (20 km) Bikila had caught up again and at 15.5 miles (25 km) the two Africans led Magee and Popov by 1:24.

The duel continued as they turned onto the torch-lit Appian Way. Bikila followed Rhadi until less than a mile from the finish where he moved smoothly away to win by 25 seconds. He finished in 2:15:16.2, breaking Popov's world best by .8 seconds, and the Olympic record by nearly eight minutes.

When asked why he ran the race barefoot Bikila replied, "We train in shoes, but it's much more comfortable without them." Pictures of his feet after the race showed he had suffered not even a blister. Combined with Rhadi's silver medal, Bikila's victory marked the beginning of the domination of Olympic distance running by Africans.

Bikila returned home an instant hero, second in popularity only to the emperor himself. But in December 1960, members of the Royal Guard attempted a coup and Bikila was jailed for a short time. Fortunately he had not been involved in the plot and was released. Those who had participated in it were hanged.

In the spring of 1963, Bikila and his teammate Mamo Wolde journeyed to the United States to run the Boston Marathon. Although both men spent several days training on the snow-covered course, neither could cope with the high winds and relative cold (low 50s Fahrenheit) at Boston that year. Bikila ran at a record pace up to 20 miles (32.2 km). Then, pierced by a cold wind blowing in from Boston Harbor, he stiffly shuffled the last six miles to finish a disappointing fifth in 2:24:43.

In 1964 at Tokyo, Bikila was not an unknown, but was still not favored to win. Forty days earlier he been operated on for appendicitis and had been able to do little training. When he arrived in Tokyo, he still limped as he walked down stairs. In addition to Bikila, Australian Ron Clarke and American Buddy Edelen were favored. The local favorite was Kokichi Tsuburaya of Japan.

Clarke jumped into the lead and ran the first five km in a very fast 15:06. Bikila caught up at four miles and he and Jim Hogan of Ireland followed Clarke through 10 km in 30:14. Nearing the nine-mile (15 km) mark, Clarke and Hogan began to drop back. At the halfway turnaround, Bikila led by five seconds over Hogan, with Clarke having fallen well behind. By the 21-mile (33.8 km) mark Bikila had stretched his lead to two minutes 30 seconds.

Bikila entered the stadium alone to the cheers of 70,000 spectators, who watched history being made as he became the first man to win two Olympic marathons. His time of 2:12:11 beat the old world best by more than a minute and a half. Looking fresh, he fell to the ground and did a few exercises, remarking to reporters, "I could run another 10 kilometers." Later, an awed Ron Clarke observed, "That was the greatest performance ever in track and field."

Some four minutes after Bikila, Tsuburaya entered the stadium to the wild cheering of his countrymen. Ten yards behind him was Basil Heatley of Great Britain, who passed the tiring Japanese runner on the last curve to finish second, while Tsuburaya held on for the bronze medal. Tsuburaya never recovered from losing the silver medal in full view of his countrymen. In January 1968 he committed suicide, leaving behind a terse note saying, "Cannot run any more."

When he arrived in Mexico City in 1968, Bikila had high hopes for his third Olympic marathon victory, although he had been hampered by a leg injured earlier in Spain. When asked about his competition, he replied, "I am afraid of no one. Mamo [Wolde] can race me, but I know I shall beat Mamo. And the others—I don't even know their names. People who want to know the names and the faces are afraid they are going to lose the game." Bikila felt that the race being at more than 7,000 feet (2,134 m) above sea level gave him an advantage despite his injury.

After nine miles (15 km) he literally fell out of the race. The pain from the stress fracture in his left fibula became so intense that he fainted. His teammate Mamo Wolde went on to win the race in a respectable 2:20:26. In 1992 Wolde was jailed as a political prisoner and as of this book's publication has not been released.

Bikila never ran another marathon. Haile Selassie promoted him to captain, and by now Bikila had become a legend to Ethiopians, as, indeed, he had to marathon lovers everywhere. In 1969, while driving a Volkswagen that had been a gift from Emperor Selassie, Bikila collided with a car and was paralyzed from the waist down. Selassie had him flown to England for treatment, but there was no hope of recovery. "Men of

**Abebe Bikila winning his second Olympic Marathon in Tokyo, 1964 (photograph by Mstislav Botashev, courtesy of Nikolai Botashev).**

success meet with tragedy," Bikila said after the accident. "I was overjoyed when I won the marathon twice. But I accepted those victories as I accept this tragedy."

In 1973, Bikila suffered a brain hemorrhage and died at the age of 41, leaving a wife and four children. The emperor proclaimed a national day of mourning and 65,000 people attended the funeral. Bikila's running captivated millions. Even as seen in scratchy old Olympic highlight films, his effortless stride and the serene, almost haunting, expression on his face are impossible to forget.

## DEREK CLAYTON—"WATCH OUT FOR THAT BLOODY TREE"

Derek Clayton brought marathoning to a new level, breaking 2:12, 2:11, 2:10 and 2:09 for the first time. He was the first to run the marathon at under a five-minute/mile pace and his 1969 world best of 2:08:33 lasted for 12 years. Clayton was born in

Lancashire, England, but moved to Australia when he was 21. After trying the mile, then the 5,000 meters, the six-foot, two-inch (1.9 m) 160-pound (72.7 kg) Clayton found his 52-second quarter speed to be too slow and moved up to the marathon.

Like Peters and Zatopek, Clayton trained very hard. He ran twice a day, seven days a week, averaging 150 miles (241 km) and occasionally more than 200 miles (322 km) a week. Clayton was self-coached and did no intervals or training on the track. His morning sessions were easy, but three days a week he ran his afternoon workout with an almost reckless intensity. On Saturday he would run a full marathon in about 2:25. Clayton, like many other marathoners, had trouble with hot weather, saying:

> I trained very hard and when you do that you are walking the line between being healthy and injured. Secondly, I relied heavily on cool weather. I have a very high sweat-rate and I'm not a good heat runner. They were the two necessary preconditions for me to perform well.

Once during his weekly marathon he found that the summer heat caused his breathing to become labored and rapid, and he felt very tired. He wrote in his book *Running to the Top* (1980):

> Since I was at the 22-mile point in the run, I decided this was going to be one time when high temperatures wouldn't defeat me. Rather than slow down, I picked up the pace. And rather than release its grip, the heat wrapped around me even tighter. I began to stagger and lose my sense of where I was. Weaving, I headed for the side of the road. It was there that, still moving at a six minute/mile pace, I ran head-on into a tree. Luckily for me it was only a small tree!

Clayton's reckless training and his supreme self-confidence produced results, but it also led to a series of injuries. He needed four operations on his Achilles tendons, two on his knees and one for a heel spur. Both his world bests came after he had been forced to take long layoffs due to injuries. This suggests he probably trained too hard or at least didn't take enough rest between his hard runs. He was also a fierce competitor. Once he missed his drink at a water-stop during a marathon. One of his competitors, running alongside, graciously offered Clayton his bottle. After taking a drink, Clayton started to give it back, but changed his mind and threw it far off to the other side of the road.

He set his first world best on Japan's fast Fukuoka course in 1967. Clayton ran the first 20 km in 59:59 and was in the lead at the halfway point (1:03:22) when local favorite Seichiro Sasakio put on an amazing mid-race surge. Sasakio caught Clayton and they ran together until Sasakio was seized by a side stitch and had to drop back. Clayton's winning time of 2:09:36 was the first marathon run under 2:10 and was not beaten at Fukuoka for 14 years.

Two months before the 1968 Olympic Games, Clayton injured his right knee. This, and the high altitude at Mexico City, prevented him from finishing higher than seventh. He was determined to atone for this setback at Antwerp, Belgium, on May 30, 1969. The course was flat, the weather cool, and Clayton pushed himself to the limit. Running at night before a huge crowd, he sped through the first 10 km in 30:06, and the second in 30:24. He began to tire at about 17 miles (27 km), but still managed the third 10 km in 30:26.

"Then fatigue set in," he wrote in his biography,

> and I began to slow down. My mind began to wander as the exhaustion became too painful to concentrate on.... The harder I pushed, the more I realized that this exhaustion wasn't a wall, it was a swamp that grew muddier and deeper the harder I went. Still I pushed on.

Despite his fatigue, Clayton ran the fourth 10 km in 30:59. On finishing the race, he asked for his time, but heard nothing through the noise. Again he asked, and heard 2:08 shouted through the mayhem. He didn't hear the seconds, but it didn't matter, he had broken 2:09. His world best of 2:08:33 lasted for 12 years.

### BUDDY EDELEN — A FORGOTTEN HERO

Leonard "Buddy" Edelen, born in Harrodsburg, Kentucky, in 1937, continued the legacy of Americans George Seward, Deerfoot and Lon Myers by going to England and becoming a world champion. Edelen was a successful college runner at the University of Minnesota, winning the Big Ten two-mile championships in 9:03 in 1958. After setting an American record for 10,000 meters he failed to run fast enough to qualify for the 1960 Olympics at that distance. In a last-ditch effort to find a qualifying race, he worked his way to Finland on a freighter, only to find no races there either.

Broke and discouraged, he advertised in a Finnish newspaper offering to teach English lessons. In two months he had earned enough to go to England, where he found work as a school teacher. With Fred Wilt, Federal Bureau of Investigation agent and former outstanding distance runner, coaching him by mail from the United States, Edelen developed a rigorous 130–150 mile (209–242 km) a week training program. He combined long runs of up to 30 miles (48 km) with speed work such as 50 × 100 meters, 10 × 800 meters in 2:12 or 40 × 400 meters in 1:08.

During his four years in England, Edelen thrived on the British club system and, to coach Wilt's dismay, Guinness Stout. Edelen frequently ran cross country meets and raced on the track at distances as short as 800 meters. In 1962 he won the British AAA 10-mile championship in 48:31.8, be-coming the first American since Deerfoot to win a British distance championship. On a cold clear day in June 1963 at the Poly-technic Marathon, Edelen surprised him-self and everyone else when he ran a world best 2:14:28. The following year, his home-town of Sioux Falls, South Dakota, raised money for his trip back to the United States, to run the Olympic marathon trials at Yonkers, New York. Although the temper-ature was 91 degrees, he was well prepared and completely outclassed the field, win-ning by 20 minutes. Unwilling to rest, five days later he ran 20 × 440 and the next day felt a tightening in his back — the begin-nings of sciatica which would make run-ning almost unbearable and eventually end his career. Five months later, running in pain, he finished a credible sixth at Tokyo, but was never again able to train or race at his former level.

Edelen was painfully aware that United States distance runners of his day were often laughed at in international races and did his utmost to change the situation. De-spite his pioneering efforts, he never got much recognition in his home country. He retired from running at age 28 and died of cancer in 1997 at age 59.

### FRANK SHORTER AND BILL RODGERS — KINGS OF THE ROAD

America produced three more out-standing male marathoners in the 1970s and early 1980s. Collectively they helped create a worldwide running boom that is still with us. Frank Shorter was born in Munich in 1947 where his father was an Army doctor. As a student at Yale, he trained under Bob Giegengack, who taught him how to coach himself and convinced him he had a bright future as a marathoner. Shorter didn't re-ally get serious about running until his se-nior year, when he increased his training mileage by switching to twice a day run-ning. In June 1969, he finished first in the NCAA six miles (29:00).

Shorter's running career really took off when he moved to Gainsville, Florida, in 1970. There he trained with Jack Bacheler, probably the tallest world-class marathoner ever. The six-foot, six-inch (2 m), 159-pound (72 kg) Bacheler finished ninth in the 1972 Olympics. Shorter had two traits that set him apart from many other marathoners. He excelled at running in the heat and had a smooth, efficient stride. Encouraged by Bacheler, who taught him to enjoy hard training and the importance of doing high mileage, Shorter improved rapidly and in December 1971 lowered his marathon time by five minutes when he ran 2:12:51 to win the Fukuoka Marathon.

The 1972 Olympic marathon field was crowded with outstanding runners. Defending champion Mamo Wolde of Ethiopia was there, along with Derek Clayton and 1968 silver medalist Kenji Kimihara. England's Ron Hill, who had run under 2:10 in winning the Commonwealth Championships in 1970, was considered the favorite by many. Shorter, who earlier in the Games had finished fifth in the 10,000 meters, was considered a possible dark horse, but few thought he would win.

In the first mile, Shorter narrowly averted disaster. He tried to shoot through a gap between a photographer's bus and a fence. Getting caught between the two, he had to stop and double back around the bus. After pounding on the bus with his fist, he soon was back with the lead group, passing five km in 15:51. "I took off at the 15-km point," Shorter later wrote.

And ran very hard to the 20-km mark. No one went with me. Why should they? Running that much faster than an even pace so early in the race was too much of a risk. The other competitors didn't know I had been training on the track to make such a move earlier than expected, recover and then hopefully resume running at race pace with a lead. I built a lead of more than a minute, eased off and cruised to the finish and the gold medal.

When he entered the stadium, the expected ovation never came. A prankster hiding outside had run in and crossed the finish line just before Shorter reached the stadium. Shorter's winning time of 2:12:20 was just eight seconds off Bikila's Olympic record.

William Henry "Bill" Rodgers, like Shorter, was born in 1947. He began running in high school in Newington, Connecticut, in 1963 and by his senior year was the state cross country champion. Rodgers was even slower than Shorter in getting started on his marathon career. From 1966 to 1970 he ran track and cross country at Wesleyan University, but his training was low key and his success only moderate. After graduation, he at first had little commitment to running, but after

Frank Shorter (right), America's most successful Olympic marathoner (United States Olympic Committee).

losing his job at a Boston Hospital he began
running 15 miles (24 km) a day.

Rodgers joined the Boston Track Club
in late 1973 and came under the coaching
of Bill Squires, who persuaded him to add
a session of long intervals to his weekly
training program. This, in addition to his
arduous 15–20 mile runs on the roads, improved Rodgers's fitness dramatically. In
March 1975 he ran his first world class race,
finishing third in the International Cross
Country Championship in Morocco. This
was the highest an American had ever
finished and an amazing performance for
someone whose training had been limited
to the snow-covered roads of New England.

A month later at the Boston Marathon,
Rodgers ran possibly his best race ever. Ron
Hill of England, who had set the Boston
record of 2:10:30, and Canadian Champion
Jerome Drayton were the favorites. By 15
km only Drayton was still with Rodgers. "I
can remember some woman yelling out 'Go,

**Bill Rodgers, who along with Shorter took
marathoning and road racing to new heights
in the United States (courtesy Bill Rodgers).**

Jerome! Go, Jerome,'" Rodgers wrote in
*Marathoning* (1982). "It irritated me, hearing a Boston spectator rooting for a Canadian. I was an unknown in my own town...
So I really poured it on." When Rodgers
reached the hills of Newton, Drayton was
no longer in sight. Because of his inexperience, Rodgers came to complete stops four
or five times during the race. These stops
were to drink and once to tie a shoelace. He
still finished in an American record 2:09:55.

Shorter beat Rodgers by seven seconds
in the 1976 U.S. Olympic trial and was favored to win the Olympic marathon in
Montreal. But this time, unlike in 1972, his
surging tactics caught no one by surprise.
It also rained during the race and Shorter,
who ran superbly in the heat, tended to
tighten up in the rain. Rodgers set the early
pace, passing five km in 15:19 and 10 km in
30:48. Then Shorter took over and led a
dozen runners past nine miles (15 km) in
46:00. Shorter surged several times to try to
drop the lead pack, but only succeeded in
reducing it to eight. Halfway through the
race Rodgers broke down. Suffering from
dehydration and cramps, he would have to
struggle just to finish.

At 15.5 miles (25 km) Shorter opened
a 30-meter gap, but could not shake Waldemar Cierpinski, an unknown former steeplechase runner from East Germany. Cierpinski, who had carefully studied Shorter's
training methods and racing tactics, had decided the way to beat the defending champion was to employ Shorter's own tactics.
When Cierpinski noticed that each of
Shorter's surges was a little weaker, he
countered with his own and just after 18.6
miles (30 km) moved into the lead. Shorter
struggled to stay in contact and at one point
cut Cierpinski's lead from 200 to 20 meters,
but the East German surged again and
Shorter could not respond.

Cierpinski was confused at the finish
and ran an extra lap, but still won in 2:09:55.
Shorter finished second in 2:10:45. Teammate Don Kardong, running a conservative

race, moved up to third place entering the stadium but was out-sprinted by Karel Lismont of Belgium for the bronze medal. Rodgers finished 40th in 2:25:14. Four years later, Cierpinski ran the marathon at the Olympics in Moscow, where he won a close race in 2:11:03.

Besides his Olympic medals, Shorter won the highly regarded Fukuoka Marathon four times, but he was hampered by injuries over the latter part of his career. After the Montreal Olympics he never ran up to his previous level in the marathon, although he excelled at shorter road races for several more years.

Rodgers ran poorly in his only Olympic race, but he also went on to have a long and highly successful career of marathon and road races, including four marathon wins at Boston and four at New York. He was a strong runner, able to run repeat miles at a 4:20 pace, "til the cows came home." He was also able to run 100–150 miles per week and maintain a racing schedule of about 35 races, year after year, without serious injury or burnout. Rodgers ran an amazing 28 marathons under 2:15 during his long career. "We're all brothers and sisters in this sport," said Rogers when he was inducted into the Road Runners Club of America Hall of Fame in 1978. "I'll see you on the roads."

Both Rodgers and Shorter worked to kill amateurism, which, despite some noble elements, had long been rife with hypocrisy and unfairness. By the mid–1980s serious and talented runners like Rodgers and Shorter could legally make a living from the sport. After the 1988 Olympic Games, the IOC voted to declare all professionals eligible for the Olympics, subject to the approval of the international federations in charge of each sport. Despite all their other achievements, Rodgers and Shorter will probably be remembered most for taking road-running and marathoning from fringe sports to being accepted by the public and engaged in by millions.

## ALBERTO SALAZAR—IT'S NOT BRAGGING IF YOU CAN DO IT

Alberto Salazar took over where Shorter and Rodgers left off. Born in Cuba in 1958, his family moved to the United States in 1960 and he grew up in Wayland, Massachusetts. In 1976 Salazar entered the University of Oregon, where he was coached by Bill Dellinger. By 1980 Salazar had won both the AAU and NCAA cross country championships and had lowered his best 10,000 meters on the track to below 28 minutes. On October 28, 1980, at New York, he ran his first marathon. Before the race he predicted he would run 2:10 and fulfilled his promise by winning in 2:09:41.

The following year Salazar again predicted his time for the New York Marathon, saying: "I really think I should be able to run 2:08." He kept his word, with almost perfect marathon weather—cloudy, cool (55 degrees)—he surged between the 16th

**Alberto Salazar (University of Oregon).**

and 17th mile and broke Jose Gomez of Mexico, his stiffest competition. His winning time of 2:08:13 beat Clayton's 12-year-old world best by 21 seconds. Unfortunately, the course was later found to be 148 meters short and Salazar lost his unofficial record.

In April 1982 Salazar ran the fastest Boston Marathon up to that time (2:08:51), being pushed all the way by Dick Beardsley, who finished only two seconds behind. Salazar again won at New York in 1982, but injuries hampered him for the rest of his career. He did have one more outstanding race in him. Despite his injuries he kept training and years later, unable to regain his speed, he moved up to an even longer race. In 1994 at age 36 he won the "uphill" version of the 54-mile Comrades ultra marathon in South Africa. The race alternates each year between running downhill and uphill. The "up" years feature a 2,600 ft. climb. Salazar won this "biggest ultra-marathon in the world" with a time of 5:38:39.

## CARLOS LOPES—
## A MASTERFUL RUNNER

Carlos Lopes not only won a gold medal and ran a world best for the marathon but became an inspiration for those who thought their running careers were over when they reached their mid–30s. He began running in his native Lisbon, Portugal, in his late teens and his first international success came when he won the 1975 World Cross Country Championship. The following year he finished second to Lasse Viren in the 1976 Olympic 10,000 meters. In March 1983, he completed his first marathon at Rotterdam. He was out-sprinted in the last few hundred meters by Robert de Castella of Australia, but still ran an impressive 2:08:39.

At the 1984 Los Angeles Olympics Lopes was 37 years old—too old, many thought, to be a contender. But he surged away from favorites Rob de Castella of Aus-

**Carlos Lopes, winner of the 1984 Olympic marathon (AAF/LPI 1984).**

tralia and Toshihiko Seko of Japan with five miles to go and won in 2:09:21, an Olympic record. Three months later Lopes was surprised in the Chicago Marathon by Britain's Steve Jones, who won with a world best 2:08:05. Six months later, in a planned world best attempt on the flat course in Rotterdam, Lopes, now 38 years old, took almost a minute off the old world best by running 2:07:12.

On April 17, 1988, Ethiopian Belayneh DinSamo improved the marathon world best to 2:06:50, a mark that stood for 10 years. Near the end of the 20th century the marathon world best plunged by 68 seconds in only 13 months.

At the 25th running of the Rotterdam Marathon on September 20, 1998, conditions were nearly perfect — sunny and windless with temperatures in the mid–40s to mid–50s (F). An unknown 28-year-old Brazilian, Ronaldo Da Costa, running only his second marathon, didn't catch the leaders until near the halfway point, which he reached in 64 minutes, 42 seconds. He then increased the pace dramatically, running the next two miles in 9:30. "I thought I must go hard to open a gap," he said later. Da Costa kept up his torrid pace and ran the second half of the race in an amazing 1:01:23 giving him 2:06:05. This slashed 3:52 off his PR and broke the world best by 45 seconds. An elated Da Costa still had enough energy to turn two cartwheels after he crossed the finish line.

Da Costa's world best challenged the beliefs that marathoners had to be from Kenya or Ethiopia or had to be born at high altitudes to be successful. The 121-pound (55 kg) Brazilian employed an eight-week program to train for Berlin, running two 22-mile (35 km) runs per week in the hills above his hometown. His mileage peaked at about 120 miles (193 km) a week. In addition to his long runs, his program included 15 repeats of 1,000 meters in about 3:00 with 20 to 30 seconds' recovery time. He also did 25 repeats of 400 meters in 66 to 68 seconds, with a recovery time of 15 to 20 seconds. After his 22 mile runs, Da Costa completed his workouts with 10 to 15 100-meter sprints. He also included jumping and bounding exercises normally used by sprinters.

Da Costa's training and racing was interrupted in September 1999, when he was the target of three kidnapping attempts. He fled to the United States, but the turmoil surrounding the attempted kidnapping plus injuries caused him to race poorly.

On a cold (36 degrees F), windy October 1999 day in Chicago, Moroccan Khalid Khannouchi became the first man to break 2:06. Two-time Boston Marathon champion Moses Tanui from Kenya was confused by the distance markers which were in both miles and kilometers and broke away at 18 miles. He later admitted that this was three miles earlier than he originally intended to make his burst. Khannouchi, who had won the 1997 race and finished second in 1998, did not go with Tanui, but kept a steady pace and overtook him between mile 24 and 25 (39–40 km). After passing Tanui, Khannouchi went on to finish in 2:05.42, a world best.

## Women's Marathon

*My philosophy has always been, "When in doubt, run harder."*— Joan Benoit Samuelson (1985)

### The Right to Run— From Melpomene to Gibb

In the six-day races of the 1870s and 1880s Amy Howard and the other pedestriennes proved convincingly that women could run long distances as well as men, although perhaps not as fast. These performances were strangely overlooked or forgotten by the governing bodies and physical fitness experts that followed.

Women wanted to run the marathons from the beginning. There was a courageous woman who tried unsuccessfully to enter the 1896 Olympic marathon in Athens. She was a 30-year-old Syros-born Greek named Stamata Revithi. The Greek Olympic committee apparently forgot her name and called her "Melpomene" (from the muse of Greek tragedy). In a practice run three weeks before the race she completed the 40-km course on her own in 4½ hours, stopping only once for about 10 minutes to suck a few oranges. Melpomene was described as "a woman of the people with marked features and a tough and lively temperament." When her request to run the first Olympic Marathon was turned down, the Greek paper *Akropolis* wrote: "The Olympic Committee deserves to be reprimanded, because it was discourteous in refusing a lady's nomination. We can assure those concerned that none of the participants would have had any objection."

The 1928 Olympic women's 800 meter final in Amsterdam proved to be a huge setback for women's middle and long distance running. This was the first time a women's 800-meter race was included in the games. Running on a hot day, some of the lightly trained women collapsed after the race. Opponents of women's running seized on the incident and managed to get all women's races longer than 200 meters dropped from the Olympic program. Interest in women's distance running waned and for the next 30 years there was little women's participation in races longer than the sprints. Finally, in 1960 the 800 meters was restored to the Olympics, spurring a revival in women's distance running.

Roberta Gibb saw her first Boston marathon in 1964 and was fascinated by the race. She planned to run the race herself in 1965, but was injured. That summer she began training for the 1966 race and in the fall unofficially entered a three-day endurance horse race. She ran 40 miles (64 km) the first day and 25 (40 km) the second before dropping out.

Convinced of her ability to finish a marathon, she wrote to the Boston Athletic Association for an application. The BAA replied that women were not capable of running such distances and were not allowed to try. Undaunted, Gibb disguised herself in a blue hooded sweatshirt and, jumping from the bushes in Hopkinton, ran the 1966 race unofficially. She removed the sweatshirt on her way to Boston and finished unofficially in 3:22 — 302nd out of 415 finishers. Gibb wrote in *To Boston with Love* (1980), "I believed that once people knew women could run marathon distances the field would naturally open up."

News of her successful run spread around the country and the next year Kathrine Switzer ran also. She mailed in her application signed K. Switzer, and on the assumption that she was a man, the BAA sent her an official number. When the press bus passed her several miles into the race, someone noticed she wasn't a man after all. "Jock" Semple, the race co-director, leaped from the bus and tried to rip off her number, but Switzer's boyfriend, a burly hammer-thrower, intervened and Semple landed on the curb. Photographers and reporters on the bus had a field day and the photos and accounts were worldwide news.

Semple considered Switzer just an-

other of the publicity seekers, many in odd costumes, trying to make the news. "To me, it's sacred," Semple said of the race. "I can't stand for them weirdies to make a joke out of it." The public outcry that followed led to the first official women's competition at Boston in 1972. Other women in other countries also struggled to be allowed to run the marathon with the result that the women's marathon became an Olympic event in 1984.

At first, women's marathon times improved so dramatically that some were writing in scholarly journals that women would surpass men in the marathon by the year 2000. By the mid–1980s the rapid descent of the women's marathon world best had leveled off at about 10 percent greater than the men's. This is consistent with the difference between men's and women's records at other distances.

There is some controversy over who was the first woman to break three hours. Nina Kuscsik, who first ran Boston in 1969, wrote in *History of Women's Participation in the Marathon* (1977) that Beth Bonner of the United States was the first. Bonner ran the New York City Marathon in 2:55:22 on September 19, 1971. But a short time earlier, on August 31, 1971, a 28-year-old Australian, Adrienne Beames, had apparently run much faster. At Werribee, Victoria, Beames finished fifth overall in a field of 18 starters with a time of 2:46:30, lowering the women's world best by more than 15 minutes! The athletic press was skeptical of the performance because Beames had run no other outstanding performances up to that time. In a 1977 marathon in Phoenix, Arizona, Beames finished in 2:46:25, so her 1971 performance may well have been legitimate.

Jackie Hansen of the United States, whose training mileage went as high as 140 miles (225 km) a week, took the women's world best below 2:40 when she ran 2:38:19 at Eugene, Oregon on October 12, 1975. Hansen won the Boston Marathon in 1973 and between 1972 and 1982 won 12 out of 18 marathons.

## GRETE WAITZ—THE WOMAN WHO OWNED NEW YORK

Taking the women's world best below 2:30 required women with experience on the track. Grete Waitz from Norway began competing in international track in 1972 at age 18. Although she ran the 1,500 meters in 4:04, she did not have a fast enough finish to beat the Eastern Europeans. After failing to make the finals in the Montreal Olympics she considered retirement, but by that time the 3,000 meters had been added to women's track. She was more competitive at the 3,000 and set two world records (8:46.6 in 1975 and 8:45.4 in 1976). But she still didn't have a fast enough finish to win at the highest level. In 1978 Fred Lebow, director of the

**Grete Waitz, nine-time winner of the New York Marathon (AAF/LPI 1984, 45214 RH).**

New York Marathon, invited Waitz to run that race although she had never run further than 18 miles (29 km) at one time. Starting out cautiously, she ran negative splits (second half of the race faster than the first) and won her first marathon with a world best of 2:32:29.

She returned the following two years and set two more world bests (2:27:32 and 2:25:41). In all, she won New York an incredible nine times. Between 1978 and 1983 she also won the IAAF World Cross Country Championships five times; in 1983 she set another marathon world best of 2:25:29 in the London Marathon and won the inaugural IAAF World Championships Marathon in 2:28:09.

Waitz's marathon career paralleled that of Jim Peters of Britain in some respects. Both were experienced track runners who moved up to the marathon after being unable to win at the highest levels on the track. Both lowered the existing marathon records by huge amounts during their careers—Peters by eight minutes, Waitz by nine minutes. Both lost the biggest marathon races of their lives—races they were favored to win. Peters lost to Zatopek in the 1952 Olympics and Waitz to Joan Benoit Samuelson in the Los Angeles Games in 1984.

Waitz trained twice a day, running 90–100 miles a week. Her morning workouts were usually easy 30 to 60 minute runs, but in the afternoon she did quality work. She did at least one track workout a week, typically 8 × 1,000 meters with one to two minutes rest or 20 × 300. Both workouts were designed to bring her maximum heart rate to 180. Her training for the marathon was the same as for her track and cross country races except that she added a weekly long run of 15 to 20 miles leading up to a marathon.

In 1992 she ran New York, not to win nor to set a record, but as a favor to Lebow who was dying of cancer and wanted to run the New York marathon for the first time.

With her encouragement he finished his 69th and last marathon in 5:32. "Fred wanted me to try to win the marathon for the 10th time," she said. "But crossing the finish line with him in 1992 meant much more to me than a possible 10th victory."

### Joan Benoit Samuelson— America's Best Marathoner

Born in Cape Elizabeth, Maine, on May 16, 1957, Joan Benoit Samuelson took part in a variety of sports as a teenager, including skiing, field hockey and track. After a track career at Bowdoin College and North Carolina State she made her marathon debut in early 1979 in Bermuda. Making a "spur of the moment" decision to run, she finished in a respectable 2:50:54. Three months later, she entered the Boston Marathon and defeated the favorite Patti Lyons with a 2:35:15 performance.

The five-foot, three-inch (1.6m), 105-pound (48 kg) Samuelson won Boston again in 1981 in 2:30:16. The following year at Boston she gave the world a preview of what women may one day do in the marathon. She ran the first mile, which is slightly downhill in 4:47, then blazed past 10 km in 31:53, the halfway point in 1:08:23 and was still under a 2:20 marathon pace at 20 miles (1:46:44). Finishing in 2:22:43, she bettered Waitz's world best by over 2½ minutes.

Samuelson was mostly self-coached and ran about 120 miles a week when she was healthy. While training for a marathon, she did little running on the track, instead preferring continuous runs of six to fifteen miles. She wrote in *Running Tide* (1987), "If I feel good for nine straight days I run hard for nine straight days. I don't pencil in any easy days—they just happen, when my body won't cooperate. I always run the way I feel." As a marathon approached, she ran 20 miles every fifth day. On the other days she did a minimum of 10 miles in the morning and six in the afternoon. The week be-fore a marathon she tapered only slightly, still running at least 80 miles (129 km).

Less than two months before the 1984 Olympic trials she began have a knee problem so severe she could barely walk. Seventeen days before the trials she underwent arthroscopic knee surgery. Fortunately, the operation was a complete success and she won the trials in 2:31. The Los Angeles Olympic marathon was the first for women and included two other great runners, Grete Waitz and Ingrid Kristiansen. After two miles the lead pack still contained at least 30 runners and Samuelson didn't feel comfortable. The pace was too slow. She picked it up a little and by three miles was 20 yards in the lead. "We weren't running very fast and I was under control," she later said. "I didn't want to take the lead, necessarily. I wanted to run my own race. So I did what felt natural and didn't have any second thoughts about it."

By skipping the first water station she

Joan Samuelson, America's best marathoner to date (AAF/LPI 1984, 45273 RH).

managed to increase her lead even further. Grete Waitz, who was expected to be her strongest competition, was suffering from a back problem and didn't give chase until it was too late. Samuelson ran alone the rest of the way, emerging from the tunnel onto the track "like a little gray mouse skittering out of a hole." She had become the first woman Olympic marathon champion finishing with 2:24:52. Waitz was second and Rosa Mota from Portugal third.

Samuelson had one more major triumph, the 1985 Chicago Marathon, where she defeated Ingrid Kristiansen by running a personal best of 2:21:21. From then on injuries plagued her career, preventing her from achieving her greatest ambition — to break 2:20.

Ingrid Kristiansen at the World Championship in Rome, 1987. She was the first woman to hold world records in 5,000 meters, 10,000 meters and the marathon (courtesy Ingrid Kristiansen).

Ingrid Kristiansen, who was described earlier, was the next unofficial world-record holder. She started her marathon career in 1980 by winning the Stockholm Marathon in 2:34:25. At her peak she ran more than 100 miles a week following the "hard/easy" approach. She trained alone and because of the cold climate, often did her speed work on a treadmill while wearing a heart rate monitor, to more accurately gauge her progress.

Kristiansen finished fourth in the Olympic marathon in 1984 but came back strong in 1985. In preparation for the 1985 London Marathon she ran mile after mile on her treadmill. In front of her she had pinned a picture of Joan Benoit Samuelson setting her world best. Every day Kristiansen imagined herself running through the streets of London, ending with a victory in a world best time. That year at the London Marathon she reached the halfway point in 1:10:10, and tenaciously hung on to record 2:21:06 and break Benoit Samuelson's world best by 1:37.

Surprisingly, Kristiansen's record proved very difficult to break. "I thought when I ran 2:21 I could break it myself the year after," she said years later. "I thought it was an easy record to break. But maybe it's a better time than I thought." Thirteen years later, Tegla Loroupe (THE-gluh luh-ROO-pay), a 90 pound (41 kg) Kenyan broke it by 23 seconds when she won the 1998 Rotterdam marathon in 2:20:47. Loroupe bettered that performance by four seconds in Berlin in 1999. Loroupe's world bests were controversial as she used male pacers in both races.

## Beyond the Marathon

*Most of us who have been running these events [ultras] for many years do not clutter our minds with over analysis of how things work. There are only three things to remember: drink like a fish, eat like a pig, and run like a turtle.*—Charlie Gabri (1996)

Ultra running covers a wide range of distances from 30 to 1,000 miles. The most popular distances over the years have been 50 miles, 100 km, 100 miles and 24 hours on the low end and six-day and 1,000 mile races on the high end. Also popular are annually contested races such as the Comrades ultra marathon in South Africa (54 miles, 450 yards, started in 1921) and the London-to-Brighton race (52 miles, 200 yards, first run in 1837 and revived in 1951). These races annually draw thousands of runners from all over the world.

After six-day racing died out in the late 1880s, not much progress was made at ultra running until Arthur Newton and the Bunion Derby runners of the late 1920s. In 1953 Wally Hayward, a South African who won the Comrades ultra marathon five times, made an assault on Newton's 24-hour record of 152 miles, 540 yards. Shooting for 170 miles, he reached 100 miles in 12 hours, 46 minutes and stopped for a shower. But the shower caused him to stiffen badly and he struggled the rest of the way. He still managed to cover 159 miles for a world best. Haywood's record lasted until 1973 when Ron Bently of Great Britain broke it with 161 miles, 545 yards (259.6 km).

## YIANNIS KOUROS— ## ULTRA RUNNER OF THE CENTURY

The first 149-mile Spartathlon race between Athens and Sparta took place in 1983 with a strong field racing over roughly the same course used by Phiedippides in 490 B.C. Among the last minute entrants was a 27-year-old unknown Greek, Yiannis Kouros. When the second-place runner reached Sparta, he was surprised to find that he had been beaten by over two and a half hours by Kouros, whose time was 21 hours, 53 minutes, 42 seconds. Rumors were rife that during the night Kouros must have

taken a ride in a car as some of the other runners were known to have done.

In July 1984 Kouros ran his first six-day race at Randall's Island, New York. By the end of the first 24 hours he had covered 162.8 miles (262 km) and was 46 miles (74 km) ahead of the next runner. Experienced observers agreed that the Greek had "blown it" and would not survive his too-fast early pace. By the end of the second day the five-foot, five-inch (1.6 m) 140 pound (63.6 kg) Kouros had covered 266.3 miles (429 km) and was still going strong. But the pace finally began to take its toll. Running stiffly on bleeding feet, he managed only 88.7 miles (143 km) on day four. On day five Kouros regained some of his lost energy and covered 93.6 miles (151 km). Littlewood's 1888 record of 623 miles (1,003 km) was now in danger. Kouros pushed on to the end, covering 635 miles, 1,023 yards (1,023.5 km) to beat Littlewood's 96-year-old record by 12 miles (19 km). The resurgence of six-day racing was short lived. Interest began to wane soon after the men's and women's 19th century records had been broken.

In 1985 Kouros returned to Athens and silenced those who doubted his 1983 Spartathlon victory. He again won easily and lowered his own record by an hour and a half. After winning the 1987 Sydney-to-Melbourne 658-mile race, Kouros returned the following year, gave the rest of the field a 12-hour start, and still won. Kouros moved to Australia in 1990 and eventually became an Australian citizen. Two factors that contributed to Kouros's success were his relatively fast best marathon time (2:24:01) and his remarkable ability to go without sleep for prolonged periods.

In 1997 Kouros produced what ultra running expert Andy Milroy described as "probably the most phenomenal endurance feat in modern times." The 41-year-old Kouros had been frustrated for a decade in his efforts to break 300 km (186.3 miles) in 24 hours. Heavy rains and injuries had thwarted previous attempts but on Octo-

Yiannis Kouros being given food and water during the 1985 Sydney to Melbourne race. He won by a huge margin in just over five days for the 960 km course (Australian Archives, Series A6180/17, Caption Number 23/4/85/13. Commonwealth of Australia copyright, used by permission).

ber 4, he was in the best shape of his life and ready for an ultimate effort.

Going out hard, he reached 100 miles in 11 hours, 57 minutes, 59 seconds. Still running strong, he passed 124¼ miles (200 km) in 15 hours, 10 minutes 27 seconds, a world record. No ultra race is easy and Kouros found it necessary to force his increasingly exhausted body on. He reached 138 miles (222 km) in 17 hours, but had a "bad patch" at 20 hours, slowing slightly. As dawn broke, his spirits began to revive and he shouted for more food to eat as he ran. He finished 24 hours with 188 miles, 1,038 yards (303.506 km), beating the old record by a whopping 17 miles (27 km). "I will run no more 24-hour races," he said. "This record will stand for centuries."

## WOMEN'S ULTRA-RUNNING

Geraldine Watson, a South African, competed in the Comrades ultra marathon unofficially in 1932 and returned to finish in 9:31:25 in 1933. The following year she took part in a 100-mile road race and, fighting strong winds, became the first woman to cover 100 miles within 24 hours, recording a time of 22:22. Despite Watson's pioneering performances women's ultra running in the 20th century did not really get started until well into the second half of the century.

Women ran unofficially in the London to Brighton race in 1972 and officially in 1980, and the Comrades ultra marathon was officially opened to women in 1977. Probably the two greatest women ultra runners of the modern era are American Ann Trason, who excels at 50–100 miles, and Eleanor Robinson from Britain, who has set world bests in races from 24 hours to six days and longer.

Ann Trason, born in 1961, is five feet four inches (1.6 m) and weighs 105 pounds (47.7 kg). A former high school track star, she tried a triathlon in 1984, but nearly drowned during the swim portion and never tried another. That same year, she was hit by a car while riding her bike, causing her to turn to running. A couple of years later she heard of a 50-mile trail race, tried it and found her sport. In 1991 she ran 50 miles on the road in five hours, 40 minutes 18 seconds for a world record for women. That same year she covered 100 miles on the road in 13 hours, 47 minutes 41 seconds for another world best. Trason has proved equally adept at track ultras. In 1995 she set the world mark for 100 km, seven hours and 48 seconds.

Trason is famous for being the only woman to win a U.S. national ultra-marathon race open to both sexes. She trains twice a day, running 90–140 miles per week. Once a week she runs a 50-mile trail run. She also lifts weights and runs track sessions consisting of 400 meter repeats with 100-meter recovery jogs.

Eleanor Robinson, born in 1947, is five feet eight inches (1.7 m) tall and weighs 129 pounds (58.6 kg). Her best time for 50 miles is 6 hours, 4 minutes; 100 miles, 14 hours, 43 minutes 40 seconds; and 1,000 miles, 13 days, 1 hour 54 minutes. She broke Amy Howard's six-day record by covering 501 miles (807 km) in February 1986, and has since improved her six-day total to 538.3 miles (867 km). Robinson runs about 100 miles a week in training at a steady pace.

# Epilogue

*Those who ignore history have no future.*
— Robert A. Heinlein

Having traced running from its beginning, one might ask, can we use this knowledge to get a glimpse of what lies ahead? The most accurate predictions are often those that go far back into the past and project past and current trends a short distance into the future. With this in mind, here are some thoughts on the future of running.

On a technical level, the current custom of timing races to the nearest 0.01 second can easily be improved on. Timing to 0.01 seconds is adequate for the present but when a large number of co–world-record holders begin to appear in events such as the 100 meters, more precise timing will be needed. The capability already exists to time running events to 0.001 second or even 0.0001 if desired. To be of any value, more precise timing must be accompanied by correspondingly precise course measurement.

The current method of starting sprint races can be improved on. Allowing a somewhat arbitrary 0.1 second for a sprinter to legally react to the gun is unappealing because it limits human achievement. There are ways to start a race fairly that do not put any limits on reaction time as the ancient Greeks so nobly demonstrated with their starting gates over 2,000 years ago. The governing bodies of track and field have been notoriously conservative in the past, so don't expect major changes in starting methods in the near future.

The effects of winds and altitude on sprint races are two areas that also need some careful thought and perhaps change. A 2 m/s head wind—the current legal limit—causes a 100-meter time to be slower by approximately 0.1 second than if the race were run with no wind. A tail wind of the same amount causes the time to be about 0.1

second faster. If the maximum allowable tailwind was reduced to 0.2 m/s, then a runner could never gain an advantage from a tail wind or be slowed by a head wind. This is because the wind would not change the time by more than 0.01 second — the accuracy of current timing. But few records would be set since the winds are rarely that calm. Some would like to see the wind limit increased to 3, 4, or 5 m/s so that more records could be set. But this would make setting a record even more dependant on a strong tailwind.

The effect of winds on a sprinter's time depends on the wind's velocity, the runner's frontal area and his or her "drag coefficient." These quantities can all be measured or estimated with reasonable accuracy. A possible solution might be to place multiple wind gauges along the track to measure the wind profile very accurately. Currently only a single wind gauge is used which has been found not to give a true picture of wind magnitude and direction over the complete race course. The wind profile from these wind-gauges could be sent to a computer that would use a "winds-effect" model to adjust the measured time for each runner to a zero-wind condition. These calculations would take only milliseconds and the "zero-wind" time could be displayed as the official time. With this approach, records could be set under any wind conditions as long as the winds-effect model was valid for those conditions.

Altitude also has a large influence on both short and long distance races. For races up to 400 meters in length, it is easier to run a fast time at high altitude, for race distances of a mile and over, it is more difficult. The altitude effect on sprint times is almost purely aerodynamic. Less dense air at high altitude results in less drag opposing the runners and makes for faster times. This effect can be modeled in much the same way as for winds and the measured times "corrected" to some standard condition. This procedure would not work for longer races

where the effect of altitude is much more complicated.

An Olympic gold medal is currently the most coveted prize in running and will probably remain so for the foreseeable future. World championships for track and the marathon and the continual addition of sometimes obscure sports to the Olympic program have not diluted the desirability of winning a gold medal in an Olympic running event.

If new running events are ever added to the Olympic program, an ultra race is a worthy candidate. Section I of this book makes the case that humans evolved to excel at running distances longer than the marathon, yet no race of this type is included in the Olympics. Safety of the runners has been cited as a reason, but two hundred years of ultrarunning, including the six-day races in the 1880s and the Bunion Derbies in the 1920s have proved that ultrarunning need not be dangerous.

A strong case can also be made for restoring cross country to the Olympic program. Dropping the sport after the 1924 Olympics was never justified. Cross country has a long tradition and is a healthy, invigorating sport that is popular worldwide.

Some countries have historically excelled at certain running events. For example, Americans have led the world at 400 meters and below since the days of Lon Myers in the 1880s. Trinidad and Namibia are also especially strong in the sprints. The Finns dominated distance races for most of the first half of the 20th century, but the Kenyans in recent years have reigned supreme. Kenya's dominance started in the late 1960s, and is remarkable since it is a country of only about 30 million. Morocco and Ethiopia are also strong in the longer races.

American women are strong at short distances as are the Germans. No country currently dominates women's distance running. One might expect the same countries that excel in men's distance running to do likewise for women. Social customs that prevent many women in those countries from competing are probably the reason why this has not occurred.

Since most of the nations of the world have now been exposed to running at its highest levels we probably have a fairly accurate picture or the relative strengths of the different countries. Yet there may still be surprises in store. The vast talent pools of much of Africa, South America and Asia remain largely untapped.

Running in many of the East European countries has declined since the breakup of the Soviet bloc. The East German "sports machine" had sophisticated talent identification, experienced coaches, good sports science and motivated athletes. It also included what the East Germans called "supporting means" or banned performance-enhancing drugs given to athletes, starting in their preteen years, sometimes without their knowledge. The East Germans were willing to go to such lengths to develop their athletes because they felt athletic prowess demonstrated the superiority of their form of government. This system produced results and may provide (hopefully without the drugs) a model for the future.

Performance enhancing drugs, primarily steroids, human growth hormone and EPO, are the biggest problem facing running today. Random drug testing, which started in 1989, was a big step forward in detecting steroid use. Effective tests for EPO are being developed but no test for HGH exists. Currently, positives drug tests are sometimes covered up and runners testing positive are routinely found innocent by their national courts and running federations. These national federations are in the untenable position of having to look out for the interests of the same people they are trying to catch.

In the six-day races of the 1880s, runners could legally use any drugs they chose.

One reporter, on entering a runner's tent without permission, counted 31 different drugs and stated that "every one was for active use." Some have suggested we return to this system — that drug testing is hopeless and runners should be allowed to use whatever drugs they want. A counter argument is that today's drugs are so effective that if they were made legal, every runner who wants to compete on a world level would be forced to use them to be competitive. Even if a solution is found to the drug problem, cloning, genetic therapy and artificial body parts are on the horizon and may be even more difficult problems to solve.

Since the late 18th century when reliable timing came into use, times for running performances have improved by 20–25 percent. Yet in that short time (on the scale of human time on earth), it is hard to see how evolution could have made the average human any faster. It is possible that the top speed for humans, which occurs for about 15 meters in the middle of a 100-meter race, has already been approached. No sprinter has improved significantly on the top speed of Bob Hayes who was timed at about 27 mi/hr (43 km/hr) in the early 1960s. But even in the 100 meters, world records are still possible by improvements in starting, reaching top speed and maintaining top speed. Where we continue to improve the most is at increasing the distance we can run a fast pace.

Two of the world's greatest milers had very similar thoughts on future improvements in running. In 1935 Jack Lovelock wrote in his diary: "And what of the ultimate for the mile — there can be no ultimate at the present time. For I am unable to see where, as our knowledge of physiology and psychology increases there can be any limit to the human capacity for speed."

In 1994, on the 40th anniversary of Roger Bannister's historic four-minute mile, Herb Elliott was asked for his thoughts on future improvements in the mile. He echoed Lovelock's sentiments when he answered: "I think we're only on the border of understanding the interface between mind, spirit and body. I believe there is a quantum leap somewhere in the equation that we have yet to discover. There are all sorts of things that are possible."

# Bibliography

In writing this history I have consulted a large number of books, magazines, newspapers and other publications. In some cases I was forced to use secondary sources which I tried to verify where possible. The following works were found to be especially valuable and are recommended for those wanting to delve deeper into running history.

## *Major Sources for Section I*

Alexander, R. McNeill. "The Spring in Your Step." *New Scientist*, April 30, 1987, pp. 42–44.

Bortz, Walter M. "Physical Exercise as an Evolutionary Force." *Journal of Human Evolution* 14 (1984): 145–155

Bramble, Dennis M., and David R. Carrier. "Running and Breathing in Mammals." *Science* 219 (1983): 251–256.

Carrier, David R. "The Energetic Paradox of Human Running and Hominid Evolution." *Current Anthropology* 25, No. 4 (1984): 483–496. [The most important reference on prehumans as running hunters.]

_____. "The Purpose of Toes." *Discover*, February 1995 p. 32.

Garland, Theodore. "The Relation between Maximal Running Speed and Body Mass in Terrestrial Mammals." *Journal of Zoology* 199 (1982): 157–170.

Lewin, Roger. *The Origin of Modern Humans.* New York: Scientific American Library, 1993. [Excellent general reference on human evolution]

Morton, Dudley J. *The Human Foot: Its Evolution Physiology and Functional Disorders.* New York: Hafner, 1964.

Newman, Russell W. "Why Man Is Such a Sweaty and Thirsty Naked Animal." *Human Biology* 42 (1970): 12–27.

Schuster, Richard. "Toeing the Line: Why the Big Toe Sometimes Causes Big Problems for Runners." *The Runner*, 1982, p. 18.

_____. "Traces of the Past: Evolution and

Running injuries." *The Runner*, 1982, p. 12.

_____. "The Ultimate Human Race: How Running Has Affected Our Evolution." *The Runner*, 1981, p. 20.

Taylor, C. Richard. "Which Consumes More Energy (Two Legs vs Four)." *Science* 179 (1973): 186–187.

Watanabe, Hitoshi. "Running, Creeping and Climbing: A New Ecological and Evolutionary Perspective on Human Locomotion." *Mankind* 8 No. 1 (1971): 1–13.

White, Tim D. "Evolutionary Implications of Pliocene Hominid Footprints." *Science* 208 (1980): 175–176.

## *Major Sources for Section II*

Broneer, Oscar. "Starting Devices in Greek Stadia." *American Journal of Archaeology* Vol 76 (1972): 205–206.

Decker, Wolfgang. *Sports and Games of Ancient Egypt*. Translated by Allen Guttmann, New Haven and London: Yale University, 1992.

Gardiner, Edward Norman. *Athletics of the Ancient World*. Oxford: Clarendon, 1930.

_____. *Greek Athletic Sports and Festivals*. Brown Reprints, 1910.

Harris, H. A. *Greek Athletes and Athletics*. 2d ed. Bloomington: Indiana University, 1967.

_____. *Sport in Greece and Rome*. Ithaca, New York: Cornell University Press, 1972.

Howell, Reet A. "The Atalanta Legend in Art and Literature." *Journal of Sport History* 16 No. 2 (1989): 127–139.

Kramer, Samuel Noah. *History Begins at Sumer: Thirty-nine Firsts in Man's Recorded History*. Philadelphia: University of Pennsylvania, 1981. [Contains the story of King Shulgi's run]

Lamont, Deane Anderson. "Running Phenomena in Ancient Sumer." *Journal of Sport History* 22 No. 3 (Fall 1995): 207–215.

Miller, Stephen G. *Arete: Greek Sports from Ancient Sources*. Berkeley: University of California, 1991.

_____. "Turns and Lanes in Ancient Stadium." *American Journal of Archaeology* 84 (1980): 159–166.

Pausanias. *Description of Greece, with an English Translation by W.H.S. Jones*. In six volumes. London: William Heinemann, 1918. [A.D. 160–170 description of Olympia]

Philostratus, the Athenian. *Philostratos' Concerning Gymnastics*. Trans. by Thomas Woody. *Research Quarterly* 7 (May 1936): 3–26.

Robinson, Rachel Sargent. *Sources for the History of Greek Athletics*. Chicago: Ares Publishers, 1927, 1955.

Romano, David Gilman. *Athletics and Mathematics in Archaic Corinth: The Origins of the Greek Stadion*. Memoirs of the American Philosophical Society Held at Philadelphia for Promoting Useful Knowledge 206 (1993).

Tzachou-Alexandri, Olga. *Mind and Body: Athletic Contests in Ancient Greece*, Athens: Ministry of Culture, 1988. [Contains some beautiful color illustrations]

Valavanis, Panos. *Hysplex: The Starting Mechanism in Ancient Stadia*. Berkeley: University of California, 1999.

Yalouris, Nicholas (ed.). *The Olympic Games*. Athens: Ekdotike Athenon S.A., 1976. [Covers the ancient games]

## *Major Sources for Section III*

Anderson, Earl R. "Footnotes More Pedestrian Than Sublime." *Eighteenth-Century Studies* 14 (1980): 56–68.

_____. "Freak Races." *Running Times*, March 1982, pp. 21–22, 24.

_____. "The Running Footmen of the 19th century England." *Running Times*, March 1981, pp. 17–20.

Depping, Guillaume. *Wonders of Bodily Strength and Skill*. Translated from the French by Charles Russell. New York: Scribner's, 1871.

Donaldson, G. "The Running Footmen: These Super Fit Servants Were the Forerunners of the Ultra Marathon Men." In *Athletics*, Wilowdale, Ont.: (1984): 22–23, 49.

Egan, Pierce. *Book of Sports and Mirror of Life*. London: Tegg, 1832, pp. 259–265

_____. *Sporting Anecdotes, A Complete Panorama of the Sporting World*. London: Neeley and Jones, 1807, 1825.

Guts Muths, Johann C. F. *Gymnastics for Youth*. Philadelphia: Brown Reprint, 1793, 1803, 1970.

Heywood, William. *Palio and Ponte: An Account of the Sports of Central Italy from the Death of Dante to the XXth Century*. London: Methuen, 1904, 1969. [Describes the Palio Foot-race referred to in Dante's Inferno]

Holliman, Jennie. *American Sports (1788–1835)*. Philadelphia: Porcupine Press, 1931, 1975.

Landes, David S. *Revolution in Time: Clocks and the Making of the Modern World*. Cambridge: Belknap Press, 1983.

Lennox, Lord William Pitt. *Fashion Then and Now*. London: Chapman and Hall, 1878. [Vol. II contains a list of 18th century pedestrian feats]

Radford, Peter. "Women's Foot-Races in the 18th and 19th Centuries: A Popular and Widespread Practice." *Canadian Journal of the History of Sport*, XXV (May 1994): 57–68.

"A Running Footman." *Frank Leslie's Popular Monthly* 5 (1876): 103.

Shearman, Sir Montague. *Athletics and Football*. London: Longmans, Green, 1888.

_____. "George Seward, the Cockfield Putter." *British Society of Sports History Newsletter* No. 9 (1999): 37–42.

_____, ed. "The Running Career of James Wantling." *Sports Quarterly Magazine* No. 13 (1980): 3–5.

Hughes, Thomas. *Tom Brown's School Days*. Houghton Mifflin, 1857, 1931. [This book did much to popularize the sport of paper chasing.]

Moss, George. "The Long Distance Runners of Antebellum America." *Journal of Popular Culture* 8 No. 2 (Fall 1974): 370–82.

Radford, Peter F. "From Oral Tradition to Printed Record: British Sports Science in Transition 1805–1807." *Stadion* VII/XIII (1986/1987): 295–304.

Rieck, Gustav. *Des Stauermannes Mensen Ernst*. Breslau, Poland: 1838. [The source of the Ernst legend]

Terry, Dave. "Britain's First Great Sprinter — James Jem Wantling." *Athletics Weekly*, January 2, 1965.

Thom, Walter. *Pedestrianism*. Aberdeen: Brown and Frost, 1813. [The first book on running]

Webster, David. *Scottish Highland Games*. Edinburgh: Reprographia, 1973.

Wheeler, C. A. *Sportascrapia, Cricket, Shooting, Pedestrianism, Equestrianism, etc*. London: Simpkin, Marshall, 1867.

## Major Sources for Section IV

Anderson, Earl R. "The Barby Hill Episode in Tom Brown's School Days: Sources and Influence." *Arete II* No. 2 (Spring 1985): 96–110.

_____. "Rugby School and the Early Years of Cross Country Running." *Proceedings of the 5th Canadian Symposium on History of Sport and Physical Education*, August 26–29, 1982, pp. 156–168.

Cumming, John. *Runners & Walkers: A Nineteenth Century Sports Chronicle*. Chicago: Regnery Gateway, 1981. [The best reference to date covering running in 19th century America]

Goulstone, John. "George Seward, the American Wonder." *Sports Quarterly Magazine* No 2 (Summer 1977): 23–30.

## Major Sources for Section V

Downer, Alfred R. *Running Recollections and How to Train*. London: Gale & Polden, 1902. [Excellent account of late 19th-century sprinting]

Harding, William Edgar. *The American Athlete*. New York: R. K. Fox, c1881.

James, Ed. *Practical Training for Running, Walking, Rowing, Wrestling, Boxing, Jumping and All Kinds of Athletic Feats*. New York: James, 1877. [Illustrations of several female pedestrians]

Jamieson, David A. *Powderhall and Pedestrianism: The History of a famous Sports Enclosure (1870–1943)*. Edinburgh: W. & A. K. Johnston, 1943. [This history of Powderhall

Stadium also describes many other 19th-century professional runners]

Lagerstrom, Ulf. *The Sprinters 1876/1914.* Published by author, 1993. [Ratings of early sprinters]

Lovesey, Peter. "Flash Harry." *Athletics Weekly,* December 25, 1982.

_____. "Harry Hutchens—Finest Sprinter of Them All?" *Athletics Weekly,* May 17, 1969, pp. 18, 45.

Lucas, John A. "Deerfoot in Britain." *Journal of American Culture* (Fall 1983): 13–19.

_____. "Pedestrianism and the Struggle for the Sir John Astley Belt 1878–1879." *Research Quarterly* 39 (October 1968): 587–594.

Lupton, James Irvine. *The Pedestrian's Record.* London: W. H. Allen, 1890. [19th-century amateur and professional records for all distances]

Milroy, Andy. *The Long Distance Record book.* Road Runners Club of England, 1989. [Excellent historical development of distance running with record progressions from 10 to 1,000 miles]

Osler, Tom, and Ed Dodd. *Ultra-marathoning.* Mountain View, Calif.: World Publications, 1979. [The first half of this book contains a well-researched account of 19th century six-day races]

Potts, D. H. *Lon.* Mountain View, Calif.: TafNews Press, 1993 [A biography of Lon Myers listing most of his major races]

Willis, Joe D., and R. G. Wetton. "L. E. Myers, 'World's Greatest Runner.'" *Journal of Sport History* 2 (Fall 1975): 93–111.

The following newspapers contain a wealth of information on 19th century running: *American Turf Register, Bell's Life, Spirit of the Times, New York Clipper, National Police Gazette, Harper's Weekly, Frank Leslie's Illustrated Newspaper, London Illustrated News, Illustrated Sporting and Dramatic News, New York Times,* and *Times* of London. The *New York Clipper* and *Bell's Life* stand out for authority and depth of coverage, but neither contain many illustrations. The *Police Gazette, Leslie's Illustrated Newspaper* and the *Illustrated Sporting and Dramatic News* are all rich sources of 19th century running illustrations.

## Major Sources for Section VI

Baker, William J. *Jesse Owens: An American Life.* New York: Free Press, 1986. [The definitive book on Jesse Owens]

Berry, Harry. *From L.A. to New York, From New York to L.A.* Lancashire, Eng.: H. Berry. [Excellent account of the 1928–29 Bunion Derbies]

Bull, Joe. *The Spiked Shoe.* Melbourne: National Press, 1960. [Professional running in Australia]

Butler, Guy. *Running and Runners.* London: Herbert Jenkins, 1938.

Clark, Ellery H. *Reminiscences of an Athlete: Twenty Years of Track and Field.* Boston and New York: Houghton Mifflin, 1911.

_____. *Track Athletics Up to Date.* New York: Duffield, 1920.

Dastoor, B. N. *Dr. Peltzer's Extract of Modern Athletic Systems.* Bombay: Owens Sports, 1960.

Doherty, Ken. *Track and Field Omnibook.* Los Altos, Calif.: TafNews Press, 1980.

Freeman, William H. "Distance Training Methods, Past and Present." *T & F Quarterly Review* 75 (4) (Winter 1975): 4–11.

Giller, Norman. *The Golden Milers.* Winchmore Publishing Services Ltd., 1982.

Gynn, Roger, and David Martin. *The Marathon Footrace: Performers and Performances.* Springfield, Ill.: Thomas, 1979. [The definitive history of the marathon]

Harris, Norman. *The Legend of Lovelock.* Wellington: Reed, 1964.

Hawn, Archie. *How to Sprint.* New York: American Sports Publishing, 1923.

Henry, Bill. *An Approved History of the Olympic Games.* Los Angeles: Southern California Committee for the Olympic Games, 1987. [One of the best of many books on the modern Olympics]

Kozik, František. *Zatopek the Marathon Victor.* Prague: Artia, 1954.

Krout, John Allen. *Annals of American Sport.* New Haven: Yale University Press, 1929. [Interesting accounts and illustrations of late 19th century American Athletes]

Lovesey, Peter. *The Kings of Distance: A Study of Five Great Runners.* London: Eyre & Spottiswoode, 1968. [Descriptions of the five greatest distance runners up to 1968: Deer-foot, Walter George, Alfred Shrubb, Paavo Nurmi and Emil Zatopek]

Mason, Percy. *Professional Athletics in Australia*. Melbourne: Rigby Publishers, 1985.

McWhirter, Ross. *Get to Your Marks: A Short History of World, Commonwealth, European and British Athletics*. London: Kaye, 1951.

Murphy, Michael C. *Athletic Training*. New York: Scribner's, 1914.

Nelson, Cordner. *The Milers*. Los Altos, Calif.: Tafnews Press, 1985. [The definitive history of the mile up to early 1980s]

Newton, Arthur H. *Racing and Training*. London: Berridge, 1949. See also *Running on Three Continents*. London: Witherby, 1940.

Paddock, Charles W. *The Fastest Human*. New York: Thomas Nelson, 1932.

Peters, J. H. *In the Long Run*. London: Cassell, 1955.

Quercetani, R. L. *A World History of Track and Field Athletics* (1864–1964). London: Oxford University Press, 1964. [This authoritative history of track and field is a classic]

Shrubb, Alfred. *Running and Cross-Country Running*. London: Health and Strength, 1908.

Thomas, James H. *The Bunion Derby: Andy Payne and the Transcontinental Footrace*. Oklahoma City, Okla.: Southwest Heritage, 1980.

## *Major Sources for Section VII*

Abebe, Tsige. *Triumph and Tragedy: A History of Abebe Bikila and His Marathon Career*. Ethiopia: T. Abebe, 1996.

Bannister, Roger. *The Four-Minute Mile*. Lyons & Burford, 1955.

Benoit, Joan, with Sally Baker. *Running Tide*. New York: Knopf, 1987.

Budd, Zola, with Hugh Eley. *Zola: The Autobiography of Zola Budd*. London: Partridge Press, 1989.

Cerutty, Percy Wells. *Athletics: How to Become a Champion*. London: Stanley Paul, 1960. [One of several interesting books by Cerutty]

Clarke, Ron, and Tregrove. *The Unforgiving Minute*. London: Pelham, 1966.

Coe, Sebastian, with David Miller. *Running Free*. London: Sidgwick & Jackson, 1981.

Duncanson, Neil. *The Fastest Men on Earth*. London: Willow Books, 1988. [Well researched accounts of Olympic gold-medal-winning sprinters from 1896 to 1984]

Elliott, Herb. *The Golden Mile*. London: Cassell, 1961.

Francis, Charlie. *Speed Trap: Inside the Biggest Scandal in Olympic History*. New York: St Martin's Press, 1990.

Greenspan, Bud. *The Olympiad Greatest Moments*. Dreamworks SKG Television, 1996. [A well-done series of eight Olympic Track & Field Videos]

Hayes, Bob. *Run, Bullet, Run: The Rise, Fall, and Recovery of Bob Hayes*. New York: Harper & Row, 1990.

Hendershott, Jon. *Track's Greatest Women*. Los Altos, Calif.: Tafnews Press, 1987.

Krise, Raymond, and Bill Squires. *Fast Tracks: The History of Distance Running*. Brattleboro, Vt.: Stephen Greene Press, 1982. [Contains a good account of the 1970s running boom in the United States]

Lawson, Gerald. *World Record Breakers in Track & Field Athletics*. Human Kinetics, 1997. [Short biographies of all the IAAF approved record holders]

Lewis, Carl, with Jefferey Marx. *Inside Track: My Professional Life in Amateur Track & Field*. New York: Simon and Schuster, 1990.

Lovesey, Peter, and Tom McNab. *The Guide to British Track and Field Literature 1275–1968*. London: Athletics Arena, 1969. [This book is indispensable to anyone researching the history of running or T&F. It contains nearly 900 annotated references. An updated version, *The Compendium of United Kingdom Athletics Literature*, by Andrew Huxtable, Peter Lovesey and Tom McNab, published by the British Library, is due out in late 2001. It is unfortunate that no similar work exists for U.S. running and T&F]

Lydiard, Arthur. *Run to the Top*. Aukland: Minerva, 1967.

Moore, Kenny. *Best Efforts: World Class Runners*

*and Races*. Garden City, N.Y.: Doubleday, 1982.

Murphy, Frank. *A Cold Clear Day: The Athletic Biography of Buddy Edelen*. Kansas City: Wind Sprint Press, 1992.

Noakes, Tim. *The Lore of Running*. Champaign, Ill.: Leisure Press, 1991.

Ovett, Steve, with John Rodda. *Ovett: An Autobiography*. London: Willow Books, 1984

Quercetani, R. L. *Athletics: A History of Modern Track Athletics, 1860–1990*. Milan: Vallardi & Association, 1991. [An update of Quercetani's 1964 book. It adds women and many color illustrations. The book was further updated in 2000]

Rudolph, Wilma. *Wilma*. New York: New American Library, 1977.

Ryun, Jim. *In Quest of Gold: The Jim Ryun Story*. New York: Harper & Row, 1984.

Snell, Peter. *No Bugles No Drums*. Auckland, N.Z.: Minerva, 1965.

Tames, Roger. *Steve Cram: The Making of an Athlete*. London: W.H. Allen, 1984.

Tricard, Louise Mead. *American Women's Track and Field: A History, 1895 through 1980*. Jefferson, N.C.: McFarland, 1996.

Waitz, Grete, and Gloria Averbuch. *World Class*. New York: Warner Books, 1986.

Wilt, Fred. *How They Train*. Los Altos, Calif.: TafNews Press, 1973. [Wilt collected training methods from a large number of runners and published them in this series of books]

# Index

Abascal, J. M. 280
Abdesselem, Rhadi 297
Abilene Christian College 236
Abrahams, Harold M. 175, 190
Achilles 17–20, 235
Acton & Taylor's Handicap 87, 90, 91
*Aeneid* (Virgil) 20
aerobic running 7, 11
Ageus of Argos 30
Agostini, Michael 237
Agricultural Hall London 140, 146, 156
Ahimaaz 17
Ainsworth, Henry 71, 73
Ajax 19, 20
*Akropolis* 35
Albert, James (Cathcart) 225, 228, 274, 294
Albison, Siah 102, 111, 112
Alexander, R. McNeil 6
Alexander the Great 30
Alighieri, Dante 42
Allardice, Robert Barclay *see* Barclay, Captain
Allied Games 172, 173
Amateur Athletic Association (AAA) 89, 117, 169, 198, 204, 254, 294, 295, 300; suspensions by 90 , 121, 210
Amateur Athletic Union (AAU) 94, 108, 165, 169, 179–181, 186, 187, 194, 195, 205, 236, 239, 240, 242, 258, 272, 303; adopts automatic timing 233; adopts 1/10 second timing 163; changes rule for picking race winner 180; doubts Don-

aldson's performances 170; invites Hägg to America 208; outraged by Duffey's article 167; suspensions by 167, 175, 183, 271
amateurism: defined 81; end of 300; origin in Britain 300; origin in USA 81; "under-the-table" payments 1, 81, 90, 203, 216, 303
"American Deer" *see* Howitt, William
"American Wonder" *see* Seward, George
*American Turf Register* 68
anaerobic running 11
*Ancient Hunters and Their Modern Representatives* (Sollas) 10
Ancient Olympic Games 22–35, 39
animal running: top speeds 5; cooling problems 5
Andersson, Arne 207–209, 217, 269
Anderson, Madame 152
Anystis 30, 37
Aouita, Said 280, 281
Apollo 17, 19, 22
Aquinas, Thomas 40
"Arkansas Flyer" *see* Carr, William
Arzhanov, Yevgeniy 265
Ashford, Evelyn 255, 256
Asian Amateur Athletic Association (AAAA) 254
Association of Track & Field Statisticians (ATSF) 256
Astley, Sir John D. 132, 140–144, 146, 157
Astley Belt races, 140–144, 146
Atalanta 17, 18, 21, 75
Athena 20

athletic clubs: Boston Athletic Association (BAA) 306; Cleveland 91; Detroit 94; Irish-American 195; Knickerbocker 221; London 96, 109, 114, 116, 120, 124; Manhattan 104, 108, 120; New Jersey 127, 128; New York 81, 94, 96, 104, 108, 109, 120, 125, 127; Optimist 248; Oxford University 210; San Francisco Olympic Club 92; Santa Monica 249, 250; Staten Island 127
*Athletic Training* (Murphy) 63, 64, 129
*Athletics and Mathematics in Archaic Corinth* (Romano) 24

Babers, Alonzo 259
Bacheler, Jack 301
Bacon, Fred E. 110, 120, 121
Baily, Donovan 249
Baker, Thane 237
Baker, Wendell 107
Banks, Ted 282
Bannister, Sir Roger 2, 158, 203, 268–272, 283, 295
"Barby Hill" run 67
Barclay, Captain: mile race 110; 1,000-miles-in-1,000 hours 58–59; race with Wood 57–58; training methods 33, 57, 63–64, 86, 156
Barker, Sam 134
Barlow, Billy 75, 76
Barlow, John (Tallick) 68, 69
Barthel, Josy 269
Barwick, Sandra 156
Bayi, Filbert 277, 278